Passing Illusions

Social History, Popular Culture, and Politics in Germany
Kathleen Canning, Series Editor

**Recent Titles**

**For a complete list of titles, please see www.press.umich.edu**

# Passing Illusions

## Jewish Visibility in Weimar Germany

KERRY WALLACH

UNIVERSITY OF MICHIGAN PRESS

*Ann Arbor*

Published in the United States of America by the
University of Michigan Press
Manufactured in the United States of America
⊗ Printed on acid-free paper

2020   2019   2018   2017      4   3   2   1

A CIP catalog record for this book is available from the British Library.

Library of Congress Cataloging-in-Publication Data

Names: Wallach, Kerry, author.
Title: Passing illusions : Jewish visibility in Weimar Germany / Kerry Wallach.
Description: Ann Arbor : University of Michigan Press, [2017] | Series: Social history, popular
    culture, and politics in Germany | Includes bibliographical references and index.
Identifiers: LCCN 2017001837| ISBN 9780472073573 (hardcover : alk. paper) | ISBN
    9780472053575 (pbk. : alk. paper) | ISBN 9780472123001 (e-book)
Subjects: LCSH: Jews—Germany—History—1918–1933. | Jews—Germany—
    Identity. | Passing (Identity)—Germany—History—20th century. | Antisemitism—
    Germany—History—20th century. | Germany—Civilization—Jewish
    influences. | Germany—Ethnic relations.
Classification: LCC DS134.25 .W35   2017 | DDC 305.892/404309042—dc23
LC record available at https://lccn.loc.gov/2017001837

# Acknowledgments

I am delighted to thank those who have supported my work on this project, which I began in Philadelphia and wrote over many years in Berlin, New York, Gettysburg, and Rockville/Washington DC. The generosity of numerous individuals, academic networks, and institutions made this book possible, and I am very grateful for their assistance. All translations are my own unless otherwise noted.

First, I would like to thank colleagues who helped the final manuscript come together, including the anonymous readers whose suggestions for revision were immensely valuable. Sam Spinner is a brilliant scholar and dear friend whose input shaped nearly every part of this book, and I cannot thank him enough. I owe much to those who read portions of the manuscript and extended their friendship along the way: Iris Idelson-Shein, Matthew Handelman, Emily Levine, Tahneer Oksman, Nicholas Baer, Brook Henkel, McKinley Melton, and Melanie Adley. In addition, Jonathan Hess and Marion Kaplan offered important feedback and have been wonderful mentors. Liliane Weissberg expertly guided me into German-Jewish Studies and advised the dissertation that led to this book.

Many scholars of German Studies and Jewish Studies have contributed to this project through conversations, conferences, and other collaborative opportunities. I would like to express deep gratitude to Darcy Buerkle, Sharon Gillerman, Atina Grossmann, Paul Lerner, Lisa Silverman, and Jonathan Skolnik, who have offered unwavering encouragement over the past few years. I have greatly enjoyed exchanging ideas with Ofer Ashkenazi, Michael Berkowitz, Marc Caplan, Mila Ganeva, Kata Gellen, Jay Geller, Jeffrey Grossman, Klaus Hödl, Dan Magilow, Rick McCormick, Gideon Reuveni, Christian Rogowski, Scott Spector, and Valerie Weinstein. A number of colleagues shared helpful feedback on invited lectures related to this book, including Russell Berman, Adrian Daub, Scott Lerner, Antje Pfannkuchen, Michael Riff, Christa Spreizer,

Kathryn Starkey, David Wellbery, Christopher Wild, and Sunny Yudkoff. Other senior scholars who have inspired and backed my work through various channels are Michael Brenner, Kathleen Canning, Bill Donahue, Sander Gilman, Raphael Gross, Martha Helfer, Susannah Heschel, Anne Lapidus Lerner (and the AJS Paula E. Hyman Mentoring Program), Frank Mecklenburg, Guy Miron, Leslie Morris, Stefanie Schüler-Springorum, David Sorkin (and the AAJR Early Career Workshop), Uwe Spiekermann, William Weitzer, Christian Wiese, and Daniel Wildmann.

I am very much indebted to the Leo Baeck Institutes in New York/Berlin, London, and Jerusalem. The Gerald Westheimer Career Development Fellowship from the Leo Baeck Institute, New York (LBINY), enabled me to extend my research leave to a full year. A grant from LBINY and the DAAD (German Academic Exchange Service) supported early research for this project. LBI London and the Studienstiftung des deutschen Volkes funded a research year in Berlin and introduced me to fantastic colleagues through the Leo Baeck Fellowship Programme. I am thrilled to work with some of these colleagues on the German Jewish Cultures book series at Indiana University Press. The Seminar for Postdoctoral Students of German-Jewish and Central-European Jewish History (sponsored by LBI Jerusalem, LBI in Germany, and Stiftung deutsch-israelisches Zukunftsforum) offered a valuable platform for presenting my work. Sincere thanks are due to the many archivists and librarians who assisted in research for this project, particularly Michael Simonson.

Gettysburg College, where I have been a professor of German Studies since 2011, supported this book by providing extremely generous research leave and funding. I especially would like to thank the other members of the German Studies Department: Laurel Cohen, Henning Wrage, Christiane Breithaupt, and Robin Oliver. Clint Baugess and the staff of Musselman Library have been very helpful in obtaining books and other materials. This project benefited greatly from conversations with other Gettysburg colleagues: Bill Bowman, Radi Rangelova, Jack Murphy, Stefanie Sobelle, Lidia Anchisi, Kurt Andresen, Rim Baltaduonis, Abou Bamba, Temma Berg, Rob Bohrer, Vero Calvillo, Ryan Dodd, Jenny Dumont, Cassie Hays, Julie Hendon, Ian Isherwood, Ryan Johnson, Nathalie Lebon, Rachel Lesser, Richard Russell, Luke Thompson, Beatriz Trigo, Gina Velasco, and Mike Wedlock. I am fortunate to have phenomenal students, including many who contributed to this project directly or indirectly; here I would like to mention Claire Bailets, Trevor Walter, Karolina Hicke, and An Sasala. Special thanks go to my three truly exceptional and meticulous research assistants: Elizabeth Topolosky, Martina Khalek, and Kim Longfellow.

I am grateful to mentors and teachers at Wesleyan University (College of Letters) and the University of Pennsylvania for my interdisciplinary training. Noah Isenberg deserves credit for encouraging me to pursue German Studies, and for instilling in me a love of Weimar culture. At Penn, Liliane Weissberg introduced me to a range of scholarly worlds. Eric Jarosinski taught me how to be a better writer. I learned a great deal from working with Catriona MacLeod, Simon Richter, Kathryn Hellerstein, Bethany Wiggin, Frank Trommler, Beth Wenger, Benjamin Nathans, and visiting scholar Stephan Braese. Additional thanks are due to Jerry Singerman and Meghan Sullivan. Many fellows at the Herbert D. Katz Center for Advanced Judaic Studies also contributed significantly to my education.

Numerous colleagues and friends have served as a sounding board for ideas related to this project. From Penn, I am grateful to Vance Byrd, Dan DiMassa, Sonia Gollance, Emily Hauze, Gabriella Skwara, Curtis Swope, Mara Taylor, Nick Theis, Caroline Weist, Conny Aust, Jennifer Glaser, Tina Ranalli, Rami Regavim, Katrin Schreiter, Ese Jeroro, and Sophie Woolston. I also would like to thank the following colleagues for kindly sharing advice and ideas: Yael Almog, Maya Barzilai, Katie Batza, LaNitra Berger, Nadine Blumer, David Brenner, Aya Elyada, Amir Engel, Jennifer Evans, Florence Feiereisen, Anat Feinberg, Kirsten Fermaglich, Ken Frieden, Uri Ganani, Christopher Geissler, Jay Howard Geller, Rachel Gordan, Udi Greenberg, Kate Haffey, Lori Harrison-Kahan, June Hwang, Sarah Imhoff, Mariana Ivanova, Daniel Jütte, Ellen Kellman, Martin Kley, Shira Kohn, Thomas Kühne, Josh Lambert, Ilse Josepha Lazaroms, Ari Linden, Stefanie Mahrer, Ted Merwin, Anna Parkinson, Elliot Ratzman, Na'ama Rokem, Sven-Erik Rose, Miriam Rürup, Anne Schenderlein, Jana Schmidt, Dani Schrire, Inbal Steinitz, Josh Teplitsky, Mirjam Thulin, Stefan Vogt, and Erica Weitzman.

Other institutions have supported and shaped my work in productive ways. The opportunity to teach a film course at the Jewish Theological Seminary came at just the right time. A short-term postdoctoral fellowship at the German Historical Institute in Washington, DC, led to many meaningful professional connections. The Women in German network has been an important resource for me for over a decade, and I am grateful to have received the Women in German Dissertation Prize in 2012. Finally, it has been a privilege and a pleasure to work with LeAnn Fields, Christopher Dreyer, Kevin Rennells, and others at the University of Michigan Press.

Friends near and far made the process of completing this project much more enjoyable. Aileen Payumo, Una LaMarche, Jeff Zorabedian, Arcelie Reyes, Liz Oppenheim, Sara Miller, Demian Szyld, Adrianne Doering Curtis,

Erin Fletcher, Niv Elis, and Abby Moses have sustained (and hosted) me for many years. Several friends from my hometown of Shaker Heights remain close, especially Rebecca Spira King, Sarah Siegel Lubow, and Adrienne Katz Kennedy. Mary Ashcraft and Meredith Petrnousek have encouraged my pursuit of German for over two decades. In New York, Jimmy Lader and Anthony Gaugler deserve many thanks for their gracious and continual support. In Berlin, I owe a huge debt of gratitude to the Luber family (especially Eva), Anna von Gall, Elena Virnik, and Lea Weik. For their friendship in Maryland, I would like to thank Fiona Grant, Heidi Mordhorst, Zack Levine, Allison Farber, Suzee Kujawa, Mitch Rotbert, Baht Yameem Weiss; the Cohen, Entel, Chang, Carin, Freedberg, Karpay, and Truland families; and the many amazing people at Temple Beth Ami who welcomed us in the warmest way imaginable.

This book is dedicated to my grandparents, Janice and Ivan Wallach, whose American Jewish encounters with the early twentieth century have been an endless source of inspiration. The courage of my other grandmother, Anne Kinney, who was born the same year as the Weimar Republic, inspires me in different ways. I would like to thank my parents, Harriet and Mark, and my stepmother, Karla, for carving an intellectual path and enabling me to go my own way. I am so pleased to live near my brother, Philip, and his delightful family, including Vera and Bina. Many thanks also to Danny, Rachel, Rachel, and Adam Kanter and my terrific extended family. The Firsheins—Joy, Dan, and Jenna—enliven holidays and every day. To Jess Firshein, my best friend, partner, and wonderful wife, whose laughter and light fill my days, I am grateful beyond words. Heartfelt thanks also go to our son, Zev, whose boundless energy makes everything more fun.

# Contents

# Introduction: Passing, Covering, Revealing

There was a widespread notion among Jews in Weimar Germany (1919–33) that, at any given moment, one could appear Jewish or non-Jewish, or "more Jewish" or "less Jewish." Jews and non-Jews alike often sized up other people to assess whether they were Jewish. Although many conceded that it was not always possible to observe Jewishness, those who tried to find it continually emphasized the idea of Jewish visibility. In other words, the belief that Jewishness could be seen reinforced the idea that it was visible.[1] Some Jews wanted to "pass," to remain invisible, hidden, or incognito as Jews; yet there were also times when it was advantageous to be recognizable. However, the acts of choosing to remain hidden and to be seen were not mutually exclusive, and they operated both in tension and in intersection with one another. Many Jews cultivated a complex identity in order to pass for non-Jewish in some contexts (such as with non-Jews or in unknown company) and yet still be perceivably Jewish in others (for example, when around other Jews).

Although some Jews proudly proclaimed their ability to pass for non-Jews, others were skeptical about invisibility and considered it deliberately deceptive. One 1925 article titled "Not at All Jewish" in the nonpartisan best-selling German-Jewish newspaper, *Israelitisches Familienblatt* (Israelite Family Pages), sheds light on these opposing perspectives:

> Everyone probably knows members of the Jewish faith who, in Jewish circles and even among non-Jewish acquaintances, relay with a certain amount of pride that in many cases non-Jews *don't take them for Jewish at all*, and that other parties were supposedly terribly surprised to learn that before them stood a confessor (*Bekenner*) of Judaism. These confessors then usually add the following addendum to this confession (*Bekenntnis*), with a hint of personality: In our family, we generally all look non-Jewish.

The article's author, identified only as W. S., goes on to chastise those who desire and are able to pass, insinuating that anyone who takes pride in being perceived as "not at all Jewish" on the basis of external appearance in fact has "nothing at all" for inner character.[2] With this criticism, the author calls attention to the phenomenon of Jewish passing and also underscores the surprise others experience upon learning that someone who doesn't "look Jewish" is actually Jewish.

Implicit here is the complex process of recognizing and revealing Jewishness, which might include an acknowledgement, admission, or confession. The key terms *confession* and *to confess* (*Bekenntnis, sich bekennen*), which appear in the above quote and in numerous other texts examined in this study, often denote an open acknowledgment akin to "coming out."[3] In other instances, they refer specifically to expressing religious affiliation. It is only when a person comes out or is "outed" as Jewish in public that Jewishness is firmly established. Without this act of identification, Jewishness, at least in select cases, could theoretically remain hidden indefinitely. Articles such as this one that criticized Jewish invisibility suggest there was strong pushback against passing. Investigating the motivations behind staying hidden, becoming visible, and giving the illusion of passing opens up a new understanding of Weimar Jewish culture.

Whereas many scholars have foregrounded the impulses for invisibility—de-Judaization, secularization, radical assimilation, self-abnegation—this book argues that there was also a pronounced desire for Jewish visibility among Jews in Weimar Germany.[4] Exploring both sides of this dialectic helps illuminate the circumstances surrounding these seemingly contradictory inclinations. Being safely visible as a Jew in the Weimar Republic entailed coming out only under certain circumstances, and staying at least partially hidden in other situations, a tendency integral to interpreting Jewish self-identification. Scholars including Michael Brenner, Michael Berkowitz, Abigail Gillman, Lisa Silverman, and Darcy Buerkle have written about the ways German and Central European Jews grappled with knowing when to foreground Jewishness and when to conceal it.[5] Revealing one's Jewishness often involved fostering "dual legibility"—that is, appearing non-Jewish and Jewish at once—and managing dual coding in order to be openly Jewish at the right time and in the right place, and in ways that were deemed fitting for a population under scrutiny.[6] As we will see, gender also was a constitutive part of the process of deciding when to engage and display Jewishness. Instead of either passing as non-Jews or overtly displaying Jewishness at all times, many Jews inhabited a state of ambiguity but adopted signifiers of Jewishness such as badges or hairstyles that were perceptible to certain observers, and especially to other Jews.[7] It became possible, even desirable, to perform Jewishness without effacing it, and to be recognizably Jewish without standing out from the crowd.

The four chapters in *Passing Illusions* examine constructions of German-Jewish visibility, as well as instances in the 1920s and early 1930s when it was concealed, revealed, or contested. Different key aspects of visibility, invisibility, and moments of encounter inform each chapter's approach. These include the ways Jewishness was detected, with a focus on racial stereotypes (chapter 1); occasions when coming out was encouraged (chapter 2); confrontational instances in which Jews were outed or silenced (chapter 3); and episodes in which misidentifications played a pivotal role (chapter 4). The concluding chapter continues the introduction's discussion of Jewish passing in comparative contexts with a focus on African American racial passing and queer passing; its final pages point to ongoing conversations about Jewish and minority visibility in the twenty-first century.

Drawing on the intersections of German and Jewish studies within a framework of cultural studies, this book aims to bridge the work of historians and literary scholars in order to probe deeper into modes of Weimar Jewish self-presentation. This study draws on many sources typically used by historians, such as periodicals, personal memoirs, and archival documents, but it also examines cultural texts including works of fiction, anecdotes, images, advertisements, and films. Through close readings, at times at the level of the precise language used, I analyze texts for nuanced clues about Jewish visibility and invisibility and their gendered layers. The texts as well as the historical circumstances of their production and reception offer valuable insights into constructions of visibility. The book's four chapters focus mainly on texts that grant access to inner-Jewish discourses about the decision to pass or to be visible, or both. This includes an examination of Jewish responses to mainstream and antisemitic stereotypes, which inform but are not at the center of my project.

Antisemitism and its manifestations in discrimination and exclusion greatly impacted Jewish identity and self-presentation but did not lead only to hiddenness or invisibility. Indeed, *Passing Illusions* calls into question scholarship that understands antisemitism mainly as a cause of self-hatred and a reason to try to hide or shed one's Jewishness (for example, through passing or conversion). By framing my discussion of antisemitism as part of a larger conversation about both invisibility and visibility, I underscore the ways in which profiling contributed to impulses to hide and to display Jewishness. The proliferation of antisemitic sentiments and stereotypes during and after the First World War produced a need for public models of Jewishness that were not considered objectionable. Parallel to the pressure to evade antisemitism by being inconspicuous was the desire to overcome such pressures by displaying Jewishness, a right that many Weimar Jews proudly exercised.

The 14 years of the Weimar Republic serve as the basis for this study partly because Jews were legally and socially positioned as fully equal German citizens. In Imperial Germany, public visibility was overly constrained by bourgeois concerns about respectability and gender roles. Even though German Jews achieved emancipation for the most part in 1871, some forms of exclusion persisted; for example, only non-Jews could attain the highest positions in the military and at universities. Many Jews converted to Christianity to gain access to such positions, though the popular view of Jewishness as increasingly racialized made conversion less useful. During the First World War, the antisemitic Jewish census (*Judenzählung*) of October 11, 1916, which implied that Jews were shirking their military duty and aimed to ascertain what percentage of Jews were fighting on the front lines, had a particularly demoralizing effect on Jews serving in the German military, and on German Jews more broadly.[8] Not until the constitution of the democratic Weimar Republic granted women and minorities equal rights in 1919 did Jews have full access to the privileges afforded other German citizens. Personal conviction was thus a driving factor in the decision to be visibly Jewish.

Precisely because German Jews were aware of potential forms of exclusion, they created and sought out spaces of refuge in which being openly Jewish was standard. Although a sense of renewed Jewish consciousness and interest in preserving Jewish distinctiveness began already in the late nineteenth century—what Shulamit Volkov has termed a "complex dialectical process of dissimilation"—Jews were able to become even more visible in part due to changing social roles after the First World War.[9] The "caesura of 1918," as Anson Rabinbach has noted, continued the process of artistically disrupting modernity and also brought about a newly politicized aesthetic.[10] Jewish subcultures emerged and immediately confronted questions of visibility that were inherently political.[11] Weimar Berlin, a thriving cultural center that attracted residents and visitors from all over the world, as well as the largest Jewish community in Germany, was particularly conducive to the production, exchange, and display of new forms of Jewish culture.[12] Writer Elias Canetti (1905–94) noted in 1928 while reminiscing about visits to Berlin's Romanisches Café: "They resulted from a need to be seen that nobody was immune to. Anyone who did not want to be forgotten had to be seen. This applied to each rank and all stations of society."[13] Weimar Jews, too, were among those who sought to be visible, though most permitted themselves to be seen publicly as Jews only under certain circumstances.[14]

The act of concealing Jewishness or another identity was not known by any specific term in early twentieth-century Germany. By invoking the term *passing* as part of the larger discourse of Jewish visibility and recognizability, this book opens up a broader set of questions about self-identification, coding/signifying identity, and ways of interpreting codes. The concept of *passing* connects the German-Jewish experience to other widely known histories of concealing, including racial passing (Black passing for White) and sexual or queer passing (nonheterosexual for heterosexual).[15] For our purposes, Jewish passing is defined as an act in which a self-identified Jew: (1) deliberately presents as non-Jewish; (2) omits information or avoids offering a corrective when taken for non-Jewish; or (3) takes advantage of privileges that result from being perceived as a member of the dominant culture.[16] As a phenomenon, passing is sometimes ephemeral and can come to an abrupt end. It does not necessarily indicate a lasting desire to abandon Jewishness completely or to become a non-Jew.[17] For passing to be successful, a socially favored identity (non-Jewish) must eclipse a disfavored one (Jewish), at least temporarily, in the eyes of the beholder. Passing prompts questions about the very existence of identifiable categories.[18] As Werner Sollors has suggested about racial passing, it "highlights an illusory sense of certainty in what is actually an area of social ambiguity and insecurity."[19] By definition, passing requires at least a short-term act of radical assimilation that is closely linked to deception. At the same time, it sometimes can be understood as an act of resistance or an attempt to control the process of signification.[20]

Passing differs to some extent from *covering*, a less extreme but no less consequential way of negotiating public displays and perception. Legal scholar Kenji Yoshino builds on sociologist Erving Goffman's book *Stigma* (1963) to define covering as downplaying but not effacing a disfavored identity to fit into the mainstream, often at the expense of one's civil rights.[21] Whereas passing pertains to the visibility of a trait, covering relates to its obtrusiveness. For example, Franklin Delano Roosevelt covered his known disability by stationing himself behind a table during meetings. In the same vein, Yoshino writes that in the legal world he felt accepted after coming out as gay, but still was instructed not to write about it, a sentiment he summarizes as "[f]ine, be gay, but don't shove it in our faces."[22] This line by Yoshino recalls an ironic quip by satirist Kurt Tucholsky (1890–1935) penned in response to the assassination of politician Walther Rathenau in 1922: "Besides: a Jew shouldn't cause such a fuss over himself. That just exacerbates antisemitism."[23] Tucholsky underscores the fact that Rathenau was killed not only because he was Jewish but also because he inhabited a prominent official position despite encouraging others to be more inconspicuous as Jews. *Covering* is an appropriate term for many precautionary behaviors of Jews in Weimar Germany who sought—or were instructed—to be unobtrusively Jewish, or to "tone down" their Jewishness. *Passing*, on the other hand, is a more apt descriptor for the acts of those who aspired to look non-Jewish.

Encounters during which conspicuous displays of Jewishness, or absences thereof, became relevant are at the heart of this book. Representations of how Jewishness became perceptible during such encounters—of how, when, and why different figures engaged with visibility by coming out as Jewish, being outed by others, passing for non-Jewish, or covering certain elements of Jewishness—drive my inquiry into a culture of perception, embodiment, performance, spectacle, and consequent judgment and repercussions.[24] I demonstrate that, under the relatively emancipated conditions of the Weimar Republic, both performances of Jewishness and textual representations of perceived Jewishness rendered Jewish difference explicitly visible and desirable under certain circumstances. At times, individuals or communities chose to acknowledge their Jewishness openly through acts of solidarity or community building, rather than concealing it in order to conform. Many Zionist circles encouraged Jews to take pride in standing out. Liberal Jews, in contrast, were more likely to seek to blend in; some considered acculturation an accomplishment that propelled them toward the goal of being "more German." Others believed Jews were incapable of passing, or that Jewish difference existed on an indelible or biological level. The recurring treatment and criticism of passing and related notions suggests that this topic warrants further exploration.

Gender played an essential role in the visual assessment of Jewishness and contributed significantly to a person's ability to pass. Bold public displays of Jewishness were still somewhat risky in Weimar Germany, where antisemitic acts of violence repeatedly targeted readily identifiable Jews. Jewish men (especially religious East Europeans) who wore distinctive garments or long beards or who carried prayer books or Jewish newspapers remained easy targets. These and other distinguishing markers made some men more recognizable as Jews than their female counterparts. Even the circumcised male body, on full display in only select public places such as bathhouses or bathing resorts, factored into visible difference on a theoretical level due to Freudian theories.[25] In fact, circumcision plays a central role in the arguments of such scholars as Sander Gilman, Jay Geller, Daniel Boyarin, and Jonathan Boyarin, who write of an indelible or ineradicable "double mark" of Jewish male difference that, though not generally displayed, nevertheless contributed to constructions of gendered Jewish visibility.[26] Not surprisingly, most discussions by these scholars of gender and Jewishness primarily consider men. For many, "the Jew" is almost always gendered male.[27]

There was even more at stake in becoming discernibly Jewish for women, whose supposedly less visible status often enabled them to integrate into the majority population to a greater extent. Sander Gilman has claimed that Jewish women have always been only ambiguously identifiable due to a lack of permanent bodily markers of difference.[28] But this point, too, evades the matter of when and how women became visible on their own terms. In contrast to their male counterparts, Jewish women were considered to be more adaptable and less recognizable. In some cases they were rendered invisible or absent, or were written out of the picture entirely.[29] It is my contention that sexist stereotypes, allegations of excess, and openly discriminatory practices compelled Weimar Jewish women to find new strategies for being subtly visible. Yet choosing to be subtly or barely visible is different from choosing invisibility; the appreciation for Jewishness shown by many Jewish observers demonstrates that understated forms of visibility were critical to the construction of Jewish self-images during this period.

In the early twentieth century, Jewishness emerged as a known quality that one could display and perceive, and which was desirable at certain times, often in Jewish-friendly spaces. Circumstances that fostered the need to pass were often temporary and fluctuated with a shift from public to private, from mainstream to designated Jewish spaces, from indeterminate to more welcoming utterances, or when new details entered a given conversation. Passing provided a provisional haven, but not one that was needed at all times; in some instances, covering unwelcome aspects of Jewish identity in public provided adequate protection. In Weimar Germany, it became less urgent to appear non-Jewish and increasingly worthwhile to be recognizable as a Jew in certain situations. It was not always the case that Jews could control their level of visibility, however. Historically, visibility was not always a choice.

## Jewish Recognizability in Western European History

Visible demarcations of Jewishness have changed significantly in the modern era. Medieval and early modern European sumptuary laws, though not always

enforced, required Jews to make themselves distinguishable by wearing material signifiers including yellow pointed hats or circular insignias, large white
ruff collars, or badges or distinctive garments of another color that represented
Jewish otherness.[30] One historian has termed these "vestimentary stigma symbols."[31] Ordinances stating that Jews were obligated to display a badge or head
covering of sorts were part of Western European legal codes for more than 500
years, from 1215 until the late eighteenth century.[32] Yellow objects remained a
marker imposed upon Jews in a variety of twentieth-century contexts, from the
yellow passport issued to Jewish women seeking residence as sex workers in
St. Petersburg, to the Star of David paired with the word *Jew* (*Jude, Jood, Juif,*
and so forth) in Nazi-occupied lands during the Holocaust and the Second
World War.[33]

With the exception of the Nazi era, markers of Jewishness generally
became much more subtle and more difficult to detect after the Enlightenment.[34] Significantly, most modern visual signifiers of Jewishness from the
late eighteenth century until 1933 were not imposed by governmental sanc-
tions but rather were adopted voluntarily by Jews. Poet Judah Leib Gordon's
1862 entreaty, "Be a man in the streets and a Jew at home," has been taken as
a summation of the Haskalah or Jewish Enlightenment, and more broadly for
the voluntary relegation of religious practice and distinctive dress to the private sphere.[35] Having acquired modern connotations, this phrase remained
well known in Weimar Germany.[36] Free choice and self-identification were
intimately linked with Jewish modernity: only in recent centuries were Jews
at liberty to choose whether to stand out or blend in, to make themselves either distinct or indistinguishable from the majority population. Adopting
modern dress and modifying or foregoing other practices made it possible for
many acculturated Jews in Western Europe to render themselves ambiguously Jewish.

In the late eighteenth century, a significant number of Jews in German-
speaking lands took steps to change their appearance as part of a general process of acculturation. Many adherents of the Haskalah strove to maintain a
separation of public and private, relegating Jewish observance to the home or
to spaces designated for prayer. Beginning with the generation of philosopher
Moses Mendelssohn (1729–86), this meant using the German language in lieu
of (or in addition to) Yiddish or *Judendeutsch*; it also entailed adopting contemporary clothing and hairstyles. Acculturation continued throughout the
nineteenth and early twentieth centuries, when baptism, conversion, intermar-
riages, and withdrawals from the Jewish community were common steps toward gaining entrance to mainstream German society.[37] Many converts stayed

connected to Jewish family members and traditions even after entry into the German mainstream. In the eyes of zealous antisemites, however, Jewish conversion represented nothing more than an extreme form of passing that posed a threat to the German population at large, and both converts and Jews were prohibited from joining certain German organizations.

Antisemitism was both a major cause of, and a response to, instances of Jewish passing. The awareness that some Jews had begun to elect to become less recognizable, along with new perceptions of race as something that was not only skin deep, prompted a virulent wave of antisemitic sentiment in the early nineteenth century.[38] Jews passing for non-Jews were perceived as dangerous, and those who wished to avoid them elaborated at length on how to spot a Jew. Performances known as Jew Farces, which portrayed Jews as unsuccessful imitators of non-Jews, taught audiences to read codes that supposedly betrayed Jewishness.[39] Prominent cultural figures, too, took up the cause of rallying against passing Jews. In one especially vicious case in 1811, German Romantic writer Achim von Arnim gave a speech titled "On the Distinguishing Signs of Jewishness" to the eating club known as the Christlich-deutsche Tischgesellschaft (Christian-German Table Society) in which he condemned "secret Jews" and warned of the unseen dangers of hidden Jewish traits. Arnim contended that Jews proudly boasted of the ability to hide their true identities, noting that he would welcome the chance to get women to uncover their "bushy moorish (*mohrenartig*) hair."[40] He further purported that Jewish men removed their beards and wore blond wigs and new clothes to appear less Jewish, and that one could always spot a Jewish woman in disguise based on her tendency to wear jewelry.[41] Even as Arnim and others sought to prevent the participation of Jews in German culture, it was becoming increasingly difficult to identify those they sought to exclude, and to distinguish between Jewish and non-Jewish Germans.[42]

For men who maintained ties to Jewish religious observance, outward symbols of Jewishness assumed a number of visible forms in the late nineteenth and early twentieth centuries. It's worth noting that this was a relatively small group. In the Weimar era, Jews in Germany numbered 550,000 to 600,000, or just under 1 percent of the total German population. Of these, only about 15 percent, or 80,000 to 90,000 Jews, identified as Orthodox or maintained a high level of religious observance.[43] Depending on place of origin, as well as denominational, prayer group, and family affiliations, a religious Jewish man might have at times worn and displayed a skullcap (yarmulke); beard; sidelocks (*peyes*); or parts of a prayer shawl worn below other clothing, specifically the shawl's tassels or *tzitzit*. He also might have worn such traditional garb as a distinctive coat or caftan, or any of a number of hats.[44] Whereas some markers rendered the wearer discernibly Jewish even from a distance, others were much more difficult to see. A skullcap could disappear under a commonly worn, mainstream style of hat; the fringes of a shawl could remain hidden underneath other layers, though some believed they should be displayed visibly. In both cases, the wearer might have chosen to suspend ambiguity by revealing these items in a private setting.

As a general rule, the more modern Jewish women in Germany became, the less overtly Jewish they appeared.[45] The beginning of the nineteenth century marked a departure from the past as women gradually adopted more modern clothing and religious practices, and married women such as Berlin salon hostess Henriette Herz (1764–1847) switched from covering their hair with cloth head coverings to wearing wigs (*sheitels*).[46] Like other symbols of modernity, wigs have been controversial from the outset, for, as one rabbi noted, "to beautify oneself with a wig . . . was as if one went uncovered, since, to the naked eye, there appeared no difference between hair and wig."[47] The majority of German-Jewish women eventually became less religious and abandoned hair covering altogether, much to the chagrin of Orthodox rabbis.[48] Among the women who continued to wear wigs, many opted to wear updated, modern wigs that were manufactured for mass consumption and were designed to be nearly invisible. In chapter 1, I investigate some of the ways that Jews were identified and became visible to each other, including both racialized and embodied characteristics, as well as material signifiers such as wigs that were worn to signal Jewish observance.

The 1920s saw the emergence of a tension between a newly discovered sense of Jewish identity and pride, on the one hand, and a deep-seated fear of antisemitic attacks, on the other. A number of incidents that took place in Berlin illustrate this point. With a population of roughly four million, approximately 173,000 or 4 percent of whom were Jewish, central Berlin generally provided a significant degree of anonymity for all of its residents.[49] Even so, the highly visible presence of the East European Jewish minority—so-called *Ostjuden*—called attention to Jewish difference. Jews from Eastern Europe made up almost 20 percent of Germany's Jewish population by 1925 and had a strong presence both in Weimar Jewish culture (as in one photomontage by Abraham Pisarek; see figure 1) and as targets of antisemitism.[50] In 1923, violent riots against Jews and "Jewish-looking" persons broke out in the Scheunenviertel district near Berlin's Alexanderplatz, which was home to many East European Jews.[51] Such large-scale acts of violence were comparable to major pogroms in Eastern Europe, the memory of which still incited fear in many

Fig. 1. View of Berlin's Grenadierstraße in the Scheunenviertel, photo-montage by Abraham Pisarek in *Israelitisches Familienblatt*, 1930. (Courtesy of the Leo Baeck Institute, New York.)

Jews. Even attending services or other events at synagogues was at times considered risky behavior. Especially in Berlin, liberal Jewish organizations including the Centralverein deutscher Staatsbürger jüdischen Glaubens (Central Union of German Citizens of the Jewish Faith; Centralverein or CV) and the Reichsbund jüdischer Frontsoldaten (National Union of Jewish War Veterans; RjF) advocated for Jewish self-defense.[52] These groups advised their members to take precautions when in proximity to a synagogue, though members of the RjF also publicly wore subtle badges to signify their status as Jewish veterans. Chapter 3 contains a longer discussion of different forms of self-defense and self-policing.

At the same time, the rise of Jewish nationalism in the form of Zionism brought with it a desire to resist certain assimilatory trends. Instead of restricting Jewishness to private spaces, some members of the Zionist pioneer movement longed to overwrite the old Enlightenment mentality with a new motto: "Be a Jew at home and a Jew out there."[53] Yet many Zionists believed that the desire to embrace Jewishness outside of one's home could be realized only in the Jewish homeland of Eretz Israel, the Land of Israel, both for safety reasons and out of conviction. Organizations that nurtured this belief grew in popularity throughout the 1920s, though Zionists remained in the minority. The Zionistische Vereinigung für Deutschland (Zionist Federation for Germany or ZVfD), for one, increased its size from fewer than 10,000 members in 1914 to an average of 20,000 in the 1920s, which notably was still less than 4 percent of German Jewry.[54] Already in the early decades of the twentieth century, some highly visible members of student and youth organizations proudly displayed Jewishness by wearing caps and badges that co-opted the medieval yellow badge. Zionists sometimes paired the color yellow with blue and white. These symbols are explored further in chapter 1.

The First World War also marked a turning point in the relationship of German Jews to Jewish culture. In response to the war and other factors including the political and economic instability of the early Weimar Republic, many Jews embraced Jewishness with newfound intensity. They participated widely in Jewish organizations, education programs, and the creation and circulation of Jewish cultural products.[55] Michael Brenner has termed this the "Jewish Renaissance," a movement that was first envisioned in 1901 by philosopher Martin Buber (1878–1965).[56] Chapter 2 considers a range of voluntary (rather than projected) public displays of certain Jewish practices, including reading Jewish publications; urban spaces of consumption that appealed to Jewish consumers; performers who embraced Jewishness on stage; and cinematic encounters with Jewishness. Close analysis of the reception of films that address Jewish topics—including the American film *The Jazz Singer* (Crosland, 1927), as well as *Leichte Kavallerie* (Light Cavalry; Randolf, 1927) and *Dreyfus* (Oswald, 1930)—offers insight into how Jewish audiences in Germany responded to such public displays.[57]

On the other hand, many Jews remained involved in the production of mainstream and avant-garde German culture and media—including literature, journalism, photography, art, music, theater, film, radio, advertisements, and design—that did not deal overtly with Jewish subjects. *Passing Illusions* responds to historian Peter Gay's argument that the contributions of Jewish Germans to German culture were indistinguishable from those of other Germans. It elucidates the social conditions and inner-Jewish discourses that influenced the creation of these cultural products.[58] By focusing mainly on texts that explicitly reference Jewishness, I demonstrate that many Jews in Weimar Germany constantly confronted issues pertaining to passing, covering, and displaying Jewish difference, which on some level amplified their experiences of difference. Though perhaps indistinguishable on most levels, Jewish cultural production originated under different circumstances, and we can interpret it in light of both German and German-Jewish histories.

The swiftly changing stakes for Jews in Germany after January 30, 1933, dramatically exacerbated the need to become less recognizable for Jews living under the Nazi regime. Already on March 1, 1933, Rabbi Max Eschelbacher wrote that many German Jews had become the "new marranos of our time," insofar as they were increasingly reluctant to acknowledge their Jewishness in public, particularly in the workplace.[59] By the late 1930s and into the 1940s, passing could grant access to rights withheld from known Jews. In some cases, passing accompanied the act of going into hiding to avoid arrest or deportation, which often meant the difference between life and death.[60] Attempts at passing under such circumstances took a range of forms, from dying one's hair blond to appear more "Aryan," to attempting to undo a circumcision.[61] But passing did not take on this magnitude of gravity until after the Nazis took power and Jewishness became a life-threatening liability on an everyday basis. In Weimar Germany, representing oneself as non-Jewish or concealing Jewishness generally served as a means to obtain privileges, rights, luxuries, power, or a stronger sense of personal safety and security. This was not always the case for other minorities who passed under vastly different circumstances.

## Passing in Comparative Contexts

Passing is by no means unique to Jews or to Germany. Members of many minority populations—both other minority groups and in other locations—pass or cover as a part of everyday life. For some, passing is difficult to live with and conveys an inauthentic sense of self. For others, it serves as a ticket to a world that they could not enter otherwise. In the interest of brevity, I discuss Jewish passing in locations outside of Germany only briefly and instead focus my comparison on other minority groups, especially racial passing among African Americans, and forms of passing associated with gender and sexuality, particularly in Weimar Germany. Whereas many acts of passing in African American or queer communities were practices sustained over time, sometimes while living as a person of a different race within a new community, or for multiple decades or a lifetime "in the closet," this was generally not the case for German Jews passing in the 1920s and early 1930s.[62] The continued potential for hostility in public settings made it advantageous for Jews in Germany to pass at times, but at other times Jewishness came with its own benefits: Jews developed networks of cultural events, social welfare programs, and commercial support for Jewish-owned businesses. Acts of Jewish passing and covering were common practice, and Jews who selectively passed as part of the integration process generally were not compelled to leave their Jewish communities. As historian Todd Endelman has pointed out, the relatively high degree of "Jew consciousness" among both Jews and non-Jews in Germany and Central Europe resulted in increased attention to how Jews presented themselves.[63]

Whereas little attention has been given to Jewish passing in Germany prior to 1933, Jewish passing elsewhere in Central Europe and beyond has been studied in more depth. Interwar Austria offers an important point of comparison given the extensive cultural transfer that occurred between Austria and Germany; there were noteworthy differences in terms of visibility. The Jewish population of interwar Vienna was roughly 10 percent (with 80 percent born outside Vienna), more than double the proportion of Jews in Berlin.[64] Due to their prominent representation in public life and culture despite Vienna's overtly antisemitic climate, Viennese Jews were even more visible and thus bore a greater burden to downplay Jewishness. As Abigail Gillman and Lisa Silverman have demonstrated, this resulted in articulations of Jewishness that were not always visible or explicit.[65] Klaus Hödl has suggested that Viennese Jewish identity was often expressed through performances and interpersonal interactions.[66] The absence of Jews and Jewishness despite a large Jewish population was even more remarkable in Hungary. In 1920, Budapest had the second-highest percentage of Jews among European cities (after Warsaw), or roughly 23 percent. In *The Invisible Jewish Budapest* (2016), Mary Gluck suggests that a type of "critical cross-dressing" or cultural masquerade served as a means for the Hungarian Jewish bourgeoisie to find its voice.[67] In Prague and

Czechoslovakia, as Scott Spector and others have shown, Jews operated between identities and many were visible primarily due to their German-language cultural contributions.[68]

Questions of passing and visibility have been treated to some extent with respect to French-Jewish and Anglo-Jewish contexts, and more scholarship on these topics has begun to emerge. Western Europe lacked the same systematic legal discrimination present in Central Europe, and, while passing was not as necessary, there was still a strong desire among Jews to be perceived as sufficiently French or English. French Jews, who have long grappled with issues of particularity and universalism, were able to achieve prominent positions in early twentieth-century France while living openly as Jews, though many favored the "public suppression of ethnicity."[69] Leora Auslander's work examines how Jews in Paris and Berlin used material culture and cultural practices to express likeness and difference from non-Jews and other Jews.[70] As was the case in Berlin and Vienna, immigrant Jews were particularly visible in Paris in the interwar period, which led to tensions between French-born Jews and those whose Jewishness was more readily apparent.[71] Endelman has suggested that Britain's "genteel intolerance" similarly caused Jews "to mute their Jewishness" in order to be perceived as English.[72] A recent volume edited by Nathan Abrams deals with the absence of visible Jews in British film and popular culture.[73]

Jewish passing in the United States has been studied most comprehensively and offers insight into how Jewishness was performed and framed in religious, cultural, and ethnic terms.[74] Some Jews passed unintentionally: for example, many Sephardic Jewish immigrants who looked and acted unlike the Ashkenazic Jewish majority were mistaken for non-Jewish Hispanics or Turks, especially by other Jews.[75] Daniel Itzkovitz has highlighted the paradoxical nature of the fluid status attributed to most American Jews, who were perceived as both White and racially other; American and foreign; and unstable in terms of gender difference.[76] For Itzkovitz, Jewish difference is "caught in the double bind of the 'chameleonic race' marked at once by indistinguishable sameness and irreducible difference."[77] Warren Hoffman's *The Passing Game* (2009) similarly links Jewishness and sexual difference. Hoffman examines texts in which Jewishness is mediated through the lens of queer sexuality, suggesting that "the beginnings of queer Jewish identity and culture in America were all about passing."[78] This also applies to German Jews on several levels.

Studying German-Jewish passing together with other forms of passing leads us to this book's claim that seeing Jewishness entails parsing a form of minority visibility that is at once gendered, queer, and racialized. Scholars

have begun to examine Jewish difference as a category akin to gender difference, and several have argued that Jewish difference intersects with sexual difference, homosexuality, and the performance of queerness (which can be understood as an often politicized identification with sexual or gender
difference).[79] Eve Sedgwick, too, has suggested that parallels between homophobia and antisemitism have yielded commonalities between coming out
as gay and coming out as Jewish, particularly in urban environments.[80] Jewish
passing in Weimar Germany indeed had much in common with queer or LGBT
passing, and negotiating the process of coming out as Jewish bore distinct similarities to coming out as a sexual minority during that time. For these and other
groups, spatial boundaries were critical to the containment and liberation of
knowledge about concealed identities.[81] Of course, coming out as Jewish differed from coming out as a sexual minority in significant ways. In most cases,
one did not need to come out as Jewish to one's own family, although some
who passed as non-Jews also attempted to conceal their Jewish past from their
children. This book's conclusion explores how commonalities between Jewish
and queer passing and coming out narratives—for example, coded and ambiguous signifiers, and protective spaces and subcultures—point to the significance of Jewish passing for queer studies.

Racial passing, particularly in African American contexts, provides an
important basis of comparison for thinking through Jewish passing in the early
twentieth century, though this approach also has notable limitations. This comparison is limited because of significant differences in the experiences of those
who either self-identified or were identified as Black or Jewish, or both. Visual
markers such as skin color have played a far greater role in the construction of
racial difference among Blacks.[82] Despite the problematic aspects of these parallels, African American and Jewish identities have been constructed according
to similar racial models at different points in history. In 1924, Virginia passed
the Act to Preserve Racial Integrity, which prohibited interracial marriage and
defined a White person as one with "no trace of other blood" (the "one-drop
rule") for U.S. racial and segregation policies. Nazi racial policies including
the Nuremberg Laws of 1935 took the American "one-drop rule" as a model.[83]
In the late nineteenth and early twentieth centuries, much of African American
identity was built around an idea of Blackness as a fixed construct. Cultural
theorist Sara Ahmed, writing about Blacks who pass for White, points out that
the very notion of being able to pass destabilizes and calls into question the
presumption of Black visibility.[84] Passing confounds widespread notions about
the visible properties of racialized difference and lends urgency to the questions of whether and how such difference can be noticed.

This is also the case for Jewish visibility: it is possible to identify only some Jews by relying on visual information, and disrupting preconceptions of what Jews look like can lead to confusion, anger, shame, or tragedy. The unreliable or incomplete visual coding of difference necessitates the use of nonvisual categories, including explicit coming out statements and other forms of naming. Weimar Jews who had the ability to pass or cover controlled the flow of information and thus empowered themselves to fit in among less friendly or unknown publics. Chapter 4 examines the consequences of several instances of passing as well as unsuccessful attempts to pass. One of the best examples of a passing narrative by a German-Jewish author, Jakob Loewenberg's cautionary drama, *Der gelbe Fleck* (The Yellow Badge, 1899; first published 1924), tells how one mother's revelation that she passed for non-Jewish caused her antisemitic son to take his own life.

Points of intersection between literary expressions of Black and Jewish identities are likely not coincidental, as several scholars have shown. Indeed, many early twentieth-century passing narratives were produced during a period that some consider the heyday of passing in American Jewish history.[85] American authors Fannie Hurst and Edna Ferber, both of German-Jewish descent, wrote stories that number among the most popular representations of African American passing, in part because of the success of films based on these novels. Lori Harrison-Kahan's work, which analyzes Hurst's *Imitation of Life* (1933) and Ferber's *Show Boat* (1926), among others, demonstrates that Black-Jewish relations and narratives of racial and ethnic passing served as a site for a feminist critique of Whiteness.[86] Whereas *Imitation of Life* deals mainly with African American passing, it also references the inability of some Jews to integrate into mainstream culture.[87] In these novels by Hurst and Ferber, as in many passing novels by African American authors, women constitute the passing subjects. In each case, a racially ambiguous character passes for White and faces the consequences of falling in love with a White man. American Jewish authors such as Philip Roth who explore racial passing often hint at the flexibility of Jewishness and Blackness to be interpreted in multiple ways.[88] Literary scholar Jennifer Glaser has suggested that the decades following the Second World War saw many American Jewish writers speaking through other minorities in acts of racial ventriloquism that enabled them to articulate their position as Jews.[89]

Theories of Jewish passing are in fact indebted to African American history. This usage of the verb *to pass* originated in the United States with the emergence of a Black population that could pass, first for free and then for White.[90] Werner Sollors has surmised that the term *passing* entered nineteenth-century American literature via citations of notices concerning runaway slaves.[91] Such notices stated, for instance, that a runaway might "endeavor to pass for a free man."[92] Written passes that could be duplicated were issued to slaves by their masters, and these papers also assisted runaway slaves hoping to pass for free men and women.[93] Current usage of *passing* became standard in the 1920s, an era of both newly restrictive laws and the Harlem Renaissance.[94] The 1920s also saw "a veritable explosion of literary work on racial passing," which historian Allyson Hobbs argues occurred "precisely at a moment when black artists celebrated blackness and racial pride."[95] The best known passing novels associated with the Harlem Renaissance include Walter White's *Flight* (1926); the rerelease of James Weldon Johnson's *The Autobiography of an Ex-Colored Man* (1912/1927); Jessie Redmon Fauset's *Plum Bun* (1928); and Nella Larsen's *Passing* (1929), which is the most often cited work on this phenomenon.[96] Like the popular novels by Ferber and Hurst, the majority of these works deal with racially indeterminate female protagonists who pass for White. Several scholars argue that the appearance of Jewish "chameleonic" figures in these passing narratives suggested that Jews were better able to move between roles or served as mediators.[97]

Ambiguous or unidentifiable bodies—especially women who are not easily classifiable—appear as a threat in Larsen's novel, as in Loewenberg's drama and other texts produced in Weimar Germany. Larsen's novel culminates with the death of Clare Kendry, who either falls from or is pushed out of a window, conceivably as a punishment for passing for White. Judith Butler's critical reading of Larsen's novel highlights the necessity of juxtaposing supposedly "marked bodies" with the "unmarked bodies" that establish a norm in both racialized and queer contexts.[98] Scholars such as Catherine Rottenberg have built on Butler's work to make a case for the role of passing in the performance of Jewishness.[99] Further, other scholars have argued that female protagonists who pass move beyond binaries to inhabit a position of hybridity.[100] Cultural texts from the Weimar period suggest that representations of German-Jewish passing reflect patterns of negotiating subject positions similar to those of other minority groups. In Weimar Germany, the creation of ambiguous or dually coded Jewish identities similarly figured as a means of challenging established cultural norms.

## Weimar Jewish Passing: Language, Difference, and Gender

The concept of *passing* goes by many names and at times goes unnamed. Although assimilation, acculturation, and other forms of integration have been explicitly referenced in German-speaking contexts for centuries, the German language contains no exact translation for *passing*. Several verbs allow for the possibility that a person could be taken for something else (*für etwas gehalten werden; durchgehen als; gelten als*), and at least one verb/noun pair renders into German the concept of adapting or conforming, potentially to the point of becoming indistinguishable (*sich anpassen; Anpassung*).[101] Another verb describes the act of fitting in (*hineinpassen*). Still, the act of maintaining the outward presentation of a different identity for a brief or sustained period of time has no direct equivalent in German. Even when a person passes for several decades, there is no adequate name for this long-term performance or transformation. One scholar has proposed that the verb *passieren* (to happen, occur, pass through) offers an appropriate translation because it implies that something must take place for passing to be effective.[102] For the most part, however, the English word *passing* is left untranslated in German-language scholarly discourse and compensates for a conspicuous linguistic lacuna.[103]

Within Jewish contexts, the decision to conceal Jewishness in public, whether voluntary or forced, indicates a controversial break with tradition that is described using a variety of contentious terms. Perhaps the best-known example, the marranos (also known as conversos, crypto-Jews, or secret Jews) with origins in fifteenth-century Spain have come to represent both transgression and proud defiance. East European Jews provide some scholars with a more recent example of a subgroup whose "ethnic anxiety" led them to forgo traits linked to Jewishness.[104] Modern movements including Zionism have at times rejected any disavowal of Jewishness outright; many Zionists believed that the liberal Jews they called "assimilationists" were passing or covering on some level.[105] Further, Jewish languages have evolved different words to characterize acts of crossing over into another realm. In Hebrew, the word for sin or transgression, *aveira*, has the same root as the verb *la'avor*, which means to pass or cross over. Yiddish, on the other hand, contains a particularly apt term for Westernized Jews who resembled non-Jews: *daytsh*, which simply means German.[106] For Yiddish speakers, to be Jewish and Western European was to be associated with Germanness, and to want to be recognized among Jews as a different, "non-Jewish looking" type of Jew.

The notion of passing for a non-Jew hinges on the presumption that there is such a thing as someone who "looks Jewish" or possesses Jewish difference. Attempts to pass destabilized fixed or precise notions of Jewishness while also reinforcing and codifying some of these same ideas about what Jews looked like. Passing in Weimar Germany also occurred in an era when, as historian Maria Makela has suggested, the blurring of identity challenged the reliability of vision as a means of assessing ethnicity, class, gender, sexuality, and other categories.[107] Like other categories of difference, the visual parameters of Jewishness—as well as its ability to be hidden or eradicated—are often blurred or contested. Many believe that Jewish difference is always visible, that Jewish bodies stand in contrast to so-called "unmarked" non-Jewish bodies. Yet the boundaries between Jewish and non-Jewish, Jewish and Christian, and so forth, are subject to constant interrogation and renegotiation. Jewish acts of crossing and transgressing these borders serve purposes of personal, familial, or professional advancement. Sustained in the long term, passing is a disavowal or transformation of identity to overcome circumstances that prevent Jews from rising to the top of a given field or group. Jews who pass temporarily occupy the space between the tenuous binaries of Jew and non-Jew, presence and absence, visibility and invisibility, known and unknown.[108]

Although the act of passing for non-Jewish can be sustained for extended periods of time, it often is restricted to a limited period that is terminated by either the passer or someone this person encounters. This book, like the texts and discourses it examines, focuses primarily on instances of Jewish passing that come to an end, as well as specific moments when an observer realizes or is informed that the other person is a Jewish "other." The process of detecting Jewishness during such encounters may involve an exchange of insider codes, or an "aha moment" that corrects for a nonrecognition or misrecognition. As Sara Ahmed has argued, an encounter with an unknown other suggests not only a meeting, but especially "a meeting which involves surprise and conflict."[109] The "not at all Jewish" example at the beginning of this introduction demonstrates that this also applies to Jewish passing. Coming out or marking the self as Jewish, and thereby ending an act of passing, causes surprise and subverts notions about what the other should look like—not only in the eyes of non-Jews but also for other Jews. Moreover, there was an ongoing struggle for power between those who would profit from exposing hidden Jewishness, and those who desired to remain unseen or to construct identity themselves. Chapter 3 examines some of the power dynamics at play in fictional surprise encounters that out female protagonists as Jews, including in Clementine Krämer's *Esther* (1920) and Ruth Landshoff-Yorck's *Roman einer Tänzerin* (Novel of a Dancer, 1933).

Both non-Jews and Jews have participated in the social construction of Jewish racial difference, as well as attempts to detect and contest it. The idea that the Jews constituted a distinct and also visibly perceptible race took root in the late eighteenth century.[110] Notions of fixed identity—the sense that a person was biologically either Jewish or not Jewish, and would remain so regardless of religious conversion, intermarriage, or other attempts to move away from Jewishness—gained traction in the German cultural landscape in the nineteenth century.[111] Once the images of different, diseased, and dangerous Jews became an accepted part of racial antisemitism, Jews responded by approaching the data in a variety of systematic and scientific ways.[112] In the early twentieth century, such Zionist scholars as Arthur Ruppin (1876–1943) and Felix Theilhaber (1884–1956) wrote extensively about the composition and decline of the Jewish population while advocating for its renewal.[113] In addition to printing pieces by Ruppin, Theilhaber, and others, the Weimar Jewish press included numerous discussions of the "race question," which is treated at length in chapter 1.

Jews who attempted to pass for non-Jews defied the medical and sociological discourses that suggested this would be impossible. The liberal Jewish position that Jews were able to fully adapt and fit in among other Germans was compromised to some extent by a widespread acknowledgment, if not acceptance, of allegations of Jewish physical difference. That Weimar Jews participated in the construction of a potentially visible form of Eastern Jewish difference reveals an implicit recognition of racialized Jewish difference, as well as a tension between identifying with this difference and desiring to distance oneself from it. For Jewish audiences, dark skin, hair, and eye coloring all rendered the body more Eastern, and thus more "authentically" Jewish. Lithographs and other popular artworks by artist Rahel Szalit-Marcus, also discussed in chapter 1, offer potent examples of how stereotypical coloring and exaggerated features coded their subjects as Jewish.

For Weimar Jews, passing figured as a means toward achieving a type of dual legibility, of appearing simultaneously non-Jewish and Jewish, depending on the viewer. Yet passing and recognizability were not always intentional or able to be controlled, and they sometimes resulted in confusion or mistaken identifications.[114] On occasion, non-Jews intentionally passed for Jews in a form of reverse passing, which further complicated matters.[115] Chapter 4 explores how names contributed to Jewish coding, including their role in the reception of the film *Überflüssige Menschen* (Superfluous People; Rasumny, 1926). It also offers a reading of the multivalent nature of passing, invisibility, and deception in the film *Mensch ohne Namen* (*The Man Without a Name*; Ucicky, 1932) to facilitate a comparison of the abilities of men and women to pass for both non-Jewish and Jewish.

Like some Jewish men, a great number of Jewish women in Weimar Germany had the ability to pass and were treated as if they were non-Jews, whether they gave this impression wittingly or unwittingly. Displaying conspicuous,

Fig. 2. Advertisement for Bihlmaier's Institute for Cosmetic Surgery in *C.V.-Zeitung*, 1932: "Your appearance determines your life." (Courtesy of the Leo Baeck Institute, New York.)

visible markers linked to biological or physical traits, especially dark hair, dark eyes, and prominent noses, made it more likely that one would be identified as a Jew. But in an age when hair dye and plastic surgery were becoming ever more popular, even supposedly innate markers included few factors that remained unchangeable. Advertisements for women's wigs and hair dye were ubiquitous in the Weimar Jewish press, and by the late 1920s ads for plastic surgery that appeared in mainstream German publications had also made their way into select Jewish publications. One series of ads for Bihlmaier's Institute for Cosmetic Surgery highlighted the significance of procedures such as "nose corrections" for personal and professional success by way of slogans such as "A woman's face is her calling card!" and "Your appearance determines your life" (see figure 2).[116] Despite the growing acceptance of racialized models of Jewishness, being recognizably Jewish in public to some extent became more of a choice and less a predetermined destiny.[117]

For some women who may have passed unintentionally, it was important to announce Jewishness on their own terms. As Liz Conor has pointed out, this was the era of the "appearing woman"; it was a time at which "modern women understood self-display to be part of the quest for mobility, self-determination, and sexual identity."[118] Jewish women, like other modern women, put themselves on display, yet also found ways to modulate what could be seen. Female protagonists in Jewish-themed literature and film began to reflect some modern impulses of the New Woman, who in Weimar Germany was both consumer and consumed commodity, herself both spectator and object of the spectator's gaze.[119] She was free to travel and walk alone, to inhabit urban public spaces such as cafés, boulevards, and department stores, and to pursue the career and lifestyle she desired (see figure 3).[120] Whereas many New Women tended toward "excessive exhibitionism," particularly with respect to the body and sexuality, Jewish women enhanced their visibility by choosing not to pass, or by covering Jewish-coded traits only in certain situations.[121] The "New Jewish Woman" established herself through public acts, for example: working for Jewish organizations, or advocating for women's rights as Jews in Jewish and non-Jewish circles.[122] Many women came out via simple declarations ("yes, I am Jewish") or made themselves subtly recognizable through performative behaviors, such as purchasing kosher products in department stores or openly reading Jewish periodicals.

Fashion, too, played a significant role in the gendered engagement with Jewish visibility; both modesty and opulence were contested signifiers of Jewishness. Chapter 3 examines how negative stereotypes regarding Jewish women's excessive or ostentatious displays led various Jewish groups to take steps

Fig. 3. Luzie Hatch with her stepmother in Berlin. (Courtesy of Ralph Hatch.)

toward policing and disciplining such behaviors. Women were instructed to adopt a simple, plain aesthetic that ostensibly would uphold traditional Jewish values. An examination of public encounters at travel destinations including bathing resorts, exemplified in Max Brod's novel, *Jüdinnen* (Jewesses, 1911), offers insight into how Jewish women were typecast according to their adherence with such instructions. Arthur Schnitzler's novella *Fräulein Else* (1924) similarly sheds light on how physical appearance and socioeconomic status impacted Jewish visibility. Negotiating, circumventing, or overturning societal expectations was essential for managing perceptions of Jewish difference as it intersected with the gendered female body.

Jewish visibility and its gendered dimensions provide an essential and previously overlooked model for understanding the complex reasons behind hiding, covering, and displaying controversial aspects of identity. *Passing Illusions* demonstrates that Jewish recognizability, similar to racial and queer visibility in many ways, is contingent on a variety of common factors: familial and social contexts; internalization and public performances of stereotypical and symbolic behaviors; and the desire for self-expression without shame, as well as the ability to be identified by others. What some observers believed they saw was not always the whole picture. Although many Jews could pass for non-Jews, a good number only gave the illusion of passing, but in fact remained visible on some level. Through its analysis of circumstances that led to instances of Jewish passing and coming out in Weimar Germany, this book offers insight into the historical quest for recognition and acceptance that remains relevant for discussions of different types of minority visibility today.

## CHAPTER 1

# Methods of Projecting and Detecting Jewishness

Being visibly Jewish hinged on a set of codes that were continually reconstituted and reinforced in Jewish cultural production: literary works, periodicals, and visual representations of Jews that were produced by Jews. In all of these forms, Jews in Germany acknowledged the visibility of Jewish difference; only in some cases did authors and artists challenge or complicate stereotypical notions of what Jews supposedly looked like. By way of example, Berlin author Sammy Gronemann (1875–1952) describes different situations in which Jewishness is revealed in his popular book of humorous autobiographical anecdotes, *Schalet: Beiträge zur Philosophie des "Wenn Schon"* (Cholent: Essays on the Philosophy of the "So What," 1927). Gronemann dubs this act of detecting and revealing a game of "hide-and-seek" (*Versteckspiel*).[1] Signs including word choice, items of clothing, hair color, eye color, and facial features convey Jewishness to observers in Gronemann's stories. Some encounters prove beneficial to one or both parties. In one situation, the narrator's traveling uncle announces his Jewishness in the Jewish quarter of a Portuguese city with the common greeting *shalom aleichem*, whereupon the local residents suddenly insist he join them for a Sabbath meal.[2] In another case, the discovery of this same uncle's prayer shawl prompts a Jewish hotel employee in Tangier, Morocco, to fill the uncle's coat pockets with kosher delicacies.

A third scenario, however, depicts the narrator's encounter with a young woman he meets while waiting for a streetcar one evening in Vienna. He offers her a cigarette, and when she emerges from the shadows, he suspects she is Jewish because she has what he describes as a "typical Oriental face." A close-up glimpse prompts him to ask directly, "Are you a Jew (*Jüdin*)?" Startled and wary of an antisemitic attack, she answers: "Yes, I'm a Jew! . . . And I'm proud of it, for your information!" She then promptly throws the cigarette back at him before disappearing.[3] During this third encounter, Jewish difference becomes recognizable in two stages: it is first projected onto a woman whose embodied traits mark her as potentially Jewish and also "Eastern" (or "Oriental"), but it remains hypothetical until she verbally discloses that she identifies as Jewish.[4] Questioned about her heritage on a dark street at night, she has no way of knowing that the questioner is merely curious and has no malicious intentions— and, in fact, is Jewish himself. Although her response makes clear that she does not wish to hide her Jewishness, her apparent fear and vulnerability to this stranger translate into a paradoxical performance of Jewish "pride" that consists of running away.

Here, racialized Jewish difference carries over into the realm of gender difference. Gendered stereotypes play a role in the transfer of information, and this woman is subjected to a gaze predisposed to perceive her as exotic or other. Indeed, racialized coding also was common in mainstream Weimar contexts, and many visual representations of dark-haired modern women were perceived as Jewish, sometimes incorrectly. Darcy Buerkle has pointed out that many 1920s images of modern or New Women were coded "Jewish-enough" even when not explicitly identified as Jewish.[5] Scholars have demonstrated that male Jews—and even Judaism itself—were feminized to the point of debasement, often due to a racialized perception of their supposedly inferior bodies.[6] Jewish women, on the other hand, were often categorized according to their presumed place of origin and individual appearance. Unlike in the first two examples above, where men make themselves recognizably Jewish through the use of language and religious objects, it is the woman's coloring and face that mark her as Jewish.

The visual grammar of Jewish difference commonly relied upon traits such as dark hair and eye color, which were interpreted as indicators of racial or ethnic Jewish background. Whereas many Central European women with blond or light brown hair were deemed less Jewish-looking, East European women—who, according to contemporary statistics, were more likely to have natural dark coloring—were considered more easily identifiable.[7] This young woman's physical qualities and dark coloring are not only those of a Jew, but specifically those of a "typical Oriental" woman, which here is code for someone with ties to the authentic Jewish culture of the East (or, in this case, Vienna as a stand-in for the East). As Gronemann's story suggests, members of German-Jewish communities internalized these potential differences and used them as a form of shorthand for reading others during moments of public encounter.[8] The performance of Jewish difference intersected with gender because many people believed it to be visible on the bodies of Eastern Jews, and particularly Eastern women.

This chapter explores a range of visually legible factors that contributed to how both Jews and non-Jews assessed Jewishness.[9] I have divided these factors into two main categories: projections of embodied types of Jewishness, including those associated with race and ethnicity; and material signifiers including clothing and religious objects. Publicly displayed acts, practices, and gestures that further contributed to visibility are discussed in later chapters. I demonstrate that, despite the strong opposition expressed by many Weimar Jews to methods of identification based on stereotyping, Jews nevertheless relied heavily on similar forms of racial, ethnic, and cultural profiling using factors in these same categories. The chapter's excursus on racial otherness positions race as a central component of the complex set of visual markers that Weimar Jews used to create notions of community and determine who should be identified as a Jew in a racial/ethnic, religious, or cultural sense.[10] By mapping out different Jewish constructions of race in the Weimar Republic, I illuminate the divisive and unifying effects of conceptualizing Jewish difference as a form of racial difference.

Although many held that Jewishness was written on the body, others believed that Jewishness could be concealed such that it was visible to only a select few. The gendered dynamics of concealing Jewishness take center stage in the chapter's second section on East/West and Dark/Light dichotomies. Resistance to stereotyping and racialized notions of Jewishness may have influenced the adoption of several difficult to spot material signifiers of Jewishness, such as small badges or nearly invisible wigs, which enabled Jews to choose to reveal Jewishness only to select observers. Modern fashions such as short hairstyles, as well as technological advances from hair dye to plastic surgery, encouraged consumers to look for Jewish difference. Yet they also made it simple for Jews to take measures to cover, disguise, or alter the body to make Jewishness more or less visible. At times, Weimar Jews used modern innovations to challenge binary, opposing, or mutually exclusive notions of Germanness and Jewishness.

## Constructions of Embodied Racial and Ethnic Difference

The process of reading embodied signifiers of Jewishness, and of choosing when to display, hide, or ignore them, was fraught with anxiety and tension during the 1920s and early 1930s. Public demonstrations of antisemitism in Germany, though intermittent, were perpetrated against anyone believed to "look Jewish." Those in search of easy targets for antisemitic violence or discrimination were especially likely to prey upon men who were readily identifiable on the basis of distinctive garments, beards, or visible Jewish objects such as prayer books. On the other hand, women's garments and hairstyles associated with religious observance generally signified modesty and thus did not stand out to the same degree. Contradictory to notions that women's bodies were less visible because they lacked permanent markers of Jewish difference such as circumcision, women were just as likely, if not more so, to be identified as Jewish based on physical characteristics. Other antisemitic stereotypes pertaining to Jewish women's alleged opulence prompted determinations of Jewishness on the basis of conspicuous displays of wealth (see chapter 3). In many cases, the bodies of both Jewish men and women, including hair and eye color, facial features, and clothing and other adornments, became objects of scrutiny.

Stereotypical visual characteristics were used to assess Jewishness both by antisemites and by others who faced the threat of antisemitism. The goal was to distinguish between "us" and "them" as easily as possible. Many Jews deemed it imperative to be able to provide at least a cursory answer to the simple question: "Is this person a friend or foe?" Without linguistic clues or verbal confirmation, and in the absence of obvious clothing or other definitive identifying markers, an appraisal of embodied, material, or performative factors provided an answer quickly, if not always accurately. Peter Gay has written that many Berlin Jews were certain they could recognize a Jew due to appearance, a way of speaking, or by subtle, elusive signs.[11] Regardless of whether the term *race* came into play, the cultural logic of the day understood Jewishness to have both a biological foundation and the same "putative visibility" commonly associated with race.[12] Although many Jews resisted the very notion of a "Jewish race"—particularly one imposed by antisemitic eugenicists posing as race scientists—they nevertheless took note of any clues that supposedly hinted at Jewishness.

Constructions of physical difference in the early twentieth century drew heavily from scientific and pseudoscientific systems developed in the eighteenth and nineteenth centuries, all of which contributed to the modern notion of being able to see embodied Jewishness. Already in the eighteenth century, thinkers emphasized the universal nature of humankind while still highlighting differences among unequal peoples. In the 1770s, Johann Caspar Lavater popularized physiognomy, the study of fixed facial features, which were examined intensively in the form of silhouettes and other visual images.[13] Shortly thereafter, Christian Wilhelm von Dohm's *Über die bürgerliche Verbesserung der Juden* (On the Civic Improvement of the Jews, 1781) posited that alleged physical inadequacies among Jews could be treated, thus calling for a kind of regeneration in the face of degeneration, as Jonathan Hess has observed.[14] Other

German scientists and philosophers steered these debates about difference in the direction of racial theories, many of which classified Jews as a distinct group among other peoples (*Völker*) or races (*Rassen*). Late eighteenth-century naturalists believed Jews to have clearly identifiable signs of innate Jewishness already from birth, as Iris Idelson-Shein has demonstrated.[15] Orientalist Johann David Michaelis conceived of Jews as an "unmixed race of a more southern people," thereby attributing Jewish difference to the climate of Mediterranean regions and the racial qualities that evolved there. In contrast to Dohm, Michaelis developed a theory of racial antisemitism that planted the seeds for later models.[16]

Racial antisemitism and nationalism went hand in hand, and the Romantic movement of the early nineteenth century continued to frame Jews as a population that was biologically distinct from Christian German society. Many Jews attempted to circumvent this classification by converting to Christianity, which prompted malicious verbal attacks from antisemites such as Achim von Arnim. Marriage to Christian Germans often accompanied conversion; both provided yet another form of access to mainstream, non-Jewish society. In some instances, converts from Judaism not only were considered different but also were accused of attempting to hide their difference by passing as non-Jews.[17] In fact, some converts relocated and succeeded at concealing their Jewish backgrounds from their descendants. Some who successfully passed managed to erase all traces of Jewishness from the historical record.[18] But many known former Jews still could not gain access to all desired rights and privileges of non-Jews. The fear that Jews were on some level undetectable, coupled with the rise of German nationalism and race science in the 1870s, and colonialist racial dichotomies more broadly, led to widespread constructions of Jewishness along racialized "color" lines.

Different chromatic or color-based systems of codes were put in place for the purpose of scientifically classifying physical characteristics as racially or ethnically Jewish. Constructions of the oppositional binary categories "White" and "Black" meant that Jews were often aligned with one or the other.[19] Interestingly, the term *white Jew*, an insult that became popular in Nazi Germany, did not refer to a Jew, but rather a non-Jew who behaved like a Jew, as Valerie Weinstein points out in her work on films made during the Third Reich.[20] Jews were not always considered White. Sander Gilman's important book, *The Jew's Body* (1991), traces historical comparisons between Jews, Blacks, and Black Africans in racial science, suggesting that Jews had crossed racial boundaries in the global imaginary. Blackness became applicable to Jews, both with respect to racial difference in the form of skin pigmentation, and as a literal color and metonymic form of shorthand for stereotypical dark hair, eyes, or skin that was not "pure" white. The term *Black* came to be associated with Jewishness more broadly, including as a referent for skin color that also was perceived as swarthy, olive, or yellow-tinted.[21] Such prominent Jewish intellectuals as Sigmund Freud (1856–1939) and Franz Kafka (1883–1924) noted that Jews were visibly different in ways that paralleled the racial difference of Blacks.[22] Many other Jews, too, internalized these projections and conceptualized Jewish difference as visible on the body, though sometimes in subversive ways.

Yellowish skin color was mapped onto literary characters leading up to and during the Weimar period. Both non-Jewish and Jewish authors manipulated racial stereotypes involving the color yellow in order to call attention to antisemitic or negative perceptions of Jews. In fact, several books by Jewish writers actively deployed such stereotypes in their satirical responses to earlier works. One widely distributed novel, Artur Landsberger's *Berlin ohne Juden* (Berlin without Jews, 1925), responded to Hugo Bettauer's novel, *Die Stadt ohne Juden: Ein Roman von Übermorgen* (The City without Jews: A Novel for Our Time, 1922). Bettauer's dystopic novel about the expulsion of Jews from Vienna was itself a parody of an earlier antisemitic text.[23] Landsberger's non-Jewish protagonist Boris Pinski is described as recognizably Jewish for anyone looking for what were considered to be Jewish racial characteristics. The "yellowish tone of his face," as well as his poor posture and nearsightedness, qualify Pinski as a "Slavic type" who can be mistaken for an East European Jew.[24]

Other literary works at the intersection of biopolitics and science fiction considered how skin color and, consequently, constructions of race and racial visibility might be altered. A short tale by Salomo Friedlaender (1871–1946; pseudonym: Mynona), *Der operierte Goj* (The Operated Goy, 1922), responded to Oskar Panizza's grossly antisemitic depictions in *Der operierte Jud'* (The Operated Jew, 1893). In this sinister story, Panizza engages modern scientific racism to suggest that Jews could be completely transformed into non-Jews only through drastic medical procedures. Panizza's grotesque descriptions of the Jewish body include the "slightly yellow skin" of his Jewish protagonist, Itzig Faitel Stern.[25] This tale prompted Friedlaender to create a character with his same surname, Professor Friedlaender, who, similar to but also as a parody of Panizza, transforms a non-Jew into a Jew through hair dye and plastic surgery. But these medicalized racial transformations apply not only to those hoping to join or leave the "Jewish race": Professor Friedlaender's success leads a former emperor to have himself "transformed into a Negro in order to escape the Bolshevist rabble."[26] Friedlaender's text concludes with the utopian fantasy that racial difference would cease to matter if one could trans-form one's race at will.[27] Yet even in their inversions of racial stereotypes, Friedlaender and Landsberger still relied upon notions of Jewish racial differ-ence. If one failed to remove the layers of irony, their characters could resem-ble figures popularized in antisemitic representations.

In 1931 in New York, African American author George Schuyler (1895–1977) published a similarly satirical work of science fiction, *Black No More: Being an Account of the Strange and Wonderful Workings of Science in the Land of the Free, AD 1933–1940*. Schuyler's satire of American race relations engaged with the futuristic possibility of transforming Blacks into Whites as a means of criticizing groups that influenced perceptions of race and upheld Whiteness as an ideal. In *Black No More*, the "unfit" peoples that one White leader of the "Anglosaxon Association" wishes to have sterilized include "Ne-groes, aliens; Jews and other riff raff."[28] An explicit criticism of the American system, Schuyler's novel also could be read as an assault on German racism and racial antisemitism. In fact, it is while studying in Germany that Schuyler's character Dr. Junius Crookman learns to whiten Blacks.[29] In this American literary work from 1931, Germany is envisioned as a site of innovative at-tempts to pass, transform, and whiten.

Cultural representations by Weimar Jewish authors and artists co-opted historically stigmatized symbols in unexpected ways, some of which turned racialized emblems of shame into celebrated images. The biblical story of the mark of Cain (Genesis 4:15) initiated a long tradition of shaming through physical markers imposed or imprinted by others. Some have argued that the mark of Cain manifested itself in the form of a dark skin color, and that Cain was "cursed with Blackness," not unlike the biblical figure Ham. Numerous African American writers in fact understood themselves as descendants of Cain.[30] In *Juden auf Wanderschaft* (The Wandering Jews, 1927), writer Joseph Roth (1894–1939) similarly linked the mark of Cain to cultural traits acquired by Jews during their centuries in Europe: "At any rate it will be difficult for them to become a nation with a completely new, un-European physiognomy. The European mark of Cain won't wash off."[31] Here Roth suggests that erasing Europeanness by unlearning values and customs would be nearly as impossible as escaping the intangible mark that made them a highly visible group. Roth's turn of phrase further racialized "Europeanness"—Europe became part of Jew-ish physiognomy—and thereby added Europeanness to the list of Cain's pos-sible curses. But the most common interpretation of the Cain story told of a mark on Cain's forehead. Talmudic commentators postulated that this sign was a letter of God's name engraved in Cain's forehead.[32] Perhaps partly in response to this last interpretation, foreheads have long been envisioned as a place for displaying various stigmas. Branding someone's forehead with a given symbol served as a punishment for alleged crimes such as sexual immorality or attempting to escape from slavery.

Such metaphorical forehead markers also recurred in Jewish contexts, sometimes as symbols of shame, and other times as indicators of Jewish pride. An eighteenth-century Yiddish folktale told of a princess born with a small golden star on her forehead, whose brothers were cursed and transformed into geese for failing to help her. Eventually, she became a kind of messianic figure who underwent suffering to remove the curse.[33] In contrast, a short story by Russian and Yiddish writer Ossip Dymow (1878–1959; pseudonym of Yosef Perelman), "The Symbol," appeared in 1928 in the largest Zionist newspaper, *Jüdische Rundschau* (Jewish Review), with a very different message. "The Symbol" ominously warned readers that any beautiful Jewish woman who deserted her people and her God risked being branded with a terrible, unspecified symbol on her forehead by members of the Jewish community. A blacksmith's daughter, Chane, receives this conspicuous red symbol with the admonition, "Your beauty was responsible for everything. One doesn't need such beauty."[34] The notion that Jews would imprint Jewish visibility onto a woman who tried to leave her community hints at the forcefulness with which some Jews imposed notions of solidarity. Or, if taken as a criticism of these practices, Dymow's story portrays otherwise less visible women as potential victims of vengeful, misogynistic attempts to render women more visible. It further illustrates the ambiguousness and fluidity attributed to Jewish women whose beauty enabled them to find acceptance outside of Jewish circles.

In stark contrast, and in what amounts to an inversion of the practice of branding a woman with a mark of shame, poet Else Lasker-Schüler (1869–1945) conceived of how a star on her forehead might mark her as someone in search of redemption.[35] Expressionist artist John Höxter's image of the poet proudly brandishing a Star of David symbol in the middle of her forehead appeared in the Jewish humor magazine, *Schlemiel*, in 1919, opposite one of her poems (see figure 4).[36] Höxter's use of this symbol echoed Lasker-Schüler's representations of stars in her poems and drawings, including self-portraits. Both Lasker-Schüler and her portraitist envisioned the Star of David as a voluntary performance of Jewishness. This explicit forehead marker compounded Lasker-Schüler's known affinity for performing Jewishness though self-fashioning that was coded Eastern and "Oriental." Further, it added to a body that—due to Lasker-Schüler's dark coloring—was already coded Jewish in a racial sense. Whereas embodied racialized Jewish coding was neither elective nor unambiguous, open displays of a Star of David indicated the ability of

Die Dichterin Else Lasker-Schüler — *Zeichnung* — John Höxter

**Fig. 4. Poet Else Lasker-Schüler, drawing by John Höxter in *Schlemiel*, 1919. (Courtesy of the Leo Baeck Institute, New York.)**

Weimar Jews to choose to disclose Jewishness and to avoid passive acceptance of the Jewishness projected onto them by others.

Cultural appropriations of stigmatized symbols and dominant stereotypes were informed and supposedly corroborated by the findings of anthropological studies, particularly with respect to coloring. The near-ubiquitous presence of certain fictional images helped generate the need for easily quantifiable data that could be incorporated into anthropological findings. As historian Andrew Zimmerman has noted, the German Anthropological Society established two "pure" types for the purpose of simplified differentiation in the 1870s: the "blond type" and the "brunette type." Blond hair, blue eyes, and white skin pointed to Germanness in the sense of the "classical appearance of the Teutons" as described in Tacitus's *Germania* in the first century CE. The opposite type, or black hair, brown eyes, and brown skin, signified something other than Germanness, including and especially Jewishness. Other iterations of these combinations—for example, brown hair and blue eyes, or blond hair and brown eyes—were classified as "mixed-form."[37] Anthropologist Rudolf Virchow's influential study, published in 1886, presented data suggesting that only 11 percent of Jewish schoolchildren in Germany were blond, whereas roughly 32 percent of their non-Jewish counterparts could be classified as the "blond type."[38]

Some scholars have interpreted Virchow's study as evidence that Jews were relatively indistinguishable from non-Jews in Germany. This was indeed how it was received in liberal Jewish circles. At the time of publication, however, antisemites used it to support notions of visible difference.[39] After Virchow, a study by Russian anthropologist Arkadius Elkind, published in 1906 in a Jewish research periodical, showed that blond hair was extremely rare among Polish Jews and uncommon among Lithuanian and Galician Jews, despite a strong presence of blond hair in those populations in general.[40] American anthropologist Maurice Fishberg wrote in his 1911 study that a beautiful Jewish woman "who looks like a Jewess" would "have generally black or brown hair" in keeping with Sephardic beauty, which historian John Efron has explored at length.[41] By the early twentieth century, both cultural perceptions and scientific findings suggested that East European Jews had darker coloring. These claims further reinforced the widespread notion that Eastern Jews were more easily detectable.

Anthropology and other emerging fields including psychoanalysis contributed to constructions of Jewishness as a race with observable characteristics that often played out along gender lines.[42] Jewish men were accused of possessing "feminine" character traits and were considered recognizably Jewish insofar as they were seen as less masculine than non-Jews.[43] The influential work of Viennese philosopher Otto Weininger (1880–1903), *Geschlecht und Charakter* (Sex and Character, 1903), played a pivotal role in feminizing the Jewish male body. Weininger, whom scholars have characterized as a pioneer of Jewish self-hatred, hypothesized that certain Jewish racial characteristics would persist despite all Jewish efforts to adapt.[44] Antisemitic thought profited from such arguments, which reinforced notions of ineradicable Jewish difference. Psychoanalysis responded to—and thereby tacitly sustained—the argument that Jewish difference was indelibly imprinted upon the male Jewish body through circumcision, yet far more difficult to detect among female Jews. As Ann Pellegrini and others have observed, one central project of psychoanalysis (including Freud's work on emasculation and castration) was to defeminize "hypervisible" circumcised Jewish men by shifting the conversation from a focus on masculinity to a new focus on femininity (including hysteria).[45] Such constructions of Jewishness became even more visible to the public eye as Jews became targets of an antisemitism that reinforced and codified these stereotypes.

Faced with a scientifically innovative type of racial antisemitism that was spreading rapidly throughout Europe, some liberal Jews argued that because Jews could assimilate entirely, they therefore had no visible racial characteristics that set them apart from other Germans—or, at the very least, they could eliminate or conceal such markers. The events of the fin-de-siècle, including the Dreyfus Affair in France, the blatantly antisemitic rhetoric of Viennese mayor Karl Lueger, and the international hoax of *The Protocols of the Elders of Zion* (1903; circulated in German translation in 1920), launched a new sense of urgency to blend in with one's surroundings (or, for many Zionists, to pursue Jewish statehood elsewhere).

Many liberal German Jews responded by trying to convince their fellow Jews to become less visible. Walther Rathenau (1867–1922) pseudonymously published a short invective, "Höre, Israel!" (Hear, O Israel!, 1897), calling upon Jews to shed all "tribal" attributes and undergo a complete metamorphosis in order to become "Jews of German character and education." In this controversial text, Rathenau suggests that the external features of Jews would cease to differ greatly from those of other Germans if they spent enough time with "native Germans" (*Stammesdeutsche*).[46] Other liberal thinkers, too, sought to combat essentialist notions of Jewishness as something inherent and ineradicable, or as a race with an unchangeable biological foundation, though most still conceived of the Jewish people as an ethnic community of descent.[47] In the wake of antisemitism experienced during the First World War, physician Fritz Kahn's *Die Juden als Rasse und Kulturvolk* (The Jews as a Race and Civilization, 1920) similarly countered the notion of a "pure" Jewish race and highlighted the role of environment in shaping development over time, with the stated aim of serving as both a "textbook and defense book."[48] Clarifying that Jews were not all alike on a racial or biological level was on some level a contribution to Jewish self-defense.

Others challenged this argument and pointed out the precariousness of the view that Jews possessed no essential differences from other Germans. In his satirical style, Zionist Sammy Gronemann argued that the liberals' position was foolish, if for no other reason than that "every street urchin could tell by looking at their noses that they were not descendants of Hermann the German."[49] For Gronemann, it made little sense to disavow Jewishness as an ethnicity when it was, as he saw it, clearly visible in the form of inherited physical characteristics. Of course, the concept of a distinctly Jewish nose appeared time and again as a controversial indicator of Jewish visibility. It was not unheard of for official German court documents to describe a wanted suspect as having the distinguishing feature of a "Jewish nose." In one instance, a contributor to the *Familienblatt* protested the official sanctioning of this stereotype as if it were a factual descriptor.[50] Noses were but one part of the body that could be considered Jewish when they took a certain shape that was deemed inferior.[51] Both inherited and acquired embodied traits contributed to constructions of Jewish difference.

The growing Zionist movement, in contrast to the liberal position, argued that Jews should declare themselves openly as Jews, and that so-called "weak," "ghetto," or bourgeois Jews could transform themselves into physically robust "new Jews" through athletic activity. The "muscle Judaism" (*Muskeljudentum*) championed by Max Nordau (1849–1923) and others encouraged gymnastics and physical training not in order for Jews to more closely resemble other Germans, but rather for Jews to achieve physical self-improvement on their own terms. Both liberals and Zionists advocated for the reform and rejuvenation of the Jewish body in different ways, though the Zionist movement was considerably more invested in reviving the Jewish body politic (*Volkskörper*), defined in part by its blood ties.[52] Part of this project consisted of raising awareness about the health of Jews as a people. Zionist social scientists Arthur Ruppin and Felix Theilhaber published extensively about the composition of the Jewish population and often attributed its decline to such social practices as intermarriage and later marriage, while still advocating for its renewal.[53] Although emphasizing physical improvement through sports was not the same as recommending a nose job, many Zionists and others assessed the Jewishness of the body along gender and racial lines, if only to reject antisemitic claims of Jewish inferiority.[54] Indeed, a range of Jewish groups addressed the question of how best to approach and discredit constructions of an allegedly inferior Jewish race.

In the 1920s, numerous German-Jewish organizations hosted cultural events and other forums for Jews to engage critically and intensively with con-

temporary racial theories about the Jewish body. Periodicals reflect how different Jewish subgroups responded to a question that received national and international attention around this time: "Is there a Jewish race?"[55] The nonpartisan
*Israelitisches Familienblatt* was instrumental in bringing ostensibly neutral
discussions of racial difference to the fore. It initially characterized Jewish difference as circumstantial and somewhat malleable, building on notions of Jewish adaptability that were becoming increasingly popular.[56] One contributor
reported on the findings of a Jewish medical doctor, Hans Bing, who, at an
event organized by the Centralverein, acknowledged the potential biological
impact of years of ghettoization and endogamy, while also stressing the theoretical ability of Jews to conform to Europeanness.[57]

In a similar vein, the *Familienblatt* reported on the work of Jewish philosopher Constantin Brunner, who was well known in Jewish circles for his
support of assimilation. The *Familienblatt* noted that Brunner (1862–1937;
pseudonym of Arjeh Yehuda "Leo" Wertheimer) maintained that the distinguishing feature of the Jewish racial type was its unlimited variability and consequent ability to resemble all other races (*Anähnlichung*).[58] Like Rathenau,
with whom Brunner had exchanged ideas, Brunner argued that assimilation
was key to both survival and success for everyone, including Jews. He stated
plainly in another text about Jews: "All life is bound to adaptation (*Anpassung*), to assimilation."[59] One controversial piece by Brunner suggested that
the Centralverein should help Jews emancipate themselves, which he argued
could be achieved if Jews were to give up their claim to difference.[60] Brunner
elsewhere pointed out that Blacks in the United States provided an example of
how a targeted racial group could make tremendous contributions to the same
culture in which it had previously met with oppression, a comparison that underscores the racial nature of even supposedly deracialized notions of Jewish
difference.[61] In their treatment of Jewishness as a racial quality, scientists and
philosophers alike argued that Jews were gifted at blending in, conforming, or
passing as non-Jewish Germans or Europeans.

As antisemitic manipulation of racial theories intensified in the late 1920s
and early 1930s, the *Familienblatt*'s position shifted toward explicit acknowledgment of Jewish racial difference, along with the need for equal rights and
privileges in the face of these alleged differences.[62] In an effort to disseminate
recent and supposedly unbiased research on race to all of their readers, the
*Familienblatt* editors included in the paper's illustrated supplement numerous
excerpts and images from race theorist Ludwig Ferdinand Clauß's work, *Von
Seele und Antlitz der Rassen und Völker* (On the Soul and Face of Races and
Peoples, 1929). In their short introduction, the editors surprisingly did not con-

test Clauß's racial categorization of Jews as predominantly "Oriental" and "Near Eastern" types, and instead embraced Clauß's objective categorization of Jews as different but not inferior.[63] According to Clauß's system, Jewishness could be assessed according to photographs, and Jews were very rarely perceived as entirely "Nordic" or "Central European," two categories associated with Germanness.[64] By cultivating an awareness of these types, the *Familienblatt* apparently sought to arm readers with a scientific basis for challenging allegations of racial inferiority, while still acknowledging notions of regionally based Jewish racial difference that excluded Jews from Germanness.

But these divisive racial theories—which grew in popularity at this time, alongside works by antisemitic race scientists such as Hans Günther—quickly put Weimar Jews on the defensive.[65] As denying the existence of Jewish difference became a less potent weapon, many Jews instead turned to countering allegations of an inferior Jewish racial aesthetic. In 1930, the *Familienblatt* organized a prize contest that encouraged mothers to send in photographs of their beautiful, even "superior" children. The editors, in a protective tone, suggested that "indeed, the typical Jewish child is infinitely more beautiful, purely expressive, and noble of race than the nationalistic racial theorists can even imagine."[66] Implied here is the manner in which racial theorists had attacked Jews as a lesser race. In response to this contest announcement, the *Familienblatt* received a large number of submissions. Photos of 20 children were pronounced finalists for "The Beautiful Jewish Child," and all were awarded prizes according to how readers ranked them (see figure 5).[67] In publicizing photos of "typical Jewish" children who did not all possess stereotypical attributes, the contest challenged antisemitic notions of aesthetic inferiority with evidence of good-looking Jewish children.[68] Such activities invited widespread Jewish participation in the process of politicizing the issue of race at the personal level. By the early 1930s, even average readers of the Jewish press both confronted and responded to the burgeoning field of nationalistic race theory, if only on the level of wanting to celebrate their own children.

In contrast to nonpartisan positions such as those taken by the *Familienblatt*, which fluctuated parallel to mainstream shifts, liberal Jewish thinkers and organizations tended to take a more aggressive defensive stance on the race question. Some broadly rejected contemporary race theories by arguing that externally visible physical features simply could not be used to distinguish Jews from other Germans, or to establish national identity at all. At the heart of the mission of the Centralverein was the idea that Jews should be treated as equal German citizens, and that they were capable of looking the part. Self-defense against antisemitism that in any way threatened this mission topped the Centralverein agenda.[69]

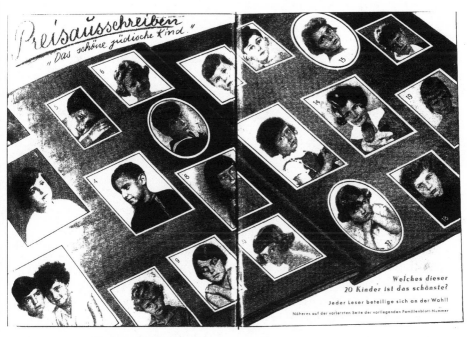

Fig. 5. "The Beautiful Jewish Child," prize contest in *Israelitisches Familienblatt*, 1930. (Courtesy of the Leo Baeck Institute, New York.)

Julius Goldstein (1873–1929), the founder and editor of the highbrow journal *Der Morgen* (The Morning), which was affiliated with the Centralverein, explicitly mentioned race among the issues the journal would address.[70] Goldstein had already explored the question "Are racial characteristics ascertainable?" in his book *Rasse und Politik* (Race and Politics, 1921), which responded in part to Virchow's work.[71] A summary of his answer was presented to members of the Reichsbund jüdischer Frontsoldaten and also appeared in its publication, *Der Schild* (The Shield), in 1925: "Whether an animal belongs to a particular animal species can be determined based on *external* features. But whether a person or a group of people belong to a nation cannot, at least not in Europe, be determined on the basis of *external* features."[72] Goldstein shifted the emphasis away from projections of Jewishness based solely on visual appraisals. His rhetoric built on the liberal Jewish political stance to argue that race science problematically invented a connection between physical appearance and the rights and privileges that come with nationhood. In a subtler manner, Goldstein discouraged treating Jews (and all humans) as if they were classifiable according to animal species rubrics.[73] In general, the RjF affirmed Goldstein's notion of Jewish inclusion in a German or European majority they had helped build.[74]

Other liberal thinkers likewise used Virchow's findings as evidence against the notion that Germans and Jews belonged to separate races and possessed certain distinctive features. Breslau attorney Ludwig Foerder (1885–1954), who was active in the Centralverein and contributed to the *Jüdischliberale Zeitung* (Jewish Liberal Newspaper), cited a long history of conversion and intermarriage to show that race and national identity could not be conflated in the case of Germanness.[75] Several years later, in 1927, Foerder parsed the basic statutes of the Centralverein to argue that its own mission undermined the fact that Jews were already fully German. He maintained that the Centralverein's goal of "fortifying the unwavering cultivation of the German disposition (*deutsche Gesinnung*)" on some level implied that Jews were not already full Germans a priori. Even more problematic for Foerder was that nowhere did the Centralverein refer to the need for the cultivation of a "Jewish disposition." He claimed that CV members deemed the formal commitment (*Bekenntnis*) to Jewishness sufficient for their purposes.[76] A similar call came from others, especially members of the younger generation of the Centralverein, to refrain from constantly referencing the need for a sense of Germanness that should have been self-evident. That their Germanness was in a state of flux was problematic; Jewishness as a constant provided a counterpoint and model of stability.[77] These voices echo the anxieties among German Jews who wished to be less visible as Jews, but more visible as Germans, yet found support for theories of visible Jewish difference at every turn.

As the Nazi party gained popularity and its teachings began to infiltrate everyday life, it became a perilous sign of non-Germanness to possess dark hair or eyes, or other physical attributes associated with "non-Aryans." In the early 1930s, Centralverein attorney Werner Cahnmann (1902–80) responded directly to race scientist Hans Günther, whose work profoundly shaped Nazi racial theories. In a booklet published in 1932, Cahnmann outlined the danger of Günther's argument for Jews in Germany, explaining that because Jews in general were deemed foreign to Europe (*europafremd*), race hygienists in Germany were essentially required to embrace antisemitism in the interest of achieving a racially "pure" Europe. Though Cahnmann refrained from addressing differences in physical appearance, he maintained that Jews had become full members of the German *Volk* through a long period of adaptation and German cultural education.[78] The Centralverein, which continued to respond directly to current racial typologies, repeated the same message in brochures that it distributed, claiming in one flyer: "There are just as many blond, blue-eyed, and tall Jews as there are dark-haired, brown-eyed, and short non-Jews."[79] Some Jews attempted to mitigate the potentially harmful effects of constructions of race to bolster the liberal argument in favor of a cultural form of German national belonging.

Yet ideology and common practice were often at odds. Although many liberal German Jews embraced theoretical arguments countering the existence of visible Jewish racial traits, they nevertheless continued to demonstrate that they believed it was possible to see Jewishness. By arguing that the Jewish body could and should be transformed, Zionist rhetoric, too, conceded that Jewish difference was imprinted on the body, albeit in such a way that it could be made less visible. Not only non-Jews and antisemites, but also many Jews, too, held that the dark coloring associated with some Jews was a telltale sign of Eastern otherness and sometimes signified an authentic form of Jewishness.[80] Jews and others found numerous ways to portray the Jewishness they observed on the streets of Germany, and while traveling; they claimed to detect it in the faces of cultural icons, and in descriptions and illustrations of literary characters. In doing so, they helped codify stereotypical notions of what Jews looked like, which by extension made it more difficult to defy the very norms they aimed to challenge. At the same time, the breadth of their representations provided a range of perspectives on Jewish visibility, which both complicated and disputed any single concept of how Jews could be detected.

### East and West, Dark and Light

Within Jewish communities in Germany, Eastern and Western Jews engaged in a nuanced process of self-differentiation that often relied on embodied physical characteristics, and which generally cast Eastern Jews as more visible and "foreign." Many German Jews used supposed differences between Western and Eastern Jewish bodies to highlight similarities between German Jews and their non-Jewish neighbors: the idea was to show that even though many (Eastern) Jews couldn't pass, others definitely could. These differences were as much constructed as based on actual places of origin or residence. From a geographical or cartographic perspective, the line between East and West was not usually clear; regional separateness and distinctiveness had blurred considerably with the waves of westward mass migration from the Russian Empire that began in the 1880s and continued into the 1920s.[81] Approximately 70,000 East European Jews migrated westward and settled in Germany during this period, many in the wake of the First World War.[82] Moscow, Kiev, and Warsaw were located in "the East," certainly—but what about Prague and Vienna? And what of Königsberg and Breslau (then in Germany, but today in Russia and Poland)?

Jews from all over Europe encountered one another in the German cities of Berlin, Frankfurt, Hamburg, and Munich, and in many other towns and villages. In Germany, the term *Westjuden* (Western Jews) came to mean Jews who were settled, modern, acculturated, able to blend in, and in touch with both the secular and the vernacular. The word *Ostjuden* (Eastern Jews) pejoratively referred to Jews who were transitory, traditional, tended toward religious observance, spoke Yiddish, and were "foreign."[83] To be perceived as Eastern was to be identified as more visibly Jewish, often at the level of embodied characteristics or coloring. As Jack Wertheimer has noted, the word "Russian" was shorthand for "Russian Jew."[84]

Even with what some scholars have termed the "Cult of the *Ostjuden*," a positively inflected obsession with the presumed authentic Jewish culture of Eastern Europe, the word *East* nearly always carried with it a stigma of sorts.[85] Many East European Jewish men who were easily recognizable due to their traditional attire or beards were stigmatized or exoticized. Already in the eighteenth century, philosopher Solomon Maimon (1754–1800) commented that adherents of the Berlin Jewish Enlightenment looked down upon those Jews who still wore long beards and who could not speak standard German.[86] Similarly, in an 1823 essay, Heinrich Heine (1797–1856) famously described Polish Jews as barbaric, bearded, fur-clad, mumbling, and smelling of garlic, though he also sarcastically claimed to prefer them to certain Western Jews.[87] In the early twentieth century, stereotypes about East European Jews encompassed both their appearance and lifestyle, which some perceived as primitive.[88] Even social workers and other supporters of Jewish migrants criticized East European Jewish households as "unhygienic" for failing to meet rationalized standards of domestic cleanliness. Women were often held responsible for the alleged filth associated with the households and bodies of impoverished Eastern Jews.[89]

In keeping with the mythologies generated by contemporary scientific findings, a typology emerged in Weimar-era cultural texts that portrayed Eastern and Western Jewish women as both physically and emotionally different from one another. The constructed differences between them encompassed embodied signifiers as well as elements of dress, personality, and even professional engagement. The stereotypical East European Jewish woman rarely possessed blond hair; her West or Central European counterpart was more likely to have light brown hair or fair skin, but likewise was not usually depicted as blond. Jewish women from the elusive "East"—including some from Austria and other nearby countries—were particularly likely to be cast as dark and exotic, and potentially also beautiful, erotic, or sensuous. Literary works by Leopold von Sacher-Masoch and other authors perpetuated and reinforced these associations in the decades leading up to and during the Weimar period. Fantasies of the "beautiful Jewess" invited special attention to women's appearance and behavior, particularly with respect to sexuality, and images of the "beautiful Jewess" were present in the literature and culture of many European traditions.[90]

Such categories also provided many who were involved in the production of German-Jewish culture with a method of criticizing Western Jewish women and idealizing women from the East. This further exoticized the Eastern other and contributed to a longing for unconventional representative models. In this vein, the inner-Jewish discourse, particularly among Zionists, portrayed Western Jewish women (*Westjüdinnen*) as assimilationist, superficial, and materialistic. In contrast, Eastern Jewish women (*Ostjüdinnen*) were upheld as more family-oriented and pious, and therefore more virtuous.[91] One contributor to Martin Buber's journal, *Der Jude* (The Jew), described the Jewish girls of Germany as "overgroomed, vain, flirtatious women who lust after money and pleasure," who could be identified by their "very slender figure[s] and fashionably cut clothing."[92] Like the mainstream figure of the New Woman, Western Jewish women were more likely to be associated with the urban life of the metropolis, whereas Eastern Jewish women often were imbued with studiousness or untainted, rural wholesomeness. Because they were coded as more distinctively Jewish, representations of East European Jewish women sometimes stood in for Jewish women as a whole.

Countless literary descriptions and visual representations portrayed Jewish female characters as visibly dark, sometimes hinting at racial otherness or foreignness.[93] Many authors included detailed passages that explicitly discussed the relationship between appearance and Jewishness, often through the eyes of one character encountering another. For instance, the eponymous protagonist in the best-selling antiwar novel, *Die Katrin wird Soldat* (Katrin Becomes a Soldier, 1930), by writer Adrienne Thomas (1897–1980; pseudonym of Hertha Adrienne Strauch), is repeatedly described using adjectives that emphasize her dark coloring. The moment when young Alsace-Lorraine native Katrin (Cathérine) Lentz's Jewishness is revealed to the reader occurs when an older friend wants to bestow upon her a decidedly non-Jewish nickname: "Maria." To his inquiry as to whether she is only a "half-Jew" with a blonde, Christian mother, she responds, "No, no, I'm the real thing."[94] Whereas Katrin is at first surprised that someone would mistake her for a non-Jew, others regard her appearance as incompatible with Germanness and inquire whether she might be French. According to the logic of accepted stereotypes and racial science,

Katrin's dark coloring made her more likely to be something other than German. The border territory of Alsace-Lorraine, with a national affiliation that was constantly in question, provided the perfect cover for a Jewish character's ambiguous appearance; its quality of being outside of the German center marked it as other. With its Mediterranean coast, France also aligned with southern regions associated with the East.

Like the girl with the "typical Oriental face" described by Gronemann, many Jewish women and men were thought to possess coloring and features commonly associated with Mediterranean regions. Implied by the broad term Mediterranean are such Southern European countries as Italy, Greece, and perhaps Spain and France, as well as what we today refer to as the Middle East. Jews from these regions were believed to have darker coloring and thus to be better at blending in with their non-Jewish surroundings than Jews in Germany. Journalist Bertha Badt-Strauss (1885–1970) summarized in the *Jüdische Rundschau* how a Jewish student from Trieste explained what it was like to live as a Jew in Italy: "We Jews are actually doing too well here in Italy! . . . You see—we are not many here; on the surface we resemble (especially to non-Jewish eyes! as we confirm later in the Venetian ghetto) the others; we fulfill the same duties and enjoy the same rights as our fellow Italian citizens." Despite this seemingly enthusiastic recommendation, Badt-Strauss's article also pointed out major obstacles of living in Italy and the growing popularity of Zionism among even those who identified as "national Italian" Jews.[95] Significantly, this description corroborates the widespread notion that many Jews looked "Mediterranean-enough" on the surface to be mistaken for Italian, and that it was not always possible to distinguish between the two. In fact, Freud's own children supposedly avoided discrimination because they looked Italian.[96] Also implied is that many Jews—or those trained to look with "Jewish eyes"— believed they were able to tell the difference between Jews and non-Jews in Italy, just as many believed they could identify Jews in Germany.

The dark coloring of Jewish women labeled "Eastern" or "Mediterranean" also came to represent their ability to perform Jewishness effectively. Writer Arnold Zweig (1887–1968) observed in his book *Das ostjüdische Antlitz* (The Face of East European Jewry, 1920) that these traits were constitutive of mass-produced fantasies about Jewish and other women, noting "that racial traits such as dark eyes and black hair, whose bearers may be pure as Luna, cannot prevent either soldier or student from wanting to make love to a dusky female Jew, Pole, or Spaniard."[97] Elsewhere Zweig reinforced these fantasies through his assessments of Jewish theater and film actresses. He also pointed out that, from a typecasting perspective, the dark features of actresses with East

European origins made them highly qualified to play Jewish or similarly "other" characters.[98] Many critics agreed with Zweig. Alfred Kerr summarily described Russian-born Maria Orska (1893–1930, born Rahel Blindermann) as "dark," and theater director Rudolf Bernauer deemed Orska especially capable of portraying "an exotic woman."[99] And although Elisabeth Bergner (1897–1986, born Elisabeth Ettel) infrequently played explicitly Jewish roles, many of her characters evoked distant lands including Italy and Russia.[100] At the same time, both Orska and Bergner were lauded for their ability to appeal to both Jewish and mainstream German audiences. Their mastery of acting was tied to the changeability commonly associated with Jews, and especially Jewish women. Traits associated with both Easternness (in the form of dark coloring or "exotic" features) and Jewishness (including the ability to hide or cover it) thus contributed to the demand for these actresses in Weimar culture.[101]

Because dark hair was considered one of the most visible signifiers of embodied Jewishness, at times it was deemed less desirable than lighter hair. The transformation of hair color was consequently a key issue for Jewish identity.[102] Women turned to different methods of disguising themselves and their hair to initiate a change of appearance. Whereas luxury wigs provided a fashionable, yet relatively expensive option for religiously observant women, hair dye also became available to the masses. In the early twentieth century, new dye formulas made it easier and less toxic for women to change their hair color. A new verb (*blondieren*) that referred to the practice of using chemicals to dye hair blond also appeared in advertisements in the Jewish press.[103] Recurring advertisements in the Centralverein's newspaper, *C.V.-Zeitung*, for the innovative hair dye "Aureol Haarfarbe" offered readers hair color in any shade, "from the lightest blond to the darkest black."[104] These ads suggest that a range of shades were in demand and could give the illusion that they were the wearer's "genuine" or "natural" hair color. Changing one's hair color could make someone look more or less Jewish; it weighed heavily in the performance of racialized Jewish traits.

Not only hair color, but also hair texture, figured as a signifier of Jewishness: curly or wavy hair has long been considered a Jewish ethnic trait. Despite—or, in some cases, perhaps due to—these associations with Jewishness, many Jewish women considered certain kinds of curls desirable during the Weimar period. Marketing strategies deployed in the Jewish press suggest that some Jewish women were interested in retaining their authentic curls, or obtaining curlier hair through various combs, lotions, and permanent wave styles.[105] One advertisement that appeared several times in *Die jüdische Frau* (The Jewish Woman), a women's magazine, made clear that the Onda-

Wellenformer would create only the "right" type of curls. A curling device used to create waves in both bobbed and long hair, its slogan read: "Onda-Wavemaker, together with Permanent Wave Fluid, also will hold in damp weather and perspiration. No Negro-Frizziness (*Negerkrause*), but rather beautiful, soft Marcel waves (*Ondulationswellen*)."[106] That a German-Jewish periodical suggested "Negro-Frizziness" was to be avoided at all costs reflects an anxiety about similarities between stereotypical Jewish and Black hair. Both were perceived as inferior and undesirable in certain cases, and both could be changed, straightened, or even covered.[107] Curly and frizzy hair types remain contested markers of Jewish difference and also continue to be broadly associated with Black hair.[108]

Hair color and texture also provided the basis for incorrect assumptions about Jewishness in instances when non-Jews were mistaken for Jews. Countless non-Jews belonged to this group of supposedly visible dark-haired "Jews"; East European or other foreign associations often contributed to their alleged visibility. Silent film actresses Pola Negri and Lya de Putti, who hailed from Poland and Hungary, respectively, were considered "Jewish-looking" non-Jews and at times were presumed Jewish.[109] In one essay from 1927, Pola Negri hypothesized what her life would have been like as a blonde, noting that the fashions and hairstyles of the day were much better suited to brunettes.[110] Irmgard Keun underscores this point in her best-selling novel, *Das kunstseidene Mädchen* (The Artificial Silk Girl, 1932), which features a naïve, non-Jewish protagonist, Doris. At one point, Doris permits herself to be taken for a Jew, hypothesizing that her black, curly hair (*krauses Haar*) might indicate Jewishness. Misguided in thinking that her companion desires her to be Jewish, she lies in response to his inquiry whether she is Jewish: "Of course—my father just sprained his ankle at the synagogue last week."[111] In Doris's case, modern technology contributes to her ability to pass for Jewish: her hair is not naturally curly, but rather the result of a permanent wave. Tellingly, it is through this experience of being mistaken for a Jew that Doris gains awareness of growing antisemitic and racist tendencies. Keun's Doris reminds the reader that racial profiling also affected non-Jewish Germans. The prevalence of images of dark-haired women made detecting Jewishness all the more complex and left much room for error.

Representations of dark coloring and other embodied characteristics were used not only to project Jewishness, sometimes erroneously, but also to help others locate Jewishness that might otherwise escape notice. Jewish artist Rahel Szalit-Marcus (1892–1942; Rahel Szalit, for short) attempted to capture Jewish difference visually through her lithographic illustrations to works of classic Yiddish and German-Jewish literature by such authors as Sholem Aleichem, Mendele Moykher Sforim, and Heinrich Heine. With a life story typical of many East European artists in the 1920s, Szalit found artistic circles in Weimar Germany that inspired and encouraged her, and she lived in Berlin until the Nazis came to power.[112] In general, her work was well received among Jewish audiences. One critic understood Szalit as a Jewish version of popular artist Käthe Kollwitz, suggesting that Szalit passionately imbued her subjects with a type of "soul" missing from Kollwitz's works.[113] Indeed, many of Szalit's images depict impoverished Eastern Jews whose cartoon-like qualities confront the viewer with an ironic visual commentary on suffering. Szalit explained that "out of a drive for self-preservation, I reach for my instinctive humor and bestow my figures with grotesque ideas (*groteske Einfälle*) that mitigate their tragedy."[114] This so-called grotesque imagery often took extreme forms. Some are snapshots of hyperbolic emotions, and others portray exaggerated, elongated, or enlarged features.[115]

Yet certain Szalit illustrations reflected embodied stereotypes of Jews so accurately that they were categorized as caricatures. Collector Eduard Fuchs, who included two of Szalit's images in his book *Die Juden in der Karikatur* (Caricatures of the Jews, 1921), was among the first to characterize her works as self-mockery (*Selbstironie*). One of Szalit's illustrations to Yiddish writer Sholem Aleichem's *Motl, the Cantor's Son* provided Fuchs with evidence that Jewish artists had begun to portray "the distinguishing characteristics of Jewish physiognomy" in a positive, even an affectionate manner (see figure 6).[116] This remark suggests that Fuchs perceived Szalit's images as deliberate representations of Jewish racial difference. That Fuchs reproduced these images in a collection of caricatures of Jews—which, as a Socialist, he viewed as a form of art and education for the masses—suggests they resonated differently or met with ambivalence among some spectators. Perhaps more significantly, Fuchs's readings of Szalit's illustrations reveal that non-Jewish observers had begun to question why Jews would choose to reproduce stereotypical features, and to what extent these potentially damaging images could be interpreted as satirical or ironic.

Whereas Fuchs interpreted Szalit's visually exaggerated figures as caricatures, the majority of Jewish critics ignored the satirical nature of such grotesque qualities and instead perceived them as authentic representations of East European tragedy and suffering, thereby creating a narrative of exceptionalism that applied only to Jewish artists. Szalit's work was in line with the Jewish Renaissance that Martin Buber had envisioned, namely an age of renewed interest in Jewish culture including art. As a female Jewish artist, Szalit was in a

**Fig. 6. Rahel Szalit-Marcus, "We're going to America," illustration to Sholem Aleichem's *Motl, the Cantor's Son*, circa 1922. (Courtesy of the Library of the YIVO Institute for Jewish Research.)**

position to repopularize so-called Semitic features as aesthetic ideals within Jewish communities.[117] Having grown up in Lithuania and Poland, Szalit was warmly praised by Weimar Jewish audiences for her ability to access and depict "the spell-binding power and the suffering of innumerable Jewish faces . . . of her Eastern Jewish home."[118] No critics writing for Jewish publications objected to Szalit's use of the same stereotypical features that, had they appeared in an antisemitic context, might have been cause for concern or outrage. Here we have another example of how Weimar Jews condoned and even welcomed visual representations of Jewish difference that they deemed to be in line with the East/West divide. As long as the only Jews that stood out in such images could be labeled "Eastern" Jews, these visual representations did not contradict notions that Western Jews were capable of blending in with their surroundings.

The participation of Weimar Jews in the construction of a potentially visible form of Eastern Jewish difference demonstrates both an implicit recognition of racialized Jewish difference and a tension between identifying with this difference and desiring to distance oneself from it. In some instances, Eastern Jewish bodies were cast as visual reminders of foreignness in order to reinforce supposed similarities between German Jews and their non-Jewish neighbors. When such Jewish-coded traits as dark hair and dark coloring were in high demand, Eastern Jewish women in particular gained visibility and prominence in Weimar culture. But the notion of foreignness applied not only to bodies with Eastern European origins; anyone with dark hair could be coded non-German and potentially French, Italian, Mediterranean, or Oriental. To be either dark-haired or Eastern was to be perceived as racially or geographically other and more visibly Jewish. Finally, there were "right" and "wrong" ways to display embodied indicators of Jewishness, and the "right" way entailed avoiding anything that could be interpreted as a sign of racial inferiority, or, in some cases (including works by Rahel Szalit), aligning visual representations of embodied difference with a sense of Eastern authenticity.

## Material Signifiers Worn or Displayed on the Body

In addition to the body itself, clothing and other items worn or displayed on the body provided a platform for making Jewishness detectable to the trained observer. Significantly, these items also could be removed. For those who contested notions of racial difference, material signifiers might have been a preferred way to make Jewishness visible. In some instances, certain colors—especially yellow, blue, and white—served as indicators of the Jewish affiliation of student groups and other organizations. Both liberals and Zionists utilized colors to represent their organizations in symbolic ways. Military badges and different types of uniforms, too, were worn on some occasions with the explicit goal of making Jewish veterans more recognizable in public. Distinctive items of clothing and other elements of traditional attire worn by religiously observant Jews, such as head coverings and prayer shawls, also indicated Jewishness when displayed.[119] Certain regular items of clothing also could be worn in such a way that they adhered visibly to standards of religious modesty.

The color yellow has a long history as a marker of Jewishness in Western Europe, though its uses changed over time, as discussed in the introduction. In contrast to earlier centuries, when Jews were legally obligated to display markers of Jewish otherness, the first few decades of the twentieth century were perhaps the only time in modern history when yellow was worn as a bold display of Jewish pride. Prior to 1933, student groups in particular mobilized previously imposed markers of Jewishness as a form of active resistance against modern antisemitism. Jewish veterans, too, made use of subtle badges that identified their wearers as Jewish. The goal was not only to actively avoid hiding one's Jewishness but also to mark oneself as unambiguously Jewish to prevent erroneous presumptions of non-Jewishness. Put another way, many Jews went out of their way to display Jewishness in order to avoid accidental passing.

Liberal Jewish students openly wore material signifiers of Jewishness to demonstrate to the broader public that Jews belonged in Germany. Members of student fraternal organizations that were part of the larger Kartell-Convent deutscher Studenten jüdischen Glaubens (Association of German Students of the Jewish Faith; abbreviated as K.C.), which was founded in the 1890s, were required to swear allegiance to the Jewish community and to agree to raise their children as Jews, presumably out of fear that they might abandon their Jewishness. In keeping with the customs of other German student fraternities, K.C. members wore distinctive colors (*Couleur*) to symbolize a particular association. With their yellow caps, sashes or bands, and pins, they presented themselves to university communities as active student fraternities and as Jews, while at the same time co-opting historically imposed markers of Jewishness (see figure 7).[120] One song of the Berlin group, Sprevia, even included an explicit reference to the medieval yellow badge: "What was previously a stigma became our badge of honor."[121] Some have referred to this movement as *Trotzjudentum* (defiant Jewishness), an animated form of Jewishness that emphasized its compatibility with Germanness and attempted to counter antisemitic stereotypes.[122] Shulamit Volkov has suggested that supporters of *Trotzjudentum* found it "shameful to convert without true faith, indecent to try to 'pass' so eagerly."[123] Displaying a yellow badge or sash was the opposite of trying to pass.

To be sure, adopting these symbols was controversial even within Jewish communities, and adherents of the liberal and Zionist movements did not always agree on the reasons or methods for displaying Jewish pride. For example, feminist leader and Zionist Rahel Straus (1880–1963) notes in her memoirs that, already in 1900, members of the liberal Bavarian Jewish student group, Badenia, like many other groups within the liberal K.C., wore yellow caps and bands to signify Jewishness.[124] Straus recalls having personally scorned these groups of young men "who wore the Jewish badge with pride" for their lack of religiosity and simultaneous disinterest in Zionism. Their relationship to Judaism seemed meaningless to her at the time.[125] Straus, along with other Zionists, feared that Jews might cease to pay attention to their Jew-

**Fig. 7. Kartell-Convent (K.C.) Jewish fraternity members at the University of Heidelberg, circa 1928. (Courtesy of the Leo Baeck Institute, New York. F 88032.)**

ishness if they achieved the liberal goal of gaining full acceptance as a group no different from other Germans.

Regardless of their fashionability among liberal Jewish students, symbols that invoked the yellow badge also became popular in Zionist student groups founded shortly after 1900. To distinguish themselves, Zionist groups sometimes paired yellow with the colors blue and white, which historically were combined in religious prayer shawls, and appeared in flags associated with the Zionist movement beginning in the 1890s. Together the three colors signified Zionism and a broader connection to Jewishness.[126] Zionist leader David Wolffsohn (1856–1914) reportedly declared that the blue, white, and yellow band worn by Zionist Jewish students reminded him of the age-old tradition of documenting Jewishness through some kind of clothing marker, implying that these bands were akin to a new kind of sumptuary or even religious accessory.[127]

Many Zionist insignias also incorporated the Star of David, which for some signified a move beyond age-old symbols. Philosopher Gershom Scholem (1897–1982) later argued that the star lacked religious connotations and thus eschewed thoughts of past glory in favor of hope for future redemption.[128]

The Kartell Zionistischer Verbindungen (Federation of Zionist Associations) adopted the colors yellow and black with an attached Star of David.[129] Many youth and sports organizations wore the Star of David with pride. One youth group carried a golden flag adorned with the star, and such Zionist sports clubs as S. C. Hakoah Berlin and Bar Kochba Berlin displayed the symbol on their uniforms.[130] As one Bar Kochba athlete noted, "every match which our team with the Star of David on their chest plays is a match of the Jewish association and in some way becomes a Jewish matter."[131] Sports uniforms contributed to Jewish prestige and publicized Jewish successes.

The veterans' association, in contrast, was wary of bold public displays of Jewish insignias and encouraged them only on certain occasions. The Reichsbund jüdischer Frontsoldaten was founded in 1919 to defend the honor of Jewish soldiers who had fought on the front lines for Germany during the First World War. It broadly aligned itself with the values of the Centralverein, and many RjF leaders were active in the CV and other liberal organizations. The RjF encouraged members to maintain a low public profile in general, but to wear the RjF's own badge (*Abzeichen*) with pride. This badge symbolized faithful military service and made members of the group recognizable to one another. Numerous small notices in the RjF's newsletter, *Der Schild*, reminded readers: "Wear your badge everywhere!" and "Wear and salute our badge!"[132] Through a small RjF symbol (sometimes paired with the word *Kriegsopfer*, or war victim) worn atop a metal pin, Jewish veterans were able to spot and show respect to each other while going about their everyday business (see figure 8). On occasion, RjF members donned this badge along with other medals and military uniforms and marched in columns through the streets of German cities. This act caught the attention of both Jews and non-Jews.[133] Public demonstrations in military uniforms exemplify one way in which Jewish men embraced, even brandished, a desire for visibility. In July 1932, the RjF encouraged all Jewish veterans to wear their military decorations as an antidote to the swastikas that others had begun to display.[134]

Toward the end of the Weimar period, badges, Stars of David, and other such symbols began to serve as dually encoded ominous warnings. Though worn as outward symbols of pride and defiance, they simultaneously hinted at the danger of being marked as overtly Jewish. As a symbol that took on new meaning in the Nazi era, the yellow badge first began to figure differently in the public eye with the boycott of Jewish stores on April 1, 1933. During the boycott, many Jewish store owners stood in front of their shops wearing military decorations in order to be more visible as loyal German citizens.[135] On April 4, 1933, editor Robert Weltsch (1891–1982) published his well-known

Fig. 8. Badge of the
Reichsbund jüdischer
Frontsoldaten, be-
tween 1919 and 1930,
pewter, silver-plated,
cold enamel, brass
pin, 2.1 x 1.7 cm. (Jü-
disches Museum Ber-
lin, photo: Jens Ziehe,
courtesy of Rosemarie
Obst.)

article on the front page of the *Jüdische Rundschau*: "Wear It with Pride, the Yellow Badge!"[136] In this article, Weltsch suggested without irony that Jews should co-opt the Star of David sign displayed in front of their stores during the boycott as a symbol of Jewish and Zionist pride. This article resonated with Jews of all political affiliations, and many Centralverein members joined local Zionist groups after the 1933 boycott.[137] Translated here as "badge," the German word *Fleck* also carries the negative connotation of a blemish, mark, or stain. During the Nazi occupation of Europe during the Second World War, the yellow star served to undo centuries of acculturation, integration, assimilation, and passing. Jews who wore this "stain" were forcibly outed as Jewish and no longer had the option of rendering themselves invisible.[138]

In addition to well-known symbols associated with Jewish youth groups, sports teams, and veterans' organizations, material objects associated with religious observance figured as distinct, if at times more subtle, external markers of Jewishness. Sammy Gronemann, whose anecdote from *Schalet* (1927) opens this chapter, was especially well positioned to comment on the use and visibility of religious objects in everyday life. An attorney and an observant Jew with an Orthodox background, Gronemann penned popular literature that resonated with German-speaking Jews from all walks of life. Due in part to confrontations with antisemitism, he joined the emerging Zionist movement in 1898 and played an important role in governing Zionist organizations after moving to Berlin in 1906.[139] His experiences as a Yiddish interpreter for the German army in Russia during the First World War contributed to the German-Jewish image of authentic Eastern Jews in several of his popular works from the early 1920s.[140] In all of his works, Gronemann translates Jewish cultural traditions and religious practices for readers with minimal knowledge of Judaism.[141] Anecdotes in *Schalet* suggest that both men and women used objects with religious connotations to display Jewishness in the 1920s.

Gronemann's sharp-witted criticisms of both older and updated traditions never missed an opportunity to highlight seemingly deceptive practices such as concealing an item originally designed to be displayed.[142] Men's prayer shawls and garments intended for everyday wear, including both head coverings and garments worn below other clothes, were concealed and exhibited in varying degrees. As Gronemann wrote in *Schalet*, the amount and type of undergarment that men revealed served as a signifier of religious affiliation and pride: "In the East one often sees long wool strands dallying under a vest or in the most unlikely places; in the West, it is shamefacedly hidden underneath the shirt, where it actually neglects its purpose to some extent. . . . On the other hand, if one wears the garment (*Arbekanfeß*), it is implied that he sports his Jewishness not only on the surface."[143] The long fringes (*tzitzit* in Hebrew) attached to the four corners of both prayer shawls and undergarments are by nature designed to stick out; their German name, *Schaufäden*, means literally "strands to be shown." Choosing to hide the fringes, as Gronemann suggests here, was a conscious decision. Yet even if the desire to blend in—whether out of shame, fear, or simply as a means of acculturation—accompanied the act of concealing the garment and also one's Jewishness, the wearer still maintained a certain degree of allegiance to Jewish ritual practice. In an age when visibility could be a threat, wearing a prayer shawl was enough to carry on the tradition. Displaying it happened only in select situations. Gronemann also pointed to a somewhat obvious but nevertheless central difference between Eastern and Western Jews: in his experience, observant Jews in the West were more likely than those in the East to try to blend in by hiding these garments.

Similarly, some religiously observant Central European women opted to display Jewish difference via subtle material signifiers, rather than through the conspicuously modest clothing and head coverings traditionally worn by married Jewish women. Anecdotes and advertisements demonstrate that although women's head coverings were nonexistent or nearly invisible by the 1920s, they nevertheless could be spotted by a trained eye if present and continued to be part of the discourse on Jewish appearance. The most salient example is what Gronemann termed the "Orthodox *Bubikopf*," a *sheitel* or wig in the shape of the ubiquitous pageboy bob haircut, or *Bubikopf* in German. These modern wigs imitated the short, bobbed hairstyles popularized by contemporary fiction and film stars the world over. Unlike the cloth head coverings and larger wigs previously worn by Jewish women, such nearly invisible wigs provided a way of clandestinely conveying Jewishness only to those observers trained to see it. Gronemann described this phenomenon as barely detectable: "The impeccable pageboy would hardly lead one to suspect that it is a wig worn in the interest of protecting an ancient Jewish tradition."[144] Its new popularity in the years following the First World War meant that bobbed hair was broadly associated with early feminism, flappers or New Women, and the rejection of traditional attire.[145] In other words, short hair itself was an unlikely signifier of either religiosity or (traditional) Jewishness. Gronemann further poked fun at the hypocritical ways in which religiously observant Jewish women donned fashionable wigs in order to adhere to Jewish laws, yet did so in the most stylish way possible, complete with ostentatious jewelry and low-cut skin-baring dresses. Orthodox women had certainly become less recognizably Jewish if a bobbed wig was the most "traditional" element of their dress and overall appearance.

Jewish women made themselves visibly modern—and perhaps also visibly Jewish—by participating in this global craze, whether in the form of a wig or a haircut.[146] Advertisements for bobbed wigs appeared throughout the Jewish press in the late 1920s and early 1930s. From the "pageboy wig" (*Bubikopf-Perücke*) advertised in the Orthodox newspaper *Der Israelit* (The Israelite), to the "newest ersatz pieces for the pageboy-evening hairstyle," women had myriad options for transforming the style, color, and texture of their hair (see figure 9).[147] Wigs were part of the overall project of reworking the religiously observant woman into one who could compete in Weimar beauty culture. Thanks to modern wigs, she could do so without giving herself away as Jewish to everyone, yet wigs also were conspicuous in their own way. One 1932 ad for a Frankfurt beauty salon reminded their *sheitel*-wearing customers, who presumably knew the feeling all too well: "Nothing is worse than when someone can tell that you're wearing a wig."[148] This salon's consultants offered tips for disguising wigs such that customers would not be discovered easily. But this line contained another implication as well: if they knew how to identify it, people could always spot who was wearing a wig. The stigma of wearing a wig always had the potential to come to light, and simultaneously to mark its wearer as potentially Jewish. Even hidden signifiers of Jewishness could make someone recognizable.

A wide range of material signifiers made it possible to reveal Jewishness to an observer trained in the language of modern Jewish symbolism. Weimar Jews had no shortage of available options for displaying Jewishness, including the newly appropriated yellow badge worn by both liberal and Zionist students, the colors blue and white and the Star of David among Zionists, the subtle badges of the RjF, as well as symbols of religious observance ranging from "strands to be shown" to impeccable wigs. The use of material symbols served as a way of resisting notions of Jewish difference as racial difference, as many of these symbols preempted the need for racial profiling or projections of Jewishness based on visual assessments of embodied characteristics. Jews were able to come out as Jewish at times simply by presenting these coded displays. If someone were wearing a uniform or badge associated with a particular Jewish organization known to the observer, it would not be necessary to puzzle over his or her coloring or facial features. The question "Are you Jewish?" could be answered before it was asked.

**Fischer's**
weltbekanntes
**Spezial - Haar - Haus**

**für Haararbeiten**
(Scheitel-Transformationen)
bietet an

**Bubikopf-Perücken mit langem
Scheitel von 45 Mk. an**

**Transformationen von 25 Mk. an**

Die tambourierten Scheitelstriche sind an
Natürlichkeit und Qualität unerreicht.

**H. Fischer, Fürth i. B.**
Nürnbergerstraße Nr. 2

Fig. 9. Advertisement for bobbed *Bubikopf* wigs in *Der Israelit,* 1929.
(Courtesy of the Leo Baeck Institute, New York.)

But the efforts of certain Weimar Jews to demonstrate that "they"—that is, a majority of Western, acculturated Jews in Germany—were capable of blending in with their non-Jewish neighbors on a physical or even a racial level was not tantamount to a universal attempt to appear non-Jewish. Some Jews pursued or played up traits such as dark or curly hair, which reflected a general tendency to embrace select Jewish-coded traits. Visual artists such as Rahel Szalit imbued their subjects with exaggerated features that Jewish critics interpreted as models of authenticity. Many students, veterans, and religiously observant Jewish men and women voluntarily adopted material signifiers that they displayed during encounters with other Jews. Such attempts to be visible constitute the subject of the next chapter, which discusses situations when Jews deliberately outed themselves despite the risks these acts carried.

## CHAPTER 2

# Coming Out as Jewish: Print, Stage, and Screen Displays

Whereas some Jews took precautions to conceal Jewishness, others openly defied such measures as part of a larger movement to avoid passing. By 1932, the decision to disclose Jewishness—to come out to the general public—had become, for some, a way of resisting antisemitism, discrimination, and the pressure to assimilate. Responses to a survey conducted by the liberal Centralverein shed light on the generational tensions that resulted:

> The younger generation doesn't want to reveal its Jewishness. They know that they are responsible for compensating for the evils committed by their parents in the Jewish arena; they do so through the precondition of a fond devotion to everything Jewish, without which the fight against antisemitism seems meaningless. But they also refuse to hush up their love for Judaism and Jewry in public, simply in order to curry favor with non-Jews.

Members of the younger generation, though reluctant to be openly Jewish in light of heightened antisemitism in schools, still felt the need to respond to their parents, who aspired to achieve at least the appearance of assimilation (*Scheinassimilation*) and would avoid doing anything "out of the ordinary" at any cost.[1] The term "public" is telling: within Jewish communities, displays of Jewishness were a central point of disagreement, particularly with respect to how to appear and behave in public to satisfy non-Jews. The Zionist *Jüdische Rundschau* expressed its solidarity with those who rejected the assimilatory trends of their parents, whom it pejoratively dubbed "the C.V. generation."[2] From the Zionist viewpoint, more C.V. members should have expressed pride in Jewishness long before 1932.

Yet despite these bold proclamations by Jews with different political leanings, it became increasingly precarious to display Jewishness in the final years of the Weimar Republic. In contrast to 1927, when Sammy Gronemann had pronounced its popularity with satirical fanfare—"Judaism has literally come into fashion: everyone's wearing it again!" (*Das Judentum ist wieder mode geworden. Man trägt es wieder!*)—the act of "wearing" Jewishness became a weighty burden only a few years later.[3] One November 1932 article in the *Israelitisches Familienblatt* punned on this phrase, specifically the dual meaning of the verb *tragen*, which can indicate both wearing and carrying. Its headline, "One 'carries' Judaism again," drew attention to the complications implicit in choosing to carry a burden. Although it supposedly had been possible to enter German society through assimilation or even baptism, the article argued that, by late 1932, people of Jewish descent could no longer find acceptance in mainstream circles. The *Familienblatt* editors concluded with a plea to acknowledge Jewishness consciously, and for the right reasons: "We also will overcome the present times, if everyone who belongs to us comes back to us; if they all, again, carry their Jewishness not as a burden, but rather with pride."[4] Encouraging people to take pride in their Jewishness was a first step toward getting them to acknowledge it openly. Although this call for Jews to come out voluntarily was among the last of its kind, it represents the culmination of a Weimar trend toward displaying Jewishness that is the focus of this chapter.

Coming out as a member of any targeted minority population—be it Jews, Blacks, LGBT communities, or others—can invite surprise, discomfort, criticism, ridicule, or even hatred. It is always complicated and often risky. No one can predict exactly how others will respond upon learning that the party in question is not only a member of a certain minority group but also one whose difference has the ability to go unnoticed, or to give an illusion of similarity that poses a silent or unseen threat. The act of coming out merges private and public spheres; it assumes a prior period of latency and concealment; it brings a (sometimes open) secret to light.[5] Disclosing or presenting Jewishness in any form in Weimar Germany entailed a delicate balancing act. Why bother to come out when faced with great risk? How was it possible to be openly Jewish in this environment without seeming "too Jewish"? What did Jewishness look like in its most nonthreatening forms?

In Weimar Germany, the concept of a "public" expression of Jewishness changed: in times prone to antisemitic outbursts and discrimination, the act of revealing Jewishness did not always mean coming out to everyone. Rather, coming out as Jewish meant presenting Jewishness such that it could be seen by other Jews, but may not have been visible to untrained eyes. There was a major difference between disclosing Jewishness to others who were likely Jewish or at least Jewish-friendly, and coming out to strangers whose affiliations were unknown. Aside from a small percentage of Jews who displayed conspicuous signifiers at all times, Jews were more likely to reveal Jewishness in safe spaces occupied by other Jews—in the presence of what scholars such as Michael Warner have termed a "counterpublic."[6] If these spaces were not available, Jewishness was thinly veiled such that it was perceptible only to those looking for it. Being visible as a Jew thus entailed coming out only at particular moments, and staying at least partially hidden in other situations. This recalls Henry Bial's concept of actors' "double coding" that could be interpreted differently by Jewish and non-Jewish audiences.[7] Among Weimar Jews, we find evidence of a web of theatrical, cinematic, and everyday performances of Jewishness that enabled Jews to be recognizable to one another.

This chapter explores how different media encouraged voluntary displays of Jewishness, both through direct forms of encouragement and in stage and screen performances that modeled Jewishness. The Jewish press, though known for its lists of antisemitic resorts and other places to be avoided, also served as a guide to navigating Jewish-friendly spaces and events. Moreover, the mere act of carrying or reading a Jewish newspaper in public coded its readers Jewish. Interactions with Weimar cultural entertainment served to educate audiences about how to display Jewishness. Prominent theater and film actors revealed their Jewishness to audiences, sometimes by relying on stereotypical gestures or behaviors, but also through engagement with Jewish themes or even with communities directly, as in the case of Irene Triesch. Finally, the Weimar Jewish reception of films that addressed Jewish topics, from *The Jazz Singer* to *Dreyfus*, sheds light on how audiences responded to cinematic encounters with on-screen Jewishness. A close look at the films praised by these audiences reveals that, in many instances, subtle displays of Jewishness garnered the most favor. These examples demonstrate that it was possible to manage visibility in order to be openly Jewish at the right time and in the right place, and in ways that were deemed fitting for a population under scrutiny.

## The Jewish Press on Where and When to Come Out

The Weimar Jewish press issued a call for visibility whenever and wherever it was appropriate, and particularly within Jewish communities. It did so through articles that emphasized the need for solidarity and devotion to Jewish causes, by advertising Jewish products and Jewish-friendly events and spaces, and by the periodicals themselves serving as important tools for displaying readers' Jewishness. Such spaces ranged from actual places in a given city or town— synagogues, naturally, but also cafés, kosher restaurants and hotels, Jewish-owned stores and offices, and certain neighborhoods—to virtual forums including the pages of the Jewish press. What made a space Jewish-friendly was the presence of numerous other recognizable Jews.[8] Inviting Jews to enter a space already populated by Jews hinged on an act of mutual recognition: both parties had to make themselves discernibly Jewish to render a space Jewish-friendly and to be able to invite in other Jews. The press played an important role in helping Jews make educated guesses about who belonged in these spaces. Behind many articles was a tacit acknowledgment of that paper's Jewish readership, often an unsubtle nod to the collective Jewish "we" (*wir*) in lieu of the modern, subjective "I" (*ich*). Newspapers and magazines aimed at all kinds of Jewish audiences shared the common agenda of addressing the timeless question: What consequences will this have for Jews? Some also raised these questions: What would it mean for Jews to display Jewishness openly, and when is this worth the risk?

Calls for Jewish pride were closely related to efforts toward making Jews more perceptible to each other. The word "pride" (*Stolz*) appeared regularly in references to Jewish self-identification both before and during the Weimar period.[9] At times, the press featured straightforward articles about prominent cultural figures who proudly and openly acknowledged their Jewishness and could serve as role models for readers. Many of these were about women and perhaps intended for women, which implies both a substantial female readership and an interest in motivating allegedly "slippery" women readers to refrain from covering and instead call attention to their Jewishness. One article about javelin-thrower Marta Jacob, who started out in the Jewish sports club Bar Kochba, extolled Jacob's relationship to Jewishness: "She is proud to be a Jew and is especially delighted about the major victories of Jewish athletes."[10] Similarly, an article about Hungarian beauty queen Böske Simon—whose Jewishness notably came to light after she had been crowned Miss Hungary, around the time she won the title of Miss Europe 1929—proclaimed: "She proudly confesses her Jewishness (*bekennt sich stolz zu ihrem Judentum*)."[11] The act of articulating Jewish pride contributed to making these women exemplary.

Explicit references to Jewish pride also could be found in literary works included in Jewish periodicals. In 1926, for example, *Die jüdische Frau* printed a poem by Ida Levy titled "Jews-Women," with these opening lines:

In dark eyes a strong-willed spirit, defiantly—
To safeguard the ancient lineage: Pride awakened (*Stolzerwacht*).
The stranger (*Fremdling*) is hated by the pure race,
Women's devotion laughs of its own volition![12]

Here, Levy calls on Jewish-coded women and other such "strangers" to combat race hatred through action in their own communities. The poem suggests that Jewish pride is called into existence both by banding together with other Jews and by defying antisemitic thought.

Defiant acts also could be quite small. Even the simple act of holding or reading a Jewish book or periodical, particularly one that displayed Hebrew lettering or included the word "Jew" in its title, was taken as a probable indication of Jewishness. It was no coincidence that Martin Buber boldly titled his journal *Der Jude*.[13] This could be problematic if one were situated in a potentially hostile environment, and some Jews went to great lengths to disguise reading material so as not to be betrayed by a book's cover or a newspaper's front page in the wrong setting. Others used Jewish periodicals as a way of "covering" religious texts. Joseph Roth hinted, perhaps sarcastically, that some Jews "came to be temple Jews, in other words: well-bred, clean-shaven gentlemen in morning coats and top hats, who wrap their prayer book in the editorial page of a Jewish newspaper in the belief it will attract less attention that way."[14] For these men, displaying a newspaper made them less conspicuous, both as Jews and as religious Jews. At first glance, a newspaper appeared a standard part of everyday life and was less obvious—and less dangerous—than a prayer book's cover. It was not considered problematic to come out as Jewish to the few who might recognize the Jewish editorial page, but to announce to the world that one had been praying was going too far.

In the Weimar period, as today, it was common practice to read in public, for example in cafés and on trains, where customers and passengers could look around at what others were reading. Newspapers and magazines were especially compatible with the fast-paced world of the Weimar metropolis; their short articles could be read easily during a commute, and many could be folded to fit in a pocket.[15] Yet displaying an obviously Jewish newspaper in public was something that some Jews avoided, and there was a divide between those who would and those who wouldn't. One loyal reader of *Die jüdische Frau*, Else B. of Steglitz, wrote to the editors in 1925 to seek advice. She explained: "Because I greatly enjoy reading your esteemed paper, I wanted to encourage a Jewish woman I know to subscribe. She very much wanted to become a reader of the paper, but, since the cover of the paper betrays its absolutely Jewish character, fears that she won't be able to read this magazine on the train."[16] The light blue cover of *Die jüdische Frau* indeed broadcast its title in large print alongside the image of a small menorah. The editor, Regina Isaacsohn (1875–1942), responded that she approved of Else B.'s decision not to pursue a subscription for her anxious friend.[17] For

Isaacsohn, there were enough others who would not hesitate to read *Die jü-dische Frau* openly; only those proud and brave enough to embrace it in a public setting were considered readers worth pursuing.[18]

On the other hand, the visible presence of a Jewish paper sometimes connected Jews to each other or to Jewish-friendly conversation partners, particularly in areas not frequented by many Jews. Periodicals that were available in waiting rooms, resorts, and elsewhere made these public spaces seem more welcoming of Jewish guests.[19] In one case, a subscription to a Jewish periodical helped someone come out as Jewish shortly after arriving in a rural setting, where everyone generally already knows who is Jewish. Sammy Gronemann explained in *Schalet* how the *Jüdische Rundschau* outed a Jewish girl working on a farm in a Bavarian village, with unexpectedly favorable results: "In the beginning one didn't know or realize she was Jewish. . . . Then one day came the *Jüdische Rundschau*, to which the young girl was subscribed. People looked surprised, but didn't say a word."[20] Later, the Zionist newspaper's arrival opened up fruitful discussions about Jewish topics, and the girl's non-Jewish hosts even requested that she invite similarly inclined, hardworking *chaluzim*, or pioneers, to join her on the farm. The moment during which this girl's Jewishness was detected was a surprise-filled one that outed her to her hosts. The girl's subscription served the purpose of revealing her Jewishness and saved her the trouble of explaining herself. Gronemann suggested with this anecdote that there might be unforeseen benefits to subscribing to a Jewish newspaper. At the same time, this story also highlights a key difference between urban anonymity—if one encounters many unknown people, it is necessary to come out again and again—and rural settings where everyone knows each other, and only a newcomer faces the task of declaring Jewishness.

Certainly, the Jewish press gave readers and subscribers regular access to a community of Jews who, by virtue of reading a Jewish newspaper, had already come out, at least to each other.[21] Itself part of the phenomenon that made Jews more recognizable, the press efficiently delivered insider information about Jewish organizations and spaces. Just as the mainstream German press thrived during the 1920s—around four thousand newspapers and magazines were published for Weimar readers on a daily, weekly, and monthly basis, with over 30 daily papers in Berlin alone—so too did the Jewish press in Germany experience its heyday during the economic boom years of the late 1920s.[22] Indeed, several scholars have referred to the Weimar Republic as the "golden age" of the German-Jewish press, which encompassed over 150 different periodicals between 1919 and 1933.[23] Although no Jewish daily paper was ever published in Germany, the three largest weekly papers—

*Israelitisches Familienblatt, C.V.-Zeitung*, and *Jüdische Rundschau*—
possessed certain attributes of German mass dailies and reached a sizeable
percentage of the potential Jewish market.[24] These and other Jewish periodicals were a central part of everyday life that provided indispensible information about Jewish communities.

Many German-speaking Jews maintained access to current events in both
German-Jewish subsets of society, and in German society at large, through
subscriptions to periodicals from both worlds. As in other free professions in
Germany such as law and medicine, Jews were disproportionately represented
in journalism and made major contributions to liberal periodicals intended for
a general German readership.[25] Many Jewish readers subscribed to or regularly
read at least one major mainstream daily newspaper, such as the *Berliner Tageblatt* or *Vossische Zeitung*, in addition to at least one Jewish periodical. For
example, the acculturated Berlin family of historian Werner Angress subscribed to three newspapers: *Berliner Tageblatt, Berliner Börsen-Zeitung*, and
*C.V.-Zeitung*.[26] Manfred Nomburg, who later immigrated to Tel Aviv, remembered that his household subscribed to the *Berliner Tageblatt* and *Jüdische
Rundschau*.[27] Whereas reading the *Berliner Tageblatt* in public marked its
reader as liberal, but not necessarily Jewish, the anecdotes above reflect the
power of a paper such as the *Jüdische Rundschau* to mark a reader Jewish instantly. The overlap between the readerships of mainstream and Jewish periodicals suggests Jewish readers learned about Jewish events and activities from
both types of papers.

In fact, both mainstream and Jewish periodicals promoted Jewish cultural
events, particularly when they were considered to be technologically innovative and thus held the potential to interest and mobilize larger audiences. In an
age when newspapers were the dominant medium of communication, periodicals kept readers informed about new developments in media and technology,
in addition to political, religious, and cultural events. For example, the question
of whether gramophone recordings of choir music should be incorporated into
religious services was hotly debated. Many argued that a "mechanical prayer
service" was a step backward if the goal was to create meaningful forms of
religiosity.[28] On another occasion, advertisements for a series of "Religious
Lectures" organized by the Berlin Jewish community appeared in a range of
both Jewish and general periodicals. One letter to the mainstream *B.Z. am Mittag* indicated that an upcoming 1932 lecture in this series might be of great
interest, even for non-Jewish readers, because it would be the first event in a
major synagogue to utilize a loudspeaker system. A few weeks later, Margarete
Goldstein (1885–1960) gave a lecture on "Home and Faith" in Berlin's new

Prinzregentenstraße Synagogue, which was known for its mixed seating and was designed specifically to accommodate events of interest to larger, secular audiences. It boasted the use of "technologically improved loudspeakers," as well as a choir and organ.[29] The loudspeaker system installed in this synagogue made it possible for lecturers to reach larger audiences. Just as the loudspeaker served as a megaphone for Jewish voices, the press served as a mouthpiece for Jewish-themed events.

Attending an event at which mainly Jews were present made it possible to preempt an official coming out act: simply being in a certain place at a designated time was enough to mark someone as Jewish. This was not always a good thing; chapter 3 discusses an instance when proximity to a synagogue on a Jewish holiday prompted antisemitic attacks. For the most part, however, public places that were known as Jewish meeting spots provided a kind of sanctuary. In Breslau, for example, the Jewish youth gathered in designated locations: in the Südpark in summer, or at the ice skating rink in the Stadtgraben in winter.[30] More formal public meetings provided important opportunities for Jews to connect with one another for reasons including political engagement, religious observance, social welfare, consumerist purposes, entertainment, and leisure activities.

Some Jewish organizations emerged because Jews found themselves shut out of other organizations or able to join mainstream German organizations only as Jews. Historian Marion Kaplan has suggested that Jewish feminists felt accepted among their non-Jewish counterparts "only when they 'closeted' their Jewishness." One leader of the Jüdischer Frauenbund (The League of Jewish Women) noted in 1930 that within interdenominational women's organizations, "those who do not call attention to their Jewishness are valued." Frauenbund leaders used this fact to encourage Jewish women to embrace Jewishness and the sense of community enabled by membership in the Frauenbund. In fact, Kaplan further notes that Bertha Pappenheim (1859–1936), the founder of the Frauenbund, used the term "half-Jews" to refer to Jewish women who covered their Jewish identity in order to join the main German women's organization directly."[31] To be sure, many social welfare and other special interest groups facilitated or maintained close ties to German-Jewish communities. But the Jewish press—and particularly the Zionist press—repeatedly pointed out the need for Jews to embrace Jewishness at all times, and not only when others deemed them Jewish. This extended not only to German Jews, but also to the American Jews who "make the discovery [of their Jewishness] when they are barred from Christian hotels or clubs."[32] The call to acknowledge Jewishness consciously, also and especially in the absence of antisemitism, reverberated loudly for both Zionists and others looking to honor authentic Jewishness throughout the 1920s.

Advertisements in the Weimar Jewish press, though an unlikely source of protection, informed prospective consumers where they could safely acquire various goods and services. Several organizations promised that the businesses advertising in their papers were fully vetted and that readers should give them priority, though it is questionable whether the editors of a given advertisement section were personally familiar with every firm. Still, *Der Schild* assured its readers: "Our advertisers are nearly exclusively comrades, buy from them."[33] Likewise, the editors of the newsletter of the Jüdischer Frauenbund explained: "The recruitment of advertisers also indirectly serves the purpose that, when making purchases, our advertisers will be given priority."[34] The Orthodox paper *Der Israelit* conducted a window display prize contest toward the end of Hanukkah in 1928, complete with a guide to lead readers from one local Frankfurt store window to the next.[35] These and other papers also referenced the kosher certifications of certain restaurants, hotels, pensions, and resorts, which guaranteed prospective customers that they would not be discriminated against and that their needs could be accommodated in these establishments. Official stamps or *hechshers* from local rabbinates, sometimes reproduced in advertisements, demarcated products including meat, wine, coffee, and soap as kosher (or kosher for Passover) according to different standards.[36]

The Jewish press also provided a way for Jewish-owned businesses to make their products and events more visible to prospective Jewish consumers, and particularly to women, who were believed to make at least 75 percent of all household purchases.[37] Department stores under Jewish ownership were well known for carrying a large selection of products for both men and women, as well as household goods and foodstuffs. Historians such as Paul Lerner have suggested that a number of department stores were closely intertwined with Jewishness and became cornerstones of Jewish life in the 1920s.[38] At Hermann Tietz and KaDeWe (Kaufhaus des Westens), which was acquired by Tietz in 1927, one could learn about seasonal sales timed to coordinate with Jewish and other holidays. It was also possible to purchase tickets for events including adult education seminars at the Jewish *Volkshochschule* and local beauty contests organized by Bar Kochba-Hakoah.

In addition, the Hermann Tietz Berlin stores provided a wide selection of products specifically for Jewish consumers, including books by Jewish authors, and kosher products that were available in separate divisions on the fourth floors of the Leipziger Straße and Alexanderplatz stores. Tietz advertised in a wide range of periodicals, thereby targeting Jewish consumers across political and denominational lines. Although these products were tucked away on high floors, it was nevertheless still a public act to examine or purchase kosher products.[39] Likewise, Kaufhaus N. Israel, instantly identifiable as Jewish due to its name, also targeted Jewish consumers with advertisements in the newsletters of the Berlin Jewish community and the Jüdischer Frauenbund, among others.[40] As Gideon Reuveni has argued, advertisements were instrumental in constructing "the Jews" as a unified group with a coherent identity despite vast differences in practice and religious observance.[41] Many such ads relied on widely recognizable Jewish symbols such as the Star of David, Hanukkah menorahs, or Hebrew lettering, sometimes with little regard for the nuances or meanings of each symbol.[42]

Articles and advertisements that encouraged readers to subscribe to a Jewish periodical, to attend Jewish religious and cultural events, or to purchase products from Jewish-owned businesses contributed in different ways to making Jewishness more visible in certain contexts. Such public forms of consumption and cultural experiences aided Jews in making themselves recognizable as Jews when the time was right. Every Jewish newspaper, every event flyer, and every publicly displayed organization's name that clearly referenced Jewishness increased the circulation of Jewish tropes in Weimar culture, thereby helping readers, attendees, members, and customers to emerge within Jewish-friendly spaces where it was safe to be openly Jewish. Seeing other cultural images, from the performances of Jewish actors on stage and screen, to Jewish characters in popular films, further instructed Weimar Jews in the language of how and when to make themselves visible.

## Acting Out on Stage and Screen

In the early 1920s, when Expressionist performances were popular on German stages, and in the subsequent years, when audiences could still recall the markers of Expressionism, audiences paid particularly close attention to actors' styles of movement. In many cases, exceptionally demonstrative gestures or facial expressions were enough to code either a performer or a character as Jewish.[43] Moreover, critics from different backgrounds attributed to Jewish performers special talents and the ability to imitate their subjects with great success. Antisemitic perspectives drew on the long-standing discourse around hidden or "chameleonic" Jews, suggesting that these skills served a larger plan to pass as non-Jewish.[44] Many Weimar Jewish cultural critics, on the other hand, ignored or co-opted such antisemitic arguments and instead praised Jewish performers' ability to enact the mentality of the majority population through a wide range of characters. In other words, many believed that what made Jewish actors so talented was their ability to pass as someone else, certainly on stage and perhaps also elsewhere. Scholars, too, have argued that theatricality is bound up with the performance of Jewishness.[45]

Even as the Jewish reception of many theater, revue, cabaret, and film actors celebrated their adaptability and fluidity, it also spotlighted performers whose Jewishness played a formative role in their career. Performers who came out as Jewish—whether in their private lives, or by performing discernibly Jewish roles, sometimes in Jewish venues—served as meaningful examples to Jewish audiences.[46] Historian Peter Jelavich has demonstrated that Jewish characters were most likely to be found in cabaret, *Jargon* (dialect) theater, and film, rather than in "high culture" such as the naturalist theater productions directed by Otto Brahm and Max Reinhardt.[47] In Imperial Germany, as Marline Otte has argued, popular forms of entertainment such as *Jargon* theaters provided Jewish performers with more opportunities to play nuanced Jewish character roles, whereas in the Weimar era, many Jewish actors rejected ethnic typecasting that fueled stereotypes.[48] Still, the Jewishness of many directors and actors did much to shape the German theater world.

Cultural critics who wrote about the talents of Jewish actors emphasized the same theme: because Jews shared a history of common experiences, it was possible for them to draw on this history in similar ways to achieve a uniquely Jewish mastery of the craft of imitation, particularly when it came to playing tragic roles. In his book *Juden auf der deutschen Bühne* (Jews on the German Stage, 1928), Arnold Zweig underscores the fact that many of the best-known and quintessential modern actors in Germany were actually foreign-born Jews with Mediterranean (and therefore "Southern," as opposed to "Northern") associations. According to Zweig, it was difficult to pinpoint what made these Jewish actors different from their non-Jewish counterparts, but it mattered that they were exposed to different and authentic foreign circumstances and languages in their early years, which subsequently influenced their "expressive gestures of the soul."[49] Similarly, critic Julius Bab (1880–1955), in his book *Schauspieler und Schaukunst* (Actors and the Art of Acting, 1926), praised the work of actor Alexander Granach and established the triumvirate of "Maria Orska—Elisabeth Bergner—Fritzi Massary" as representative of the mastery of acting in general. Bab suggested that not only the body language and gestures of these actresses but also a shared "blood relationship" of sorts was responsible for their success.[50] Interestingly, none of these actors was known for playing explicitly Jewish roles, and several had fairly ambivalent personal relationships to Jewishness.[51] Yet they were considered identifiably Jewish not only because of their physical characteristics, as discussed in chapter 1, but also based on their use of gestures and movement.

At times, Jewish critics went so far as to determine that Jews possessed a certain genius when it came to imitation. Many actors were deemed capable of eliminating or downplaying gestures or other signs of Jewishness if necessary to create a given character. Doris Wittner (1880–1937), a journalist whose articles appeared regularly in the *Jüdisch-liberale Zeitung*, expressed views in line with Zweig's: for Wittner, the Jewish ability to fit in was a result of experiencing exile for thousands of years. She wrote in 1925: "The external fate of being always foreign, often condemned to servitude, gave the Jew the genius of adaptation (*Anpassung*)."[52] Wittner further argued that Jewish women were at the forefront of literary and cultural trends in part because their "genius of adaptation" made them natural performers on stage and screen, as well as highly successful writers and thinkers.[53] To be sure, the experiences of being Jewish or foreign, or both, may have been instructive for actors learning to conceal their Jewish identity in order to play non-Jewish characters or to perform for non-Jewish audiences. Whether critics attributed so-called Jewish talent to a biological component or to collective experience, they stressed taking pride in one's Jewishness or Jewish origins as a key component in how actors made themselves recognizably Jewish for Jewish audiences.

Though largely overlooked by scholars, Irene Triesch (1877–1964) offers an example of an actress whose open affiliation with Jewishness and active public involvement with the Berlin Jewish community after 1925 earned her a warm reception in Weimar Jewish circles.[54] In contrast to many performers, Triesch actively sought out work performing for Jewish audiences. Like many of her fellow actresses including Orska, Bergner, and Massary, Triesch was raised in Vienna and came to Berlin in her twenties. Prior to 1925, she had a successful stage career starring in tragedies by Henrik Ibsen, Friedrich Schiller, Arthur Schnitzler, William Shakespeare, and others. As part of Otto Brahm's company in the Lessing Theater in Berlin before 1914, Triesch was best known for her rendition of Nora in Ibsen's *A Doll's House* (1879). In fact, critic Alfred Polgar (1873–1955) attributed this theater's "peculiar change in tragic emphasis" to Triesch's outstanding performance as Nora.[55] Not surprisingly, Doris Wittner aligned Triesch with other Jewish actors, noting, "there hardly could have been a better performer standing in for the people of 'thousand-year-old pain.'"[56] When it suited them, critics easily could detect traces of Jewishness in Triesch's performances.

Still, Triesch was also capable of performances that showcased deliberately non-Jewish interpretations of character roles.[57] Director Rudolf Bernauer noted that she mastered the art of presenting language in a nuanced way, "without using emphatic gestures."[58] Triesch's husband, renowned Scottish pianist Frederic Lamond, instructed her how to interpret "Nordic" characters such as Rebecca West in Ibsen's *Rosmersholm* in a more reserved and thus less "typically Jewish" way. In the postscript to Lamond's memoirs, which Triesch wrote shortly after his death in 1948, she recounts how he gave her notes and defined the "Nordic" essence in contrast to her: "You are too much Irene and not sufficiently Rebecca! . . . Rebecca—think of it—is a Nordic being; and we in the North express our feelings differently from you who come from the South! [W]e speak more softly, with more reluctance, hesitatingly."[59] Whereas Lamond's comment might refer to cultural differences between Scotland and Central Europe, "South" also might refer to so-called "Mediterranean" Jewishness. Triesch's repressed performance of Rebecca was received enthusiastically; a review in the *New York Times* commented on "the admirable restraint Mme. Triesch put upon her acting, a restraint that the world has been taught to consider not exactly a dominant characteristic of German actresses."[60] In the United States, the term *German* denoted foreign, Jewish, and other actors who frequented European stages. At times, many non-Jews were taken for Jews due to their Germanic last names.[61] But in Germany, even performances by Jewish actors that downplayed gestures, and therefore might have seemed less Jewish, did not always prove "German enough" for some critics.[62]

In the late 1920s, Triesch left the theater and began applying her skills elsewhere, including as a dramatic entertainer within the Berlin Jewish community and as the voice behind one Jewish-themed film project. Beginning in 1926, she gave readings that were featured and reviewed in a wide range of Jewish periodicals. A drawing of Triesch by well-known painter Max Liebermann (1847–1935) adorned an invitation to a February 1927 benefit for the Jüdische Altershilfe, an organization to help elderly Jews in Berlin. In addition to famous works by Johann Wolfgang von Goethe, Charles Baudelaire, Franz Werfel, and others, Triesch performed overtly Jewish texts including Heine's poem "Princess Sabbath" and several Bible excerpts. Journalist Bertha Badt-Strauss reported that she heard a knowledgeable member of the Jewish community approvingly sanction Triesch's reading of scripture with the comment: "She read it as correctly as a midrash!"[63] For some listeners, Triesch's voice functioned as a kind of Weimar-era biblical commentary.

Moreover, Triesch's vocal contribution to a short animated silhouette film demonstrates Triesch's ability to update an ancient Jewish story for different audiences. The short film *Chad Gadjo* (One Kid, 1930; also *Ein*

*Lämmchen, The Little Goat*, and *L'agneau*) by Julius Pinschewer (1883–1961) is one of his only films to focus on Jewish motifs.[64] In fact, Pinschewer is known primarily for his artistic animated advertising films. As Pinschewer's first film with no ultimate goal of advertising a commercial product, it stands out in several ways.[65] For one, the film was made with voiceover soundtracks in multiple languages including German, Hebrew, English, and French.[66] Although "Chad Gadjo" is a widely known Aramaic and Hebrew folk song, writer Uriel Birnbaum (1894–1956) originally composed the text of the song used in the film for a 1920 book of *Chad Gadjo* drawings by his brother, Menachem Birnbaum (1893–1944), thereby lending it greater credibility within a modern German-Jewish context. The film's Hebrew soundtrack also helped it stand out as an innovative work, as synchronized sound technology was still new and there had not yet been many sound films made in Hebrew. One Berlin Zionist newspaper eagerly anticipated the release of *Chad Gadjo* several months before its completion.[67]

Irene Triesch recorded the voice track for only the German version of Pinschewer's film, which was approved by the censorship office in May 1930 and screened at the Marmorhaus in Berlin, along with several other short films produced by Pinschewer-Film-AG.[68] The German version was also the only version of the film to include the brief frame story of a nonanimated "real" family sitting down to a Passover Seder, which situates the animation as a narrative performance that is part of the Seder.[69] The film's opening intertitle explains: "*Chad Gadjo* serves as the conclusion of the religious celebration that takes place on the evening of the Pesach Festival in the Jewish family according to the ancient custom." The holiday rituals that the family performs on screen include the distribution of matzah and a blessing over the wine. In the background, a conspicuously placed Hanukkah menorah unnecessarily codes the scene as Jewish, a trick used in other films to designate a scene (or actor) Jewish when it was not otherwise marked as such.[70]

Triesch's voiceover, which begins with the film's silhouette animation, serves as a constant reminder of the real people sitting around the table and the actual Jewish rituals to which the animation is linked. Further, her clear-spoken German reins in the potential of the animation to be a marker of foreignness or something exotic.[71] Indeed, the strong, expressionistic angles of the silhouettes naturally lend themselves to this curious story about gruesome deaths. The animation portrays the old folktale of a child whose father buys a little sheep (or goat) that is eaten by a cat, which sets off a long chain of ominous events and killings leading to a final appearance by the Holy One. At the same time, these figures—which Pinschewer created together with his collaborator, Rudi Klemm (1904–55), and which build on animation work popularized by Lotte

Reiniger—also recall the *Had Gadya* watercolor series (1919) by El Lissitzky (1890–1941), whose modern artistic interpretation of this Jewish legend employed Yiddish words and East European visual symbols.[72] In Pinschewer's film, Triesch takes on the first-person voice of the child, depicted as feminine through a skirt, who delights in her pet sheep.[73] The pitch of her voice is higher when repeating the refrain in which the child laments the fate of its pet ("Little lamb! A little lamb"); it is lower and more suspenseful when narrating the rest of the story. With her work on this film, Triesch created a more permanent and widely distributed legacy of her spoken performances of Jewish texts.

In addition to performances that elucidated age-old texts and traditions in ways that spoke to modern Jewish audiences, Triesch also impressed through her willingness to make public appearances even when it became less safe to do so. On one occasion in late 1932, she read aloud from the Bible during a newly instituted Friday evening Reform service. The Berlin Jewish Reform community's newsletter noted that Triesch, who had "acquired quite a following as a performer of the Bible" and "who feels strongly connected to Judaism," was asked to participate partly to demonstrate that the Reform movement supported women's right to stand in the pulpit. The newsletter included a photograph of Triesch, her gaze directed heavenwards, ever the performer in decorative earrings (see figure 10).[74] One critic, who in fact disapproved of Triesch performing during a prayer service, observed that she was brave to perform Jewish roles openly: "Because even if Irene Triesch is known to be a Jewish woman, it nevertheless means something that, although most others are cowards, she is reminding the public at this time so demonstratively of her Jewishness."[75]

An April 1932 article by writer Max Brod (1884–1968) in the *Jüdische Rundschau* corroborated this by suggesting that, with German nationalism on the rise, entertainers who "looked Jewish" were safer playing Jewish roles than German ones.[76] But Irene Triesch, an exception because she earned iconic status in both Jewish and mainstream spheres, proudly participated in public Jewish acts for years before the Nazis made similar forms of typecasting obligatory for Jewish performers who remained in Germany.[77] Triesch exemplified how Jewish actors could appeal to audiences by making themselves widely known as recognizable Jewish figures. Though perhaps risky, some of her performances were admired in part because they broadcast her Jewishness so clearly.

## More or Less Out: The Reception of Jewish Film Characters

The thriving visual culture of the Weimar period—from photography and the illustrated press, to increasingly popular media forms including film—was in-

Fig. 10. Irene Triesch as pictured in the Berlin Jewish Reform community's newsletter, 1932. (Courtesy of Universitätsbibliothek J. C. Senckenberg, Goethe Universität, Frankfurt am Main. S 36/F06887.)

strumental in shaping the ways in which Jewishness became visible. New ways of displaying and disseminating images inundated viewing publics with pictures designed to provoke, inform, and inspire reflection. Several popular films addressed the topic of Jews or Jewish-coded individuals passing or assimilating into mainstream culture. Scholars including Valerie Weinstein and Richard McCormick have written about the acts of passing and masquerade that take place in the films of filmmaker Ernst Lubitsch (1892–1947).[78] For example, in the comedy *Meyer aus Berlin* (Meyer from Berlin; Lubitsch, 1918/1919), a Jewish-coded Berliner attempts to pass himself off as an Alpine hiker. In another film from the early 1920s, *Das alte Gesetz* (The Ancient Law; Dupont, 1923), which one critic boldly dubbed "the first Jewish film," an actor who is the son of an Orthodox rabbi cuts off his sidelocks to transition from life in a Galician shtetl to performing on a Viennese stage.[79]

Rarely, however, were cinematic images of Jews entirely uncontroversial, for Jewish audiences found fault with all sorts of performances. In fact, even before debates about film began in earnest, the Centralverein regularly protested against Jewish comedians who told Jewish jokes in cabarets.[80] Some moving-image portrayals, Jewish critics argued, conveyed insufficiently authentic forms of Jewishness; others exaggerated Jewishness to the point of mockery. Film as a medium was believed to give viewers the illusion of reality and was regarded suspiciously because of its perceived persuasiveness. Further, like the liberal press, the German film industry was imbricated with discourses of Jewishness and Jewish influence, due in part to disproportionately high levels of involvement by Jews as filmmakers, cinema owners, and critics.[81] Rising levels of antisemitism amplified the stakes for Jewish spectators, who knew that on-screen portrayals had the ability to influence the German population at large.

During the late 1920s and early 1930s, film reception achieved a decidedly more prominent position in the Jewish press, and critics shared their interpretations of on-screen Jewishness with a variety of Jewish audiences. This body of criticism falls into two broad categories: (1) analysis of films that included problematic portrayals of Jews or Jewishness; and (2) praise for films that productively depicted Jews without the use of caricatures or stereotypes.[82] The second category suggests that Jewish audiences welcomed the opportunity to recognize and identify with discernibly Jewish film characters, particularly in realistic performances that refrained from entering the realm of antisemitic representation. In general, films that did not explicitly engage with Jewishness or Jewish characters, or employ well-known Jewish actors, did not receive significant attention in the Jewish press, though their titles may have appeared in film programs (*Spielpläne*) in papers such as the *Jüdische Rundschau*. What is surprising is that Jewish film spectators and critics writing for Jewish audiences devoted their energy to locating unequivocally positive depictions of Jewishness that often were so inconspicuous that they were nearly invisible. The remaining subsections of this chapter examine how critics and audiences assessed whether films and specific characters should be interpreted as Jewish or even "too Jewish," and how they demonstrated support for Jewishness when expressed proudly in certain ways.

*Problematic Depictions and Antisemitic Representations*

Critics writing for liberal, Zionist, and other Jewish publications were united in their dislike of perceived antisemitism and misrepresentations of Jewishness. Even though they were eager to locate films that treated Jewishness in a productive way, Weimar Jewish cinemagoers and critics remained deeply wary of depictions of Jewishness that verged on antisemitic caricatures. Perhaps they saw too many plays and films with Jewish characters—often coded as East European—who served as the brunt of a joke or the laughing stock of the whole movie. Or maybe they were all too aware of the similarities between stereotypical Jewish figures on screen and in antisemitic publications.[83] Not surprisingly, most of the visibly Jewish characters targeted in such jokes were male characters. Female Jewish characters, in contrast, could be found mainly in supporting or small roles, if they were present at all. Directors, actors, and scriptwriters all struggled to express Jewishness in such a way that it could be seen, yet did not cross the line into disputed territory through characters who could be interpreted as mocking or antisemitic. The reception of films that featured problematic depictions of Jews pointed out some of the pitfalls of relying on typecasting and stereotypes, and also underscored the fine line between films with a Jewish focus and those with a markedly antisemitic bent.

Critics Hans Wollenberg (1893–1952) and Max Kolpenitzky (1905–98), among others, maintained that a range of films contained damaging antisemitic portrayals, including military-themed films with nationalistic underpinnings. Wollenberg and Kolpenitzky, who had both experienced antisemitism firsthand, wrote that such films perpetuated a generally unfavorable image of Jews.[84] Their articles instructed readers of Jewish periodicals to be attuned to the nuances of problematic characters as well as the contexts in which they viewed such films. Films that these critics charged with antisemitic connotations include *Die dritte Eskadron* (*The Third Squadron*; Wilhelm, 1926), *Die Stadt ohne Juden* (*The City Without Jews*; Breslauer, 1924), *Brennende Grenze* (*Aftermath*; Waschneck,

1927), and feature films (*Großfilme*) made by the German film production company Ufa including *Durchlaucht Radieschen* (His Highness, the Radish; Eichberg, 1926/1927) and *Mensch ohne Namen* (*Man Without a Name*; Ucicky, 1932), which featured such characters as an insurance salesman and a ruthless attorney that were imbued with stereotypical traits.[85] Further, other reviewers argued that *Die Stadt ohne Juden* increased the negative visibility of Jews by putting Jewish wealth and prominence on display.[86]

Wollenberg, a First World War veteran and well-versed film critic, was particularly opposed to pejorative depictions of Jewish characters in military roles. He went to great lengths to contest antisemitic assertions that Jews were the driving force behind the film industry.[87] In 1927, Wollenberg, who also edited the mainstream film publication *Lichtbild-Bühne* from 1927 to 1933, summarized in the *C.V.-Zeitung* his fear that the typecasting nature of films was "predestined to exaggerate the Jewishness of the Jew, that is, to show the Jew not how he is in reality, but how old, popular stereotypes envision him."[88] One compelling example Wollenberg cites is Mischka Rappaport, the character played by actor Siegfried Arno (1895–1975) in *Die dritte Eskadron*. The film's joking intertitles label Rappaport a hapless soldier and a bowlegged Jew who answers a lieutenant's question: "How did you come to this regiment?" with the retort: "I didn't come, my emperor summoned me."[89] The humor in this and other exchanges derives from the Jewish character's literal interpretation of the questions and his supposed ignorance. Rappaport pronounces himself Jewish (the intertitle uses the word *mosaisch*, a euphemistic term referring to Mosaic law) but also is coded Jewish through antisemitic stereotypes such as bowleggedness and a strained sense of patriotism. Because Rappaport's actions, gestures, and sensibility code him as Jewish, they simultaneously render his self-identification unimportant.

Along with other critics, Wollenberg faulted everyone who contributed in even the smallest way to the construction of stereotypical Jewish characters. Among those he blamed were "Jewish performers who hire themselves out for such roles for commensurate fees"; "Jewish directors [who] turn up to make scenes of this sort"; "Jewish title writers, who include the corresponding texts"; and "Jewish businessmen, who as filmmakers are ultimately accountable for these goings-on!"[90] By calling for self-reflection in the creation of Jewish characters as a response to Jewish self-mockery in film, Wollenberg's articles aimed to help filmmakers and viewers transform the way Jews were depicted on screen. This debate about self-mockery in film, theatrical performances, and cabaret continued for several years. One report published in the *C.V.-Zeitung* in 1931 cited several prominent critics including Wollenberg on "the question of the display of Jewish characters." This article sums up the contribution by critic Rudolf Arnheim (1904–2007) as follows: "The Jew in cinema, whether good or bad, beautiful or ugly, has the same task we all have in life: to be not only a Jew, but [also] a person."[91] But a lack of character depth and borderline inappropriate jokes could be misinterpreted easily, and, for some critics, defeated the purpose of depicting realistic Jewish characters on screen.

It mattered not only how one interpreted such characters, and who created them, but also where one viewed a potentially controversial film. Critics argued that viewers in rural areas or towns with small or no Jewish populations were more likely to misinterpret stereotypes of Jews. Songwriter and scriptwriter Max Kolpenitzky wrote in 1927 in the *Jüdische Rundschau* and *Israelitisches Familienblatt* about his encounter with impressionable small-town cinemagoers while viewing the Ufa film, *Durchlaucht Radieschen*:

> Many people take everything offered here at face value, and are accustomed to carrying over these impressions into everyday life. Anyone who has visited these countless small cinemas even once—after all, they make up the bulk of the cinemas—will easily notice how peals of laughter that sound different from the usual laughs always ring out when this kind of "Jewish type" appears.

Kolpenitzky pointed out that Jewish character types on German screens often figured as the brunt of potentially harmful jokes, which audiences in smaller cinemas interpreted more harshly. He elaborated that by "Jewish type," he meant everything from clothing manufacturers to "the old, stooped Eastern Jew with a grungy caftan and flowing sidelocks."[92] Another critic pointed out how ludicrous the Jewish character in *Brennende Grenze* appeared, noting: "The Jew trembles exaggeratedly in comical fear, secretly passes the sergeant some money, and runs away, bowlegged. . . . I don't have anything against the depiction of bad Jews, but they should be characters and not caricatures."[93] The visibly Jewish appearance of certain minor Jewish characters instantly marked them as different and of lesser value than the film's protagonists. Instead of bringing characters with emotional depth or other value to the film, the "Jewish type" represented a category of men with exaggerated faults and shortcomings.

The same visual markers recurred on screen and in Jewish film criticism: Jewish men became visible in an objectionable way whenever they embodied stereotypes, from the banal (Jews wear beards, sidelocks, and caftans) to the despicable (Jews are bowlegged, weak, ignorant, ruthless, and involved in treacherous money-related schemes). In contrast, critics praised films with less stereotypical or nonstereotypical portrayals of Jewish characters that focused instead on aspects of authentic Jewish life. Some of these ideal films presented Jewishness in a subtle way, whereas select films put it front and center and thereby exemplified what it meant to screen positive images of Jewishness.

### *Positively Out: Model Jewish Films*

Overt references to Jewishness in Weimar cinema were relatively uncommon, and only a handful of German films dealt extensively with topics related to Jewish life. But Jewish-identified avid filmgoers sought out these few films with explicitly Jewish themes, whether they included Jewish role models worthy of emulation, starred famous Jewish actors and actresses, or simply provided a basis for discussion and criticism. Numerous German and Austrian films with easily identifiable Jewish themes or players received positive attention in the Weimar Jewish press. Among these are such historical works as *Das alte Gesetz* and *Dreyfus* (Oswald, 1930); the occasional military or entertainment film with positive or neutral depictions of Jewish characters, for example *Leichte Kavallerie* (Light Cavalry; Randolf, 1927); American films *Potash and Perlmutter* (Badger, 1923), *The Jazz Singer* (Crosland, 1927), and *Disraeli* (Green, 1929); and Zionist and other documentary-style films that claimed to offer authentic glimpses into Jewish life. Reviews in the Jewish press explained how viewers might interpret and parse these films for accurate representations of Jewish behavior, tradition, and matter-of-fact, unexaggerated Jewish self-presentation or obvious examples of Jewish pride.

The popular films about American Jewish acculturation that enjoyed a warm reception in the Weimar Jewish press touched on many themes familiar to Jews in Germany, including the integration of Old World elements into the New World, tensions between tradition and modernity, and the performance of Jewishness in the public sphere. Writer Carl A. Bratter, an American immigrant from Germany, reviewed Montague Glass's comedic Potash and Perlmutter stories in the *C.V.-Zeitung*. According to Bratter, these stories about Jewish owners of a ready-to-wear clothing business were well positioned to provide humorous and authentic insight into what it was like for struggling German and East European Jewish immigrants working in the American garment industry.[94] Screenings of Clarence Badger's *Potash and Perlmutter* film at Berlin's Ufa-Palast am Zoo in 1924 received special attention in the *Yidishe ilustrirte tsaytung* (Yiddish Illustrated Newspaper), which deemed the film worthwhile not only because of its hilarity and famous actors but also because audiences had the opportunity to view live fashion shows in conjunction with this film.[95] Several top Berlin fashion houses engaged models to participate in a live show after the third act.[96] Film was thus more than an on-screen medium; at times it provided an occasion for a live experience of other industries relevant to Jewish communities. Combining a film screening with a live fashion show further increased the visibility of Jewish participation in both the American and German fashion industries. It also put a variety of actual participants in the German *Konfektion* or ready-to-wear sector, from designers to models, on par with the film's actors as examples of how connections to Jewishness could be displayed publicly and inoffensively.[97]

Not surprisingly, the American film that made the greatest impact in German-Jewish circles was *The Jazz Singer* (Crosland, 1927), which appealed to Jewish viewers through its portrayal of acculturation and its treatment and rejection of passing on several levels. This famously innovative early sound film—a part-talkie that still relied on some intertitles—tells of a cantor's son, Jakie Rabinowitz (Al Jolson), who changes his name to Jack Robin and leaves New York's Lower East Side to pursue a career as a jazz singer on Broadway, where he meets dancer Mary Dale. Ultimately, and not without inner conflict, Jack misses his Broadway premiere to sing Kol Nidre in his dying father's stead. German-Jewish critics extolled *The Jazz Singer* for utilizing synchronized sound as an opportunity to showcase East European cantorial melodies. For Jewish filmgoers in Germany, *The Jazz Singer* also offered a further glimpse of authentic Jewish life and religious practices transplanted to America. The film's focus on the performance of identities by way of Americanization, blackface minstrelsy, and Broadway and synagogue appearances enabled German viewers to consider how American Jews might have passed or covered their Jewishness, and how Jewishness figured as a form of racial otherness in American contexts.

The reception of *The Jazz Singer* in Germany, where it was known as *Der Jazzsänger*, exemplifies the different types of film reception across the spectrum of Weimar Jewish cinemagoers. Jazz music became extremely popular in Berlin in the mid-1920s, and images of Black jazz musicians, including one in a photograph titled *Charleston* by Yva (1900–1942; pseudonym of Else Neuländer-Simon), were splashed across the covers of illustrated magazines well before the film made it to German cinemas.[98] When a silent version of *The Jazz Singer* first premiered in Germany at Berlin's Gloria-Palast on September 18, 1928, the film was already an international sensation; one early ad in *Der Israelit* cited its tremendous box office success in New York.[99] Some reviews praised the film's authentic treatment of Jewish elements while simultaneously marveling at its many innovations, including Jolson's performances. Other responses to the film pointed to its ambivalent portrayals of Jewishness, particularly with respect to Jack's behavior. As one reviewer of the silent version put it, "To report on the so-called Jewish content of this film is particularly difficult."[100]

Jazz was itself a contested art form, and the German right criticized *The Jazz Singer* as part of a broader rejection of American and Jewish culture. In fact, reactionary critics regarded jazz as created by Blacks and marketed by Jews.[101] The image of a Black jazz musician marked with a Star of David later became the face of *Entartete Musik* (Degenerate Music), an exhibition similar to the Nazi exhibition on degenerate art.[102] One 1928 article in the *C.V.-Zeitung* pronounced the film's plot to be steeped in "sentimentality" and "kitsch," underscoring the fact that the *Deutsche Zeitung*, a right-wing German newspaper, had cited the film as an example of the horrific nature of Jewish "clannishness" (*Versipptheit*).[103] Jolson became further entangled with controversial films when another film in which he starred, *The Singing Fool* (Bacon, 1928), premiered in June 1929 as the first fully synchronized American sound film shown in Germany.[104] Joseph Goebbels even called for the withdrawal of the "pan-Jewish propaganda" of *The Jazz Singer* from German cinemas when the sound version was released in Germany in late 1929, though Ufa did not pull it.[105]

These and other antisemitic responses to the film prompted the *Familienblatt* to respond with humor. It ran a satirical cartoon of a Black jazz singer with this caption: "In order to appease [the antisemitic press], in the future 'Triumphantly we want to defeat France' will be sung in lieu of the Kol Nidre melody."[106] By proposing a German military song as an accompaniment to the most decidedly Jewish parts of the film, this cartoon highlighted the absurdity of attempting to overwrite the popular film's Jewishness at the level of sound—especially when doing so would not eliminate its visual depictions of racial otherness. Yet even these critical or defensive treatments of *The Jazz Singer* in Jewish newspapers demonstrate sympathy with its willingness to broadcast a sense of Jewish pride in a major feature film.

Advertisements for late 1929 screenings of the sound version of *The Jazz Singer* in Berlin's Gloria-Palast cinema emphasized the film's striking performances of song and identities. One ad in the *Berliner jüdische Zeitung* declared the film an unforgettable tearjerker: "There is no conceivable purer pleasure. Al Jolson's chanting of Kol Nidre remains unforgettable; perhaps even more enchanting is his jubilant bittersweet song, 'Mammy.' No one should be ashamed of breaking out in tears from this film."[107] Emotional responses to hearing Jewish melodies in this early sound film were bound up with familial ties and Jewish experiences. Playing up another aspect of the film, the Berlin *Gemeindeblatt*, the newsletter of the Berlin Jewish community, ran a full-page ad of Jolson performing in blackface against a black background (see figure 11).[108] Here, the focus is not explicitly on Jewishness; only small lines of text at the bottom reference Kol Nidre and Jewish music. It is not possible to make out the outline of the figure in this promotional image, which also was distributed widely in the United States. Rather, only the whites of his eyes, the "mask" of white around his mouth, a white shirt collar, and white gloves are visible.

The image of the Black American jazz singer offered German Jews an alternative way of representing Jewish difference on screen. In these German ads and reviews, Jolson's Jack Robin becomes memorable and visible not through his Blackness, but through the white accents that contrast with and offset Blackness. This recalls Michael Rogin's argument that blackface minstrelsy provided Jewish immigrants with a means to become (White) Americans.[109] Many German reviews and ads contained only text; the one image repeatedly selected to depict the main character was not that of a "typical" Jew, but rather a Jewish man performing Blackness. Jewishness is referenced only in the fine print. In this case, the German-Jewish press's conflicted relationship with screen representations of Jews resulted in a fascination with a figure who looked nothing like most German Jews. With its images of a Jew "passing" for a Black man, the press pointed to other models that, though a contested form of representation in their own right, nevertheless deflected from the usual antisemitic stereotypes.

In mainstream Weimar circles, images of Black jazz singers with Jewish connections reinforced the conflation of Jewishness with other racialized minority identities.[110] In another film made several years later, *Moritz macht sein Glück* (*Moritz Makes His Fortune*; Speyer, 1931), actor Siegfried Arno impersonated Jolson in blackface.[111] Arno's character, Moritz Meyer, is booed offstage at a fashion ball after lip-synching to an English recording of Jolson. Shortly thereafter, Moritz is unable to remove the black makeup from his face, and he is fired (and promptly rehired) from his job at Meyer & Co., a ready-to-wear clothing store, for this and other antics. Arno's role in this film reveals his mastery of a type of "screen passing" that involves acting and perhaps overacting to call attention to stereotypical aspects of racialized roles—including Jolson's.[112] With its unambiguous reference to *The Jazz Singer*, the use of blackface contributes to coding Moritz as Jewish. His exaggerated efforts to scrub away the makeup represent a daily struggle with stigmatized forms of otherness. For some performers, blackface was not the only way of expressing anxiety about racial and ethnic difference. Many Jewish comic performers made

Fig. 11. Advertisement for *The Jazz Singer* in the Berlin *Gemeindeblatt*, 1929. (Courtesy of the Leo Baeck Institute, New York.)

themselves identifiably Jewish through the use of Jewface, which relied on fake beards and used face putty to create exaggerated hook noses.[113]

But in Germany, some of the best ways to depict Jewishness on screen included highly subtle characters and realistic documentaries. The illustrated supplement of the *Israelitisches Familienblatt* regularly featured still images and promotional photos for films that seemed relevant in some way for Jewish viewers, even when the films were only questionably Jewish. Chapter 4 comments further on the *Familienblatt*'s tendency to misidentify Jewishness and to generalize about what might count as Jewish in a film. In 1929, for example, the paper featured an article on *Disraeli*, an English-language sound biopic about British prime minister Benjamin Disraeli. The editor observed: "Even though very little is shown here that is Jewish per se (*wenig an sich Jüdisches*), it nevertheless fills us with particular satisfaction to see someone placed into the center of European veneration who was so closely linked to Judaism, and who took every opportunity to emphasize this."[114] This comment suggests that depicting something intangible such as great respect for Jews—or even for one exceptional Jewish politician—was significant in that it provided a positive representation of Jewishness that was barely perceptible.[115]

In contrast to films with very little Jewish content "per se," several documentary films clearly portrayed Jewish life in order to educate viewers about a particular topic. These films generally were sponsored by one or more Jewish organizations. For instance, the "charity film," *Ein Freitag Abend* (One Friday Night, 1926), directed by Gertrud David and produced by the Zentralwohl-fahrtsstelle der deutschen Juden (Central Welfare Agency of German Jews), provided insight into social welfare practices in different Jewish contexts. Used in part to raise money and recruit volunteers, the film was screened for audiences in 60 Jewish communities, and 21 times in Berlin, with over 15,000 viewers in Berlin alone.[116] A still image of a Sabbath dinner appeared in the *Familienblatt*'s illustrated supplement and provided evidence of the film's depictions of Jewish ritual.[117] Viewers recognized prominent social welfare workers including Henriette May, Minna Schwarz, and Lina Wagner-Tauber. Regina Isaacsohn declared that the film also was instructive insofar as it depicted women fulfilling important cultural obligations outside the home.[118] The film not only made visible a kind of work that it is often invisible, but it also increased the visibility of Jews in the field of German social work.[119]

Documentary films that introduced the Land of Israel to those who had not yet traveled there were of paramount importance to the Zionist cause. Some of these silent "Palestine films" also were lauded for their ability to disseminate positive images of Jewish culture in a modern and compelling fashion.

Spectators took particular pride in visual depictions of the land, anything relating to the Hebrew language, and portrayals of traditional Jewish rituals.[120] In 1925, the "Palestine film," *Eretz Israel*, which included images of the inauguration of the Hebrew University in Jerusalem, was screened, first privately at an event at the Grüngard salon, and then publicly at a Berlin theater. Sammy Gronemann offered a short lecture to accompany the film's private screening, which indicates its importance among the Zionist elite.[121] However, not all "Palestine films" were well received. In order to engage spectators on behalf of Zionist causes, a film had to be visually compelling. One review of a documentary made by the Palestine Film Company, *Eine Reise durch Palästina* (A Journey through Palestine, 1928), took the film to task for its bland and boring presentation of the land, lack of coherent narrative, poor cinematography and use of technology, as well as its notably unrecognizable faces, interiors, and landscapes.[122] In other words, on-screen representations of the Land of Israel were deemed usable only when they were done well. Being able to identify faces and places was part of the process of recording visual history and delivering it to the Jewish masses.

Other "Palestine films" were deemed more successful in their use of compelling and recognizable visual imagery. The documentary *Frühling in Palästina* (Spring in Palestine, 1928), a joint venture of the organizations Keren Hayesod and Keren Kayemeth, attempted to compensate for the mistakes of previous films by conveying information about local culture more effectively. German director Willy Prager edited footage assembled by J. Ben Dow and J. Gal-Eser in Palestine to ensure the film met the demands of the modern viewer. Five shorter films were created from the longer version in the hope that the film would reach more viewers if each part stood on its own.[123] The film premiere met with great success, and several December 1928 screenings were advertised widely in the *Jüdische Rundschau*.[124] With a variety of engaging subjects including the observance of Jewish festivals in Jerusalem and Tel Aviv, women's roles, the region north of the Jordan River, and such exports as oranges and matzah, *Frühling in Palästina* had something for everyone.

Films that captured the events of Zionist organizations such as sports clubs were also in high demand. One short amateur documentary film, *Makkabäer. Ein Film jüdischer Sportjugend* (Maccabees: A Film of Jewish Young Athletes; Simmenauer, 1930), received highest praise for its realistic depictions, including the absence of staged shots. This fast-paced film focused on the Jewish athletes and prominent guests who attended the 1929 Maccabi World Congress in Ostrava, Czechoslovakia.[125] As one reviewer noted about the film's premiere in Berlin, where "only a flag was missing": "The good shots and the familiar faces inspired much joy and excitement, and the five filmmakers . . . were called up amidst resounding applause from the audience, who were thrilled with the presentation."[126] This reviewer emphasized the fact that the people shown here—some of whom are mentioned by name in the film's intertitles—were familiar to certain viewers. The film thus presented these subjects as entirely "out," and as fully committed participants in the project of displaying recognizable Jewish activities to spectators interested in model behavior.

*Desirable Displays of Jewish Women in Film*

In Weimar Jewish circles, film was known as a medium that could be particularly influential for female spectators, both because of the medium's realistic qualities and the supposedly impressionable nature of women.[127] One film critic, Heinz Ludwigg, explicitly addressed the gendered dimensions of spectatorship in a 1925 article for *Die jüdische Frau*, while also calling attention to the central role of women as consumers of film: "You have no idea, my dear lady, how very important you are to the propaganda directors of film studios and movie theaters. . . . [T]herefore, my dearest, the posters and images are tailored primarily to your taste, and therefore, my most adored one, the psychological layer of the ads is produced for you."[128] This type of direct address, which was not uncommon in Jewish periodicals, presented the culture industry as one that was bound up with Jewish women's tastes and consumer needs. Likewise, in a well-known 1927 series of feuilletons published in the mainstream *Frankfurter Zeitung*, critic Siegfried Kracauer (1889–1966) commented on the impressionable nature of shopgirls at the movies, noting that "sensational film hits and life usually correspond to each other because the Little Miss Typists model themselves after the examples they see on the screen."[129] With an ironic tone of condescension similar to Ludwigg's, Kracauer, too, observed what these "little" girls would take away from each film, including the desire for a successful love relationship and the importance of wealth for overall happiness. As film theorist Mary Ann Doane has suggested, the female gaze was often censored and even negated, and womanliness or femininity itself was considered a kind of performance or masquerade.[130]

Whereas these Weimar-era critics were careful to note the roles of women as spectators, and Wollenberg, Kolpenitzky, and others focused on stereotypes of Jewish men in film, critics infrequently commented on the presentation of Jewish women in film. The vast majority of recurring Jewish character types were male; female Jewish characters were neither cause for laughter, nor generally deemed worthy of comment. And despite an abundance of Weimar visual images of women that were coded Jewish, so-called authentic performances of Jewish female characters on screen were barely identifiable as such. In the following analysis of two exemplary and widely distributed films, Rolf Randolf's *Leichte Kavallerie* (1927) and Richard Oswald's *Dreyfus* (1930), and their favorable reception in the Jewish press, I argue that the most desirable displays of Jewishness were, paradoxically, highly subtle or visually absent, particularly with respect to women. In part because the Jewishness of female characters often was constructed through relationships to male characters, or merely encoded by way of darker coloring, the most coveted cinematic encounters with female Jewish characters were unremarkable. Gender stereotypes often were reinforced even when Jewishness was displayed in inoffensive ways.

The film *Leichte Kavallerie*, of which no known copies exist today, is set in Galicia in October 1914. A weary squadron of Austrian troops is billeted at various homes in a small Eastern town. Rabbi Süß (Albert Steinrück) and his daughter, Rahel (Elizza La Porta), are assigned to provide temporary accommodations for Lieutenant Rüdiger von Starhemberg (André Mattoni) (see figure 12). The rabbi fears for his daughter and attempts to send her to a relative in Vienna before the inevitable happens, but to no avail: Rahel and the lieutenant fall in love. After a climactic scene in which the rabbi contemplates killing his daughter's non-Jewish lover but is unable to do so, Rahel helps German troops rescue Starhemberg's squadron from a surprise attack by the Russian army. In one of the final scenes, she visits him in the hospital; the implication is that he will heal and they will enjoy a happy life together.[131] Most reviews of *Leichte Kavallerie* described it as a military film that combined tales of espionage and battle on the eastern front with a story about a love affair between a Jewish woman and a Christian man.[132] Kracauer, who pronounced it a "watered-down remake of *Hotel Stadt Lemburg*," pointed out that its scenes in the trenches heightened private desires and paved the way for "good kissing."[133] The Jewish press, too, emphasized the film's main love story, though with a condemnation of intermarriage.[134]

Most significant about this film's reception is that its understated style of performance is what held the greatest appeal for Jewish spectators. In a full-page illustrated feature story, the *Familienblatt* praised *Leichte Kavallerie* for authentic, yet not exaggerated, depictions of Jewish life: "Although the ending's prospective intermarriage is of course unacceptable for us Jews, this film nevertheless deserves our interest due to its many fond, realistic depictions of the Jewish milieu in Galicia. Above all, it is deserving because the director has

Fig. 12. Cast of characters in *Leichte Kavallerie* (Randolf, 1927), in *Illustrierter Film-Kurier* 9, no. 688 (October 1927), 7. (Courtesy of Stiftung Deutsche Kinemathek.)

steered clear of all exaggerations, which are unfortunately so common in films about Jews."[135] The elements of Jewish life presented in this film are deemed worthwhile primarily because of their subtlety. Aside from one reference in the intertitles to the rabbi donning a prayer shawl as he prepares to go to synagogue, no other scenes seem to treat Jewish life as such. Instead, Jewishness becomes most significant as an obstacle to intermarriage. Interestingly, both Rabbi Süß and his daughter were played by non-Jewish actors, a fact not mentioned in the review.

In *Leichte Kavallerie*, Jewishness is defined—and redefined—as an "Eastern" form of difference that separates the "Eastern" from the "Western" troops and other characters. Rahel, played by Romanian-born actress Elizza La Porta, possesses stereotypically Eastern dark eyes and hair.[136] Like other cinematic rabbis' daughters, such as Miriam in *Der Golem, wie er in die Welt kam* (*The Golem: How He Came Into the World*; Wegener, 1920), Rahel initially seems to be at the mercy of overprotective male guardians, yet she still manages to pursue relations with a non-Jew.[137] (Coincidentally, actor Albert Steinrück played the rabbi/father in both *Der Golem* and *Leichte Kavallerie*.) Rahel is most remarkable because of her heroic act of aiding military troops, a traditionally masculine act. She remains in control, which, as film scholars Patrice Petro and Heide Schlüpmann have argued about other characters, reflects a repositioning of the Weimar female subject as more androgynous and thus able to pursue freedom from patriarchal authority.[138] But Rahel's Jewishness is suppressed and overwritten by "Western" German values. Instead of exaggerating Jewishness, she essentially abandons it; the new reality she represents is not one that can properly accommodate Jewishness. The *Familienblatt*'s reception hints that Rahel's role in saving the squadron counterbalances the transgression of intermarriage only to a limited extent.

The German-Jewish press's strong approval of Rahel's character reveals a tacit preference for Jewish characters who did not "act Jewish" or display undesirable traits associated with Jewishness. By focusing mainly on the rabbi and his daughter, the *Familienblatt* entirely overlooked the performances of other Jewish characters. Nowhere did its review mention approval or disapproval of the figure of the Jewish merchant, Moritz Wasserstrahl, played by Siegfried Arno. Other reviews notably credited Wasserstrahl, whose name is mocked throughout the film (he is called Wasservogel, Wasserkrug), for supplying the film with humor. Turning the focus to women, who generally were depicted as less overtly Jewish compared to male characters, was a way of covering the most objectionable stereotypical performances of Jews such as those performed by Arno. As one review in the general press put it: "Elizza la Porta is not entirely balanced. . . . But she is beautiful and young and instinctively makes the right gestures."[139] Restrained female characters provided the German-Jewish press with a way of accessing the "right" kind of visibility for Jews.

Richard Oswald's *Dreyfus*, a very different film with questions of Jewish belonging and antisemitism (and another understated Jewish woman) at its heart, received more coverage in Jewish periodicals than any other Weimar film.[140] *Dreyfus* is thus one of the most important German-Jewish films of the era with respect to understanding Jewish spectatorial desire. A commercially successful early historical docudrama that premiered at Berlin's Gloria-Palast on August 16, 1930, *Dreyfus* received favorable reviews in both the Jewish press and the general press. Richard Oswald (1880–1963, born Richard Ornstein), who participated in the production of over 100 films, is best known today for films such as *Anders als die Andern* (*Different from the Others*, 1919; see the conclusion). He also figures prominently in several recent scholarly studies of Weimar cinema.[141] S. S. Prawer has argued that Oswald's willingness to deal with the problems encountered by Jews carried over from his early silent films to sound film; Ofer Ashkenazi has suggested that many of Oswald's later silent films also treat Jewish identity more implicitly.[142]

*Dreyfus* opens with a speech by attorney and C.V. deputy chairman Bruno Weil (1883–1961), whose book provided the basis for the film's script. The rest of the film showcases the well-known historical events that took place from 1894 to 1906: French-Jewish captain Alfred Dreyfus (Fritz Kortner) is wrongly accused, sentenced, and sent to prison for transmitting military secrets to the German government. Eventually, after a long imprisonment and intervention by writer Emile Zola (Heinrich George), Dreyfus is exonerated thanks to proof that Major Esterhazy (Oskar Homolka) is the real traitor. The film also exposes the vicious political plot against Dreyfus. Another key player is Dreyfus's wife, Lucie (Grete Mosheim), who stands by her husband throughout his long ordeal.

Oswald's film leaves no doubt that its highly politicized message was designed to counter antisemitism. The Jewish victim is clearly identified and marked as such from the outset: the camera tracks General Boisdeffre's finger as it points first to the word "Jew" (*Jude*) and ends on "Dreyfus." The word *Jude* is uttered out loud at least four times, once as part of an exclamation by Colonel Picquart: "Whether Jew or Christian, there is only one kind of justice." Further, the casting of Fritz Kortner (1892–1970, born Fritz Nathan Kohn) in this role was far from coincidental, as Kortner was repeatedly cast in Jewish stage roles, including negative portrayals such as his recurring stage role of Shylock.[143] As Dreyfus, Kortner—whose physical characteristics and talent at embodying Jewish characters made him a regular target of antisemitic fantasies—again played a character whose Jewishness was linked inextricably to alleged culpability.[144] Doris Wittner commented that the way Kortner roared the phrase "I am innocent" countless times gripped "not only the ears, but also the souls of the listener."[145] Another critic commented that Kortner's screams became "a stirring memory not only for the generation that lived through this trial, but also a reminder to our youth."[146] Oswald himself had been the subject of antisemitic attacks, and he had faced much resistance in bringing the Dreyfus Affair to the German screen. Oswald later wrote in a letter to Kracauer: "At that time one needed a certain amount of audacity to make a film in which the Jew is innocent."[147] Still, there were also many leftist filmgoers who longed for a pro-Jewish, anti-Nazi film in August 1930, just one month before the German elections.[148] Kortner observed in his autobiography that cinemas were overflowing with Germans bitter about the antisemitic persecution of Dreyfus.[149]

Although the Jewish press raved about the potential of *Dreyfus* to effect political change on behalf of Jews, its attention to Lucie Dreyfus was circumscribed and focused on her ability to downplay Jewishness.[150] In fact, *Familienblatt* editor Will Pleß commented mainly on the ability of film and theater actress Grete Mosheim (1905–86) to appeal to "the greater public."[151] Indeed, the fair-haired, blue-eyed Berliner was perceived as able to portray Jewishness such that it was not visually legible, and therefore amenable to both mainstream and Jewish audiences. Although Mosheim's father was Jewish, her mother was not, and she was raised in a Christian household; she later recalled learning that her father was Jewish at age 14.[152] Her appeal also may have stemmed in part from her modest upbringing in Berlin-Kreuzberg. She often played members of the lower social classes, such as her starring roles as Susi Sachs in Oswald's *Arm wie eine Kirchenmaus* (*Poor as a Church Mouse*, 1931) and Eliza Doolittle in Shaw's *Pygmalion*. Further, several roles required her to play women in distress, from Gretchen in Goethe's *Faust* to the lead role in *Cyankali* (Cyanide; Tintner, 1930), which dealt with abortion rights.

Appearance and especially blondness figured significantly into the ways others assessed Mosheim's Jewishness or lack thereof. According to Kortner, who referred to her as "the blond half-Jew (*Halbjüdin*)," she appealed to people from all walks of life.[153] One article even described her as "internally blond."[154] Critics Rudolf Arnheim and Alfred Kerr praised her general inconspicuousness and opacity, and her fellow actor and friend Hubert von Meyerinck described her as "the blonde Grete, who was German in the best sense of the word."[155] When asked whether and how she employed gestures in her silent film roles, Mosheim responded: "Few; the fewer, the better, even in silent film."[156] Only in one film role, that of Lucie Dreyfus, did Mosheim play a char-

**Fig. 13. Grete Mosheim and Fritz Kortner in *Dreyfus* (Oswald, 1930). (Courtesy of Stiftung Deutsche Kinemathek.)**

acter who, because of her husband, was marked as Jewish.[157] Yet even in this pro-Jewish, highly political film, Mosheim's appearance and performance were desirable precisely because she managed not to act or "look Jewish" and to avoid exaggeration of all kinds.

In *Dreyfus*, the quiet heroism of Lucie Dreyfus serves as a foil to the grand deeds of male heroes (and antiheroes), in part because of its inconspicuousness. Prawer suggests Mosheim plays a "wholly assimilated wife."[158] The film's mise-en-scène and costumes further contain and conceal her Jewishness and her character. Lucie Dreyfus is at times positioned in the background of the frame. Many close-ups and other shots of her are partially obscured by prison or window bars or a dark mourning dress, hat, and veil (see figure 13). Mosheim's character is not the center of attention, as in other films about women's rights, but rather the shadow. Her cries of "he is innocent" are but an echo to her husband's much louder and more memorable screams. In what at the time was the best-known Weimar film with an explicitly Jewish topic, the only Jewish woman in the film is blond, acquiescent, and barely visible.

Film criticism in the Weimar Jewish press reveals that Jewish audiences welcomed the opportunity to identify with positive images of Jewish characters even when difficult to locate. Performances of Jewishness that were deemed realistic or authentic, especially those that avoided exaggeration and overwrought stereotypes, resonated with filmgoers and critics in search of favorable visual models. Many female characters were constructed in relation to male characters; some of their performances of Jewishness were subtle enough that they did not provoke controversial reactions. The most highly praised cinematic encounters with Jewish women included such characters as Rahel Süß, a rabbi's daughter who abandons her Jewish home in Galicia, and Lucie Dreyfus, the wife of a famous French Jew who openly exhibits nothing that is specifically Jewish. Both characters were played by actresses who avoided attributes of appearance and behavior that would have coded them "more Jewish."

In Weimar Germany, the most desirable Jewish female characters either were not coded as particularly Jewish or were barely visible at all—yet their mere presence was enough to carve out a space for the representation of Jews on screen. It was difficult to identify these women as Jewish because they effectively passed for non-Jewish were it not for the context of the story. But barely visible is very different from invisible, and the enthusiastic reception of such on-screen representations of Jewishness suggests that subtle forms of visibility were critical to the construction of Weimar Jewish self-images. In fact, favorable visualizations of Jewishness facilitated the process of Jewish self-identification and choosing to come out. In the absence of such positive depictions, or when the focus turned to policing members of the Jewish community to prevent them from mirroring stereotypical representations, voluntary acknowledgments were not always possible, as the next chapter demonstrates.

## CHAPTER 3

# Hostile Outings: When Being Seen Was Undesirable

Weimar Jews engaged in some form of passing or made themselves less visible for a variety of reasons, including threats to their well-being. Fear of repercussions for being discernibly Jewish—which, in some cases, simply meant appearing well off or fashionable—influenced the ways Jews marked themselves and instructed each other with respect to dress. Even within Jewish communities, women who displayed expensive tastes or dressed in a flashy way, especially on Jewish holidays or in proximity to synagogues, were accused of incurring unnecessary attention that could prompt antisemitic acts. Jews thus observed and policed each other with respect to how they presented themselves in public. One liberal Jewish response was to encourage women to do a more effective job of conforming to mainstream demands by covering themselves and their Jewishness. Upper-class travel destinations, such as summer vacation resorts, were especially dangerous places to be identifiably Jewish. Throughout the 1920s, the Centralverein consistently warned Jewish travelers to avoid summer vacation spots known to be antisemitic, including nearly every Bavarian bath and resort.[1]

One short anecdote from July 1925 illustrates how resort politics could force Jewishness into the public eye, and how the hostility of self-policing arose in an attempt to prevent the hostility of antisemitism. This anonymous feuilleton published in the *Israelitisches Familienblatt* is titled "The Blonde and the Brunette." It tells of two women who meet at a vacation resort without knowledge of the other person's relationship to Jewishness. The brunette is intelligent, modest, an excellent mother, and is declared Jewish from the outset; the blonde, in contrast, is described only as slender, elegant, and also a mother. The blonde loudly proclaims that she cannot abide the Jewish women at the resort who are always overdressed, and whose ostentatious accessories cause them to resemble "jewelry store windows," a metaphor common in stereotypical representations of Jewish women that evokes not only excess but also the need to put it on display.[2] With more than a hint of hostility, the blonde at first outs the other Jews at the resort whose appearance and behaviors are in line with common antisemitic stereotypes. This initially deflects attention from her and makes it easier for her to conceal her own identity. When the two women meet for breakfast one morning, the blonde, who has been complaining of hunger, orders bread with cheese, whereas the brunette chooses roast meat. The brunette remarks that the blonde should order meat to satisfy her hunger, whereupon the blonde responds with the punch line: "Not for anything . . . my parents were very Orthodox, and I was raised strictly, I eat only kosher."[3] The blonde's choice to come out as Jewish even after berating her fellow Jews demonstrates a rejection of their Jewish-coded behaviors, as well as a hesitance to associate with obvious targets of antisemitism.

This story normalizes passing and suggests that it exists only in the eyes of the beholder. At first, the blonde passes for a non-Jew in the eyes of the brunette, and in what is conveyed to the reader. The blonde is marked as "less Jewish" within the narrative precisely because she is juxtaposed with the brunette and others who are coded Jewish. But it quickly becomes clear that the blonde's unfriendly act of outing others is but a precursor to the act of revealing her own identity. Although the blonde seems to be temporarily passing, or at least covering, to avoid being mistaken for a stigmatized other, she is quick to come out when her Jewish identity is challenged. Paradoxically, the widespread act of covering Jewishness ultimately contributes to marking this "slippery" blonde "more Jewish" than others who are easier to identify.

Stereotyping based on both physical characteristics and material signifiers influenced Jews across the board, and it is not surprising that a blonde character who did not fit those stereotypes had the ability to trick the reader. In fact, deceptive blonde female characters stood in the international limelight at this time, thereby reinforcing cultural and social distinctions based on women's hair color. Also well known in Germany was American author Anita Loos's *Gentlemen Prefer Blondes* (1925), about the ditzy, yet remarkably shrewd blonde, Lorelei Lee (later immortalized by Marilyn Monroe in the 1953 film).[4] One advertisement in the Berlin *Gemeindeblatt* for Kleinol Henna Shampoo used the German translation of Loos's book title as an advertising slogan: *Männer bevorzügen blond.*[5] Alongside growing right-wing nationalism that privileged so-called "Aryan" coloring, blond became the dominant hair color shown in German magazines by the early 1930s.[6] Indeed, the performance of blondness as a means to appear "less Jewish" and "more German" became critical to the survival of many Jews who passed as non-Jews in Nazi Germany.[7]

This chapter explores how antisemitic and other attacks—whether anticipated or actual—affected Jewish relationships to visibility and modes of self-
regulation during a time when concealing Jewishness was not a matter of life
and death, but rather one of feeling safe, comfortable, and unashamed. Because
outing people as Jewish, either without their permission or by calling attention
to them in unwanted ways, had the potential to cause harm on a number of
levels, accusations of Jewishness took different forms. Most obviously, antisemitic attackers who targeted Jews and "Jewish-looking" people on the street
participated in malicious attacks entangled with the act of publicly humiliating
Jews. Consequently, many Jews aimed to protect themselves by remaining inconspicuous in public. As violent incidents increased in frequency and sever-
ity, Jewish institutions were established to come to the aid of Jews in distress.
Even as some Jews took defensive measures, others engaged in forms of surveillance or self-policing—of "ethnic, racial, and sexual regulation" that challenged the autonomy of the individual—to prevent Jews from inviting such
attacks.[8] In these cases, hostility was directed inward and Jews deployed stereotypes against each other, and particularly against Jewish women, ostensibly
as a means of fending off more severe attacks.

Stereotypes also were used as a means of identifying new people in resort
towns. In Max Brod's novel *Jüdinnen* (Jewesses, 1911), in which all characters
are Jewish, one character is continually outed as an "Eastern" Jewish woman
to underscore differences among Jews. Another novella set mainly in a resort
town, Arthur Schnitzler's *Fräulein Else* (1924), addresses Jewish visibility by
way of a young woman who is made visible against her wishes. The chapter's
final section about the sometimes antisemitic treatment of women who are revealed to be Jewish examines two novels in which dancers are outed during
surprise visits, as well as how Jewish beauty queens were received after their
Jewishness came to light. Reflected in all of these examples, from historical
events to literary representations, is an ongoing struggle for power between
those who attempted to profit by exposing hidden Jewishness, and those who
desired to remain unseen or to construct identity on their own terms.[9]

### Violence, Self-Defense, and Spilled Secrets

Sporadic violent attacks against Jews were a harsh reality of life in Weimar
Germany. The victims of such attacks included visible Jews and others who
were identified as likely Jews. These attacks took place in both major cities
(Berlin, Cologne, Breslau) and less populated areas, particularly—but not

exclusively—during the years of economic crisis toward the beginning and the end of the Weimar Republic.[10] Examples of several major attacks in Berlin illustrate what was at stake for Jews who could be identified, as well as how Jewish communities responded. With the creation of a secret Jewish defense organization, a small group of Berlin Jews prepared to provide aid in part by remaining underground to avoid discovery. Yet this organization's secret identity was jeopardized when other Jewish organizations referenced it in their publications. Spilling the "secret" Jewishness of any person or group was thus potentially threatening, especially for an organization whose purpose was to defend against such acts.

Attacks perpetrated against East European Jews in Germany are among the best known and least surprising antisemitic violence of this era. On November 5 and 6, 1923, at the height of the economic crisis and hyperinflation, antisemitic agitators led mobs in a violent pogrom in Berlin. Jews with East European backgrounds constituted a majority of those assaulted. The mobs specifically targeted the Scheunenviertel district near Alexanderplatz, where they ransacked Jewish homes and Jewish-owned shops, and attacked and robbed "Jewish-looking" people including many street hawkers.[11] For some, this pogrom signaled the end of a long history of successful Jewish assimilation.[12] It also contributed to tensions between German Jews and East European Jews. In part due to feelings of shame, embarrassment, or even basic fears of the other or being seen as other, many Jews in Germany rejected the idea of the stereotypical *Ostjude* and, with it, the conspicuous attire of Eastern Jews.[13]

But not only East European Jews were targets of antisemitism on the streets of Berlin. As other Jews also became targets of random violent acts, the Jewish community developed new strategies for combating this violence. Several years after the Scheunenviertel riots, on Sunday, March 20, 1927, paramilitary SA men (the Brownshirts of the Nazi Party) assaulted pedestrians assumed to be Jewish in several locations in Berlin and Cologne. The violence in Berlin started with a National Socialist attack on Communists, first at Berlin's Lichterfelde-Ost station and then on a train going to the centrally located Kurfürstendamm. This wide boulevard—home to many famous cafés, cinemas, and shops—had been the place to see and be seen in Berlin West since 1900. A large number of Jewish businesses and organizations, too, maintained offices on or near the Kurfürstendamm, including the Reichsbund jüdischer Frontsoldaten and several K.C. fraternities.[14] Jewish economist Kurt Zielenziger (1890–1944) argued that the Kurfürstendamm itself served as a symbol of Jewish affluence and entrepreneurship.[15] In antisemitic circles, it earned the moniker "Cohnfürstendamm."[16] As a preface to the 1927 attack, Joseph Goeb-

bels, as Gauleiter of Berlin, led a crowd of ten thousand in a demonstration at
the nearby Wittenbergplatz; attacks against "Jewish-looking" people broke out
in cafés on and near the Kurfürstendamm shortly thereafter.[17] The *C.V.-Zeitung*'s
report on this attack declared it "pogrom-like" and a sign of National Socialist
terror.[18] During the 1927 attack on this centrally located street, German police
stood by and did not intervene while National Socialists violently beat Jews.

Lack of police support during the 1927 attacks seems to have been one
catalyst for the formation of a secretive group called the Jüdischer Abwehr-
dienst (Jewish Defense Service), also known as the JAD.[19] Members of the
JAD supposedly rushed to help get things under control when, on September
12, 1931, the first day of Rosh Hashanah, a number of Jews fell victim to another particularly violent evening attack on the Kurfürstendamm.[20] Several
hundred National Socialists in plainclothes, whom observers at first took for
harmless passersby because they wore neither uniforms nor badges, suddenly
set upon Jews and "Jewish-looking" people walking along the Kurfürstendamm
and in Café Reimann. Many had come directly from High Holy Day services
at the Fasanenstraße and other nearby synagogues.[21] The National Socialists
used fists, clubs, sticks, and even more dangerous weapons to beat many Jews
senseless. As journalist Max Reiner (1883–1944) noted, these victims were
"recognizable in part because they were dressed in celebratory attire for the
Jewish New Year."[22] In this case, the majority of people attacked did not necessarily possess embodied attributes associated with Jewishness, nor did they
usually wear attire that marked them as distinctly Jewish in public. Rather, they
simply donned holiday finery to attend religious services on one occasion.

The secret Jewish Defense Service soon became embroiled in an inner-
Jewish controversy about its own urgent need for invisibility when other Jewish groups indiscreetly brought it into the public eye. The nonpartisan JAD,
which consisted of members from the union of Jewish war veterans (RjF) and
from the Zionist sports organizations Makkabi and Bar Kochba, supposedly
had 250 to 300 members in Berlin and maintained ties to the Berlin police. The
JAD reportedly operated as an extralegal organization and kept no minutes of
its meetings. Shortly after the 1931 Kurfürstendamm attacks, a debate ensued
when Jewish newspapers outed the organization's existence despite its wish for
total secrecy. The RjF was charged with having called attention to the JAD's
existence in an article in *Der Schild* that referenced the precautionary "Surveillance and Intelligence Service" (*Beobachtungs- und Nachrichtendienst*) made
up of RjF members and others.[23] This single reference resulted in a press feud
in several Jewish newspapers.[24] In response, the JAD planned a meeting with
members of the RjF and CV to put an end to the dispute, but members of the

RjF cancelled the meeting. On November 6, 1931, representatives of the JAD wrote an urgent letter to Berlin Jewish community leader Wilhelm Graetz (1879–1974), noting: "It is through these publications that we are most damaged, indeed downright endangered, and this is born of an abnormal amount of irresponsibility when the delicate question of Jewish self-protection is written about publicly."[25] The authors of this letter threatened that the defense service would be forced to shut down if these organizations would not take responsibility for the harm they potentially had caused.

Although it is not known whether printed references to this secret defense organization actually caused it to cease operations, the fact remains that the act of outing the organization, even to Jewish reading publics, was perceived as highly detrimental and damaging. The parameters of the Jewish public sphere provided a limited sense of security, but not enough to protect groups that hoped to shore up their reserves by remaining invisible. To be sure, the Kurfürstendamm attacks and other violent incidents alarmed Weimar Jews and provided evidence of the pressing need for caution in public places, and for defense organizations that could take over when caution was not sufficient. It was likely in an attempt to assuage concerned readers' fears of such dangers that the editors of *Der Schild* decided to spill the secrets of this small defense organization, which today exists as little more than a footnote in the history of German-Jewish organizations. The JAD argued that its desire for secrecy should win out over the need for public knowledge or transparency. For the JAD, it was strategic to err on the side of invisibility and to avoid being revealed in any form. The history of the JAD teaches us that the pursuit of secrecy and invisibility was complicated by the spread of news and rumors, even in inner-Jewish publication contexts that targeted Jewish readers. Then, as today, the public dissemination of even the slightest indicator of a hidden identity could cause a media explosion and lead to discovery.

## Self-Discipline and the Policing of Women's Conspicuous Jewelry and Attire

Along with the fear of physical harm, the specter of the potential public humiliation that came with being outed closely informed how Jews in Weimar Germany interacted with one another and attempted to regulate the public image of Jews. Visibility factored heavily into the fear of harm; conspicuousness and obtrusiveness played a significant role in anxieties about humiliation. As Peter Gay has noted, German Jews in the 1920s did not hesitate to voice their embarrassment at spectacles created by other Jews. Gay wrote that Jews had been taught for centuries to be inconspicuous by wearing only approved items and attending only certain events; he further observed that strong feelings about proper ways of appearing led to tensions within Jewish communities.[26] German Jews certainly highlighted differences between themselves and Jews from Eastern Europe and sometimes held the latter responsible for Jewish public visibility. Self-policing within Weimar Jewish communities also often came with gendered dimensions. Women became prime targets of inner-Jewish accusations and were charged with various forms of excess or accused of disloyalty whenever their fashion choices reflected objectionable stereotypes.

Within Jewish circles, whether women were at liberty to display luxury items including jewelry—which could be interpreted as indicators of Jewishness—was a matter of great contention.[27] Two liberal organizations, the RjF and the Centralverein, took it upon themselves to mandate the public behavior of Jewish women. Whereas many of the German-Jewish men who belonged to these organizations already had abandoned such public markers of religious observance as head coverings, prayer shawls, and other distinctive clothing, liberal women, in contrast, had been coded Jewish mainly through embodied characteristics and stereotypes about opulence and excess. Rarely did Jews (at least not Jews writing under their own names!) explicitly instruct women to change their hair color or alter their facial features in order to appear less Jewish. Instead, both men and women accused women of carelessly displaying Jewishness simply by wearing everyday items of great value or by following other extreme fashion trends. Attempts to regulate women's fashions and overall appearance figured as a means of preventing non-Jews from identifying and discriminating against women who supposedly made themselves and others in their proximity more visible.[28]

Highly conspicuous displays of wealth such as expensive clothing and jewelry were coded as Jewish within the German imagination long before the Weimar period.[29] Already in the early nineteenth century, antisemites such as Achim von Arnim specifically referenced jewelry in discussions of how to spot a Jewish woman.[30] Antisemitic and other caricatures contributed to the propagation of stereotypes about Jewish women as nouveaux riches or parvenus, suggesting they married for titles, wealth, and jewelry in particular.[31] One caricature from 1850, "The Expensive Jewelry," which was published in the mainstream satire magazine *Fliegende Blätter*, accentuated stereotypes of opulence and intermarriage as an acculturation strategy.[32] It also exaggerated the subject's nose to make her look more stereotypically Jewish (see figure 14). Its caption read: "my wife, the baroness, wears her jewelry twice or maybe three

**Fig. 14. "The Expensive Jewelry," caricature in *Fliegende Blätter*, 1850.**

„Hören Sie, Baron, Ihre Frau Gemahlin trägt da einen Schmuck, wie ich in Paris und London keinen schöneren sah!"

„Recht hab'n se, Herr Graf; recht hab'n se, und was die Hauptsach is — mein' Frau, die Baronin zieht'n an im Jahr zweimal, vielleicht auch dreimal, und kost' ihr allemal sechzehnhundert Gulden, wenn mer berechnet die Prozent für's Capital, was ich hab' gegeben für die Stauer!"

times a year, and it costs her about 1,600 Gulden each time, if one considers the interest on the capital that I invested in the jewels!"[33] The word "baroness" referred to the practice of Jewish women marrying non-Jewish members of the nobility in order to improve their own social standing. This is but one example of how acculturated so-called Three-Day-Jews (*Drei-Tage-Juden*) who went to temple only a few times per year were targeted for displaying wealth on those occasions; it was common practice to wear one's best or new clothes on the Jewish High Holidays.[34]

Similar caricatures that targeted the ways Jewish women flaunted wealth could be found the world over in the 1920s. One sensationalist Australian newspaper featured a woman dripping with jewelry; the caption played on the word "jewelry" by way of a hyphen: "Jew-els."[35] Another cartoon from 1920 in the Berlin-based Jewish humor magazine, *Schlemiel*, blamed tensions between East European and German Jews on the alleged greed of bourgeois German-Jewish women. A small line of text that appeared above an image of two fashionably dressed women provided context by quoting from a recent newspaper notice: "To mitigate the housing shortage, the *Ostjuden* should be expelled." The cartoon's caption below read: "Just think, Lu, now that I have rented an eight-room apartment, I can invite two friends over at the same time."[36] This cartoon attacked Jews who wished harm upon other Jews, suggesting that certain German Jews wanted their East European counterparts out of Germany. At the same time, the caption subtly connected women's bourgeois and supposedly self-indulgent entertaining practices to a general undercurrent of resentment directed at East European Jews. The cartoon thus reflected the sentiment that women in particular should be held accountable for desiring lavish symbols of wealth in excess of what they needed. It further conflated Jewish women with avarice, selfishness, and oppression of the (Jewish) other.

Prominent Jewish figures also took aim at Jewish women for their consumerist impulses. For instance, Walther Rathenau's pseudonymous "Hear, O Israel!" (1897) chided Jews for hiding the "strange and exotic beauty" of Jewish women under "bales of satin, clouds of lace, and nests of diamonds."[37] Following his assassination in 1922, Rathenau, the first German Jew to be elected to as high an official position as foreign minister, remained highly respected in the majority of Jewish communities.[38] Despite the fact that Rathenau often castigated women, Jewish women's magazines featured regular tributes to Rathenau and his ideas. In one passage reprinted in *Die jüdische Frau* in 1925, Rathenau cited the modern bourgeois division of labor—men as wage earners, women as household purchasers—as responsible for having created "one of the most unpleasant phenomena of our time: the Luxury Woman." Here Rathenau further argued for the "condemnation of purchasable happiness, silly jewelry, and disdainful idleness."[39] Other Jewish organizations took a similar stance toward self-policing by claiming that successful ambiguity was contingent on both gender and subtlety of appearance.

One of the most extreme examples of institutional self-policing among Weimar Jews was the self-discipline movement (*Selbstzuchtaktion*). In the early 1920s, members of the RjF instituted a widespread campaign with the goal of silencing, or at least quieting, supposedly excessive acts or displays of luxury by Jews that were considered objectionable or offensive. This included an attempt to suppress variety and cabaret performances by Jewish actors whose lowbrow jokes made Jews a public target.[40] The Centralverein echoed this sentiment by focusing on the acts of certain Jewish performers, as discussed in chapter 2.[41] In keeping with the mission of the self-discipline movement, publications of the RjF supported self-monitoring on a broader level and advocated for the adoption of a simple, unadorned style to avoid attracting unwanted attention. Many of its admonitions were vague and only obliquely referenced displays of wealth and other specifics of undesirable behavior. One leaflet proclaimed: "The RjF endorses strict self-discipline and simplicity in the conduct of one's life!"[42] Another contained the missive: "Out of the inns of gluttony! Away with the mad pursuit of pleasure! Down with the vain baubles! *Back to simplicity and serious living!*"[43] The values upheld here are the same ones championed by many conservative religious groups: simplicity, restraint, and, to some extent, self-effacement. However, they found little resonance among Jews who had become comfortable embracing success in the public eye. As historian Donald Niewyk has suggested, this campaign by Jewish war veterans was by far its most controversial method of combating antisemitism.[44]

Though not directed only at women, such actions by the RjF were often framed in gendered terms that presumed women to be perpetrators of the "crimes" of opulence and ostentation. In fact, the first supplement to *Der Schild* contained a section allocated to Jewish women that included this message: "You all know that *true refinement* manifests itself best in *plain garb*, that ornate gaudiness is only a sign of *uneducated taste*, that everywhere a display of exterior belongings betrays the *lack of inner wealth*."[45] This passage threatened women that they would appear uneducated and emotionally impoverished if they wore anything that looked expensive or even decorative. Under the guise of protecting all Weimar Jews from the surrounding "world of hate," the RjF honed in on women as potentially ostentatious and therefore culpable for being visibly Jewish.

RjF member and attorney Adolph Asch (1881–1972) wrote in his memoirs of his involvement in a group that sought to discipline Jewish women by accusing them of behavior and attire that invited attacks. Not surprisingly, few others were as forthright about their participation in this movement. According to Asch (though contested by scholars), Asch was a founding member of the Berlin branch of the Self-Discipline Organization (Selbstzuchtorganisation), which issued explicit warnings to other Jews to avoid ostentation in public, and especially at sea resorts.[46] In 1922, published pamphlets were distributed in synagogues around the holidays to remind congregants "to guard the dignity customary before and after the divine services on the High Holidays, and especially to ask Jewish women to avoid all showy luxury in clothing and jewelry."[47] Asch wrote of the supposed success of these pamphlets: he described how one wife of a moneylender took these warnings to heart and appeared at the second High Holy Day service wearing much less jewelry than at the first.[48] Elsewhere Asch suggested that rabbis themselves distributed these pamphlets to their own congregants.[49] In this instance, religious observance became intertwined with self-presentation and its connection to Jewishness. For Asch, pamphlets about concealing Jewishness constituted a kind of religious lesson about women's modesty. Having faced accusations of being a "hidden Jew" while in a student fraternity, Asch spent decades addressing the question of outward presentations of Jewishness.[50] In his telling, his own experiences led him to instruct others to cover allegedly obtrusive elements of Jewishness. Downplaying Jewishness, for Asch, was a way to obscure its stigma.

The Centralverein's quest to promote Jewish self-defense also included advocating for subtlety in general, including among Jewish women, though it did so more ambivalently than the RjF. The CV called for a deeper level of Jewish self-awareness already with its founding in 1893.[51] During the Weimar period, this often took the form of notices or warnings in the CV newspaper. Like those published by the RjF, the CV's notices framed admonitions as preemptive responses to possible antisemitic attacks or accusations. One contained a vague reminder by the Association of Rabbis in June 1922 that every individual was also a representative of the collective: "Judgment will be passed quickly on Jewish men and Jewish women, and will become a judgment against the Jews. On all of his paths, every one of us should remain conscious of the fact that the dignity of Jewry is entrusted to him, to his course of action, his speech and activities. . . . True refinement reveals itself in the simplicity, in the dignity of life."[52] The same key words used by the RjF also appeared in the *C.V.-Zeitung*, including "simplicity" or "plainness" (*Schlichtheit*), a thinly veiled reference to the pressure to be inconspicuous and to cover anything in violation of that goal. Likewise, "true refinement" (*Vornehmheit*) set a lofty behavioral and moral goal while implying the difficulty of reconciling displays of material wealth with such morals. Even the Association of Rabbis conveyed the urgency of remaining inoffensive and thus rendering oneself above the judgment of others. According to this rationale, the mistakes of the individual reflected poorly on and could have consequences for the group as a whole, and thus no Jews had the right to incur this risk by behaving in an unbefitting manner.

The president of the Centralverein, Ludwig Holländer (1877–1936), responded to pressures for Jews to remain less noticeable by situating the issue of Jewish visibility in the context of the modern impulse to be seen as fashionable. His oft-cited article, "Self-Dignity," published on the front page of the *C.V.-Zeitung* on August 10, 1922, opened by citing the demands of the so-called enemies of the Jews: "See to it that the Jews improve, that they don't behave conspicuously, don't flaunt, don't haggle, that they display only humility, and only then will we amend our judgment." Holländer questioned this demand for invisibility among Jews, noting that non-Jews, too, were equally guilty of such showy behaviors. Holländer hypothesized that Jewish women's "sense of beauty" might be in jeopardy if they were compelled to make drastic changes to their aesthetics. He posed additional difficult questions about Jewish visibility: "Should women stop putting on jewelry, should everything fashionable be banned? Where is the boundary? To be sure, it exists where the aesthetic sense is susceptible to being disturbed. But different eyes see differently. Indeed, one should answer this question: 'Where is the boundary of jewelry, of striving toward a compliance with looking modern?'"[53] The word "modern" stood in for the concept of looking non-Jewish, of blending in with one's forward-moving and upwardly mobile surroundings. On some levels, the desire to look modern meant acting in accordance with external pressures, including some that invited comparison with Jewish stereotypes.

As spelled out in this text, the problem for Holländer lay not only in owning or wearing luxury objects but also in rebuking others—particularly women—for flaunting jewelry publicly. In a world of varied aesthetic sensibilities, Holländer hints that certain groups unfairly held others to unattainable standards. While famously acknowledging the perspective that "stepchildren must be doubly good," Holländer ostensibly attempted to shift the emphasis from blaming Jews to encouraging them to elevate their sense of self-dignity. Yet by repeatedly echoing the words of his opponents, and by questioning them without refuting them, Holländer contributed to the growing campaign against conspicuous attire and luxurious modern fashions that coded women as Jewish. Both the Centralverein and the RjF focused on Jewish women in discussions about concealing Jewishness. Just as women were considered to be more adaptable, and thus better able to pass, they also were held accountable for failing to do so.

Conservative religious Jewish groups, too, actively criticized modern styles that followed mainstream trends and moved away from the traditional Jewish emphasis on distinctiveness. Precisely because they sometimes embraced so-called "sinful" or luxurious modern styles, Jewish women remained more susceptible to criticism than their male counterparts. Rabbinic councils and others advocated for Jewish women to dress modestly and to eschew the latest styles by avoiding short skirts, revealing clothing, and high heels. That some women supposedly showed too much skin led the editors of the Orthodox paper *Der Israelit* to claim that these women were engaged in "thoughtless mimicry of un-Jewish fashion." Additionally, the editors encouraged Jewish women to reject modern, degenerate styles and to resist the temptation "to justify vanity ethically." To combat this practice, *Der Israelit* supported recovering the ancient Jewish traditions of *tznius*, or modest dress. The editors argued that only through modesty would the Jewish people become worthy of redemption.[54] Again, the trope of mimicry described the behavior of those Jews who attempted to resemble non-Jews, or, in this case, those who adopted modern fashions. Wearing so-called "modern" dress meant "looking non-Jewish," which ran counter to the goals of some religious Jews.

When Jewish women added their opinions to inner-Jewish debates about modern women's fashions, they represented a variety of viewpoints. Some reiterated the importance of cultivating external simplicity in order to focus on inner moral values, whereas others made a strong case for being permitted to take part in current German fashion trends, which were themselves political. The Jüdischer Frauenbund ran its own self-discipline campaign on behalf of simplicity. As Marion Kaplan has suggested, the Frauenbund, too, propagated negative images of Jewish women by cautioning women and girls to avoid ostentation.[55] In 1925, Else Fuchs-Hes (1889–1978), a member of the Frauenbund and several other Jewish women's organizations, argued in the *Familienblatt* in favor of a similarly conservative perspective, namely that Jewish women needed to be true to themselves and could do so by resisting the superlative clothing fashion of the day: skirts that were potentially too short, stockings that were too gaudy, heels that were too high, hair that was too short.[56] Doris Wittner, in contrast, took up the cause of liberal Jewish women, arguing that they should be granted the freedom to wear the latest fashions. Barring them from doing so, Wittner daringly claimed, would be tantamount to imposing Christian or antisemitic restrictions on Jewish expression.[57]

Toward the end of the Weimar period, however, most contributors emphasized the drawbacks of being conspicuous as a Jew. Regina Isaacsohn, who edited *Die jüdische Frau* in the mid-1920s, later reaffirmed her belief that women needed to present Jewishness in a proud but inconspicuous manner. She argued in the *Jüdisch-liberale Zeitung* in 1931 that women were in a position to enlighten others and to prevent attacks through "self-disciplining," which could take the form of quieting other Jews who exhibited embarrassing or objectionable behaviors. Isaacsohn wrote that she especially supported the act of "putting those co-religionists who make themselves unpleasantly noticeable in their place," claiming it would be advantageous in all cases for Jews to monitor each other rather than to permit themselves to be policed by members of other religions or antisemites.[58] Immediately following the Kurfürstendamm attacks in September 1931, CV representative Alfred Wiener asked Rabbi Leo Baeck to respond to accusations that "tactless" Jewish women wearing conspicuous jewelry and furs had provoked the attacks. Baeck's short text on the front page of the *C.V.-Zeitung* again reminded readers of the need to embrace "simplicity and genuineness" in the face of "crudeness (*Rohheit*)."[59] Another article by Isaacsohn in *Der Schild* in November 1931 added a "woman's voice" to the RjF's ongoing discussion about self-presentation: "At every time, but especially at present, it is important to bring into public view opportunities that demonstrate that—and how—every Jewish person can contribute to weakening the amount and intensity of antisemitism."[60] Concerns about being publicly outed, policed, or attacked by others led many Jews to support inner-Jewish regulation of displays of ostentation or anything coded Jewish, which operated both within and counter to the broader historical framework of the surveillance of Jews by other regulatory bodies.[61]

### Deciphering Jewish Difference in Resort Towns

The spa vacation towns located in southern Germany, Austria, Switzerland, Italy, and what was then Bohemia or Czechoslovakia provided particularly fertile ground for encounters between unknown entities. These towns were frequented by a growing number of middle-class Jewish visitors in the late nineteenth and early twentieth centuries.[62] Since only people who were relatively well off could afford to travel to a distant resort town in another country, trips to spa towns were themselves demonstrations of some degree of wealth. Unlike in their hometowns or neighborhoods, where many people already knew which families were Jewish, resort towns took Jewish populations out of context and placed them into new situations where coming out as Jewish was often necessary. Many people, like the blonde in the anecdote at the beginning of this chapter, carefully controlled information about their Jewishness in order to avoid antisemitic responses. Others, like the brunette, had no trouble being readable as Jewish from the outset. But the ability to out oneself in such a resort setting was limited by others who sought to differentiate between resort town guests. In these settings, observers were faced with the task of "telling the difference" between Jew and non-Jew, as well as Western and Eastern Jews; these distinctions were not always readily apparent and were sometimes invented.[63] In spa territory, as elsewhere, Jewish guests took steps to avoid being outed by others or inviting negative attention, while still making themselves recognizable to those who wanted to find other Jews.

Because most spa towns were relatively small and not always inclusive, the knowledge that someone was Jewish could spread quickly and serve as either a liability or an asset. Attracting unwanted attention—often understood within the context of "resort antisemitism" (*Bäder-Antisemitismus*)—in such resorts was fairly common; a good amount of the self-policing that occurred within Jewish communities aimed to prevent wealthy or well-off spa guests from being too conspicuous. Other locations within Germany offered fresh air and rejuvenation and were more easily accessible to middle-class Germans, though northern islands such as Borkum were known hotbeds of antisemitism.[64] Within small towns, just as in urban settings, clothing, jewelry, and noisy behavior were faulted with making Jews identifiable as such. Whereas women were accused of dressing ostentatiously and wearing too much jewelry, men were held responsible for being too loud. Both men and women were encouraged to practice "genteel restraint" (*vornehme Zurückhaltung*) while out in public on their vacations.[65] In certain cases, public knowledge that a professional was Jewish proved advantageous. For example, Lotte Hirschberg recalled that her husband, Josef Hirschberg, was hired to fill a position in the Silesian bathing town Altheide because of the town's desperate need for a Jewish doctor. Because Hirschberg was the only Jewish doctor, all of the Jewish spa guests sought him out, and the family prospered there until his practice was boycotted in April 1933.[66]

In many instances, the contained spaces of spa towns gave rise to a dichotomy between "us" and "them," a sense of wanting to belong that was at odds with suspicions about the potentially hostile other. Historian Mirjam Zadoff, in her book *Next Year in Marienbad: The Lost Worlds of Jewish Spa Culture* (2012), describes the ritual of sizing up other visitors while walking through a resort town: "Observers on the promenades were avidly engaged in 'decoding the body,' seeking to deduce from the appearance and habitus of the person confronting them something about his or her character." Zadoff further describes how Kafka, who wrote of his love for several Czech spa towns in 1916, nevertheless felt as if he were "a Chinese" going home when he visited these places, a possible allusion to the fact that Jews sometimes were perceived as foreigners even in their hometowns.[67] It was not unusual for guests to spend a considerable amount of time on the promenades in these towns. Some families who visited spa towns had photos taken there on every visit; figure 15 shows one such family, the Esbergs, in Marienbad in 1928.

Non-Jews and Jews were not the only two groups that evaluated each other while walking in resort towns; "Western" and "Eastern" Jews also engaged in such practices.[68] The tensions that arose between Western and Eastern

Fig. 15. Esberg family vacationing in Marienbad, 1928. (Courtesy of the
Leo Baeck Institute, New York, Marianne Steiner Collection.)

Jews were portrayed in the form of various fictional encounters in several Yiddish novels about these spas. Israel J. Singer's novel, *The Brothers Ashkenazi*
(1936), tells of a Jewish man from Lodz, Poland, who put on his high silk top
hat at the Austro-Hungarian border so as not to embarrass his wife in front of
the Germans. In Sholem Aleichem's satirical epistolary novel, *Marienbad*
(1917), many supposedly pious young women ceased to wear their traditional
wigs once in Marienbad.[69] These and other literary examples speak to the ways
spa towns provided a space for performing Jewish identity differently. New or
no head coverings coded their wearers as more or less Jewish or Eastern, or
both: the use of a top hat made the Polish Jew appear more German, and the
removal of a wig made a religious woman appear less visibly Orthodox. Such
performances also helped people to avoid detection by others who might out
them as Jewish.

Other literary works, such as Max Brod's novel *Jüdinnen* (1911), offer a
potent reflection of how Jews interacted with and even maliciously outed one
another in a resort town setting. Brod, best known not for his own writings but
rather as Kafka's friend and editor, published several popular literary works
with Jewish themes both before and during the Weimar period. *Jüdinnen* was his

first novel on a Jewish topic. Despite being based in Prague, Brod regularly contributed to Jewish and mainstream periodicals in Germany and was arguably an important intellectual figure in Weimar culture.[70] In the 1910s, Brod became an avid Zionist who shared many of Buber's Zionist ideals.[71] His writings served as a forerunner for debates that later unfolded in Jewish and especially Zionist periodicals about different types of Jewish women.[72] In fact, *Jüdinnen* was extremely successful and was reprinted four times within five weeks of its publication in 1911, and at least 25,000 copies were published by 1922 in multiple print runs. Excerpts also appeared in several mainstream periodicals, suggesting that the text found its way into popular culture and was a talking point in many different circles, including during the early Weimar years.[73]

Setting *Jüdinnen* in Teplitz, a fashionable health resort and spa town northwest of Prague, enabled Brod to focus on the tensions that accompanied public displays of Jewishness and divergent political positions within Jewish communities. Located not far from the Czech-German border, Teplitz was known for catering to a largely Jewish population of summer guests. The town served as a vacation destination among the German-speaking Jewish bourgeoisie beginning in the late eighteenth century, and over 10,000 Jewish guests spent time recovering in Teplitz's thermal baths between 1836 and 1932.[74] Within the novel, all of the central characters are Jewish, and Jews thus play a wide range of oppositional roles, from liberal to anti-Zionist and self-hating.[75] Characters do not come out as Jewish, but rather as more in line with Western or Eastern Jewish types.

In *Jüdinnen*, the 17-year-old male protagonist, Hugo Rosenthal, who remains politically aloof and whom some scholars read as representative of Brod himself, observes Olga Großlicht transform from a girl into a young lady from one summer to the next. Olga's origins in the Bohemian town Kolin mark her as a variant of the "spiritually superior" Eastern Jewish woman.[76] Hugo comments on the way in which "her thick black hair, her strong nose, her large juicy mouth . . . only appeared to enhance the expression of worry that lay in her eyes."[77] Through the eyes of Hugo, Brod biases readers in favor of Olga's open displays of Jewishness by way of her stereotypically Eastern coloring and demeanor. Olga represents the healthy, athletic country girl in contrast to the sickly city girl, Irene Popper.[78] As a counterpart to Olga (who Irene assumes speaks Yiddish), the light-haired and gray-eyed Irene represents a vilified liberal who easily passes for a non-Jew. Irene, the coddled offspring of a mother who plays the marriage market on behalf of her children, engages in "Western behavior" and represents the Western Jewish women whose lives revolve around external appearances.

In the penultimate chapter of the novel, the conflict between Irene and Olga reaches its culmination when Irene initiates an abusive game designed to publicly humiliate people by exposing how others perceive them. The game, "Rudeness (*Grobheiten*)," a kind of public "roast," invites participants to comment anonymously on one person who steps away; this person then returns and is required to respond to the written insults. Nußbaum, the first subject of the game, is accused of being a conceited, inveterate bachelor. Olga is pronounced someone who is "beautiful," "often knows more than she lets on," and who "chases after all the men."[79] The reader is left to assume that the last remark, which enrages Olga, was maliciously made by Irene in order to embarrass her adversary. In the act of exposing Olga's weaknesses, Irene instead brings to light the fact that others perceive her favorably, which is in keeping with her image as a stereotypical Eastern Jewish woman, here and elsewhere idealized by Brod. Hugo and others deem Olga's supposed identifiability and transparency both desirable and aesthetically pleasing. Within a small resort town setting where everyone was Jewish, it was not Jewishness that remained to be exposed, but rather the different Jewish types and what they revealed about Jewish culture.[80]

Another well-known literary work with a resort town backdrop, Arthur Schnitzler's *Fräulein Else* (1924), closely analyzed the power dynamics of visibility at play within a Jewish family and its social circles. In Schnitzler's novella, which is set around 1900 but reflects the financial anxieties of the 1920s, 19-year-old Else T. travels with her cousin Paul to the Italian resort town of San Martino di Castrozza, in the Dolomites. Narrated through Else's inner monologue, much of the story takes place at a grand hotel there.[81] Else also exchanges numerous letters and telegrams with her parents back in Vienna. Although the word *Jew* appears nowhere in the novella's pages—itself an act of covering—Else grapples with a physical appearance that, despite being under constant scrutiny by others, does not reveal her Jewishness.[82] The daughter of a wealthy Viennese attorney, Else exists in a world where it is generally known that she and her family are Jewish but nonetheless are relatively accepted as affluent members of society.

Else is conflicted about her ability to pass; she passes without trying, though she corrects for misperceptions only in her thoughts. She subtly references her own Jewishness once, in the context of an inner monologue prompted by an encounter with Herr von Dorsday, an art dealer and family friend. In Else's view, Dorsday's attempts to seem refined are unable to disguise his Eastern Jewish origins:[83]

No, Herr Dorsday, I'm not taken in by your smartness and your monocle
and your title. You might just as well deal in old clothes as in old pictures.
– But, Else, Else, what are you thinking of? – Oh, I can permit myself a
remark like that. Nobody notices it in me. I'm positively blonde, a reddish
blonde, and Rudi looks like a regular aristocrat. Certainly one can notice
it at once in Mother, at any rate in her speech, but not at all in Father. For
that matter, let people notice it. I don't deny it, and I'm sure Rudi doesn't.[84]

In this case, Jewishness exists between the lines as a pointed, if ambivalent "it,"
though it clearly informs Else's perception of how the world views her and her
brother, Rudi.[85] She is careful not to disavow Jewishness even as she avoids
mentioning it explicitly, though she can't help but condescend to Jews with
Eastern origins and false titles of nobility. The character of Else is a product of
her time: instead of seeking only to blend in, she claims not to be opposed to
Jewish visibility, yet Jewish conspicuousness remains something to be avoided.
Given the confines of the familial and societal structures that surround her, a
nominal desire for both (Jewish) visibility and empowerment as a young
woman proves paradoxical.

Fräulein Else's ultimate suicide inserts Else into a legacy of Jewish female
characters who suffer as a result of their visibility or lack thereof. Like the
mother in Jakob Loewenberg's drama discussed in chapter 4, Else's physical
appearance and blondness obscure her recognizability as a Jew and imbue her
with a kind of social fluidity. Notably, the 1929 silent film based on Schnitzler's novella (set not in Italy but in St. Moritz, Switzerland) starred dark-
haired actress Elisabeth Bergner in the role of Else. Bergner replaced Else's
blonde invisibility with a character more likely to be perceived as Jewish, particularly in light of Bergner's own Jewish background (see figure 16).[86]

But, visible or not, Else's Jewishness only compounds her vulnerability as
a woman. It is during the shameful moment when she is first instructed by her
bankrupt parents to seek financial assistance from Dorsday that she underscores their mutual Jewishness. Whereas Else views Dorsday as someone who
cannot evade his connections to Jews who trade in used textiles ("you might
just as well deal in old clothes")—a jab at poor East European Jewish immigrants and others who eked out an existence as street peddlers—her conclusion
is that her cosmopolitan, middle-class Viennese background and her appearance elevate her to a status above his parvenu opulence. Earlier in the novella,
Else notes: "But I don't like him. He's a social climber. What good does your
first-class tailor do you, Herr von Dorsday? Dorsday! I'm sure your name used

**Fig. 16. Elisabeth Bergner in** *Fräulein Else* **(Czinner, 1929). (Courtesy of Stiftung Deutsche Kinemathek.)**

to be something else."[87] In fact, both his name and attempts at self-fashioning suggest to Else that Dorsday has tried too hard to conceal his origins in order to fit into mainstream society. The act of going to great lengths to cover Jewishness ironically makes it easier to spot. Else's ambiguousness, in contrast, is achieved effortlessly, though ultimately has more damaging effects. Again it is the Jewish woman who struggles with articulating her visibility, whereas the Jewish man cannot avoid it.

Unlike other female characters who passed or converted and thereby caused the deaths of loved ones, Fräulein Else turns the situation on herself. Taken by Dorsday for a powerless young woman who would be willing to reveal herself to him fully—that is, show herself in the nude, as per his request—she opts to terminate this moment of sexualized hypervisibility and removes herself from the situation by way of suicide. Dorsday's request to see Else's uncovered body in exchange for a huge sum of money renders her vulnerable through precisely that which she previously had managed to avoid: being seen in ways that made her uncomfortable. Her predicament focuses the reader's attention on the male observer's attempt to police the female body. Accustomed to being able to pass, or at least to remain generally inconspicuous, Else is unprepared for the moment when her naked body becomes the object of the male gaze. Her resistance to being outed, though it comes too late to spare her this indignity, takes the form of a drive toward invisibility through her own absence.

In their literary depictions of Jewish life in resort towns, Brod and Schnitzler alluded to the tensions and pressure inherent in public encounters with unknown others. Interactions between Jews, even when the different parties already knew each other to be Jewish, were complicated by inner-Jewish political tensions, competitiveness, financial troubles, and gendered power dynamics. Scenarios in which some Jews made others still more visible and, in the cases of *Jüdinnen* and *Fräulein Else*, also publicly humiliated them, served as reflections of the impulse to get ahead by portraying someone else in a negative light. References to Jewishness were but one piece of the equation. Other components—Eastern Jewish affiliations, family ties, and local networks—all became fodder for a system that privileged those who were willing to expose others to gain the upper hand.

## Women's Careers Interrupted: Of Dancers
## and Beauty Queens

Whereas some women were advised to make themselves or their bodies inconspicuous, those whose physical appearances were tied to their professional endeavors, including professional dancers and beauty queens, had no choice but to put them on display. Female performers frequently starred in cabaret and revue acts in Weimar Germany. Take, for example, Josephine Baker and the Tiller Girls, who visited Berlin; or Marlene Dietrich's risqué song and dance performances as Lola Lola in the film *Der blaue Engel* (The Blue Angel; von Sternberg, 1930).[88] But the women who achieved the greatest success as cabaret dancers or as beauty queens were generally not known to be Jewish; in fact, when their Jewishness became known, it caused serious backlash. This section examines two literary works from the beginning and end of the Weimar era— Clementine Krämer's *Esther* (1920) and Ruth Landshoff-Yorck's *Roman einer Tänzerin* (Novel of a Dancer, 1933)—in which dancers were outed as Jewish by the arrival of relatives or others, as well as historical instances in which beauty queens became antisemitic targets once their Jewishness was uncovered.[89] In these cases, the surprise of suddenly learning about the Jewishness of a person presumed to be non-Jewish served as a catalyst for uncharitable gossip, slander, and even violence.

A lesser-known novel, Krämer's *Esther* tells of the transformation of a girl from a provincial *Judendorf* (the fictional, predominantly Jewish village of Haiderstadt) into a cosmopolitan dancer who lives in Munich and also performs in Berlin.[90] It thus anticipated several literary works of the New Objectivity (*Neue Sachlichkeit*), a German cultural movement in the late 1920s that emphasized realistic, concrete scenarios using straightforward language and imagery. Such novels as Vicki Baum's *Menschen im Hotel* (Grand Hotel, 1929) and Irmgard Keun's *Das kunstseidene Mädchen* (The Artificial Silk Girl, 1932) featured similar tales of girls from the provinces who took on what was perceived to be morally compromising work in the modern metropolis, such as cabaret dancing, modeling, or, in a more extreme form, prostitution.[91]

However, Krämer's *Esther* differed from other works of Weimar popular culture in that it was published exclusively for Jewish readers. *Esther* only ever appeared in serialized installments in two leading weekly Jewish newspapers, through which it might have reached as much as 20 percent of the potential Jewish market: first in the *Allgemeine Zeitung des Judentums* (Universal Jewish Newspaper), and then under the title *Die Tänzerin* (The Dancer) in the *Israelitisches Familienblatt*, both in 1920.[92] It is likely that the editors of the *Familienblatt* changed the title either to advertise its plotline about a female dancer or to enhance its appeal to an audience further removed from religious Judaism (the title *Esther* invoked the biblical book of Esther).[93] Although it likely found few readers outside of Jewish circles, *Esther*, as a rare novel that appeared in two different widely circulated Jewish newspapers, contributed significantly to the body of German-language serialized literature by Jews and for Jews that had been in place since the 1830s, as Jonathan Hess and Jonathan Skolnik have documented.[94]

Clementine Krämer (1873–1942, born Clementine Sophie Cahnmann) spent much of her childhood in rural areas in southern Germany, near Alsace and in the Black Forest.[95] Like the protagonist of *Esther*, Krämer relocated to Munich, where she became active in social work for the organization B'nai B'rith. She taught German language and literature courses to girls from Galicia, Rumania, and Russia. A founding member of the Munich branch of the Jüdischer Frauenbund, Krämer was also an activist for the Jewish feminist and pacifist movements, and for liberal Judaism. Additionally, she was a prolific journalist who published dozens of articles, stories, and vignettes in general and Jewish periodicals. Elizabeth Loentz has noted that Krämer carefully reserved stories about Jewish issues and identifiably Jewish characters for Jewish publication; this was typical for Jewish women journalists of the period.[96] When Krämer's husband's banking firm collapsed in 1929, her career as a writer came to an end, and she worked as a saleswoman in a Munich textile store until the late 1930s. Her attempts to leave Germany failed, and in 1942 she was deported to Theresienstadt, where she perished.[97]

Krämer found greater success writing for Jewish audiences than for general publication spheres.[98] It is likely that *Esther* found favor in part because it bridged the gap between classic Jewish literature and German popular culture of the 1920s. As in other works of modern German-Jewish literature, Krämer's glossed Yiddish and Hebrew terms translated Jewish concepts as well as Sabbath and holiday traditions for acculturated readers. She thereby instructed her readers to remain close to the Jewish people even when faced with modern distractions. Yet, at the same time, Krämer paradoxically introduced into Jewish literary circles the notion of an exemplary modern woman who temporarily sublimated her Jewish identity to become a cabaret star. Like her biblical namesake, Krämer's Esther adapts and passes for a non-Jewish woman; her beauty and glamorous exterior elevate her social status.[99] Through its inclusion of tropes drawn from both the Bible and contemporary culture—from the process of outing oneself as Jewish, to the antisemitic responses this could elicit—Krämer's work implicitly treats the intersections of religious affiliation and disavowal, adherents to traditional and popular belief systems, and reciprocal relations between German and Jewish modernities.

But *Esther* is also a Jewish *Bildungsroman* about coming of age and transformations with respect to Jewish identity. Young Esther Stein's upbringing in Haiderstadt is fairly traditional, though tensions regarding acculturation have begun to permeate its culture. Esther's father, who wants her to have the freedom to choose her own husband, passes away when she is 16. When a shrewd businessman, Liepmann Schuhrmann, subsequently asks to marry her, Esther leaves at the urging of a cousin, who points out that her options are to marry or find a more promising future for herself. The bohemian world of the city presents Esther with a number of challenges, and she solicits help from non-Jews to acclimate to Munich and find work as a dancer. Despite her talent for dancing, which she first discovers at a Jewish wedding, she has no formal training. The prima ballerina does not deem Esther's skills sufficiently impressive for her to train with the ballet, and Esther must find her way by dancing at the Körbchen Cabaret. Walter Grünerz, the cabaret's non-Jewish pianist, becomes a fixture in her life, though she ends their relationship to win the affection of Peter Pattendorff, an educated bourgeois citizen of Jewish heritage. A brilliant literary scholar, Peter lectures on Goethe and the modern period; when Peter meets Esther, he is writing a pamphlet titled "Modern Judaism." From Peter, Esther learns how to become modern without abandoning Jewishness, though she still views herself as a parvenu of the worst kind.[100]

In its manipulation of Jewish tropes, Krämer's narrative style follows the same trajectory as Esther's religious and cultural transformation. Whereas the beginning of the novel is filled with descriptions of Jewish rituals and glossed Germanized versions of Yiddish and Hebrew terms (for example: *Kalle* and *Choson* for bride and groom; *Chein*, a Yiddish word meaning kindness, grace, and charm; and a line from a Sabbath prayer), these traces of Jewish culture are later supplanted by mainstream topics.[101] Once Esther relocates to Munich, superstition and secular learning take over the role previously played by Jewishness. Jewish references reappear when Esther interacts with people from her village, such as when the Haiderstadt rabbi visits and pleads with her to return home, reminding her that the name Esther was conveyed to the honorable biblical queen only after she married King Ahasuerus. Like the biblical Esther, Esther Stein no longer represents innocence because she is willing to put herself and her beauty on display. According to the rabbi, she is considered in Haiderstadt to be a fallen woman, a kind of "prodigal daughter." Esther's stage name, "Sterstein," plays on the meaning of her first name in Hebrew (star; *Stern* in German) while simultaneously covering her Jewishness. This new name also masks Esther's Jewishness within the world of the novel: Peter, like King Ahasuerus, is later surprised to learn that behind this ambiguous exterior is a Jewish girl.[102]

As a cabaret dancer, Esther Stein generally operates outside of Jewish circles. It takes a public appearance by someone from her past to out her as Jewish and put her Jewishness in the spotlight.[103] Soon after the rabbi's visit, Liepmann Schuhrmann makes an unwelcome appearance during one of Esther's performances. He hurls insults at the stage and calls her a whore; a media scandal promptly ensues, which also serves as publicity for Esther's act:

> Already the next morning, the following headlines appear in the newspaper: "Scandal in Cabaret," "Roosters in the Basket (*Körbchen*)," "The Diva and her Lovers." Even the antisemitic paper says: "It cannot be denied that this Star from Zion (or just from Przemyśl?) with a bitter, one almost could say awkward charm, perhaps is destined to blaze new trails for the art of dancing." And so on in this way.[104]

Of the different newspapers covering this incident, only the antisemitic paper references Esther's Jewishness, with a jab at the East European Jewish origins of many such dancers. Krämer's readers, of course, were in on the many secrets of Esther's private life; they could imagine the shame Esther experienced upon being targeted as a female cabaret dancer, and a Jewish dancer at that.[105] Moreover, readers of the Weimar Jewish press would have been intimately familiar with Esther's struggle to acculturate, and some could have sympathized with Esther's need to pass in order to distance herself from her Jewish background. That a man from Esther's past arrives and draws public attention to her Jewishness underscores the ambiguousness of female characters made visible only through their relationships to Jewish men.

After years of sublimating her Jewishness to her career as a dancer, Esther rediscovers a connection to Jewishness through her relationship to Peter. She embraces—and perhaps co-opts—the titles given to her by the antisemitic papers, including "Star from Zion" and "Salome from Yerushalayim (Jerusalem)." She moves from confessing her Jewishness to confessing her personal indiscretions, stating: "Because the most difficult thing still remains to be said: Despite the fact that I, as I've told you, was not chosen to be an artist, I've nevertheless led the life of a dancer."[106] Krämer's use of the word chosen (*auserwählt*) invites a comparison with "the chosen people." Whereas Esther is not destined to be a dancer of the highest caliber, she still can reconcile her membership in a different elite group with her profession of choice. The novel *Esther/Die Tänzerin* thus culminates in a plea aimed at German-Jewish readers on behalf of the modern woman, a forerunner of the New Woman, who seeks a number of freedoms: to escape the gendered confines of convention (including many religious traditions), to choose her own partners, to practice a controversial profession, and to disclose information about herself at will. Krämer's protagonist does not seek to evade Jewish laws and traditions entirely, but rather renders herself ambiguous such that she may control when Jewishness becomes relevant. The modern Esther-figure, like the biblical queen, avails herself of a number of strategies to negotiate successfully the intersections of Jewish and mainstream worlds.

Ruth Landshoff-Yorck's *Roman einer Tänzerin*, which was penned in the final years of the Weimar Republic but first published many decades later, in 2002, describes a strikingly similar situation in which a dancer is outed as Jewish against her will by the arrival of an overtly Jewish figure from her past. This roman à clef, a fictional work with thinly veiled references to "real life" figures, barely disguised its representation of dancer Lena Amsel (1898–1929) in the form of protagonist Lena Vogel. (In German, *Amsel* means blackbird, and *Vogel* simply means bird.) In addition to knowing Amsel personally, Landshoff-Yorck also shared a lover (Karl Vollmoeller) with her. In fact, Amsel, the daughter of a Jewish manufacturer from Lodz who made her career in Berlin, Vienna, and Paris, was widely known for her numerous lovers and husbands and for her famous death in a Bugatti car race in 1929. Weimar authors from Annemarie Schwarzenbach to Klaus Mann referenced Lena Amsel and even her Jewish background in their works from this period.[107] However, neither Lena Amsel nor Ruth Landshoff-Yorck widely publicized their connections to Jewishness or maintained strong ties to Jewish communities prior to 1933.[108]

Ruth Landshoff-Yorck (1904–66, born Ruth Levy) was born and raised in Berlin; she used the last name of her mother, Else Landshoff, until she married David Yorck von Wartenburg in 1932.[109] Her uncle, publishing magnate Samuel Fischer, introduced her to an array of prominent literary and cultural figures. She studied acting with Max Reinhardt and debuted as an actress in the Expressionist vampire film, *Nosferatu* (Murnau, 1922).[110] Celebrated for her love of motorcycles, fast cars, and bobbed hair, she also became known in mainstream Weimar circles as a journalist who published in the *Berliner Illustrirte Zeitung* and *Die Dame*. Landshoff-Yorck's first novel, *Die vielen und der Eine* (The Many and the One), appeared with Ernst Rowohlt Verlag in 1930; it, too, included a brief reference to Lena Amsel.[111] In early 1933, Landshoff-Yorck received and reviewed a proof of her completed book, *Roman einer Tänzerin*, which Rowohlt had planned to print under the modified title, *Leben einer Tänzerin* (Life of a Dancer). Literary scholar Walter Fähnders has suggested that her handwritten marks on the proofs imply a desire to publish the book "at the last minute" despite the changing conditions for Jews in Germany and the growing need to be inconspicuous. Her planned changes consisted of eliminating the words "Jew" and "Jewish" in several instances—for example, "good Jewish God" would become "good God"; "little Jewish girl (*Judenmädchen*)" would be "little girl"—as well as deleting all passages referencing Jewish holidays such as Passover.[112]

The editorial alterations made by Landshoff-Yorck in 1933 paralleled the actions of her protagonist, Lena Vogel, to remain inconspicuous as a Jew despite her Jewish upbringing in Poland. Landshoff-Yorck nevertheless coded her character Jewish from the first pages of the novel. Lena Vogel supposedly had herself baptized in order to marry one of her lovers, though it was unclear which one she would marry at the time; her "hard dark hair surrounded her wide face like a cloud" during a performance. Landshoff-Yorck describes Lena Vogel's career as follows: "Dancing was in any case already a pretext, though for what was not obvious."[113] Though Lena's Polish origins and foreignness are no secret, it is not until her Uncle Fränkel from Lodz arrives and interrupts her at work in the Viennese Tabarin revue theater that her connections to Jewishness become explicit: "The man . . . was a small, nimble Eastern Jew in a caftan, with carefully twisted sidelocks. Cerni immediately thought of Lena's practice of brushing her tightly curled hair (*ihre straffen krausen Haare*) around a curling stick in the evenings. She now looked astounded." Lena's uncle's *peyes* invite a comparison with the texture of her own dark hair, and his presence prompts her to acknowledge her Jewishness by associating with him in public. She performs the role of his niece happily and conspicuously: "She was apparently less concerned with proclaiming her pride in her Jewishness than her pride in the fact that she dared to proclaim her Jewishness as the wife of one, no, several aristocrats, as the girlfriend of many."[114] Lena Vogel's own personal and professional successes took precedence over the rules of the Eastern world from which she came.

The arrival of Lena Vogel's uncle outs her as Jewish in a public setting and thereby exposes her as someone who successfully covered Jewishness in order to be accepted within mainstream culture. Soon after, she breaks from her husband, who is surprised to learn that she previously had kept such company; her identity as "a little Jewish girl from Lodz" was not one that he had been forced to confront.[115] In both Krämer's *Esther* and Landshoff-Yorck's *Roman einer Tänzerin*, neither of which reached mainstream Weimar readers, two dancers are able to leave their Jewishness in the past until it comes back to haunt them. The two protagonists were not openly acknowledged as Jews, but rather were marked as such only by the overt Jewishness of male relatives from a German-Jewish village and Lodz, Poland. The humiliation experienced by Esther Stein, and the shock and subsequent personal troubles of Lena Vogel, suggest that such acts of outing women as Jewish were neither welcome nor constructive.

The two Central European Jewish women who were crowned as both national and international beauty queens in 1929—and who also were outed as Jewish due to this success—exemplified the aesthetic values promoted by those who engaged in self-policing in the German-Jewish press. They were restrained, elegant, and not particularly visible as Jews. Specifically, they did not look stereotypically Jewish. Both had fairly light coloring and light brown or blondish hair. To the general public, Erzsébet "Böske" Simon (Miss Hungary, 1909–70; also Elizabeth Simon) and Lisl Goldarbeiter (Miss Austria, 1909–97), who were crowned Miss Europe and Miss Universe, respectively, appeared modest and ambiguous enough so as not to draw attention to themselves as Jews. They, too, took a page from the biblical Esther, who was renowned for her beauty and initially passed for non-Jewish. It was only after they were crowned as national beauty queens that their Jewishness became publicly known; it is unclear whether they would have advanced so far at the national level had they been identified as Jewish at an earlier stage. Exactly who first outed them as Jews is unknown, though contributors to the Jewish press were quick to capitalize on the fact that these beauty queens were both of Jewish descent.[116] The antisemitic attacks that occurred soon thereafter serve as evidence that it was safer to hide one's Jewishness as a woman in the public eye, particularly if one wished to get ahead professionally.

Böske Simon was first crowned Miss Hungary in Budapest, and then defeated women from 16 other countries to win the Miss Europe pageant in Paris in February 1929, which understandably earned her international attention from non-Jews and Jews alike. After her victory in Paris, Jewish papers began to feature articles about and images of Simon, whom they gladly deemed a model Jewish woman (see figure 17).[117] The mainstream Hungarian press celebrated Simon's European victory as having brought honor to the Hungarian people. But, Parisian accolades notwithstanding, Simon was terrorized by rioting antisemitic students upon her return to Budapest after it had become known that she was Jewish. Prevented from meeting her train at the station, the students reportedly tracked her down and taunted her with pejorative names such as "Miss Palestine"; they also stopped the local movie theater from showing a newsreel about her victory. After a celebratory ball, she was harassed at home with cacophonous music underneath her window. The antisemitic *Völkischer Beobachter*, too, slandered her as a spoiled "little Jewish girl (*Judenmädel*)" who supposedly fell victim to the antics of French industrialists.[118]

Still, the Jewish press continued to emphasize Simon's Jewishness even when she became a target. She was continually compelled to discuss it to the point where it became onerous. The *Familienblatt* reported that Böske Simon came from a religious Jewish home in which the Sabbath and holidays were strictly observed. Supposedly her main desire was not to have a theater or film career, but simply to marry a Jewish man. It reprinted a Parisian Jewish journalist's interview with the beauty queen: "'Is it true that you are a Jewish woman (*Jüdin*)?' Miss Europe's little face became animated: 'Everywhere I go, I get this question! Yes! I am Jewish. . . . I don't deny my ancestry, although now it is mentioned so often that it has almost become oppressive.'"[119] Simon's beauty catapulted her into the public eye; her Jewishness became a secondary source of fascination for the media. But only her beauty was voluntarily exhibited and discussed. Time and again, she was pressured by all sides into acknowledging her Jewishness, which sometimes served as a liability.

The case of Lisl Goldarbeiter was slightly different: although the Jewish press and antisemites alike considered her Jewish and treated her accordingly

Nr. 38 / 28. Februar 1929

Fig. 17. Beauty queen Böske Simon: "The most beautiful woman in Europe—a Jewish woman!" (Courtesy of the Leo Baeck Institute, New York.)

once this information became public, Goldarbeiter did not identify much with the Jewish community until the late 1930s. After submitting a photograph to a popular Viennese newspaper and attending only one high tea event, Goldarbeiter was crowned the first Miss Austria in January 1929. Soon thereafter, she came in second to Böske Simon in the Miss Europe competition, before winning the title of Miss Universe in Galveston, Texas, on June 11, 1929. In her acceptance speech, she emphasized the fact that she had competed on behalf of Austria and Vienna: "I am very, very happy and hope that I have been successful in offering the great and proud American people . . . a good opinion of Austrian women and my hometown of Vienna."[120] Jewishness was not central to Goldarbeiter's identity, nor did she proclaim her victory relevant for Jews.

Though Goldarbeiter never openly acknowledged her Jewish background, the *Familienblatt* persisted in explaining that her father was a Viennese Jew with a small clothing business, and that a Jewish girl had been crowned the most beautiful in the world. Ironically, the *Familienblatt* argued that the ability of this girl with chestnut-colored hair and grayish-blue eyes to win renown for Jews was based solely on her unique look and "genteel appearance" (*vornehme Erscheinung*), an allusion to her ability to pass for a bourgeois, non-Jewish Austrian.[121] The newspaper used Simon's and Goldarbeiter's victories to argue for the superiority of Jewish beauty, while also pointing out disparities in the treatment of men and women. One contributor noted that both countries regularly discriminated against Jewish men: "And now, a real Austrian or Hungarian man 'cannot tolerate a Jew[ish man] / But he gladly chooses their daughters.'"[122] The ability of Central European Jewish women to blend in—or to use their beauty as a means to gain recognition—at times facilitated special access to mainstream European cultures that their male counterparts were not afforded.

Yet Lisl Goldarbeiter, too, was attacked and even physically mobbed by angry crowds when she returned to Europe after being crowned Miss Universe. Motivated by antisemitism and by the failure of Romanian contestant Magda Demetrescu to win, the crowd that greeted Goldarbeiter during a September 1929 visit to Bucharest reportedly screamed, "Magda is our weight! We want no slender beauty queens here!" This expression of solidarity with the Romanian contestant also was accompanied by a blatantly antisemitic remark directed at Goldarbeiter: "Let's make her eat some pork!"[123] It was not only the Jewish press that insisted Goldarbeiter be considered as a Jewish woman, but also antisemitic hecklers. The more public attention the beauty queens' Jewish backgrounds received, the greater the backlash against their victories.

A wide range of situations serve as reminders of the reasons people opted to hide or downplay their Jewishness. Examples include antisemitic attacks in the street, attempts to maintain the covert status of a secret defense organization, and acts of self-policing, as well as literary and other scenes in which Jews are outed or humiliated by being put on display. Anxiety about being outed accompanied the fear of being attacked or humiliated. In many cases, it was safer or just simpler to leave Jewishness unmentioned. Responses to these anxieties, and to the painful surprise that often accompanied learning about a previously hidden identity, contributed to the desire of some Jews to pass as non-Jews. The next chapter addresses recorded instances of successful passing and instances when Jewishness was falsely assessed, as well as their broader consequences.

CHAPTER 4

# Mistaken Identifications and Nonrecognitions

Suddenly realizing that someone was not the person he or she had claimed to be—or had been presumed to be—revealed not only the complex identity of the passing subject but also incorrect assumptions on the part of the observer. Whether it took the form of a voluntary coming out, a hostile outing by another party, or a negotiation of mistaken identities, the abrupt termination of a sustained act of passing had the potential to cause confusion, anger, scandal, and tragedy. It further challenged stereotypes about what Jews looked like, how they acted, and to what extent it was possible to detect Jewishness based on observed qualities. Anxiety about passing reflected a desire to avoid being seen or mistaken for something undesirable, whether it was a Jew, a non-Jew, or a certain kind of Jew.

Discussions of Jewish visibility emphasized the stakes of being able to distinguish correctly between Jew and non-Jew, and between Jewish types. Because deliberately obscuring Jewishness was frowned upon in Zionist circles, deliberations about passing often pointed out its drawbacks. In one 1926 article in the *Jüdische Rundschau*, Zionist Moses Waldmann (1885–1954) compared the act of Jews trying to blend in with their surroundings—which he alleged was most common among liberal Jews—with the habits of the color-changing chameleon. In doing so, he joined a long line of European critics who made this comparison, though some did so as a compliment.[1] Waldmann, however, put an unfavorable spin on chameleonic tendencies and radical assimilation by proposing that Jews could be categorized into two opposing factions: "fearful Jews" and "self-evident Jews." He defined a fearful or chameleonic Jew as "a Jew who is afraid of being caught as a Jew, namely a Jew who fundamentally perceives the fact of his Jewishness as a stigma (*Makel*)." In this comparison of passing with the ability to change color, Waldmann's argument implicitly gestured toward a racialized form of Jewishness, though he also asserted that the fearful Jew's "mutation (*Abart*)" could not be detected by way of skin color.[2] Significantly, it was not the fearful Jew's appearance that gave away Jewishness, but rather his or her behavior. Chameleonic tendencies, namely passing or trying to pass, paradoxically made Jew-ishness all the more visible.[3]

According to Waldmann, many fearful or chameleonic Jews were espe-cially afraid of being mistaken for East European Jews, from whom they tried to distance themselves. Faced with rising nationalistic antisemitism, these fear-ful Jews attempted "to demonstrate that the *Ostjuden* represented a completely different type of Jew and emphatically rejected being mistaken for them."[4] It was not only Jewishness that figured as a stigma to be avoided but also charac-teristics associated with Eastern Europe that accentuated the stigma of Jewish-ness even further. In countless cultural texts from this period, Eastern Europe-anness or Russianness signified Jewishness. Of course, Jewishness was not always stigmatized; in many cases, Jews from Eastern Europe were idolized or upheld by German Jews as more authentic. But even those who held great re-spect for East European Jewry likely avoided the conspicuousness associated with East European difference. Most German Jews who hoped to avoid being seen as the "wrong" kind of Jew would not voluntarily perform Russianness.

Mistaken identities had the potential either to provide sanctuary or to pose a threat, depending on whether Jewishness was perceived as a socially favored or disfavored identity. The pursuit of favored identities resulted in intentional passing; passers counterbalanced their hidden selves with the masked selves that they showed to the world. The ongoing performance of a non-Jewish iden-tity presumably gave access to a broader set of rights and privileges and allevi-ated the sense of stigma associated with Jewishness. Other cases of mistaken identity were less entangled with deceptive misleading and more concerned with distracting observers from potentially obtrusive markers. At times this took the form of emphasizing differences between East European and other Jews. Covering or downplaying any potentially conspicuous aspects of Jewish-ness, or fashioning them in an ambiguous manner, also sometimes resulted in misinterpretations of identity.

In its examination of German-Jewish texts that explicitly treat instances of passing, misrecognition, or nonrecognition, this chapter establishes that these situations, too, led to impactful moments of encounter. Putting an end to sustained acts of passing by correcting a misperception could result in the loss of privileges and access, or could have even more severe consequences, both for those who passed and their immediate family members. The fate of the in-dividual could cause a crisis of identity for the collective. Cultural products including literature and film suggest that such discourses about passing con-stantly occupied and interested Weimar Jews. And although a genre of passing novels never emerged in German-Jewish contexts as it did among African

Americans, a number of publications and cultural products of the 1920s and early 1930s similarly reflect the many anxieties that surrounded Jewish visibility. For some, passing ran counter to Jewish pride; its successful execution was sometimes couched in discourses of self-hatred, total assimilation, and even self-erasure.

This chapter explores the phenomena of misrecognitions and nonrecognitions to highlight different responses to perceived intentionality and deception. At the same time, it points to the coincidental nature of other mistakes in perception. A short drama about German-Jewish passing by Jakob Loewenberg exemplifies the tragic consequences of deceiving one's own relatives: an anti-semitic son's sudden discovery that his mother had kept her Jewishness secret prompts him to take his own life. Misidentifications and nonrecognitions also occurred in situations where Russianness was conflated with Jewishness. Jewish-sounding names, though generally presented as extravisual information, nevertheless informed how spectators interpreted visual representations in certain films. The Jewish reception of the Soviet-German film *Überflüssige Menschen* (Superfluous People; Rasumny, 1926) reveals that ambiguity paired with stereotypically Jewish names was enough to mislead even Jews who were well prepared to detect Jewishness. In addition, complex representations of passing, nonrecognition, and Jewish caricature in the film *Mensch ohne Namen* (*The Man Without a Name*; Ucicky, 1932) point to the role of relative positioning in establishing Jewish visibility. The presence of a known Jew could impact whether nearby others were coded more or less Jewish. Not everyone was able to pass or was given license to do so, and others managed to blend in only by making concessions. What these texts have in common is anxiety about (mis)-recognition, and all of these examples showcase attempts to pinpoint Jewishness by way of accepted codes known to both reveal and mislead.

### The Tragic Consequences of Passing

Jakob Loewenberg's one-act drama, *Der gelbe Fleck* (The Yellow Badge), perhaps the most salient example of a passing narrative by a modern German-Jewish author, focuses on the psychological impact of one Jewish mother's decision to pass. A teacher and writer who was active in the liberal Jewish community of Hamburg, Loewenberg published many works that explicitly addressed Jewish themes. This short play of only seven scenes was written in 1899 but first published in a 1924 collection of writings by the same name. It most likely was never performed.[5] The drama's cautionary tale is set in an unnamed major provincial city, "around 1880 and—in the present." Hans, an antisemitic member of a student dueling fraternity, is called home by his mother, who informs him that his sister, Martha, has become engaged to a Jewish doctor, Richard. The mother also circuitously informs Hans that she herself is a Jewish woman, noting that her blondness served as an entry ticket to non-Jewish society. Because she was "so blond" and "so beautiful," she was able to marry a Christian man, after which she moved with him to another town and spent many years passing as a non-Jew.[6] Upon learning that he has a Jewish mother, Hans locks himself in his room and commits suicide with one of his dueling pistols.

I argue that in Loewenberg's drama, the "yellow badge" symbolizes both Jewish visibility and invisibility. It represents not only the medieval sumptuary stigma forced upon Jews to make them more easily discernible, but also a blonde woman's ability to pass as non-Jewish due to physical traits associated with racialized Germanness. But *Der gelbe Fleck* also was written and published during one of the only periods in history when the yellow badge that previously had been imposed on Jews was worn anew as a symbol of pride. It was also during this era that race science began to define Germanness and Jewishness as chromatically distinct from one another; blondness and lighter coloring were considered a clear indicator of Germanness. This play thus epitomizes the contradictions inherent in Jewish visibility during the Weimar period. Precisely because Jewishness was not imposed through legal or regulatory mechanisms and therefore was often difficult or impossible to see, Jewish visibility was mired in racialized stereotypes about Jewish appearance and coloring. Women were often the catalysts for discussions of Jewish passing. In this and other instances, female characters are depicted as slippery, mercurial, and generally less readable. Because women were perceived as the least likely to be recognized as Jews, they were portrayed as more likely to pass, and were positioned as figures with much to lose if they became visible at the wrong moments.

Scholars have largely overlooked Loewenberg's writings in general, and this drama in particular.[7] Much of what we know about Jakob Loewenberg stems from information compiled by his son, Ernst Loewenberg, who immigrated to the United States in 1938.[8] Jakob Loewenberg (1856–1929) was born and raised in a liberal Jewish home in Niederntudorf, a Westphalian village near Paderborn. After studying philosophy and languages in Marburg and Heidelberg, where he was a member of a dueling fraternity, Loewenberg moved to Hamburg in 1886, where he supervised a well-known private girls' school from 1892 until his death in 1929. In addition to being a teacher, Loewenberg was a prolific writer of prose, poetry, and a few dramas, a substantial portion of which dealt with the German-Jewish experience. He was also an active member of the Centralverein.[9] During his lifetime, Loewenberg was considered within Jewish circles to be an important Jewish writer. In 1925, for example, the *Jüdisch-liberale Zeitung* included Loewenberg in a survey about how Jewishness impacted the work of German authors; also surveyed were such prominent cultural figures as Max Brod, Siegfried Jacobsohn, Arthur Silbergleit, Ernst Toller, Arnold Zweig, and Stefan Zweig.[10] In addition, Loewenberg's poems and articles often appeared in Jewish newspapers including the *Jüdisch-liberale Zeitung*, *C.V.-Zeitung*, and *Israelitisches Familienblatt*. Even the Zionist *Jüdische Rundschau* printed a somewhat reluctant obituary for Loewenberg in 1929, which bespeaks his familiarity beyond partisan allegiances.[11]

The title *Der gelbe Fleck* appropriates the yellow badge as a liberal warning symbol. After all, the word *Fleck* can also mean blemish, mark, or stain. According to his son, Loewenberg chose the title of *Der gelbe Fleck* in response to a painful awareness of rising antisemitism after the First World War—and in defiance of the consequently poor treatment of German Jews. Writing with the bias of hindsight, Ernst claimed in 1970: "Loewenberg felt that a period was approaching when Jews would again have to show the yellow badge as in the Middle Ages."[12] Regardless of Jakob Loewenberg's sense of what was to come, he manipulated a powerful example from the past to shed light on the contemporary situation of German Jews. That the play was first published 25 years after being written hints that its message became more urgent in the 1920s, yet still suggests that the work remained largely unknown for many years.[13]

The medieval badge also played a role in the reception of Loewenberg's drama. The badge was familiar to many as a symbol of oppression, and it remained a constant reference point for student groups and others who sought to co-opt it. One 1925 advertisement for the book in the *C.V.-Zeitung* explicitly referenced the yellow badge's medieval origins, though it failed to draw specific connections between this symbol and the political situation of the 1920s.[14] In 1926, not long after Loewenberg's drama finally appeared in print, the *Jüdische Rundschau* published a seemingly unrelated cover story that also bore the title "Der gelbe Fleck." This article accused German-Jewish communities of metaphorically stigmatizing "foreign" Jews—and assigning to them a virtual distinguishing marker akin to the yellow badge—by depriving them of rights.[15] Here we find additional self-awareness of the tension between Jews of German and East European descent, as well as the allegation that Jews stigmatized each other. In some ways, this article anticipated the *Jüdische Rund-*

*schau*'s famous article of April 4, 1933, in which editor Robert Weltsch declared in the face of the Nazi boycott of Jewish-owned businesses that all Jews in Germany should wear the yellow badge of Jewish difference with pride.[16] Whereas Zionist groups politicized the badge as a controversial and multivalent symbol of persecution and pride, Loewenberg's drama added a liberal valence to the symbol's role in Jewish discourse about historical oppression. It advocated for limited acceptance of the badge's visibility and a rejection of the pursuit of total Jewish visibility.

The two yellow symbols in Loewenberg's drama serve as contradictory and gendered indicators of how to see Jewishness. Yellow is an indisputable sign of Jewishness, but it is also the exact opposite: its presence as a hair color symbolizes the absence of Jewish traits. In the dispute with his mother that constitutes the central action of the drama and its entire sixth scene, the law student Hans overtly references the badge with the assertion that Jews should still be required "to wear the badge as back in the Middle Ages." This remark comes just after Hans's comment that he has never met a Jew, and shortly before his mother reveals her own Jewish background. Loewenberg suggests that for Hans and others schooled in antisemitic rhetoric, some Jews remain invisible, for "a prejudgment is stronger than the truth." Hans is unable to recognize Jews, and especially Jewish women, who do not meet stereotypical descriptions. Before revealing herself as Jewish, his mother asks him directly what would happen if he fell in love with a Jewish woman. Hans replies, "With a hook-nosed black Jew-whore (*schwarze Judendirn*)!" to which his mother responds: "There are also straight-nosed, blonde ones."[17] Hans's mother attempts to complicate his understanding of Jews by dismantling common stereotypes and pointing out that Jews come in all shapes and sizes.

Simple though this lesson about diversity among Jews may seem, it was actually a more complex message from which liberal Jewish audiences had much to learn. Hans's mother cautions Hans that he must objectively verify information about Jewishness himself rather than accept the biased viewpoints of others as truth. In fact, the *C.V.-Zeitung* advertised Loewenberg's drama to readers who were exposed on a daily basis to pervasive stereotypes about Jewish appearance. At the same time, the newspaper also regularly contributed to the construction of Jewish appearance by affirming, rather than challenging, these widespread images. Numerous articles instructed readers to downplay conspicuous elements of Jewishness including luxury goods, jewelry, and any behavior that was coded stereotypically Jewish.

The mother is depicted as having followed such directives to the extreme. Her true identity is further obscured through namelessness—she is called only

*Mutter*, though the other characters all possess first names. For the mother, blond hair itself is both a type of disguise and a stigmatized badge that prevents her from being recognizable and thereby burdens her with the option of passing. Only in the second scene, when Martha (Hans's more open-minded sister) states that her mother is Jewish, does the reader become aware of this fact. As we learn from the mother's coming out story, this symbolic mask provided the means to make a different life possible. When her husband was initially denied professional opportunities because he married a Jewish woman, the pair relocated to another town where he found work. Although this move enabled them to live in relative anonymity, living a lie also meant severing ties to their respective families. In lieu of family, the mother relied on the help of a non-Jewish maid named Christine, who unknowingly spent two decades raising the children of a passing Jewish woman. Christine later proclaims that she would be unwilling to work for a Jewish family or to help raise Jewish children. Hans's membership in his fraternity, too, was predicated upon presumed non-Jewishness. Though originally founded by both non-Jews and Jews, the fictional fraternity, like many fraternities in the 1880s, eventually became increasingly German nationalist and prohibited Jews from continuing as members.

The mother describes for Hans the torment she personally suffered because she chose to pass:

> Can you imagine what it means to go around for years under a mask, to hear one's own self denigrated and insulted, and to need to keep silent? I have cursed my face, my hair, my name, which betrayed my heritage to no one, reminded no one to be more considerate. . . . Oh, if only I had been true, perhaps my son would now be defending his mother rather than being ashamed of her.[18]

The mother refers to passing as wearing a mask, a theme that recurred elsewhere in Weimar Jewish culture—and, indeed, worldwide—sometimes in the context of masquerade or costume balls (see figure 18).[19] Passing provided her with temporary immunity to antisemitic discrimination, though not without emotional cost. But because passing made her vulnerable to discovery, it also prevented her from defending the Jewish people.

In contrast to the mother, who passes without difficulty, Loewenberg portrays certain Jewish men as more perceptibly Jewish in appearance. In fact, the mother notes that Martha suspected her future fiancé's Jewishness at first glance. The mother describes Martha's initial response to Richard, "where one could in fact see that he was a Jew and could ask, annoyed: How did he come

Fig. 18. "Carnival," cartoon by Fritz Julian Levi in *Schlemiel*, 1920: "The time of the universal unmasking has come. Off with the mask, sir!" (Courtesy of the Leo Baeck Institute, New York.)

to be in our house?"[20] But Martha protests that she was not irritated, but merely surprised, because at the time she believed there had never been a Jew in their house. Martha further notes that she fell in love with him once her mother confided that she herself was Jewish and that Richard was Martha's cousin. The ease with which Martha comes to terms with her mother's personal history suggests Martha is not alarmed by the fact that Jewish identity could be concealed. In Martha's case, new knowledge of her Jewish background and Richard's kindness help reshape her understanding of Jewishness.

Hans's experience is the opposite of Martha's. Instead of opening doors, his mother's act of coming out as Jewish has the potential to prevent him from participating in his beloved fraternity and from supporting the German nationalist cause of which he is so proud.[21] Throughout the drama, Loewenberg emphasizes the irreconcilability of Jewishness with Hans's quest for German honor through typically masculine acts. For example, Hans first appears in his mother's house with a bloody slash on his forehead that he received in a duel with a Jewish student—which could be interpreted as a mark of Cain of sorts. This polarity between non-Jewish and Jewish students also recalls the antisemitic turn in German universities in the 1880s and 1890s, particularly among the *Corps* students in dueling fraternities.[22] In fact, the first German-Jewish fraternity was formed in 1886 as a result of Jewish exclusion from other fraternities.[23] Hans's position becomes untenable when he is Judaized and disempowered through the awareness that his mother has been concealing her Jewishness. The attempt to force Hans away from his fixed viewpoints is not successful. Ultimately, the drama characterizes Hans as ashamed, humiliated, and unable to bear the burden of his mother's and sister's choices. Fraught with anxieties surrounding his masculinity, Hans cannot reconcile his identity as a proud German Nationalist with the surprise of his own family's Jewishness. Yet it is Hans's mother who is cast as responsible for imposing this situation, and who bears the blame for Hans's death.

If we read Loewenberg's drama as a tragedy, then it makes sense to read the mother as a type of tragic heroine, albeit one who makes decisions that are not depicted as unambiguously heroic. The mother is the only character to appear in all seven scenes of the play, and her actions dictate the dramatic conflict. It is she who has borne the yellow badge's burden, both because she grew up in a Jewish milieu and because her coloring enabled a form of escape to a non-Jewish one. Loewenberg's decision to write a drama suggests that this German-Jewish passing narrative was best told through suspenseful dialogue focused on the present moment. No background information about the mother's past is provided to the reader; we never learn what it was like for the mother to live as a Jew during her youth, only about her life while passing and afterward.

Because the reader (or viewer) of the drama never experiences the mother as anything other than someone who passed, its focus is not on Jewish life, but on living as a formerly concealed Jew whom others have taken for a non-Jew. The presentation of her identity is complicated by external circumstances relating to antisemitism, racial prejudice, and the honor and social standing of her family. At the same time, the mother admits that she also participated indirectly in antisemitic culture. To this end, one contemporary critic described the drama as having prompted "inner disgust at the disgrace of racial hatred," though it is left open-ended whether this jab refers to hatred of Jews by non-Jews, or to Jewish self-hatred.[24] The drama further warns of a type of nationalism that would have people such as Hans choose death over Jewishness. As the play tells it, only the onset of a severe illness prompts the mother to reach out to her sister and her sister's son, Richard, who live openly as Jews. The mother's ultimate choice to contact someone from her family suggests that she would rather continue her life as a known Jew than die while maintaining her assumed identity. Sadly, her desire and ability to discard her mask do not carry over to her son. In Loewenberg's drama, passing comes with its own stigma that can be transmitted and cause harm to others.

Although Loewenberg's drama *Der gelbe Fleck* contains only one fictional story about the consequences of passing for non-Jewish, tales of similarly tragic events can be found in other accounts and personal memoirs that deal with conversion to Christianity. Conversion, which often occurred under different circumstances than passing, was in many cases a more publicly acknowledged form of gaining access to the same privileges.[25] Todd Endelman has suggested that conversion should be considered alongside radical assimilation as another Jewish mode of adaptation that, more often than not, was not undertaken out of conviction.[26] One *Schlemiel* cartoon by illustrator and artistic director Menachem Birnbaum made fun of Jews for using conversion—or other means of distancing themselves from Jewish communities—as a symbolic means of escape from what others perceived as racial identity.[27] In this cartoon, a well-dressed Black gentleman asks a sheepish couple for advice: "I heard that you resigned from Judaism! How does one do that? I would like to resign (*austreten*) from the Ethiopian race!"[28] In addition to leveling a charge against Jews who abandoned their heritage, this cartoon offered a subtle comment on the significant differences between Jewish and Black visibility, and the fact that many Blacks did not have the option to pass for White.[29]

According to Ernst's recollections of his father, Jakob Loewenberg was unable to tolerate Jews who took advantage of the societal access that conversion provided. Indeed, his novel, *Aus zwei Quellen* (From Two Sources), which some have interpreted as semiautobiographical, describes a hero who rejects conversion.[30] In one of his poems, "Baptized" (*Getauft*), Jakob Loewenberg goes further and castigates former Jews for acts of dishonorable selfishness in trying to free themselves of shame: "Speak, have you chosen in your heart / What your mouth devoutly confesses (*bekennt*)? . . . Not that you forgot that of the fathers / And have chosen another alliance: / No, it's that we ever possessed you / That is what pains and torments us!"[31] In this poem, baptism prompted by anything other than true devotion is deemed the ultimate betrayal. Further, the act of outwardly embracing a religion should match the heart's desire.

Fiction supposedly meets fact in another story, "Der Herr Professor" (1912/1924), which was likely based on a newspaper notice about the suicide of a Jewish teacher whose son converted to Christianity.[32] This story was also included in Loewenberg's *Der gelbe Fleck* volume in 1924 and was reprinted in the *Israelitisches Familienblatt* in 1925. In this reversal of the drama *Der gelbe Fleck* along generational lines, the son converts to Christianity in order to gain access to a university professorship closed to Jews. The father protests:

> No internal struggles? Not even a trace of conviction? Religion as a technicality? But the truth is no technicality. . . . If you convert and voluntarily become a confessor of another religion (*wenn du dich zu einer andern Religion bekennst, freiwillig bekennst*), and don't do it out of conviction, then you are a liar, a perjurer, a miscreant; then I cannot grieve for you, then I must condemn you.

Six months after learning that his son has converted, the father repeats his plea for his son to return to Judaism. When the son refuses, it is the father who drowns himself in the Donau River and leaves behind a suicide note.[33] Here, the child turns away from Jewishness instead of the parent, and it is the parent who kills himself in shame as a consequence. In both *Der gelbe Fleck* and "Der Herr Professor," the characters who die are not the ones who crossed over into the Christian realm, but rather their immediate family members. Families are torn apart by the secrets and stubborn silence of those who passed or converted, whether for several decades or only a few months. In these examples, Loewenberg's characters seek a true and authentic sense of self, and passing and conversion are thought to undermine or hinder this search.

An unrelated nonfictional memoir contains a similar story of a son who died by suicide upon learning that his mother came from a Jewish family, suggesting that incidents like the ones portrayed in Loewenberg's writings still occurred in 1920s Europe. Alice Lieberg wrote of befriending Susanna Dybwad and her twin sister while studying in Geneva; the twins also had a brother who worked as a chemist in a large company. Lieberg recalled that the three Dybwad siblings, who previously had no knowledge of their Jewish ancestry, suddenly learned that their mother was a baptized Jew. Once this came to light, the Dybwad brother lost his job and committed suicide.[34] That the mother underwent a religious conversion ceremony did nothing to mitigate the consequences of this information. Because she had kept her background a secret, it was equally shameful and resulted in the loss of a job, which subsequently led to lost honor and lost life. In this instance, as in Loewenberg's fictional accounts, one family member's attempt to circumvent the barriers posed by Jewishness led to the death of another.

These accounts describe how divulging previously concealed information about Jewish ancestry or conversion prompted male family members who themselves did not pass or convert to commit suicide. Representations of the shock of unveiling Jewishness suggest that the stigma of newly discovered Jewishness, coupled with a damaged sense of honor, outweighed the stigma of suicide in many cases. This was also the case for other supposed violations of male honor; the trope of men committing suicide appeared regularly in other German-Jewish literary works from around this time. For example, Ludwig Jacobowski's *Werther, der Jude* (Werther the Jew, 1892), a creative adaptation of Johann Wolfgang von Goethe's novel, *Die Leiden des jungen Werthers* (The Sorrows of Young Werther, 1774/1787), features a Jewish male protagonist who identifies with a German nationalist fraternity and shoots himself when faced with several major failures.[35] Suicide within German-Jewish communities was also a hotly debated subject in the Weimar Jewish press. Many articles focused on determining the causes of the rising suicide rate, often concluding that economic crisis was a primary impetus.[36] As Darcy Buerkle has shown, Jewish women, too, regularly died by suicide, though their deaths were more likely to be omitted from the historical record.[37] Schnitzler's *Fräulein Else*, which is discussed in chapter 3, describes a Jewish woman's literary suicide.

Loewenberg's works and other examples suggest that the disgrace brought about by uncovering Jewishness (or revealing that one had abandoned it through conversion) was magnified when it came in the form of a surprise announcement later in life. The period of its latency caused the secret to fester and increased its potential to cause harm. Those who were raised Jewish, in contrast, were not subjected to the kind of sudden shock that came with discovering Jewishness or Jewish heritage at a more advanced age. A misidentification could become fatal if it became clear that the passing subject had intentionally deceived or defied other family members. In addition to appearance, names contributed greatly to the way people were identified and could be altered to avoid or amplify the potential for misidentifications.

## Russian and Jewish-Sounding Names, and Other Points of Confusion

In early 1928, the *C.V.-Zeitung* and *Jüdische Rundschau* both published articles on a minor news item regarding the name change of the non-Jewish Lithuanian prime minister Augustinas Woldemaras (also: Voldemaras), who visited Berlin around that time. The story in the *C.V.-Zeitung*, taken from the Polish newspaper *Czas* (Time), focused on the national affiliation of the prime minister, who previously had been known as Herr Waldemar. He was the son of a German colonist and had spent different parts of his life in Polish, Russian, Ukrainian, and Lithuanian surroundings. The *C.V.-Zeitung* noted that Waldemar underwent "unusual transformations" (*ungewöhnliche Metamorphosen*) and eventually added the final syllable "as" to his name to become "Woldemaras," a man who more easily could be identified as "an ardent supporter of the independence of the Kingdom of Lithuania."[38] A response in the form of a letter to the *Jüdische Rundschau* editor, by someone writing under the pseudonym Politicus, took issue with the *C.V.-Zeitung* republishing this story, which seemingly had nothing to do with Jewishness or the self-defense of Jews. Politicus satirically inquired: "Is it [the Centralverein's] goal to show that not only Jews take part in assimilation, but rather that this virtue is also present among other peoples? In citing the example of a European prime minister, does [the Centralverein] wish to justify those Jews who add a syllable to their name or attempt to make it conform (*anpassen*) to their environment in another way?"[39] The *Jüdische Rundschau*'s inquiry into the motives behind this article on name changing sheds light on the different forms of sensitivity to names within Jewish communities. Whereas the Centralverein might have viewed the genesis of Woldemaras's name as a mere human-interest story, this *Jüdische Rundschau* contributor perceived it as a political comment on capacities for assimilation.

With its focus on the relevance of Woldemaras's "as" for Jewish communities, this debate reminds us that names were widely considered a controversial and key indicator of Jewishness in Germany and elsewhere. Weimar Jewish newspapers printed discussions about the implications of choosing biblical and therefore "Jewish" first names for children (Isaak, Reuben), noting that many

German Jews had turned away from this custom, and that Germanized nick-
names often replaced any Jewish first names still in use (Max for Mosche, Zilli
for Zipora).[40] The history of Jewish family names provided a constant source of
fascination for journals such as *Jüdische Familien-Forschung* (Journal for Jewish
Genealogy).[41] For our purposes, it is equally important to note that surnames
often were behind mistaken identifications, and that stereotypically Jewish-
sounding names sometimes caused the same confusion as visual, racialized
Jewish-coded attributes including coloring or facial features. Similarly, Jews
with names that did not sound Jewish were sometimes accused of having changed
their names. Elias Canetti, for one, wrote that he was wrongly accused of changing his name from Kahn to Canetti in order to hide his Jewish background.[42]

Indeed, certain names and the practice of name changing were imbued
with symbolic power on political and even legal levels. Historian Dietz Bering
has pointed out that even though antisemitic publications used presumed Jewish names such as Cohn and Isidor to insult or deride Jews, the percentage of
Jews who sought name changes during the Weimar period was proportional to
that of the general population. Bering interprets this as an indicator that con-
spiratorial theories of widespread Jewish name changing largely serviced an
antisemitic agenda of accusing Jews of trying to remain undetected.[43] With
respect to the parallel and more prevalent trend of American Jewish name
changing, historian Kirsten Fermaglich has argued that American law permitted Jews to shed this manifestation of the broader racialized stigma that marked
Jews, whereas other groups such as African Americans were prohibited by law
from passing for White.[44]

Still, in Weimar Germany, a few prominent Jews modified their names to
make themselves less legible as Jews or as Jews with East European backgrounds. For example, poet Mascha Kaléko (1907–75, born Golda Malka Aufen),
together with her first husband, Saul, added the French accent *aigu* to the letter
"e" in "Kaléko" circa 1930. The addition of this accent may have been designed
to distract from the fact that the name "Kaleko" has a pronunciation similar to
that of the word for "cripple" in Russian and Yiddish. The French accent, on the
other hand, made the name seem less Russian—and therefore less Jewish—and
more ambiguously West European. It is possible that the added accent was partly
responsible for the incorrect perception that many people harbored regarding
Mascha Kaléko's Jewishness. In fact, several books of her poetry were published
by mainstream German publishing houses in 1933 and 1934, and it was not
widely known that she was Jewish until 1935.[45] Had Kaléko's name more clearly
revealed her Jewish background, her works probably would have been banned
from publication already in 1933. This was also the case for other Jewish artists,

such as the photographer Yva, whose pseudonym likely helped her continue working in Berlin well past 1933.[46]

Jews were among those who were prone to misinterpreting the coding of names, and many participated in profiling on the basis of names alone. One exemplary notice in the *Israelitisches Familienblatt* commented in January 1933 that Kurt Bondy (1874–1972), a psychology professor at the University of Göttingen, had been accused of being a "Jew and Socialist" and had been removed from his position as director of the Juvenile Delinquent Center at Eisenach. The title of the *Familienblatt*'s article, "The Name is 'Suspicious,'" hinted that Bondy's removal was in part due to his name, despite the fact that Bondy was "most definitely not Jewish, but rather Protestant"—or so the *Familienblatt* alleged.[47] But it was in actuality the *Familienblatt* that was incorrect: Bondy was raised Jewish and later became a leader of various Jewish organizations before escaping to the United States in 1939.[48] In this instance, the *Familienblatt* assumed that Bondy's last name had caused others to mistake him for a Jew (which he was), and had therefore been misinterpreted (which it had not). This was not the first time the *Familienblatt* inaccurately assessed Jewishness on the basis of names.

Though mistaken identifications had effects ranging from mildly humorous to scandalous or life altering, in the case of Alexander Rasumny's film *Überflüssige Menschen* (1926), there was very little at stake. No interpretation of this film was likely to lead to the loss of life or even a job. The confusion as to whether the film held value for Jewish audiences, as suggested by the *Familienblatt*, is nevertheless significant because it reveals how a few stereotypical elements led to the interpretation of a film as Jewish even in the absence of unequivocal signifiers of Jewishness. To be sure, this often occurred with films that were determined to be antisemitic—the German-Jewish press regularly called out negative representations of Jews—but *Überflüssige Menschen* was at no point interpreted as anti-Jewish. The reception of this film instead suggests that Jewishness was in the eye of the beholder.

Unlike other films promoted by the Jewish press that treat Jewishness explicitly (see chapter 2), *Überflüssige Menschen* is only nominally, if at all, a Jewish film. It has no obviously Jewish characters, stars only one actor known for his Jewishness (Bruno Arno) in a minor role, and features scenes of female nudity that generally were frowned upon in Jewish circles. Its sole diegetic traces of Jewishness are the names of several characters, as well as an inconsequential wedding scene that is potentially—but not conclusively—coded Jewish. *Überflüssige Menschen* is an example of a film that, because of its Russian/Soviet components, was characterized as sufficiently Jewish to warrant a mention in the Jewish press. Its alleged Jewishness calls into question how and why Weimar films were determined to be Jewish. In the following analysis, I posit that certain signifiers of Russianness and Easternness came to be mistaken for Jewishness.

A slapstick melodrama, *Überflüssige Menschen* is known in film history as the first in a series of Soviet-German coproductions that were produced and distributed in Germany by Prometheus-Film. In fact, Prometheus originally intended this film to serve as a follow-up to the wildly popular Soviet film *Battleship Potemkin* (Eisenstein, 1925), which met with great success in German cinemas. To this end, Prometheus, together with Phönix-Film, engaged a high-profile cast including Heinrich George, Albert Steinrück, and Werner Krauss. (Krauss, who starred in *Mensch ohne Namen*, returns as a key figure later in this chapter.) Prominent actors notwithstanding, *Überflüssige Menschen* proved to be a commercial failure, which Bruce Murray has suggested might have been a result of not meeting the filmgoers' expectations for powerful social critique that they associated with Russian directors after *Potemkin*. According to Murray, plans for *Überflüssige Menschen* were formally announced in July 1926, and the film premiered in Berlin's Capitol cinema on November 2, 1926, where it was screened for only one week. It was shown again, apparently in revised form, in several locations in December 1926.[49] The film was later presumed lost for decades until it resurfaced in the late 1970s in a film archive in East Germany, after which it was restored, screened, and televised with a musical accompaniment by Werner Schmidt-Boelcke.[50]

*Überflüssige Menschen* is set in a Russian village before the First World War. Its plot is adapted from multiple short stories by Anton Chekhov including "Romance with a Double Bass" (1886) and "Rothschild's Fiddle" (1894).[51] The story centers on members of a local group of musicians who make up an orchestra of sorts—including Mendel Rothschild, the percussionist (Arno); Sigajew, the double bass player (Eugen Klöpfer); Balagula, the trombonist (George); and Bronsa, a violinist and coffin-maker (Steinrück)—who are enlisted to perform first at a wedding, and then at the engagement celebration of Mayor Duboff's daughter, Ola (Elza Temary).[52] On the day of her engagement, Ola goes swimming. The double bass player, Sigajew, happens to be swimming nearby when Ola's younger brother steals her clothes as a prank. Sigajew comes along and offers to hide Ola in his large instrument case. Ola scandalously arrives at her engagement party naked, and her fiancé, Lukin (Hans Brausewetter), is dismayed to discover her hiding in the bass case. Lukin then blackmails Ola's father for a dramatically increased dowry. Throughout the film, the local policeman, Suka (Krauss), patrols the village and keeps order.

There are no explicit references to Jewishness in the film aside from several stereotypically Jewish names and a few potential symbols that may or may not be present. Whether the film portrays any aspects of Jewish life remains unclear even upon close scrutiny of its visual imagery and intertitles. The opening shot, for example, depicts a bustling street scene in the village, with crosses atop church steeples in the background. To be sure, the film is partly based on "Rothschild's Fiddle," which contains a message of Jewish and Russian reconciliation, though the film simply refers to "motifs by Chekhov" and does not mention the title of this story specifically. And although a minor character in the film harkens back to the eponymous character of Chekhov's story, Mendel Rothschild is so insignificant in the film that he is not referenced again by name after the opening sequence in which he is introduced as the hapless "notice poster" (*Zettelankleber*) and "timpanist in the town orchestra." In Chekhov's story, the "Jews' orchestra" is conducted by "Moisey Ilyitch Shahkes," who is clearly coded Jewish.[53] But in the film, the conductor for the small group of musicians is known only by the ambiguous name of Schachkes and has no other indicators of Jewishness. Bronsa, who in the literary version represents a non-Jew who is regularly invited to play with the Jewish orchestra, is also coded Christian in the film: at one point, he is shown mourning his daughter in a cemetery replete with crosses and gravestones engraved in Russian. Finally, aside from two intertitles that reference the musicians playing at a "wedding in the house of Jankel Leisermann," no explanation is provided as to how Jankel Leisermann relates to the other characters, whether this is a Jewish celebration, or who gets married at his house. Instead, the focus in this scene is the orchestra's relative inability to collect itself and perform satisfactorily.

Yet this tangential wedding scene (and perhaps other unnamed factors) was enough to prompt *Familienblatt* editors to praise the film in a discussion of "new Jewish films" in December 1926. Perhaps there was a shortage of films to discuss at this time, or maybe someone invited the *Familienblatt* editors to promote *Überflüssige Menschen* to Jewish audiences. In any case, this article, which presumably coincided with the film's second run, provided little information about the film's content. As a form of explanation, the editors wrote only: "Finally, we mention the charming German-Russian cooperative film *Überflüssige Menschen*, which indeed is not Jewish as such, but contains a proper Jewish wedding, of which we here reprint an image."[54] As depicted in the film still in the *Familienblatt*, this wedding scene is shown primarily in long shots; tall candlesticks are visible on several long tables, and a strategi-

Fig. 19. Wedding scene in *Überflüssige Menschen* (Rasumny, 1926) in *Das Magazin der Phoebus-Theater*, no. 23 (November 1926), 1. (Courtesy of Stiftung Deutsche Kinemathek.)

cally placed painting on the wall might (or might not) portray a man wearing a prayer shawl (see figure 19, which is the same image). When we first see the wedding party and guests enter, they immediately sit down to eat. The bride's father appears to be wearing a head covering of sorts; her mother also wears a nondescript loose-fitting cloth head covering that could be in keeping with Russian or Christian tradition. Some of the male guests have beards, and many wear hats. The dancing that ensues could be categorized broadly as East European. Very little, if anything, in the scene is discernibly Jewish, and, because only postceremony festivities are shown, many elements associated with traditional Jewish weddings—a canopy, the breaking of a glass, a rabbi—are nowhere to be found. If one looks beyond names and ignores the fact that this wedding takes place in the home of Jankel Leisermann, it is easy to overlook or disregard any other potentially Jewish elements of the scene.

Aside from the names "Mendel Rothschild" and "Jankel Leisermann," the spectator cannot be certain that the Russian village has many Jewish residents. Rather, the film's focus is on culture coded non-Jewish in part by the implied consumption of pork. The film's promotional and censor materials entirely omit references to the wedding at the Leisermann house aside from the two intertitles mentioned above.[55] Beyond the orchestra members, none of the people involved in the wedding scene are included in official cast lists and must have been played by extras. In contrast, the second celebratory and decidedly non-Jewish venue at which the orchestra plays, Ola and Lukin's engagement celebration, takes center stage in the film. Ola and her fiancé are typically Russian; they are the classic stuff of Chekhov's prose. Ola's father, the mayor of the village, bears the surname "Duboff"; her fiancé is listed only as "Geometer Lukin" (Surveyor Lukin), a typical Russian surname. Moreover, Ola and Lukin's engagement includes a festive meal of the food most unlikely to appear at a traditional Jewish celebration: a huge smoked pig, shown for several seconds in a close-up that dissolves into the local policeman, Suka (Krauss), licking his fingers greedily in a form of mild social commentary about the role of the village police. The film thus visually overwrites the possibly Jewish wedding scene with the far more memorable image of a succulent pig. If the first wedding scene is coded Jewish, perhaps it is through the conspicuous absence of such a pig.

Whereas the Jewish press praised the authentic Jewishness of *Überflüssige Menschen*, the general press criticized the film's lack of cohesion. Only some reviewers made an offhand reference to the Jewish wedding scene or to Mendel Rothschild. In his short summary for *Lichtbild-Bühne*, Hans Wollenberg, a film critic who was often among the first to comment on a film's Jewish or antisemitic components, mentioned nothing about Jewishness. In a longer review, Wollenberg referenced "the Jewish wedding (*Judenhochzeit*)" only once in a list of memorable scenes. But Wollenberg's review also maintains that the film is Russian through and through, concluding that a comparison of *Überflüssige Menschen* with Gerhard Lamprecht's *Menschen untereinander* (People to Each Other, 1926) could shed light on the differences between Russian and German cultural psychology.[56] For Wollenberg, *Überflüssige Menschen* depicted a foreign milieu, though not a Jewish one. Another review summarized the film at length without mentioning the Jewish wedding scene, though it briefly cited "Bruno Arno as a mildly annoying, smartly portrayed figure (a little Jew-character [*Jüdchen*])"; a different review referred to Arno's character as a "forgotten Jewish lad."[57] The word *Jew* notably appears nowhere in the biting review by Herbert Ihering, who sometimes made backhanded antisemitic remarks about Jewish actors.[58] The absence of thorough attention to Jewishness in all reviews is itself noteworthy: in this film, Jewishness, if present, blended in with Eastern Europe.

In recommending *Überflüssige Menschen*, the German-Jewish press presented this film as Jewish by default when it was certainly Russian, but contained no unambiguous or significant representations of Jews. A few Jewish-sounding names, a story set in a Russian village, and a wedding without a pig were sufficient to render aspects of this film Jewish for a reviewer in search of "new Jewish films." But one must ask whether the anonymous *Familienblatt* editor who included it actually saw the film, or simply ran its promotional photo after being told that the film included a Jewish wedding scene; the latter seems more likely. The Jewish press rarely promoted films that featured any nudity, as *Überflüssige Menschen* does in the scenes of Ola swimming and riding in the instrument case. In fact, only one Jewish magazine advertised the 1929 film version of *Fräulein Else* starring Elisabeth Bergner, which, in contrast, was relatively successful and likewise briefly played on scopophilic spectatorial desire by putting women's naked bodies on display.[59] In both cases, Jewishness is present only in the literary works on which the films were based; the viewer is not confronted with any overt signs of Jewishness. Though on display as objectified, even fetishized, women, Ola and Else are not (perceptibly) Jewish characters, though Else is coded Jewish if one is familiar with extrafilmic circumstances such as Schnitzler's novella or Bergner's background.

Ultimately, the questionable Jewishness of *Überflüssige Menschen* played little role in the overall reception of the film; only the Jewish press grasped at Russianness as a Jewish signifier. Chekhov's stories, known for their generally ambivalent and sometimes harsh representations of Jews, provided the ideal subject matter for a film that was just Russian enough to be vaguely Jewish, though not "Jewish as such." The perplexingly different interpretations of this film reveal that Russianness served as a symbol of exotic foreignness and of non-Germanness: in other words, Russianness sometimes passed for Jewishness. But the possibility remains that Jewishness is not present at all in this comedic Soviet-German coproduction, and that this film, like the case of Woldemaras, served mainly as a metaphor about the incorporation of, or assimilation into, another tradition. Simply by adding an "as," Waldemar made his name sound more Lithuanian; by downplaying Jewish-sounding names and marginalizing Jewish characters, *Überflüssige Menschen* made itself Russian enough for mainstream German audiences. Other German films, too, incorporated Russian elements that symbolized both foreignness and Jewishness on some level.

### Deception, Jewish Caricature, and the Unrecognizable Man Next to the Known Jew

The Ufa sound film *Mensch ohne Namen* (*The Man Without a Name*, Ucicky, 1932) offers a compelling example of a film in which tensions related to mistaken identity are entwined with ambivalent depictions of Jewishness. Like numerous films made after the First World War, its story reflects the trauma experienced by German soldiers who were presumed dead and returned home to find their wives remarried. One such film from 1921 was supposedly based on a true story reported in the newspaper *B.Z. am Mittag*. In another well-known film directed by Richard Oswald, *Dr. Bessels Verwandlung* (The Transformation of Dr. Bessel, 1927), a wounded German soldier passes for French and at one point also is mistaken for a Jew by several East European Jews. This character becomes aligned with Jewish otherness by way of association, for, as he notes: "You are mistaken, I am not a Jew! But I know what it means to be hunted and persecuted."[60] Significantly, many stories about war veteran returnees focus on how these men establish the authenticity of their claims to former identities. *Mensch ohne Namen*, like other such films, teaches a lesson about performing one's most authentic self. As a film from the final year of the Weimar Republic that has received limited scholarly attention, it merits close examination as a widely known text about passing as German.

In *Mensch ohne Namen*, former automobile factory owner Heinrich Martin (Werner Krauss) went missing in 1916 while fighting in the Great War. He returns to Berlin in 1932 and attempts to verify his identity after 16 years of amnesia. Some of his time away was spent working at an automobile factory in the Soviet Union, where the film's opening scene takes place. In fact, the first words he speaks in the film are in Russian. But it turns out that Heinrich Martin was declared dead long ago, and, in the meantime, his best friend, Alfred Sander (Mathias Wieman), has taken over Martin's factory and has married his wife, Eva-Maria (Helene Thimig). Taken for a new immigrant from Russia, the "foreign" protagonist is initially ostracized by German society and thus rendered a nameless outcast who must assimilate and adhere to social and legal norms to make himself visible again. Although he is convinced that his loyalty to Germany in the First World War will bring justice, the court rules against him (and against his Jewish-coded attorney, Erwin Gablinsky, played by Fritz Grünbaum), forcing Martin to seek a new life and a new name. He chooses the name "Gottlieb Leberecht Müller" and contents himself with a new love, Grete Schulze (Maria Bard), and new friends including Julius "Jule" Hanke (Julius Falkenstein) and Gablinsky. The film provides the viewer with no conclusive evidence as to whether the central character is the same Heinrich Martin who went missing or just someone passing for him.

Non-Jewish actor Werner Krauss plays Russified veteran Heinrich Martin, whose goal upon reentering Germany is to pass for and be accepted as himself and as German, and in doing so is coded Jewish yet aligned with Germany.[61] But the juxtaposition of Krauss's character with Erwin Gablinsky, an attorney who—partly because he is played by a Jewish character actor—is obviously coded as an East European Jew and cannot pass for a non-Jew, sets up Heinrich Martin as someone who is better able to blend in. Martin is notably willing to make major sacrifices, including that of his own name, to be recognized as German. In my reading of *Mensch ohne Namen*, it is not Grünbaum's Gablinsky, but rather Krauss's Heinrich Martin, who is a plausible cipher for the German-Jewish experience. The seemingly despicable Gablinsky serves as the insufferable East European foil to Martin's restrained, more assimilated character. Unlike Gablinsky, Martin is able to move away from his Russian past. Both the film's title and story point to the importance of naming for understanding someone's identity; the similarities between the names of the Jewish actors and their characters underscore the roles of Jewish names. The film teaches that, with the proper compromises, it is possible for an "outsider" to find acceptance in German society—but only if he is able to go unnoticed.

The film resonated differently with mainstream German and German-Jewish audiences. Its premiere at Berlin's Ufa-Palast am Zoo on July 1, 1932, met with tremendous applause and was deemed a great success by mainstream critics Herbert Ihering and Fritz Olimsky.[62] In contrast, lead actor Werner Krauss was initially so embarrassed by the film that he and his wife, Maria Bard (who played Grete, his stenographer and love interest in the film), made sure to be out of town on the day of the premiere. Several days prior, Krauss wrote to a friend that they were happy to miss the premiere of "our terrible film" and that they wanted to be far away so as not to hear the complaints "when the Kurfürstendamm grumbles loudly."[63] Krauss later described the film as relatively insignificant given its otherwise impressive cast and the qualifications of the film's screenwriter, Robert Liebmann (1890–1942), who had written screenplays for such highly successful Ufa sound films as *Der blaue Engel* (1930) and *Der Kongreß tanzt* (The Congress Dances, 1931).[64] It should be noted that, despite Krauss's protestations, it was Krauss's performance that redeemed the film for some viewers. Audiences in New York in late 1932 and in Jerusalem in early 1933 praised Krauss in particular.[65] While no one classified it as a "Jewish film," its portrayal of Gablinsky was provocative enough to warrant commentary from a Jewish perspective.

Although the mainstream German reception of the film was generally positive, the German-Jewish press condemned *Mensch ohne Namen* for creating an exaggerated image of a "typical Jew" in the form of the haggling, ruthless attorney, a "shyster" lawyer (*Winkeladvokat*) played by Fritz Grünbaum.[66] Along with comic performers Siegfried Arno, Bruno Arno, and others, Grünbaum was highly visible as a Jew precisely because these Jewish actors often were type-cast in similarly eccentric roles (see chapter 2). In keeping with the trend among some liberal German-Jewish film critics and spectators to blame Jewish per-formers who enacted negative portrayals of Jewish characters, the *Jüdische Rundschau* took Grünbaum to task for his supposedly caricatural portrayal of Erwin Gablinsky.[67] One L. Mischkowski, a guest contributor to the *Jüdische Rundschau*, described the "shyster" lawyer type in this film as "the incarnation of artful shiftiness, obtrusiveness, impertinence, loudmouthedness, and indis-cretion. [The type] is portrayed in the form of a pronounced Eastern Jewish caricature with a fleshy nose, rubbery lips, large mouth, and so forth." Predict-ably, Mischkowski held Grünbaum responsible for agreeing to be typecast be-cause of his appearance and manner of speaking, noting that the film prompted audiences in small-town theaters to laugh at this image of a stereotypical Jew.[68] Not known for printing extensive film criticism, the *Jüdische Rundschau*'s tacit endorsement of this opinion suggests it did not object to the argument that Ga-blinsky's performance of Jewishness lent itself to antisemitic stereotypes and agitation, and thus was guilty of enabling propagandistic imagery.

It is unclear who was responsible for creating this example of a stereo-typical Jew. It is also not certain whether Gablinsky was the product of antise-mitic motivations or self-satire, or perhaps both. In 1932, the German film production company Ufa already had a reputation for privileging humor that distorted the image of "the Jew." One 1930 article in the *C.V.-Zeitung* pointed out that certain Ufa sound films easily could be perceived as antisemitic "Hitler propaganda."[69] Ufa's history of unsympathetic portrayals of Jews indeed might have impacted the way some filmgoers interpreted *Mensch ohne Namen*. Some viewers were likely watching for obnoxious Jewish-coded characters who could not pass.

The individuals involved in the making of *Mensch ohne Namen* certainly had very different and complex relationships to Jewishness; their paths di-verged only a few months after the film's release. Whereas Fritz Grünbaum and screenwriter Robert Liebmann were considered Jewish by the Nazis and were murdered at Dachau and Auschwitz, respectively, Werner Krauss and di-rector Gustav Ucicky each made numerous propaganda films after 1933. Actor Julius Falkenstein (1879–1933) had a different story: though a known Jewish comedic actor, he received special permission to continue making films after the Nazi rise to power. Despite this, internal Ufa correspondence suggests that he was not to be offered major roles, and he made only one more film before his death in December 1933.[70] Incidentally, Falkenstein, like his character, went by the nickname "Jule," which differs by only one letter from the word

*Jude*. It likely was no coincidence that the actor's last name became the more Germanic-sounding name "Hanke" in the film.[71]

There is no disputing that director Gustav Ucicky (1898–1961), an illegitimate son of Gustav Klimt who achieved a moderate level of success during the Weimar era, became an opportunistic Nazi sympathizer very soon after making *Mensch ohne Namen*.[72] A number of Ucicky's films, especially *Flüchtlinge* (*Refugees*, 1933) and *Heimkehr* (*Homecoming*, 1941), received great acclaim under the Nazis for their overtly propagandistic messages.[73] As Eric Rentschler has observed, Ucicky enjoyed A-list status in Nazi Germany. His film adaptation of Kleist's *Der zerbrochene Krug* (The Broken Jug, 1937) was known to be among Hitler's favorites.[74] During the early 1930s, Ucicky's sound films focused primarily on famous historical battles, including two "Prussian films"—one of which, *Yorck* (1931), also starred Werner Krauss in his first sound film—as well as *Morgenrot* (*Dawn*, 1933), which was dedicated to the U-Boot heroes of the First World War and premiered a few days after Hitler took power.

Compared to Ucicky's other films that deal with military themes, *Mensch ohne Namen* is the only one that focuses on the aftermath of war, rather than war itself. Though not a military film, *Mensch ohne Namen* attracted a similar audience and was to some extent received as such.[75] Additionally, *Mensch ohne Namen* was connected in subtle ways to the historic battles referenced in Honoré de Balzac's novella from 100 years prior, *Colonel Chabert* (1832), on which Liebmann's screenplay was loosely based. Balzac's story centers on Chabert, an officer thought to have died in 1807 in the Napoleonic battle of Eylau, which included some Prussian involvement.[76] Werner Krauss highlighted what for him was a notable difference between the novella and the film, namely that Chabert's wife does not recognize Chabert, whereas in the film Eva-Maria recognizes Heinrich Martin but denies that she does.[77] Contrary to Krauss's interpretation, Balzac's text suggests that Chabert's wife recognizes Chabert but plays dumb, and it remains unclear in the film whether Eva-Maria or anyone else actually recognizes Martin. But one notable difference is Balzac's depiction of the attorney character: Derville is a philanthropic, gracious man, a "good soldier" who generously gives Chabert a daily allowance to help him get back on his feet.[78] Balzac's lawyer bears no resemblance to the "shyster" lawyer in *Mensch ohne Namen*, though Derville may have served as a source of inspiration for the far more benevolent character of Julius Hanke, who first encounters Heinrich Martin on the street and offers him a place to stay in Berlin. In short, major changes to the figure of the attorney were made by Liebmann or Ucicky, or perhaps even by Grünbaum.

A cabaret, theater, and film performer active mainly in Vienna and Berlin, Fritz Grünbaum (1880–1941) was known for a dramatic persona that embodied several Jewish clichés. Many associated him with "typical Jewish humor" and the "jargon joke (*Jargonwitz*)."[79] His ironic jokes walked the line between self-deprecating humor and satire, inviting both laughter and mockery. Together with actor Karl Farkas (1893–1971), Grünbaum introduced to Vienna the *Doppelconférence*, a cabaret dialogue in which two actors play a smart character (*der Gescheite*) and a dumb character (*der Blöde*). Naturally, Grünbaum always played the fool to Farkas's cleverer and better-looking part.[80] In these and other cabaret acts, Grünbaum often ridiculed his own height, hair loss, and overall appearance in rhymes: "Yes, that I, when put to the judgment of observation / Effectively amount to a mistake of creation. / Don't call my concerns small (*kleinlich*) / Being as small as I am is really shameful."[81] Grünbaum was and still is the subject of many caricatures; he even served as one inspiration for the character of Adolf Grünbaum in Dani Levy's satirical Hitler film, *Mein Führer* (2007).[82] It was expected that Grünbaum, along with Falkenstein, would provide *Mensch ohne Namen* with comic relief as he did for other films. For example, Grünbaum similarly served as the brunt of innocuous jokes in *Arm wie eine Kirchenmaus* (Oswald, 1931).

Filmgoers were predisposed to view portrayals of Jewish lawyers in a certain light. The stereotype of the ruthless Jewish lawyer was omnipresent on stage and screen by this time and likely colored Fritz Grünbaum's performance of Gablinsky.[83] Long forbidden from practicing more than a few select professions, many German Jews worked in law and medicine, resulting in a disproportionately large percentage of Jewish attorneys.[84] One oft-quoted line from Ferdinand Bruckner's 1928 drama *Die Verbrecher* (The Criminals) goes so far as to suggest that "the lawyers are all Jews."[85] Indeed, the professional title *Rechtsanwalt* or *Advokat* was linked to Jewishness on many levels. In his memoirs, attorney Adolph Asch described how, upon revealing his profession, the party to whom he was speaking immediately took this to be a proclamation of his Jewishness.[86] It is not surprising that Grünbaum, too, almost became an attorney before he turned to acting.[87] In keeping with widespread antisemitic perceptions of Jewish lawyers, Erwin Gablinsky is slick and scheming; he speaks and moves quickly, interrupts, smiles gleefully, and peppers his speech with Yiddishisms such as *nebbich* (poor thing). He first offers to take Heinrich Martin's case for a fee of 20 percent, but, after a brief attempt to negotiate, he immediately drives the price up to 30 percent.

Although his main goal is ostensibly to help Heinrich Martin, Gablinsky's character is also self-serving, and the film highlights qualities that enhance his visibility as a stereotypical Jewish lawyer. Confronted with accusations that his portrayal of Gablinsky could be read as antisemitic, Fritz Grünbaum defended himself in a letter to the editor of *Die neue Welt* on August 19, 1932: "It is clear that I couldn't portray a shyster lawyer as an elegant and noble gentleman. He is in his physical guise one of those types of characters who can be found in the remote outskirts of all metropolitan areas."[88] Grünbaum further claimed to have suggested changes to several scenes to lend his character greater personal depth. Although these scenes supposedly were filmed, they have not been preserved. Günter Krenn argues that Ucicky's final cut eliminates Grünbaum's usual ironic inflections and makes his character seem one-dimensional.[89] In addition, in the majority of shots camera angles and the mise-en-scène position Gablinsky behind or next to a taller character, or even seated, such that Gablinsky appears shorter than all other characters.[90] This height differential is especially apparent in the courtroom scenes where Heinrich Martin stands next to the seated Gablinsky.[91] The spectator literally looks down on Gablinsky in many instances, thus maximizing his visibility as a person of lower status.

One scene near the end of the film presents a particularly salient juxtaposition of characters that are coded with Jewishness and otherness in different ways (see figure 20). Gablinsky arrives at Grete's apartment for a celebratory round of coffee and cake; he brings with him Heinrich Martin, who has just returned from a court-mandated stint in a psychiatric clinic. Jule is also present. From the moment Gablinsky enters the room, he is ridiculed and made to seem even smaller by the placement of the other characters. Audiences were already familiar with the infectious laugh of Maria "Migo" Bard, who played Cilly in *Berlin-Alexanderplatz* (Jutzi, 1931); here, her bald humor privileges Martin while targeting the impatient Gablinsky. Gablinsky's suggestion in this scene that "foreign words are always suspicious" seems at first to be self-reflexive due to his own dubious behavior. But in the larger context of the film, it is Heinrich Martin who must grapple with the suspicion placed upon him and his foreignness.

Werner Krauss's body of work and controversial career choices complicate my argument that Heinrich Martin is not only coded Jewish but also figures as a representative German Jew. Krauss, who often played lead roles, was known as the man of a thousand faces, the quintessential "chameleon" performer, and one of the greatest actors of his time.[92] Krauss's most famous Weimar role was Dr. Caligari; he starred in other noteworthy silent films, including roles as the eponymous Jewish protagonist of *Nathan der Weise* (Nathan the Wise, 1922), the butcher in *Die freudlose Gasse* (*The Joyless Street*, 1925), and of course the local Russian policeman in *Überflüssige Menschen*. But many of

**Fig. 20.** *From left:* **Julius Falkenstein, Fritz Grünbaum, Werner Krauss, and Maria Bard in** *Mensch ohne Namen* **(Ucicky, 1932). (Courtesy of Stiftung Deutsche Kinemathek.)**

his roles were far from sympathetic to Jews. In Nazi Germany, Krauss was among the actors who agreed to play despicable Jewish characters. Herbert Ihering suggested that the Propaganda Ministry likely remembered Krauss's Shylock on Max Reinhardt's stage in 1921.[93] Although Krauss reprised this role in 1943, he is most notorious for playing multiple Jewish roles in *Jud Süß* (Jew Süss, Harlan, 1940), including Rabbi Loew.[94] Krauss's contributions to this overtly antisemitic Nazi propaganda film caused him to be banned from performing in Germany after 1945.[95] In other words, both before and after Heinrich Martin, Werner Krauss played many Jewish characters (as well as other characters that were coded Jewish) in different kinds of films.

Heinrich Martin's fight to recover his own identity is both a process of self-recognition and a disavowal of the Russianness and foreignness he has known since 1916. Here it is worth recalling that, also in 1916, German Jews fighting in the First World War were subjected to a Jewish census to determine whether they were represented proportionately on the frontlines. Just as Jewish soldiers were deeply offended by this accusation of disloyalty, Heinrich Martin takes it as a personal affront that his own Iron Cross goes ignored as he attempts to validate his identity. One clerk who sees his Russian documents directs him to the Foreign Office; nothing Martin does can substantiate his constantly repeated and ignored claim: "But I am a German." He repeats this unsuccessful plea to be seen as Heinrich Martin during his court hearing, at which Gablinsky argues that people can become unrecognizable through changes to their facial features, such as when a grenade changes the shape of a person's nose. This line invokes the phenomenon of nose jobs as a form of Jewish assimilation, and it also highlights the nose as an object of particular scrutiny in legal matters of identification.[96]

In addition to Heinrich Martin's face, other parts of his body also contribute to making him unrecognizable and help convince others that he is an imposter. Eva-Maria testifies that she does not recognize the man claiming to be Heinrich Martin, and Alfred Sander presents the ripped uniform the "real" Heinrich Martin was wearing when he died, which suggests Martin should have a huge scar on his left side. When asked to show the scar in order to prove his identity, Martin insists: "I am no imposter! I am Heinrich Martin, I demand justice. . . . There is simply no scar there at all! . . . I am a German, Your Honor. I fought for Germany. I love my home country. You wish to prohibit a German from being a German? Is that justice? You are no judge; you are a dog, a dog! Justice! Justice! Justice!" The absence of a visible scar on Martin's left side now marks him as an invisible other, and as someone who has the potential to shed or disguise his difference. The judge concedes that he views Martin as unreliable and does not buy his claim. This scene also makes it difficult for the viewer to believe Martin's story, though the film remains sympathetic to his cause in general. Heinrich Martin is one of the many alleged imposters of Weimar cinema; as Noah Isenberg has suggested, the "feeling of having been duped" and a general sense of insecurity characterized the early years of the Weimar Republic and carried over into representations in film.[97]

Heinrich Martin's frantic, repeated calls for justice as he is dragged screaming from the courtroom recall another film largely made up of courtroom scenes that was released two years earlier and widely celebrated by the Jewish press: Richard Oswald's *Dreyfus*.[98] Both films portray a quest for justice for innocent men, with Dreyfus wrongly accused because he was Jewish, and Martin unable to authenticate his former identity, which he lost while fighting for Germany. Yet despite Heinrich Martin's claim to Germanness, he is neither recognized nor believed; there can be no justice for him in the German system in 1932. Instead, his only option is to sever every association with his former self and his otherness and to pass as someone new. With the dissolve from the courtroom to the psychiatric clinic, an assimilatory filmic strategy that calls to mind Valerie Weinstein's concept of "the dissolve of the Jew," Heinrich Martin fades into oblivion.[99] After his forced rehabilitation, the court recognizes Heinrich Martin's right to citizenship on the condition that he takes a new name. The film effectively erases Martin and replaces him with a newly reformed and renamed man, who as such is recognized by the German system.

Martin's new state-imposed and state-sanctioned name symbolizes forced subservience to government power, in addition to all of the privileges that being acknowledged by the state affords. The ritual of taking a new name at baptism was naturally familiar to many German Jews who converted to Christianity, including some who changed their names but kept their initials. For instance, one anecdote told of a Jew named Mausche Lövysohn who, on the way to his baptism, declared he wished to be known as "Martin Luther" so that he might keep the same initials.[100] Borrowing the last name of a young court clerk present at the hearing, Heinrich Martin is metaphorically baptized and reborn as Gottlieb Leberecht Müller, a man with new access to rights and privileges. In response to hearing Martin/Müller's new name, Grete comments: "Müller and Schulze, that's the way it should be," affirming that these two people belong together and hinting at the fact that they both posses stereotypical German last names, which roughly translate to miller and sheriff.[101]

The film *Mensch ohne Namen* models an adaptive process of making otherness disappear in the Weimar era, when a mistaken identity could lead to social stigma and the loss of privileges. Several of its characters are coded Jewish, and the contrast between them highlights how each one represents his respective category. Falkenstein's Jule Hanke offers an additional counterpoint: Hanke is a likable and unassuming character with no legible Jewish qualities whatsoever. One could even argue that it is Jule who passes all along, for at no time does this character become visible as a Jew or allude to the Jewishness of the actor.[102] Likewise, Gottlieb Leberecht Müller learns to eclipse his otherness by permitting the German court to discipline him and mold him into someone else. But he cannot pass for German until he becomes an assimilated, compliant individual who demonstrates genteel restraint; someone who is less like the stereotypically Jewish Erwin Gablinsky, and more like members of the court. Only incognito, under the guise of a new identity, does he subsequently gain acceptance, if not recognition, in Germany. The indicators of Martin/Müller's Jewishness—that he is perceived as Russian, that his nose and face may no longer resemble the original, and that his demand for justice can be honored only if he is "baptized" with a new, typically German name—support a reading of a Russified Jew trying to pass for a German non-Jew, whereas Gablinsky is never able to pass and remains the brunt of the joke. Martin/Müller demonstrates that passing is possible, if not always desirable. Grünbaum and his character, on the other hand, both serve as painful reminders of how clear signs of Jewish visibility could lead to exclusion.

Cases of mistaken identity were abundant in Weimar Germany, where many Jews passed for non-Jews, and others discouraged simple identification by other means. The legendary possibility of a parent (such as the mother in Jakob Loewenberg's *Der gelbe Fleck*) revealing a previously concealed Jewish background to her grown children—and its potentially horrific consequences—haunted audiences that on a daily basis confronted the option to pass. Female characters who passed successfully reflected widespread perceptions that Jewish women were more likely to be able to disguise their Jewishness. A desire to uncover the true identity behind the mask often led to misidentifications, misnomers, or unusual choices regarding what could be considered Jewish, with a general emphasis on Russianness and East Europeanness as potential symbols of Jewishness. Names often played a role in different processes of (mis)identification. And, in some instances, as in the film *Mensch ohne Namen*, the presence of a highly visible Jewish figure made it possible for others to pass by remaining invisible or by taking a new name, and with it a new identity. Texts from the final years of the Weimar period hint that passing became a more appealing, even necessary, option as rising antisemitism made it increasingly risky to display Jewishness openly.

# Conclusion: German-Jewish Passing in Comparative Contexts

Whereas the four main chapters of this book examine instances when Jewish visibility was concealed, revealed, or contested in Weimar Germany, the concluding chapter remains focused on the 1920s and 1930s but extends its scope beyond Germany. Here I consider intersections and similarities between representations of Jewish passing and different models of racial and sexual passing, which I argue support a reading of Jewish visibility as gendered, racialized, and queer. In order to understand why and when Jewish passing occurred or was rejected in Weimar Germany, it is useful to consider better-known contemporaneous examples of African American passing and queer passing, as well as scholarly work on these subjects that offers a larger framework within which to situate German-Jewish passing.[1] In comparing representations of passing by Jews, African Americans, and queer individuals, it is not my intention to collapse or undermine significant differences between them or the circumstances of their production. On the contrary, I would suggest that key differences offer insight into why some groups thematized and criticized passing at length, whereas Weimar Jews alluded to it less intensively or more obliquely. Studying passing helps us to understand different paths that minority groups took, or might take, toward achieving productive forms of visibility and, consequently, better and fuller access to civil rights and an overall sense of safety and well-being.

Historically, in the wider American cultural landscape, the term *passing* has referred to acts carried out by minorities with far fewer legal rights than Jews. Passing for White or passing for heterosexual provided professional or personal upward mobility or political sanctuary. The secrecy and privacy afforded by passing were prompted by more than a drive to fit in or assimilate: racial antisemitism, racism, and homophobia all led to concealed identities. Eugenics movements and other attempts to reinforce White supremacy had a significant impact on minority groups in both Germany and the United States. At the same time that the proto-Nazi movement slowly took root in Germany, the Ku Klux Klan experienced a major resurgence in the United States.[2] Jews and Blacks were similarly targeted in the United States, and German antisemitism was increasingly contingent on racialized notions of Jewishness. Queer or LGBT visibility, too, was—and still is—the subject of persecution on multiple levels and put people who were open about sexual difference at risk. In consulting different accounts of passing, we find motivations for passing as well as methods of coming out without forfeiting the rights and protections that passing might enable.

For Weimar Jews, as for others grappling with the perils of being recognized, writing about the restrictions of "forced" invisibility served as a means of heightening awareness of that group's visibility. Jewish discourses on passing, which came to the fore even while Jews made advanced strides toward attaining equal legal status and civil rights, suggest that Jews sought visibility partly because of the conflicting messages conveyed by the tenuousness of their social positions. The impulse for middle-class acceptance and respectability in the face of discriminatory measures such as the Jewish census of 1916 simultaneously informed the desire to blend in and the need to defend civil rights—including the right to be publicly visible—by way of a "resolidarization" of or renewed focus on Jewish life.[3] In other words, passing and other forms of radical assimilation became more urgent partly because Jews who objected to passing politicized the topic through culture. The renewal of Jewish cultural identity or "Jewish Renaissance" provided occasions to criticize those who passed or rejected Jewishness. Weimar Jews who passed may have hoped to circumvent forms of antisemitic discrimination that, legal freedoms notwithstanding, still prevented them from rising to the top of a given profession.

But perhaps it is because Weimar Jews were comparatively well off in terms of their legal rights and access to high-level positions that inner-Jewish conversations about Jewish passing were more understated than parallel conversations within other minority groups.[4] Despite the many random acts of antisemitic violence in the 1920s and early 1930s, Weimar Jews did not live in constant fear of being lynched, blackmailed, arrested, or imprisoned. In the years shortly before the Nazi rise to power in 1933, the stakes for German-Jewish passing were not as high as the stakes for African Americans or queer populations. Afro-Germans and other people of color in Weimar Germany, too, often faced more overt forms of racism and discrimination.[5] Both the choice to pass and the decision to criticize those who passed took place within a framework of resistance to social pressures and exclusionary measures rather than in response to oppressive legal restrictions. Similarly, when American Jews passed or wrote about passing during this period, they did so in response to subtle forms of institutionalized antisemitism, such as more restrictive immigration laws or university quotas for Jewish students, and not because of laws that drastically limited their civil rights.[6] In comparing discussions of Weimar Jewish passing with those of racial and sexual passing, it is thus not surprising to find fewer, and less conspicuous, deliberations on Jewish passing.

A comparative approach reveals that representations of Weimar Jewish passing possess significant commonalities with texts about passing and visibility produced by or for other minority groups. Numerous works associated with the Harlem Renaissance condemn arbitrary notions of Blackness and Whiteness as defined according to visible attributes. Because Jewishness was to some extent conceptualized as a distinct race or ethnicity, its perceptibility, too, was assessed along racial lines, and Jewish passing narratives similarly deconstruct racial stereotypes. At the same time, the ability to recognize Jewishness was firmly grounded in a set of coded signifiers that, in some ways, more closely parallel those used in establishing queer visibility in a world accustomed to closetedness. Historian Jennifer Evans has recently made the case for avoiding the "expectation of invisibility" in the queering of German history; the same could be said of how we read Jewishness.[7] Finally, the gendered aspects of Jewish visibility are further entwined with depictions of racial and queer visibility, and many passing narratives focus on female characters imbued with the ability to pass. The so-called transformations undergone by women who passed also differ to some extent from those of their male counterparts: women are portrayed as more ambiguous, more slippery, and thus better able to pass. By focusing on attributes shared by (or distinctive to) representations of several forms of passing, we come to a deeper understanding of how the quest for visibility affects different minority groups, both historically and in the present day.[8]

## Points of Intersection in African American and Jewish Passing Narratives

African American and Jewish passing narratives reflect the fact that different kinds of minority visibility were under scrutiny in the 1920s. When passing became the central topic of discussion, it was often the subject of criticism: messages about the potential drawbacks of racialized passing abound in African American novels, as in Jewish and other texts produced in Germany and the United States. Indeed, Adam Meyer has proposed that a more accurate term for the African American passing novel would be the "*anti*-passing novel," a term that can apply to any treatment of passing that addresses its harmful effects on individuals and their respective communities.[9] Similarly tragic consequences, ranging from ostracism to suicide, befall many characters who pass (and their relatives) in both Jewish and African American accounts of passing. Some passers—for example, the mother in Jakob Loewenberg's *Der gelbe Fleck* (The Yellow Badge, 1898/1924; see chapter 4), and Mimi Daquin in Walter White's *Flight* (1926)—find themselves compelled to return to their groups of origin, thereby teaching a lesson about the disadvantages of passing. Further, some works criticize passing not only in a narrow sense for one particular group but also by taking a stand against the actual phenomenon of passing. These works sometimes employ broad, general terms (e.g. "foreigner," "different") or concepts (victims of historical persecution, mob violence) to gesture subtly toward solidarity with other minorities who turn to passing as a strategy.[10] Writers also align Blacks and Jews less explicitly through parallel story lines, or emphasize the common ground within their histories.[11]

The visibility of passers hinged to some extent on how observers interpreted and responded to the signals and codes of would-be passers.[12] Some believed that certain codes were perceptible only to other group members, or were impenetrable to those not "in" on the secret knowledge necessary to decode them.[13] Membership supposedly enhanced familiarity with these codes and any code-switching that might occur. It was thought to be easier to spot Jewishness if one were Jewish, Blackness if one were Black, or queerness if one were queer. Jews in Europe and the United States felt that they were well equipped to recognize other Jews by way of distinguishing signs.[14] In a similar vein, Ralph Ellison controversially suggested that Blacks had a special eye to detect those who were passing as White.[15] Audre Lorde later wrote about her search for other Black lesbians, "Doesn't it take one to know one?"[16] Such arguments hint at essential instincts to see through acts of passing, but they also suggest that members of a certain group were more attuned to passing, and that outsiders were sometimes oblivious to the symbols used within a group.

Other writers contested the assertion that membership in a group could guarantee the ability to spot a passer by ridiculing the idea that any casual observer could tell who was passing based on visual characteristics alone. Arthur Schnitzler's Fräulein Else states plainly: "Nobody notices it in me. I'm positively blonde."[17] In Nella Larsen's *Passing*, Irene Redfield comments to a friend: "Nobody can [tell]. Not by looking. . . . There are ways. But they're not definite or tangible."[18] For the most part, passing narratives reflect the widespread assumption that other members of a minority group who could identify a passer still would not betray that person.[19] Those who posed the greatest danger were outsiders who learned to read hidden or subtle codes, particularly those who engaged in profiteering or blackmail by exposing those who passed.

The moral stakes of deception also played an important role in concealing Black and Jewish identities. For passing to occur, both deception and a suspension of disbelief, or a willingness to categorize someone based on limited information, needed to be in place. By this logic, both the passing subject and anyone fooled by the passing subject ("the dupe," in Amy Robinson's phrasing) were complicit in overlooking missing pieces of the puzzle.[20] W. E. B. Du Bois, in a review of Nella Larsen's *Passing*, suggested that many passing novels were in fact about the moral issue of "a person's right to conceal the fact that he had a grandparent of Negro descent."[21] Many passing narratives interrogated precisely these ethical questions: In what cases are lies by silence or omission justifiable? How could people live with deceiving members of their own family? Is it more acceptable to mislead strangers?[22] By focusing on the consequences or even punishments for passing, literary narratives attempt to answer these questions by explaining the reasons why people pass, but nevertheless promising pain for those who make "wrong" choices about hiding their "true" selves. At the same time, they also point a finger at the observer who cannot see—or does not look—beyond that which is perceptible to the eye.

Passing novels of the Harlem Renaissance chronicle the experiences of characters whose indeterminate identities straddle, cross, or transgress the color line of racial segregation brought about by Jim Crow laws.[23] Most often these characters are light-skinned Black or biracial women who pass for White. Other racial, ethnic, sexual, class, and religious identities come into play, but usually in connection with the categories of Black and White. Passing for White generally necessitates an ongoing performance sustained over time and in a new location, often New York City. It demands the invention of a new personal history and family tree, the adoption of new attitudes, and an erasure or obfuscation of one's past. For some who pass, fear of discovery extends to anxiety about the physical appearance of offspring, a trope linked to notions of racial purity that reinforces the randomness of racial visibility and its transmission over generations.

Constructions of Jewish visibility and histories of Jewish persecution inform or provide a counterpoint to notions of African American identity in many instances. This is exemplified by one brief mention of a Jew in *The Autobiography of an Ex-Colored Man* (1912) by James Weldon Johnson (1871–1938): "He knew that to sanction Negro oppression would be to sanction Jewish oppression."[24] Several articles in the Weimar Jewish press contained analogous messages about African American identity. A response by Edith Falk to the

1928 German translation of Johnson's autobiography drew a similar parallel: "In the struggle for recognition in the global community, both the Jews and the Negroes come up against such similar difficulties among those to whom they lend their strengths as enrichments."[25] Anna Nussbaum, who edited *Afrika singt* (Africa Sings, 1929), a selection of German translations of African American poetry by Johnson, Du Bois, Langston Hughes, Claude McKay, Jean Toomer, and others that was reviewed in the *Jüdische Rundschau*, pointed to the broad relevance of racial solidarity among Blacks: "A commitment (*Bekenntnis*) to one's race irrespective of language, citizenship, and religion seems to us to be a productive, creative feeling."[26] In her review of this volume, Martha Weltsch emphasized the common exilic or diasporic (*Golus*) experiences of African Americans and Jews: "The suffering of a people that lives as a pariah among peoples, scorned and trampled, enslaved and shunned, and yet still aware of its worth, full of longing for a better life, freedom, spirit, and humanity, and full of pride for the strength and beauty of its own blood—is that not a world of emotions and experiences that is akin to ours?"[27] The term "pride" is especially noteworthy; Weltsch, too, focuses on the importance of "racial consciousness" (*Rassenbewusstsein*) more broadly. References to Jewish characters in African American literature serve as a reminder of the relevance of the Jewish experience for African Americans. Other texts in the German-Jewish press demonstrate how Jews portrayed African American experiences as similarly limited by legal and social restrictions.[28]

Racially ambiguous female characters are central to African American passing novels, thus establishing a category of women who manipulated (mis)-perceptions of themselves in order to avoid discrimination. The most prominent examples in works by African American authors include Mimi Daquin in Walter White's *Flight* (1926), Angela Murray in Jessie Redmon Fauset's *Plum Bun* (1929), and Clare Kendry in Nella Larsen's *Passing* (1929). A contested figure, the mixed-race or biracial character—sometimes characterized as a "tragic mulatta"—both defies racial stereotypes and subverts them in different ways.[29] Because they are racially indeterminate, these women are portrayed as more susceptible to reclassification by themselves or others. Teresa Zackodnik has argued that African American women writers portrayed mulatta figures who "talked out of both sides of their mouths" and thereby used "double-voiced discourse" to reach both African American and White audiences.[30] Double or dual coding also was a common occurrence among portrayals of and by Weimar Jews; Jewishness was often displayed or discussed in hidden ways such that it was visible only to those who knew how to perceive it.[31] It is not only authorship and audience that are at stake for our purposes but also how all of these representations relate to Jewish passing.

Walter White's *Flight* (1926), a clear entreaty for those who could pass to remain part of their Black communities of origin, also makes a subtle plea for members of Jewish communities to do the same. Walter White (1893–1955), who personally was light-skinned and able to pass, was a director of the NAACP for several decades. He even worked undercover to investigate activities of the Ku Klux Klan.[32] White's background, political involvement, and familiarity with African American history are imprinted upon *Flight* in many ways. The novel follows protagonist Mimi Daquin from New Orleans to Atlanta, Philadelphia, Harlem, and elsewhere in New York. Mimi's heritage is Creole and African American; she was raised Catholic; her skin is described as ivory white, and her hair as reddish gold. Her red-blond hair alone marks her as other in both Black and White communities.[33] Profoundly influenced by the terrors she witnessed as a child during the Atlanta race riots of 1906, Mimi Daquin does not pass until rumors of her past—she became pregnant but refused to get married—resurface in Harlem years later. Cast out of Harlem and left with no viable alternatives, Mimi passes for White only in the final third of the novel; in its last pages, she returns to Harlem.

Mimi Daquin, who passes for White in order to earn acceptance and a better living, finds her parallel in Sylvia Smith, who passes for non-Jewish. Mimi also idolizes other New York Jews who do not pass.[34] Both Mimi and Sylvia can pass for French, which elevates them to upper-class status in the fashion world, and they find work at an elite French-inspired New York designer fashion house. Again we see that Frenchness can be a cover for Jewishness, as for other minority identities. Sylvia also changed her last name, Bernstein, in order to pass. But Sylvia's name is not the only factor that might betray her Jewishness: in explaining her background, White describes how Sylvia's "dark" face bears the very "mark of Israel" that she generally attempts to conceal.[35] The text racializes the external appearance of both Mimi and Sylvia, inviting the reader to understand how both were categorized based on their coloring, names, and other intangible elements that recall the stigmatized "mark of Cain" (see chapter 1).

Further, Mimi's encounters with other Jews intensify with the introduction of characters who are both racist and antisemitic. Mimi identifies with the "sad, weary faces" of the Lower East Side, who, "like her own race, had known bitter persecution." The older generation of women with "heavy wigs" and "men with magnificent beards" in fact "appealed to her more than almost any type she had ever seen."[36] Mimi's connection to them grows as her husband, Jimmie Forrester, disparages Jews together with other minorities: "This Klan's stirring up things all over—little rough, maybe—but these kikes and Catholics and niggers got to be kept under control."[37] Jimmie's urge to control both Catholics and Blacks targets Mimi personally. His inclusion of Jews, a group with which Mimi has already aligned herself via Sylvia and visits to the Lower East Side, affects Mimi by extension.

Significantly, attending a show that includes a theatrical blackface performance by a Jew is what first inspires Mimi to put a stop to her own everyday performance of Whiteness. While attending this production, which bears similarities to the play that served as the basis for *The Jazz Singer*, Mimi's companion comments, "'the only good spots in the show are the dirty ones,' furnished as they were by a Jewish comedian in blackface."[38] By implying that there is something objectionable—even "dirty"—about Jews performing Blackness to entertain predominantly White downtown audiences, *Flight* triangulates the concepts of Jewishness, Blackness, and Whiteness. As constructs, they are both dependent on and at odds with each other. Jimmie's variety of Whiteness is achieved in part through a disingenuous appreciation for the performance of race, ironically often by Blacks or Jews. Moreover, the Jewish comedian is positioned here as one who, by performing Blackness, in fact highlights his own Jewishness and otherness with respect to the audience. The unpleasantness of this display galvanizes Mimi into returning to Harlem. *Flight*'s protagonist learns how to embrace her own culture from both positive and negative models of Jewish visibility and authenticity, much like those who engaged with Jewish visibility in Germany.

Much studied and often cited in scholarly conversations about passing, Nella Larsen's *Passing* (1929) offers additional crucial insights into how passing endangered those who passed, as well as the vast differences between the experiences of passers and those who could pass but did not. The daughter of a White Danish mother and a Black West Indian father (who went missing when she was young), Nella Larsen (1891–1964) struggled to find acceptance within her own family. Eventually she found her way to Harlem.[39] Larsen's *Passing* reflects on racially charged public and private encounters and visual appraisals; it contemplates what it means to wear the mask of a different race in some contexts, while removing it in others. The novel is told largely from the perspective of an unreliable narrator, Irene Redfield, who reencounters her childhood friend, Clare Kendry, when both seek relief from the summer heat in a restaurant on a hotel rooftop.[40] Both Irene and Clare can pass for White, though only Clare chooses to pass for an extended period. Irene, in contrast, frowns on passing and does so only selectively in certain public social situations.[41] When Clare falls from a sixth-floor window at the end of the novel, it remains unclear whether she falls of her own accord, or perhaps is pushed, either by her own husband, Jack, a White racist who had just learned her secret, or by Irene, who suspected Clare of having sexual relations with Irene's husband, Brian (who is Black and not able to pass).

In comparing Larsen's *Passing* with German-Jewish passing narratives, Larsen's juxtaposition of two female characters is especially striking. As part of its lesson about minority visibility, Larsen's references to hair and eye color set up Irene and Clare as a complex meditation on the stereotypes of the blonde and the brunette. In other words, Larsen's novel about two African American women reactivates broader debates about body aesthetics, pitting light coloring that is supposedly Northern or Central European against dark coloring associated with Eastern Europe, Africa, and many other parts of the world. Similar to the *Familienblatt* anecdote about the Jewish blonde and brunette who meet in a resort town (see chapter 3), and the mother in Loewenberg's *Der gelbe Fleck*, Larsen's blonde, Clare, is the least recognizable and thus most likely to capitalize on her ability to deceive the viewer. The brunette, in contrast—in this case Irene, who has black curly hair and brown eyes—is portrayed as proud and more forthcoming about her race. A "blonde beauty" with gold hair and ivory skin, Clare has no trouble concealing her background, though at one point Irene observes that Clare's black eyes are particularly "exotic" and could be considered "Negro eyes."[42] Clare's blonde hair, however, aligns her with Europe; that she possesses both light and dark features makes her all the more mysterious. Larsen's description of Clare's eyes recalls numerous descriptions of Jewish women's dark eyes.[43] Indeed, Clare's conspicuous displays of her beauty and wealth also parallel the allegedly ostentatious displays for which Jewish women were criticized, and for which African American women, too, sometimes came under fire, particularly with respect to bright-colored clothing.[44]

In novels including *Flight* and *Passing*, as in Loewenberg's *Der gelbe Fleck*, passing women stand out in sharp relief against bigoted men. Mixed-race female characters who supposedly threaten racial purity are already passing when they become romantically involved with racist White men; these men prove to be the undoing of the passing personas of Mimi and Clare. In Loewenberg's drama, in contrast, the mother only passes for non-Jewish after her marriage to a Christian man meets with disapproval. She keeps her secret not from her husband, but from her children. Whereas Loewenberg's mother takes the risk of revealing her Jewishness to her children, the protagonists of 1920s passing novels by African American authors tend to avoid confrontation and do not voluntarily come out as Black to their family members, but rather attempt to release themselves from the bonds of passing through other means.

In all of these narratives, female characters take the lead in grappling with whether to pass in part as a means to marry both out and up, though they pay a high price for leaving family and other ties behind. Women have had greater access to upward mobility via marriage throughout history. Their bodies and self-expression serve as sites for the performance of Blackness/Whiteness or Jewishness/non-Jewishness, both in life and in literature. But whether Black passing for White, or Jewish passing for non-Jewish, most women in passing narratives eventually become discontented and undergo some kind of return to their previous lives. Until this return occurs, the risk of being discovered hovers over the female passing subject, who is faulted and punished for her changeability.[45] In many stories, male characters who suddenly learn that their loved ones were passing become angry, violent, and unpredictable. Because of their supposed fluidity and consequent opportunities to pass, women were tasked with making choices that would model pride and public visibility for others in their respective minority groups. Proud New Women figures (including the New Negro Woman and the New Jewish Woman) represent the opposite of concealment and passing.[46] Their existence challenges the notion that passing was considered acceptable by all women who could pass. Just as gender figures into racial passing, gendered aspects of visibility are also intertwined with sexual passing.

### Reading the Codes: Parallels between Queer Passing and German-Jewish Passing

Sexual or queer passing was extremely common in the early twentieth century, and finding a way to come out without endangering the self posed a constant challenge to populations of sexual minorities who had long been considered invisible. Gender, too, was an important piece of this puzzle, due to widespread blurring of gender and sexuality in the early twentieth century, as well as a different kind of passing that occurred during and after the First World War, when women assumed new gender roles to achieve greater equality.[47] In Germany, Paragraph 175 of the German Criminal Code made homosexual acts illegal beginning in 1871, which led to the active persecution of men who engaged in homosexual conduct. Such restrictive laws and punitive measures created a need for queer scenes to exist mainly behind closed doors—in nightclubs and other private meeting spaces, for example—even while public displays of sex and sexuality proliferated and became more widely accepted.[48]

At the same time, modern impulses for self-expression offered harsh criticisms of the legal and social policies that made closetedness necessary. As queer scenes flourished in the Weimar period, the notion of rejecting sexual passing in favor of coming out in certain contexts gained momentum, and even supposedly secret clubs were well known and frequented by both locals and tourists. Weimar Germany thus saw parallel periods of queer and Jewish flourishing during which queer and Jewish communities deemed passing a necessary evil in some cases, yet encouraged subtle forms of visibility at the right time and in the right place. The complex coding used to display sexual identities was similar in many ways to signs that indicated Jewishness. Identifying members of a particular group required both literacy in this set of codes and occasions to see them.

Because both Jewishness and queerness have been posited as forms of difference that are not presumed to be immediately visible on the body, consciously displayed visual or behavioral coding becomes necessary in order to signify these identities. For centuries, sumptuary laws dictated that European Jews be marked as such with a yellow badge, hat, or white collar; only in the modern period did Jews begin to regulate external displays of Jewishness. Whereas the traditional dress associated with East European Jews served as an obvious marker for some, other Weimar Jews relied on material signifiers including badges and uniforms, and Jewish periodicals that they carried or read openly. In queer communities, coding took different forms, for example: nontraditional gender presentation (masculine women or feminine men) via clothing, hairstyles, or accessories such as monocles; subscribing to queer periodicals including *Die Freundin* (The Girlfriend), *Garçonne*, or *Der Eigene* (The Unique One); and mentioning coded terms including the word *Freundin* and the names of particular venues.[49] Some of these forms of coding, such as women with short hair, seemed unremarkable in light of larger Weimar trends. As one scholar has noted, "inconspicuous passing was not forbidden."[50] Other forms of coding were more noticeable and came with greater risk.

Many queer studies scholars proceed from the assumption that a would-be passer is actively involved in the process of choosing when and how to reveal sexuality in either coded or overt forms, a notion that is contingent on queer subjects having the ability to pass. Eve Sedgwick, for example, draws on Michel Foucault to point out that closetedness is itself a performance initiated by the speech act of silence.[51] This multilayered silence, however, may be regulated or controlled by others operating either within or outside of the queer community. Additionally, some individuals may have been unable or less able to conceal sexual difference. Other scholars have advocated for reading queer visibility in conjunction with racial visibility and Blackness, thereby making the case that "multiple axes of oppression" taken together can expand our understanding of the circumstances for the concealment and display of different identities.[52] Just as including racialized Black (or Brown) bodies may complicate the visibility of certain queer figures, it is also worth considering to what extent racialized Jewish bodies come into play. In the case of someone who is immediately taken for Jewish based on physical characteristics, is that person's Jewishness more visible than his or her sexuality? Likewise, if a Jew cultivates the ability to pass for a non-Jew, is that person better equipped to conceal a given sexuality?[53] In addition to intersections of queer and Black or Jewish visibility, it remains crucial to consider the power of the individual to determine both subjectivity and visibility, and to remember that queer (in)visibility may not always have been a choice, either due to legal restrictions or to other ways in which queerness might have been imprinted or projected onto the body.

Historically, rejecting queer passing was not always a viable option. Rather, passing was seen as a necessity for those who potentially would face imprisonment or worse if reported to the authorities. Blackmail was extraordinarily common, as illustrated in the "education film (*Aufklärungsfilm*)" *Anders als die Andern (Different from the Others*, 1919).[54] This film, which was directed by Richard Oswald (who also directed *Dreyfus*, 1930), was among the first films to deal openly with homosexuality. Oswald collaborated with German-Jewish sexologist Magnus Hirschfeld (1868–1935), who was relatively open about his own homosexuality. Hirschfeld estimated that one out of three homosexuals had been blackmailed.[55] Like cultural works from this period that deal with Jewish and racial passing, *Anders als die Andern* considers suicide as a possible ramification of queer passing or forced closetedness. The film's protagonist, Paul Körner, reads in the newspaper about others—a factory owner, a respected judge, a student—who commit such an "incomprehensible deed" (suicide) just before a wedding day or on other occasions for "unknown reasons." Instead of introducing suicide later in the narrative, the film opens with this problem and works backward, thus boldly confronting the fact that queer individuals from all walks of life might be susceptible to acts of harm.

The recuperation of both queer sexualities and Jewishness involved pronouncing them respectable, untainted identities that did not need to be concealed. *Anders als die Andern* brings to light the specific experiences of homosexual men as an oppressed group.[56] The Jewishness of the film's creators remains unstated, yet perhaps informed their attention to minority visibility on some level. Magnus Hirschfeld elsewhere wrote that he felt stigmatized as a Jew; Jews were especially visible insofar as they were disproportionately represented among doctors and sexologists.[57] The reception of *Anders als die Andern*, too, was bound up with antisemitic reactions and sparked a discussion about homosexuality and Jewishness in the journal *Film-Kurier*.[58] The film's intertitles advocate plainly for the acceptance of homosexuality: "Love for one's own sex can be just as pure and noble as that for the opposite sex. This orientation is to be found among many respectable people in all levels of society." The words used here to justify and instill pride in homosexuality are the same terms found in German-Jewish self-defense discourses that described Jews as "purely expressive" and "noble of race" in response to antisemitic allegations.[59] Passing is not referenced explicitly; the desire for the freedom to fully embrace one's identity is analogous to resisting instructions to conceal, cover, or pass.

Even while they sometimes advocated for queer visibility, Magnus Hirschfeld and his Institut für Sexualwissenschaft (Institute for Sexual Science), founded in 1919, also offered guidance for those who wanted or needed to pass. During the First World War, Hirschfeld instructed queer individuals, as well as heterosexual women, to help them enter the military and pass as "normal" soldiers.[60] The term *transvestite* entered the popular lexicon in conjunction with Hirschfeld's 1910 work, *Die Transvestiten* (The Transvestites), which theorized the spectrum of individuals who cross-dressed. Accounts of both male-to-female and female-to-male passing appeared with some frequency in the mainstream Germany media of the 1920s.[61] Hirschfeld also pioneered sex changes for hermaphrodites (intersex) and transgender people.[62] Sander Gilman has argued that the 1907 memoir of N. O. Body (1885–1956; pseudonym of Karl M[artha] Baer), who was born with ambiguous genitalia and later worked with Hirschfeld to undergo a gender reassignment process, contains a "double passing" insofar as it further conceals the author's Jewish background by describing it as "exotic" and "French."[63] Both terms instantly mark the author of this memoir as someone who inhabited a marginal position in German society; for a reader accustomed to looking for double meanings, it would be possible to interpret "exotic" and "French" as code for Jewish.

Anxieties about antisemitic and homophobic backlash contributed to the self-presentation and self-monitoring of both Jewish and queer communities. In the same way that Jews advised each other to avoid jewelry and other displays of opulence, select queer communities engaged in self-policing to make certain that their peers avoided excess and appeared respectable in public. Historian Laurie Marhoefer points out that for some homosexual men this meant engaging in commercial sex to keep their sex lives secret and thereby minimize the risk of blackmail or arrest. Middle-class women, as historian Marti Lybeck has noted, were similarly worried about respectability, and advertisements for lesbian bars assured readers that their events were "restrained and dignified."[64] In the case of transvestites, as Marhoefer and Katie Sutton have shown, appearing respectable involved embracing simple, elegant bourgeois fashion—and rejecting gaudy jewelry—in order to achieve "gender authenticity."[65] At other times, it entailed emphasizing that only select people should appear at public events, namely those who would be sure to refrain from open displays of desire in mixed company. Lybeck suggests that at events of the German League for Human Rights, for example, only "respectable and impeccable (*einwandfrei*)" people were welcome, which excluded both homosexuals and prostitutes.[66] These acts of self-policing also recall the notion that members of a group were best qualified to detect passing. Those who could detect passers were charged with helping them stay "in the closet" so as not to invite negative attention to the group as a whole. This was accomplished not only by passing as non-Jewish, as White, or as nonqueer, but also by passing as an upstanding member of the middle class, another privileged group that at times was grossly inhospitable to minorities.

Because public spaces required caution, private gatherings figured as "safe spaces." Just as Weimar Jews sought out Jewish-friendly spaces where they could openly display Jewishness, queer individuals in Weimar Germany also frequented locations where they did not need to pass, such as rooms in private organizations that supported them. Berlin's nightlife also provided particularly rich access to queer meeting spots and places of encounter, including scores of bars and underground clubs frequented by different social groups (Hirschfeld estimated that there were roughly 100 gay bars by 1923); the most famous was perhaps the Eldorado, a nightclub popular among transvestites, artists, and tourists that was immortalized in the writings of Klaus Mann and Christopher Isherwood.[67] But these spaces provided only limited protections. Because members of certain organizations feared being outed, some organizations began addressing members by pseudonyms and sending mail in plain envelopes.[68] Such actions parallel those of the secret Jewish Defense Service that attempted to cover its tracks entirely, yet they stand in contrast to the position taken by Jewish editors who advocated proudly displaying Jewish periodicals in public despite the risks.[69] These and other measures suggest a greater sensitivity to—or simply more dire consequences for—being outed as queer.

Other queer-themed films of Weimar cinema, too, serve as reflections of the anxieties surrounding minority visibility and coming out. Whereas displays of Jewishness on screen were often relatively subtle (or antisemitic), performances of gender inversions regularly took center stage in Weimar culture, and questions of how to reveal homosexual or homoerotic identities also made their way to the screen. Alexander Doty has argued that heterocentrist films and other texts can provide a glimpse into "queer moments" that stand in contrast to, but often operate within, the nonqueer.[70] In other words, queer moments might pass as nonqueer within a larger plot or framework. Such films as *Ich möchte kein Mann sein* (*I Don't Want to Be a Man*; Lubitsch, 1918) and *Der Geiger von Florenz* (*Impetuous Youth*; literally: The Fiddler from Florence; Czinner, 1926)—both made by Jewish directors in Germany—suggest a fascination with these moments as exemplified by cross-dressing subjects in popular culture.[71] These films demonstrate how far gender-bending masquerades could go, while at the same time alluding to the homoerotic impulses behind some instances of cross-dressing and drag. It is not clear whether the relationships that evolve between cross-dressing female-to-male subjects and their male counterparts demonstrate the abilities of these counterparts to see through acts of passing, or whether the men are in fact attracted to (women passing as) men.[72] Passing itself becomes a cover for queerness: the observer who pretends not to see or who cannot detect the passer becomes aligned with queer desire.

Jewish passing and queer passing bore many similarities in the early twentieth century, from the performance of specific codes in public or in private, to the manipulation of otherness such that it was less visible at certain times. The threat of public attacks, humiliation, and shame led members of these and other minority groups to contemplate suicide, as reflected in cultural representations of their struggles with coming out, even to family and close friends. Both groups underwent processes of self-policing with the goal of ensuring a greater degree of protection for the Jewish or queer population as a whole. Choosing to perform or display one's Jewishness or queerness, when it was a choice, was directly linked to potential consequences. Yet even while passing provided a kind of sanctuary at times, cultural texts by and for members of Jewish and queer communities suggest that passing often was accompanied by a counterimpulse for visibility and the desire to be known as oneself.

Weimar Jews developed and instructed each other in subtle codes that would make them recognizable to other Jews. To be sure, most Jews were familiar with how to alter or present their appearance and behavior in order to pass for non-Jews, but many never took these measures, and some engaged in only certain practices at designated times. Others passed or covered on some level, whether by modifying racialized indicators of stereotypical Jewishness (dyed hair, nose jobs) or by downplaying performative aspects of Jewishness (exaggerated gestures, overt expressions of religious observance) in public. Still, even those who passed or covered may have demonstrated affiliation with Jewish communities in other ways, perhaps by continuing to prioritize Jewishness in Jewish-friendly spaces away from the public eye. Cultural texts and other examples from this period suggest some Jews wore subtle markers of Jewishness that could be seen only by those trained to see them, from inconspicuous badges to barely detectable head coverings.

The history of the Jewish quest to be seen, and at times to be invisible, is one that intersects and parallels similar pursuits by other minority groups in the early twentieth century. By examining these struggles together, we stand to gain a more precise grasp of how members of minority populations worked to construct the definitions and boundaries that shaped each group's visibility. The recurrence of cultural narratives about African American, queer, and Jewish passing hints at an imperative for minority visibility that was complicated by historical events, legal and sociocultural restrictions, and the emergence of a modern sense of pride among stigmatized groups. Racism, racial and other forms of antisemitism, and homophobia served as reasons to pass in many instances. Internalized forms of discrimination and the drive to get ahead personally or professionally led other individuals to pass either selectively or on a more permanent basis. An awareness of how other minorities approached their unprivileged positions, or attempted to gain power through passing, circulated through and with cultural texts and responses to them. In short: Jewish passing did not occur in a vacuum, nor did resistance to Jewish passing emerge entirely independent from other influences. The history of German-Jewish passing is both representative of and intertwined with the histories of other movements geared toward minority visibility and acceptance. Scholars of African American studies and queer studies, among other fields, may find it useful to consider how elements of the Weimar Jewish experience could inform projects on other minority groups.

From the history of German-Jewish passing, as well as its connections to other forms of passing in the early twentieth century, we also gain insight into resonances for present-day discourses of minority visibility. These conversations are all the more urgent in an age when acts of violence regularly take Black, Brown, and queer lives in the United States. The politically divisive events of 2016 have empowered the Ku Klux Klan and other White supremacy groups in new ways, and Jews, Muslims, people of color, LGBT individuals, and other minorities may find themselves revisiting questions of visibility in the interest of self-protection. Antisemitic violence has also escalated in Europe in recent years—especially in France and the U.K., but also in Germany—and whether twenty-first-century Europe is safe for Jews is a matter of ongoing debate and concern, particularly with the rise of several right-wing political parties. With the benefit of hindsight, many scholars scour the years that preceded the Holocaust for portentous signs of what was to come. Antisemitic riots and attacks, but also different Jewish impulses to blend in during the Weimar era, sometimes are taken as indications of undeniable discord. In fact, historically significant years, especially 1929 and 1933, are often invoked in discussions about where European Jews stand today, and whether Jews worldwide should take precautions to conceal Jewishness.[73] However, I would like to suggest that we also have much to learn by studying historical counter-impulses for Jewish visibility, which teach us that the Weimar Republic was more than a brief period in which discriminatory measures anticipated far more extreme Nazi acts of persecutions and violence. Rather, the years from 1919 to 1933 represent a distinct era of resistance to everyday oppressions and humiliations, and of searching for chances to be open about Jewishness in public.

The choice to display Jewishness, as well as other minority identities that were not readily legible, was—and is—bound up with the expectation that someone else would be able and would choose to see it. To be unable to see a Black woman or man whose skin does not appear black, or a queer individual whose difference is not perceptible, is not only the "fault" of the unseen subject but also of the observer with a limited understanding of how to discern Blackness or queerness. This also applies to Jewishness, though, as this book demonstrates, historical perceptions of Jewish appearance were less stable or even illusory, and determining how to identify Jews was often half the battle for the observer. In teaching readers how to see Jewishness, Weimar Jewish texts both deconstructed notions of racialized visibility and established insider codes similar to those used to establish queer visibility, as well as appropriate times and places to make use of them. Whether these codes were detected hinged on observers (some Jewish, many non-Jewish) who either read or ignored various signs of Jewishness. The same holds true today: to act as educated observers, we must probe beyond what is immediately visible to perceive forms of difference that might otherwise escape notice. We must learn not only to read the codes, but also to be receptive to their presence.

# Notes

## INTRODUCTION

1. Germany was not alone in perpetuating the notion that Jews could be assessed on the basis of visual characteristics. In the 1940s and 1950s, a number of sociological studies in the United States attempted to determine to what extent live subjects and photographic portraits could be assessed as Jewish, and with what degree of accuracy. Judgments were made on the basis of physical appearance as well as verbalization, regional accent, gestures, and name. One study conducted among undergraduates at the University of Pennsylvania determined that speech and gesture are stronger determinants than appearance. Interestingly, the female population was dropped from this study and was not factored into its findings. See Leonard D. Savitz and Richard F. Tomasson, "The Identifiability of Jews," *American Journal of Sociology* 64, no. 5 (March 1959): 468–75, here 474, 471n11. See also Sander L. Gilman, *Making the Body Beautiful: A Cultural History of Aesthetic Surgery* (Princeton: Princeton University Press, 1999), 192–93; and Matthew Frye Jacobson, *Whiteness of a Different Color: European Immigrants and the Alchemy of Race* (Cambridge: Harvard University Press, 1999), 171–99.

2. W. S., "Garnicht jüdisch," *Israelitisches Familienblatt* 27, no. 50 (December 10, 1925): 10; italics in original.

3. Katie Sutton has similarly identified the recurring trope of *sich bekennen* (to confess, to acknowledge openly) within the autobiographical writings of Weimar transvestites. Katie Sutton, "Sexological Cases and the Prehistory of Transgender Identity Politics in Interwar Germany," in *Case Studies and the Dissemination of Knowledge*, ed. Joy Damousi, Birgit Lang, and Katie Sutton (New York: Routledge, 2015), 85–103.

4. See, for example, the work of Sander Gilman and Peter Gay, who study the impulse for invisibility. Steven Aschheim and Jeanette Malkin also have written about the need to hide and conceal Jewishness in public. See Steven E. Aschheim, "Reflections on Theatricality, Identity, and the Modern Jewish Experience," and Jeanette Malkin, "Transforming in Public: Jewish Actors on the German Expressionist Stage," in *Jews and the Making of Modern German Theatre*, ed. Jeanette R. Malkin and Freddie Rokem (Iowa City: University of Iowa Press, 2010), 21–38 and 151–73.

5. See Michael Brenner, *The Renaissance of Jewish Culture in Weimar Germany* (New Haven: Yale University Press, 1996); Michael Berkowitz, *The Jewish Self-Image in the West* (New York: New York University Press, 2000); Abigail Gillman, *Viennese Jewish Modernism: Freud, Hofmannsthal, Beer-Hofmann, and Schnitzler* (University

Park: Pennsylvania State University Press, 2009); Lisa Silverman, *Becoming Austrians: Jews and Culture Between the World Wars* (New York: Oxford University Press, 2012); and Darcy C. Buerkle, *Nothing Happened: Charlotte Salomon and an Archive of Suicide* (Ann Arbor: University of Michigan Press, 2013).

6. Dual coding differs from code-switching in that it enables both identities to come through simultaneously. Henry Bial has theorized the "double coding" that was used by American Jewish performers to communicate different messages to Jewish and mainstream audiences, with reference to W. E. B. Du Bois's formulation of "double consciousness." Henry Bial, *Acting Jewish: Negotiating Ethnicity on the American Stage and Screen* (Ann Arbor: University of Michigan Press, 2005), 16–20. John Efron, too, draws on Du Bois to suggest that the "double consciousness" of German Jews led to "an acute self-consciousness." John M. Efron, *German Jewry and the Allure of the Sephardic* (Princeton: Princeton University Press, 2016), 7. Paul Mendes-Flohr has written about the dual or "bifurcated" (*zweiseitig*) nature of German Jews, a term he borrows from philosopher Walter Benjamin. Paul Mendes-Flohr, *German Jews: A Dual Identity* (New Haven: Yale University Press, 1999), 51 and 94. David Wertheim has suggested that Jews attempted "to have it both ways" in the polarized climate of the Weimar Republic. David J. Wertheim, *Salvation through Spinoza: A Study of Jewish Culture in Weimar Germany* (Leiden: Brill, 2011), 213. Till van Rahden uses the term "situational ethnicity" to refer to the social contingency of expressions of Jewishness. Till van Rahden, *Jews and Other Germans: Civil Society, Religious Diversity, and Urban Politics in Breslau, 1860–1925*, trans. Marcus Brainard (Madison: University of Wisconsin Press, 2008), 8–9.

7. Leora Auslander similarly points out that "clothes and carriage allow Jews to recognize each other while allowing them to 'pass' among those not raised in a Jewish milieu." Leora Auslander, "The Boundaries of Jewishness, or When Is a Cultural Practice Jewish?," *Journal of Modern Jewish Studies* 8, no. 1 (2009): 47–64; here 49.

8. The count determined that a proportionate number of Jews were stationed at the front. See Werner T. Angress, "The German Army's '*Judenzählung*' of 1916: Genesis—Consequences—Significance," *Leo Baeck Institute Year Book* 23 (1978): 117–38; Michael Brenner, "The German Army Orders a Census of Jewish Soldiers, and Jews Defend German Culture," in *Yale Companion to Jewish Writing and Thought in German Culture, 1096–1996*, ed. Sander L. Gilman and Jack Zipes (New Haven: Yale University Press, 1997), 348–54; Anton Kaes, *Shell Shock Cinema: Weimar Culture and the Wounds of War* (Princeton: Princeton University Press, 2009), 111; Tim Grady, *The German-Jewish Soldiers of the First World War in History and Memory* (Liverpool: Liverpool University Press, 2011); and Brian E. Crim, *Antisemitism in the German Military Community and the Jewish Response, 1914–1938* (Lanham, MD: Lexington Books, 2014), 10–13, 107–8.

9. Shulamit Volkov, *Germans, Jews, and Antisemites: Trials in Emancipation* (New York: Cambridge University Press, 2006), 263; and Shulamit Volkov, "The Dynamics of Dissimilation: *Ostjuden* and German Jews," in *The Jewish Response to German Culture from the Enlightenment to the Second World War*, ed. Jehuda Reinharz and Walter Schatzberg (Hanover, NH: University Press of New England, 1985), 195–211. On the term *dissimilation*, see Jonathan Skolnik, *Jewish Pasts, German Fictions: His-*

*tory, Memory, and Minority Culture in Germany, 1824–1955* (Stanford: Stanford University Press, 2014), 5–9.

10. Anson Rabinbach, *In the Shadow of Catastrophe: German Intellectuals between Apocalypse and Enlightenment* (Berkeley: University of California Press, 1997), 7.

11. See the essays in Michael Brenner and Derek J. Penslar, eds., *In Search of Jewish Community: Jewish Identities in Germany and Austria, 1918–1933* (Bloomington: Indiana University Press, 1998), especially Jacob Borut, "'Verjudung des Judentums': Was There a Zionist Subculture in Weimar Germany?," 92–114.

12. Rachel Seelig has argued that the Jewish culture of Weimar Berlin was "the product of a unique encounter in a particular time and place," namely one that brought together Eastern and Western Jews as well as German, Hebrew, and Yiddish. Rachel Seelig, *Strangers in Berlin: Modern Jewish Literature between East and West, 1919–1933* (Ann Arbor: University of Michigan Press, 2016), 8.

13. Elias Canetti, *The Torch in My Ear*, trans. Joachim Neugroschel (New York: Farrar, Straus and Giroux, 1982), 301. Translation cited in Sabine Rewald, Ian Buruma, and Matthias Eberle, *Glitter and Doom: German Portraits from the 1920s* (New York: Metropolitan Museum of Art, 2006), 148.

14. Insofar as I engage with discourses of self-regulation and the regulation of others, it is worth referencing Michel Foucault's argument that people police themselves in part by voluntarily seeing and agreeing to be seen, and that the economy of visibility correlates to exercising power. For the purposes of this study, however, the impulse to be seen represents resistance to a larger (self-)regulatory mechanism of concealment. Michel Foucault, *Discipline and Punish: The Birth of the Prison*, 2nd ed., trans. Alan Sheridan (New York: Vintage Books, 1995), 187.

15. Throughout this study, the capitalization of the terms *Black* and *White* indicates that they refer to culturally constructed and racialized social groups. I use the terms *sexual* and *queer passing* more or less interchangeably, and I understand the umbrella term *queer* to encompass LGBT identities.

16. I follow dictionary conventions in using the terms *passing for* and *passing as* interchangeably. Here I differ from scholars such as Pamela Caughie, who maintains that passing *for* something signifies a firm position, but that passing *as* is a metaphor that indicates one has no position or a fraudulent one. Pamela L. Caughie, *Passing and Pedagogy: The Dynamics of Responsibility* (Urbana: University of Illinois Press, 1999), 25 and 179. Additionally, I assume that passing refers to one widely acknowledged specific act, rather than a more dynamic or multidirectional one, as P. Gabrielle Foreman has suggested was prevalent in the nineteenth century. For example, Foreman cites the case of Ellen Craft, who passed for both White and male to escape from slavery in 1848 with her husband, William Craft, who posed as her slave. P. Gabrielle Foreman and Cherene Sherrard-Johnson, "Racial Recovery, Racial Death: An Introduction in Four Parts," *Legacy* 24, no. 2 (2007): 157–70; here 159. On the Crafts, see also Marjorie Garber, *Vested Interests: Cross-Dressing and Cultural Anxiety* (New York: Routledge, 1992), 282–85; Marcia Alesan Dawkins, *Clearly Invisible: Racial Passing and the Color of Cultural Identity* (Waco, TX: Baylor University Press, 2012), 31–46; and Allyson Hobbs, *A Chosen Exile: A History of Racial Passing in American Life* (Cambridge: Harvard University Press, 2014), 45–49.

17. My definition diverges from Todd Endelman's definition of Jewish passing as "the attempt to flee the Jewish community by assuming a non-Jewish identity and hiding evidence of Jewish birth and upbringing." Todd Endelman, *Leaving the Jewish Fold: Conversion and Radical Assimilation in Modern Jewish History* (Princeton: Princeton University Press, 2015), 16.

18. See Elaine K. Ginsberg, "Introduction: The Politics of Passing," in *Passing and the Fictions of Identity*, ed. Elaine K. Ginsberg (Durham, NC: Duke University Press, 1996), 1–18; here 4.

19. Werner Sollors, *Neither Black nor White, Yet Both: Thematic Explorations of Interracial Literature* (Cambridge: Harvard University Press, 1997), 250.

20. Linda Schlossberg, "Introduction: Rites of Passing," in *Passing: Identity and Interpretation in Sexuality, Race, and Religion*, ed. María Carla Sánchez and Linda Schlossberg (New York: New York University Press, 2001), 1–13; here 3. See also Gilman, *Making the Body Beautiful*, 331; and Hobbs, *Chosen Exile*, 132.

21. Kenji Yoshino, *Covering: The Hidden Assault on Our Civil Rights* (New York: Random House, 2007), xi; and Erving Goffman, *Stigma: Notes on the Management of Spoiled Identity* (1963; repr., New York: Simon and Schuster, 2009), 102–3, 129–30. Historian Deborah Hertz has applied Yoshino's model to German-Jewish history in the early nineteenth century. See Deborah Hertz, "Masquerades and Open Secrets, Or New Ways to Understand Jewish Assimilation," in *Versteckter Glaube oder doppelte Identität? Das Bild des Marranentums im 19. und 20. Jahrhundert/Concealed Faith or Double Identity? The Image of Marranism in the 19th and 20th Centuries*, ed. Anna-Dorothea Ludewig, Hannah Lotte Lund, and Paola Ferruta (Hildesheim: Georg Olms Verlag, 2011), 57–79.

22. Yoshino, *Covering,* 18–19.

23. Kurt Tucholsky, "Mr. Wendriner Makes a Phone Call," in *Berlin! Berlin! Dispatches from the Weimar Republic*, trans. Cindy Opitz (New York: Berlinica Publishing, 2013), 96–97; here 97. Abbreviations have been removed for clarity. This article was originally published on July 6, 1922, in *Die Weltbühne* under the pseudonym Kaspar Hauser.

24. On the notion of coming out as Jewish, see Jon Stratton, *Coming Out Jewish: Constructing Ambivalent Identities* (New York: Routledge, 2000); Daniel Itzkovitz, "Passing Like Me," *South Atlantic Quarterly* 98, nos. 1–2 (1999): 35–57; Daniel Itzkovitz, "Secret Temples," in *Jews and Other Differences: The New Jewish Cultural Studies*, ed. Jonathan Boyarin and Daniel Boyarin (Minneapolis: University of Minnesota Press, 1997), 176–202; and Eve Kosofsky Sedgwick, *Epistemology of the Closet* (Berkeley: University of California Press, 2008), 75.

25. Additionally, circumcision occasionally offered the evidence needed to ascertain a person's identity on a legal level. This was the case for Adolf Beck, a Norwegian imprisoned in London, who was pardoned when it was determined that he had been mistaken for John Smith, a criminal and a circumcised Jew. See Deborah Cohen, "Who Was Who? Race and Jews in Turn-of-the-Century Britain," *Journal of British Studies* 41, no. 4 (2002): 460–83. On debates about circumcision, see Robin Judd, *Contested Rituals: Circumcision, Kosher Butchering, and Jewish Political Life in Germany, 1843–1933* (Ithaca: Cornell University Press, 2007).

26. See Sander L. Gilman, *Jewish Self-Hatred: Anti-Semitism and the Hidden Language of the Jews* (Baltimore: Johns Hopkins University Press, 1986); Sander L. Gilman, *The Jew's Body* (New York: Routledge, 1991); Sander L. Gilman, *Freud, Race, and Gender* (Princeton: Princeton University Press, 1993); Jay Geller, *On Freud's Jewish Body: Mitigating Circumcisions* (New York: Fordham University Press, 2007); Jay Geller, *The Other Jewish Question: Identifying the Jew and Making Sense of Modernity* (New York: Fordham University Press, 2011); and Jonathan Boyarin and Daniel Boyarin, "Self-Exposure as Theory: The Double Mark of the Male Jew," in *Rhetorics of Self-making*, ed. Debbora Battaglia (Berkeley: University of California Press, 1995), 16–42.

27. Scholars including Marion Kaplan and Barbara Hahn have explicitly challenged the omission of women from the category "Jews" and from the writing of German-Jewish history. Marion A. Kaplan, *The Making of the Jewish Middle Class: Women, Family, and Identity in Imperial Germany* (Oxford: Oxford University Press, 1991), vii–viii; and Barbara Hahn, *The Jewess Pallas Athena: This Too a Theory of Modernity*, trans. James McFarland (Princeton: Princeton University Press, 2005), 30.

28. Sander L. Gilman, "Salome, Syphilis, Sarah Bernhardt, and the Modern Jewess," in *The Jew in the Text: Modernity and the Construction of Identity*, ed. Linda Nochlin and Tamar Garb (London: Thames and Hudson, 1995), 97–120.

29. See Buerkle, *Nothing Happened*, and Lisa Silverman, *Becoming Austrians*.

30. Badges, along with other material signs of otherness, contributed to what Mitchell Merback has termed a "veritable 'iconography of antisemitism' within European art," which is often tied to yellow symbols. Mitchell B. Merback, introduction to *Beyond the Yellow Badge: Anti-Judaism and Antisemitism in Medieval and Early Modern Visual Culture*, ed. Mitchell B. Merback (Boston: Brill, 2008), 1–29; here 6. Not all badges and distinctive clothing items worn by Jews were yellow—some were blue or red—and authorities sometimes changed the color simply to charge a fee. See also Alexander Maxwell, *Patriots against Fashion: Clothing and Nationalism in Europe's Age of Revolutions* (New York: Palgrave Macmillan, 2014), 51–52; Sabine Doran, *The Culture of Yellow: Or, the Visual Politics of Late Modernity* (New York: Bloomsbury, 2013), 5–8, 159–88; Flora Cassen, "From Iconic O to Yellow Hat: Anti-Jewish Distinctive Signs in Renaissance Italy," in *Fashioning Jews: Clothing, Culture, and Commerce*, ed. Leonard J. Greenspoon (West Lafayette, IN: Purdue University Press, 2013), 29–48; Marjorie Garber, "Category Crises: The Way of the Cross and the Jewish Star," in *Queer Theory and the Jewish Question*, ed. Daniel Boyarin, Daniel Itzkovitz, and Ann Pellegrini (New York: Columbia University Press, 2003), 19–40; and Garber, *Vested Interests*, 224.

31. Robert Jütte, "Stigma-Symbole. Kleidung als identitätstiftendes Merkmal bei spätmittelalterlichen und frühneuzeitlichen Randgruppen (Juden, Dirnen, Aussätzige, Bettler)," *Saeculum* 44, no. 1 (1993): 65–89; here 67. Cf. Roland Barthes's term *vestimentary signifier*. Roland Barthes, *The Fashion System*, trans. Matthew Ward and Richard Howard (Berkeley: University of California Press, 1983), 22.

32. See Guido Kisch, "The Yellow Badge in History," *Historia Judaica* 19, no. 2 (1957): 89–146. Additionally, historian Cornelia Aust is currently at work on a study of the dress and appearance of Jews in the early modern period. A portion of this project is

available online as "Jüdische Kleiderordnungen: Die visuelle Ordnung der früh-neuzeitlichen Gesellschaft."

33. The yellow passport was also referenced in German cultural texts about Eastern Europe, such as in the film *Der gelbe Schein* (*The Yellow Ticket*, Illés and Janson, 1918).

34. David Sorkin has argued that the endeavor to become indistinguishable led to the formation of a community that was invisible even to itself, suggesting that German Jews had to define their community. David Sorkin, *The Transformation of German Jewry, 1780–1840* (Detroit: Wayne State University Press, 1999), 6–7, 123, 177.

35. This statement applied specifically to the Russian Haskalah but is often, at times erroneously, applied retrospectively and more broadly to the Haskalah in other parts of Europe. See Michael Stanislawski, *For Whom Do I Toil? Judah Leib Gordon and the Crisis of Russian Jewry* (New York: Oxford University Press, 1988), 49–51.

36. A variation of this phrase was used by Zionists in Weimar Germany, as discussed below. See J. Ch. Brenner, "Zehn Jahre Hechaluz," *Jüdische Rundschau* 33, no. 23 (March 20, 1928): 165.

37. Roughly 25,000 Jews converted to Protestantism and Catholicism in Imperial Germany from 1880 to 1919. See Monika Richarz, "Demographic Developments," in *German-Jewish History in Modern Times*, vol. 3, *Integration in Dispute 1871–1918*, ed. Michael A. Meyer and Michael Brenner (New York: Columbia University Press, 1997), 7–34; here 15–16. See also Deborah Hertz, *How Jews Became Germans: The History of Conversion and Assimilation in Berlin* (New Haven: Yale University Press, 2007); Todd M. Endelman, "Gender and Conversion Revisited," in *Gender and Jewish History*, ed. Marion A. Kaplan and Deborah Dash Moore (Bloomington: Indiana University Press, 2011), 170–86; and Endelman, *Leaving the Jewish Fold*.

38. On race as not only skin deep, see Iris Idelson-Shein, *Difference of a Different Kind: Jewish Constructions of Race during the Long Eighteenth Century* (Philadelphia: University of Pennsylvania Press, 2014), 139.

39. On Jew Farces, see Katrin Sieg, *Ethnic Drag: Performing Race, Nation, and Sexuality in West Germany* (Ann Arbor: University of Michigan, 2002), 38–41.

40. Achim von Arnim, "Über die Kennzeichen des Judenthums," in Ludwig Achim von Arnim, *Texte der deutschen Tischgesellschaft*, ed. Stefan Nienhaus (Tübingen: Max Niemeyer Verlag, 2008), 107–28; here 109, 113. Translation cited in Martha Helfer, *The Word Unheard: Legacies of Anti-Semitism in German Literature and Culture* (Evanston, IL: Northwestern University Press, 2011), 65. See also Hertz, *How Jews*, 79–83.

41. Arnim, "Über die Kennzeichen," 115, 124. Martha Helfer carefully explicates Arnim's methods for sniffing out "the Jew," suggesting that Arnim "needs the Jew precisely to exclude 'the Jewish' from Christian German society." Helfer, *Word Unheard*, 66.

42. On changes in Berlin Jewish dress, see Steven M. Lowenstein, *The Berlin Jewish Community: Enlightenment, Family, and Crisis, 1770–1830* (New York: Oxford University Press, 1994), 44–46.

43. See Monika Richarz, "Jewish Women in the Family and Public Sphere," in Meyer and Brenner, *German-Jewish History*, vol. 3, 68–102; here 82. For additional population statistics, see Sharon Gillerman, *Germans into Jews: Remaking the Jewish Social Body in the Weimar Republic* (Stanford: Stanford University Press, 2009), 22.

44. Steven Aschheim differentiates between what he terms "Caftan" and "Cravat" types of Jewish men. Steven E. Aschheim, *Brothers and Strangers: The East European Jew in German and German Jewish Consciousness, 1800–1923* (Madison: University of Wisconsin Press, 1982), 58–79.

45. On women and the privatization of Jewishness along gender lines, see Paula E. Hyman, *Gender and Assimilation in Modern Jewish History: The Roles and Representation of Women* (Seattle: University of Washington Press, 1995); and Marion A. Kaplan, "Tradition and Transition: The Acculturation, Assimilation, and Integration of Jews in Imperial Germany—A Gender Analysis," *Leo Baeck Institute Year Book* 27 (1982): 3–35.

46. In memoirs composed in the 1820s, Henriette Herz described her aversion to the headdress (*Kopfzeug*) worn by most married Jewish women and the unofficial dispensation she received to wear a wig, and later to display her own hair. Henriette Herz, "Memoirs of a Jewish Girlhood," in *Bitter Healing: German Women Writers from 1700 to 1830: An Anthology*, ed. Jeannine Blackwell and Susanne Zantop (Lincoln: University of Nebraska Press, 1990), 303–31; here 319, 328.

47. R. Katzenellenbogen (sixteenth-century Padua), cited in Leila Leah Bronner, "From Veil to Wig: Jewish Women's Hair Covering," *Judaism* 42, no. 4 (1993): 464–77; here 472. On both women's and men's use of wigs, see Lowenstein, *Berlin Jewish Community*, 45–56.

48. Kaplan, *Making of the Jewish Middle Class*, 80.

49. See Esra Bennathan, "Die Demographische und wirtschaftliche Struktur der Juden," in *Entscheidungsjahr 1932. Zur Judenfrage in der Endphase der Weimarer Republik*, ed. Werner E. Mosse and Arnold Paucker (Tübingen: Mohr Siebeck, 1966), 87–134; here 94. The Jewish population of Berlin—which constituted 32 percent of German Jewry, and owned approximately half of all German-Jewish businesses—was concentrated in six central districts: Wilmersdorf, Charlottenburg, Mitte, Schöneberg, Prenzlauer Berg, and Tiergarten. See Christoph Kreutzmüller, *Final Sale in Berlin: The Destruction of Jewish Commercial Activity, 1930–1945*, trans. Jane Paulick and Jefferson Chase (New York: Berghahn Books, 2015), 75, 79.

50. "Eine jüdische Gasse im Berliner Norden," *Israelitisches Familienblatt* 32, no. 26 (June 26, 1930): 127. See also Thomas Raschke, ed., *Das Scheunenviertel. Spuren eines verlorenen Berlins* (Berlin: Haude & Spener, 1994), 112. This photomontage by Abraham Pisarek (1901–83) might have served as a response to antisemitic caricatures of Jews in the Scheunenviertel. See Aschheim, *Brothers and Strangers*, 222; Gillerman, *Germans into Jews*, 24; and Jack Wertheimer, *Unwelcome Strangers: East European Jews in Imperial Germany* (New York: Oxford University Press, 1987), 81. On Pisarek, see Joachim Schlör, ed., *Jüdisches Leben in Berlin, 1933–1941. Fotografien von Abraham Pisarek* (Berlin: Edition Braus, 2012). On the innovative use of photography in Weimar culture, see Daniel H. Magilow, *The Photography of Crisis: The Photo Essays of Weimar Germany* (University Park: Pennsylvania State University Press, 2012), 119–25.

51. On antisemitic violence in Weimar Germany, see Kreutzmüller, *Final Sale*, 99–102; Stephanie Seul, "Transnational Press Discourses on German Antisemitism during the Weimar Republic: The Riots in Berlin's Scheunenviertel, 1923," *Leo Baeck Institute*

*Year Book* 59 (2014): 91–120; David Clay Large, "'Out with the Ostjuden': The Scheunenviertel Riots in Berlin, November 1923," in *Exclusionary Violence: Antisemitic Riots in Modern German History*, ed. Christhard Hoffmann, Werner Bergmann, and Helmut Walser Smith (Ann Arbor: University of Michigan Press, 2002), 123–40; Dirk Walter, *Antisemitische Kriminalität und Gewalt: Judenfeindschaft in der Weimarer Republik* (Bonn: Dietz, 1999); Cornelia Hecht, *Deutsche Juden und Antisemitismus in der Weimarer Republik* (Bonn: Dietz, 2003); and Trude Maurer, *Ostjuden in Deutschland, 1918–1933* (Hamburg: H. Christians Verlag, 1986).

52. On Jewish self-defense organizations, see Avraham Barkai, "The Organized Jewish Community" and "Political Orientations and Crisis Consciousness," in *German-Jewish History in Modern Times*, vol. 4, *Renewal and Destruction 1918–1945*, ed. Michael A. Meyer and Michael Brenner (New York: Columbia University Press, 1998), 71–101 and 102–26; Avraham Barkai, *"Wehr dich!" Der Centralverein deutscher Staatsbürger jüdischen Glaubens (C.V.) 1893–1938* (Munich: Beck, 2002); and Ulrich Dunker, *Der Reichsbund jüdischer Frontsoldaten 1919–1938. Geschichte eines jüdischen Abwehrvereins* (Düsseldorf: Droste, 1977). On the impact of Jewish organizations on Jewish visibility, see Peter Pulzer, *Jews and the German State: The Political History of a Minority, 1848–1933* (Detroit: Wayne State University Press, 2003), 13.

53. In German: "Sei Jude zu Hause und Jude draußen." J. Ch. Brenner, "Zehn Jahre Hechaluz," 165.

54. Moshe Zimmermann, *Die deutschen Juden. 1914–1945* (Munich: R. Oldenbourg Verlag, 1997), 32.

55. The turn toward Jewish culture also responded in part to the "Kunstwart-Debate" of 1912, in which journalist Moritz Goldstein famously struck out against the notion of a German-Jewish symbiosis. Goldstein declared that "those Jews who are completely unaware, who continue to take part in German cultural activities, who pretend and persuade themselves that they are not recognized" were in fact grave enemies of Jewish success because they denied the way Jews were perceived. Moritz Goldstein, "Deutsch-jüdischer Parnass," *Der Kunstwart* 25 (1912): 281–94; here 283. Cited in Moritz Goldstein, "German Jewry's Dilemma: The Story of a Provocative Essay," *Leo Baeck Institute Year Book* 2 (1957): 236–54; here 244. See also Steven E. Aschheim, *In Times of Crisis: Essays on European Culture, Germans, and Jews* (Madison: University of Wisconsin Press, 2001), 64–72; and Mendes-Flohr, *German Jews*, 46–48.

56. Michael Brenner, *Renaissance*, 24.

57. For a discussion of how the visual language of films correlates to the Jewish experience of desiring not to be perceived as other, see Ofer Ashkenazi, *Weimar Film and Modern Jewish Identity* (New York: Palgrave Macmillan, 2012), 15.

58. See Peter Gay, *Freud, Jews and Other Germans: Masters and Victims in Modernist Culture* (New York: Oxford University Press, 1978), 99; and Peter Gay, *Weimar Culture: The Outsider as Insider* (1968; repr., New York: W. W. Norton, 2001).

59. Max Eschelbacher, "Die Sammlung der Zerstreuten. Vom neuen Marannentum unserer Tage," *Jüdisch-liberale Zeitung* 12, no. 23 (March 1, 1933): 1–2. Jonathan Skolnik contends that Hermann Sinsheimer's novel, *Maria Nunnez: Eine jüdische Überlieferung* (1934), written after the Nazi seizure of power, depicts marranos as "thinly veiled stand-ins for a great many German Jews in the 1930s." Skolnik, *Jewish Pasts*, 154.

60. Numerous autobiographical accounts discuss episodes of passing in Nazi Germany. See, for example, Anita Witt, *Passing: Growing Up in Hitler's Germany* (Lexington, KY: CreateSpace Independent Publishing Platform, 2014); and Reha Sokolow and Al Sokolow, with Debra Galant, *Defying the Tide: An Account of Authentic Compassion during the Holocaust* (Jerusalem: Devora Publishing Company, 2003).

61. See, for example, the discussion of Agnieszka Holland's film *Europa, Europa* (1990) in Jonathan Boyarin and Daniel Boyarin, "Self-Exposure as Theory," 22. See also Gilman, *Making the Body Beautiful*, 137–44.

62. Catherine Rottenberg contrasts Black and Jewish experiences in New York City to argue that Blacks faced greater pressure not to deny their Blackness by passing, which often resulted in relocating to a new neighborhood. Catherine Rottenberg, "The Making of an Icon: Early Representations of Harlem and the Lower East Side," in *Black Harlem and the Jewish Lower East Side: Narratives out of Time*, ed. Catherine Rottenberg (Albany: State University of New York Press, 2014), 29–42; here 39.

63. Endelman, *Leaving the Jewish Fold*, 111–12.

64. Wolfgang Maderthaner and Lisa Silverman, "'Wiener Kreise': Jewishness, Politics, and Culture in Interwar Vienna," in *Interwar Vienna: Culture between Tradition and Modernity*, ed. Deborah Holmes and Lisa Silverman (Rochester, NY: Camden House, 2009), 59–80; here 67; and Lisa Silverman, *Becoming Austrians*, 14.

65. Gillman, *Viennese Jewish Modernism*, 12; and Lisa Silverman, *Becoming Austrians*, 8. Further, Steven Beller has pointed out that the "negative consciousness" of Jewishness in Vienna—a desire to have escaped Jewishness, or pride in appearing non-Jewish—acknowledged Jewishness by dwelling on its absence. Steven Beller, *Vienna and the Jews, 1867–1938: A Cultural History* (New York: Cambridge University Press, 1989), 73–76.

66. Klaus Hödl, "The Blurring of Distinction: Performance and Jewish Identities in Late Nineteenth-Century Vienna," *European Journal of Jewish Studies* 3, no. 2 (2009): 229–49. See also Klaus Hödl's book-in-progress on the Jewish presence in Viennese popular culture around 1900.

67. Mary Gluck, *The Invisible Jewish Budapest: Metropolitan Culture at the Fin de Siècle* (Madison: University of Wisconsin Press, 2016), 192. Gluck borrows this term from Elaine Showalter.

68. Scott Spector, *Prague Territories: National Conflict and Cultural Innovation in Franz Kafka's Fin de Siècle* (Berkeley: University of California Press, 2000), 5. See also Marsha L. Rozenblit, "Jews, German Culture, and the Dilemma of National Identity: The Case of Moravia, 1848–1938," *Jewish Social Studies* 20, no. 1 (2013): 77–120.

69. Paula E. Hyman, *The Jews of Modern France* (Berkeley: University of California Press, 1998), 131.

70. Leora Auslander, "'Jewish Taste?' Jews and the Aesthetics of Everyday Life in Paris and Berlin, 1920–1942," in *Histories of Leisure*, ed. Rudy Koshar (Oxford: Berg, 2002), 299–318.

71. See Nadia Malinovich, *French and Jewish: Culture and the Politics of Identity in Early Twentieth-Century France* (Oxford: Littman Library of Jewish Civilization, 2008), 5–6; and Paula E. Hyman, *From Dreyfus to Vichy: The Remaking of French Jewry, 1906–1939* (New York: Columbia University Press, 1979).

72. Todd M. Endelman, *The Jews of Britain, 1656 to 2000* (Berkeley: University of California Press, 2002), 247. See also Deborah Cohen, "Who Was Who," 469.

73. Nathan Abrams, ed., *Hidden in Plain Sight: Jews and Jewishness in British Film, Television, and Popular Culture* (Evanston, IL: Northwestern University Press, 2016). This volume points to Jewish directors in interwar Britain such as Alexander Korda, who downplayed Jewishness and wrote Jewish characters out of his films, and to the greater visibility of Jewish characters after the Second World War.

74. Norman Kleeblatt defines Jewish passing in an American postwar context as "radical assimilation and clear separation of public persona from private self." Norman L. Kleeblatt, "'Passing' into Multiculturalism," in *Too Jewish? Challenging Traditional Identities*, ed. Norman L. Kleeblatt (New York: Jewish Museum, 1996), 3–38; here 5.

75. Aviva Ben-Ur, "Funny, You Don't Look Jewish! 'Passing' and the Elasticity of Ethnic Identity Among Levantine Sephardic Immigrants in Early 20th Century America," *Kolor: Journal on Moving Communities* 2 (2002): 9–18.

76. American Jews were racialized in different ways as their status within American culture shifted. See Elliott R. Barkan, Hasia Diner, and Alan M. Kraut, eds., *From Arrival to Incorporation: Migrants to the U.S. in a Global Era* (New York: New York University Press, 2008); Jacobson, *Whiteness*; and the scholarship of Karen Brodkin and David Roediger.

77. Itzkovitz, "Passing Like Me," 38–39.

78. Warren Hoffman, *The Passing Game: Queering Jewish American Culture* (Syracuse, NY: Syracuse University Press, 2009), 10.

79. On the intersections of queer passing and Jewishness, see Boyarin, Itzkovitz, and Pellegrini, *Queer Theory*; Matti Bunzl, *Symptoms of Modernity: Jews and Queers in Late-Twentieth-Century Vienna* (Berkeley: University of California Press, 1999); Ann Pellegrini, "Whiteface Performances: 'Race,' Gender, and Jewish Bodies," in Boyarin and Boyarin, *Jews and Other Differences*, 108–49; and Ann Pellegrini, *Performance Anxieties: Staging Psychoanalysis, Staging Race* (New York: Routledge, 1997). On Jewishness as a category akin to gender, see Lisa Silverman, *Becoming Austrians*, 6–7; and Maderthaner and Silverman, "Wiener Kreise," in Holmes and Silverman, *Interwar Vienna*, 62–64.

80. Sedgwick, *Epistemology*, 75.

81. Recent scholarship demonstrates that safe spaces for queer scenes or subcultures emerged in Weimar Germany, where the performance or free expression of these identities was often reserved for private spaces. See Katie Sutton, *The Masculine Woman in Weimar Germany* (New York: Berghahn Books, 2011); Katie Sutton, "'We Too Deserve a Place in the Sun': The Politics of Transvestite Identity in Weimar Germany," *German Studies Review* 35, no. 2 (2012): 335–54; and Laurie Marhoefer, *Sex and the Weimar Republic: German Homosexual Emancipation and the Rise of the Nazis* (Toronto: University of Toronto Press, 2015).

82. Frantz Fanon expressed frustration with the limits of comparing Blacks and Jews in his 1952 book: "The Jewishness of the Jew, however, can go unnoticed. . . . His acts and behaviors are the determining factor. He is a white man, and apart from some debatable features, he can pass undetected. . . . I am the slave not to the 'idea' others have of me, but to my appearance." Frantz Fanon, *Black Skin, White Masks*, trans. Rich-

ard Philcox (New York: Grove Press, 2008), 95. See also Bryan Cheyette, "Frantz Fanon and the Black-Jewish Imaginary," in *Frantz Fanon's* Black Skin, White Masks: *New Interdisciplinary Essays*, ed. Max Silverman (Manchester: Manchester University Press, 2005), 74–99.

83. See Clarence Lusane, *Hitler's Black Victims: The Historical Experiences of Afro-Germans, European Blacks, Africans, and African Americans in the Nazi Era* (New York: Routledge, 2003), 95–99; Larry A. Greene and Anke Ortlepp, eds., *Germans and African Americans: Two Centuries of Exchange* (Jackson: University Press of Mississippi, 2011); Eric J. Sundquist, *Strangers in the Land: Blacks, Jews, Post-Holocaust America* (Cambridge: Belknap Press of Harvard University Press, 2005), 182–86; Emily Miller Budick, *Blacks and Jews in Literary Conversation* (New York: Cambridge University Press, 1998), 67; and Hobbs, *Chosen Exile*, 128–29, 132. Several scholars have argued that constructions of race in Germany after the Second World War also built on American models of race. See Rita Chin, Heide Fehrenbach, Geoff Eley, and Atina Grossmann, *After the Nazi Racial State: Difference and Democracy in Germany and Europe* (Ann Arbor: University of Michigan Press, 2009).

84. Sara Ahmed, "'She'll Wake Up One of These Days and Find She's Turned into a Nigger': Passing through Hybridity," *Theory, Culture & Society* 16, no. 2 (1999): 87–106; here 87, 91. See also Sara Ahmed, "Some Striking Feature: Whiteness and Institutional Passing," presented at *Disrupting Visibility: The Politics of Passing*, June 12, 2105, Goldsmiths, http://feministkilljoys.com/2015/06/14/some-striking-feature-whiteness-and-institutional-passing/

85. Endelman, *Leaving the Jewish Fold*, 183.

86. Lori Harrison-Kahan, *The White Negress: Literature, Minstrelsy, and the Black-Jewish Imaginary* (New Brunswick, NJ: Rutgers University Press, 2011), 15. See also Daniel Itzkovitz, introduction to Fannie Hurst, *Imitation of Life*, ed. Daniel Itzkovitz (Durham, NC: Duke University Press, 2004), vii–xlv. The 1934 film version of *Imitation of Life* differs from the novel in that it challenges the ability of the passer (Peola Johnston) to sustain the loss of her family by having her return to attend her mother's funeral, after which Peola subsequently reenters the Black community. This corrective to Hurst's original ending to some extent positioned Hurst's work within the movement to counter African American passing, though Hurst remained a controversial figure.

87. Hurst, *Imitation of Life*, 36–37. When Bea Pullman celebrates her wedding at the Hotel Rudolph in Philadelphia, Hurst describes some members of its "wealthy Semitic clientele" as "heavy-busted, Oriental-eyed girls in heavy authentic jewelry." Further, several scholars have suggested that the use of the pseudonym "B. Pullman" is part of a strategy to pass as a man to be successful in business. See Harrison-Kahan, *White Negress*, 138; and Lauren Berlant, *The Female Complaint: The Unfinished Business of Sentimentality in American Culture* (Durham, NC: Duke University Press, 2008), 113–18.

88. For example, Philip Roth's *The Human Stain* (2000) tells of an African American male protagonist who successfully passes as a Jew for his adult life. Other works by Philip Roth, notably *Goodbye, Columbus* (1959) and *The Plot against America* (2004), also discuss Jewish recognizability. On Roth, see Sundquist, *Strangers in the Land*, 513–23; and Jennifer Glaser, *Borrowed Voices: Writing and Racial Ventriloquism in the*

*Jewish American Imagination* (New Brunswick, NJ: Rutgers University Press, 2016), 95–108.

89. Glaser, *Borrowed Voices*.

90. Ginsberg, "Introduction," *Passing and the Fictions of Identity*, 5.

91. Sollors, *Neither Black*, 255–56.

92. Graham Russell Hodges and Alan Edward Brown, eds., *"Pretends to Be Free": Runaway Slave Advertisements from Colonial and Revolutionary New York and New Jersey* (New York: Garland Publishing, 1994), 139, 193.

93. Hobbs, *Chosen Exile*, 36–41.

94. Passing Road (Route 625) in Essex County, Virginia, stands as a testament to Virginia's Act to Preserve Racial Integrity (1924). Essex borders Caroline County, which was home to Mildred and Richard Loving, plaintiffs in the 1967 Supreme Court case that invalidated the 1924 act. See Brooke Kroeger, *Passing: When People Can't Be Who They Are* (New York: Public Affairs, 2003), 47, 55–56. On the Virginia Act's role in amplifying the need to pass, see Hobbs, *Chosen Exile*, 128–32.

95. Hobbs, *Chosen Exile*, 178.

96. Carl Van Vechten's controversial novel *Nigger Heaven* (1926), which glosses *passing* as "i.e., passing for white," also helped popularize the term, though Van Vechten was White and affiliated only by association with the Harlem Renaissance. See Sollors, *Neither Black*, 247–84; here 247; and Hobbs, *Chosen Exile*, 178–79.

97. Harrison-Kahan, *White Negress*, 84; Glaser, *Borrowed Voices*, 99; Itzkovitz, "Passing Like Me"; and Sundquist, *Strangers in the Land*, 67.

98. Judith Butler, *Bodies That Matter: On the Discursive Limits of Sex* (New York: Routledge, 1993), 170.

99. Catherine Rottenberg, *Performing Americanness: Race, Class, and Gender in Modern African-American and Jewish-American Literature* (Lebanon, NH: Dartmouth College Press, 2008), 6.

100. Sara Ahmed, "She'll Wake Up." Laurence Roth posits something similar with respect to Jews, namely that forms of "kosher hybridity" in American Jewish contexts enable a kind of "cultural straddling." Laurence Roth, *Inspecting Jews: American Jewish Detective Stories* (New Brunswick, NJ: Rutgers University Press, 2004), 4.

101. Several recent essays explore the notion of German-Jewish *Anpassung*. See, for example, Liliane Weissberg, "Der Jude als Paria. Stationen in der Geschichte einer Idee im Diskurs der Assimilation," and Julius H. Schoeps, "Deutschlands Juden und ihr Anpassungsbemühen. Der Versuch, Bilanz in einer nach wie vor kontrovers geführten Debatte zu ziehen," in *Was war deutsches Judentum? 1870–1933*, ed. Christina von Braun (Berlin: De Gruyter Oldenbourg, 2015), 117–33 and 277–93.

102. Aischa Ahmed, "'Na ja, irgendwie hat man das ja gesehen'. Passing in Deutschland—Überlegungen zu Repräsentation und Differenz," in *Mythen, Masken und Subjekte. Kritische Weißseinsforschung in Deutschland*, ed. Maureen Maisha Eggers, Grada Kilomba, Peggy Piesche, and Susan Arndt (Münster: Unrast, 2005), 270–82.

103. For examples of the English word *passing* in German-language scholarship, see Aischa Ahmed's article cited above; Nike Thurn, *"Falsche Juden". Performative Identitäten in der deutschsprachigen Literatur von Lessing bis Walser* (Göttingen: Wallstein Verlag, 2015), 69–97; and Geertje Mak, "'Passing Women' im Sprechzimmer von Mag-

nus Hirschfeld: Warum der Begriff 'Transvestit' nicht für Frauen in Männerkleidern eingeführt wurde," *Österreichische Zeitschrift für Geschichtswissenschaften* 9, no. 3 (1998): 384–99.

104. See Janet Liebman Jacobs, *Hidden Heritage: The Legacy of the Crypto-Jews* (Berkeley: University of California Press, 2002), 30–31; Gilman, *Jewish Self-Hatred*, 270; and Ludewig, Lund, and Ferruta, eds., *Versteckter Glaube oder doppelte Identität? /Concealed Faith or Double Identity?*.

105. Aschheim, *Brothers and Strangers*, 94.

106. On the figure of the *daytsh*, see Dan Miron, *The Image of the Shtetl and Other Studies of the Modern Jewish Literary Imagination* (Syracuse, NY: Syracuse University Press, 2000), 26–31.

107. Maria Makela, "Rejuvenation and Regen(d)eration: *Der Steinachfilm*, Sex Glands, and Weimar-Era Visual and Literary Culture," *German Studies Review* 38, no. 1 (2015): 35–62; here 56; and Maria Makela, "Mistaken Identity in Fritz Lang's *Metropolis*," in *The New Woman International: Representations in Photography and Film from the 1870s through the 1960s*, ed. Elizabeth Otto and Vanessa Rocco (Ann Arbor: University of Michigan Press, 2011), 175–93.

108. I intentionally omit the pairing German/Jewish, which was not understood as an oppositional pair by many German Jews. See Todd Samuel Presner, *Mobile Modernity: Germans, Jews, Trains* (New York: Columbia University Press, 2007), 7.

109. Sara Ahmed, *Strange Encounters: Embodied Others in Post-Coloniality* (New York: Routledge, 2000), 6.

110. Iris Idelson-Shein has demonstrated that eighteenth-century European Jews revised and adapted emerging anthropological discourses about race to suit their own needs. Idelson-Shein, *Difference*, 4.

111. Mitchell Hart has noted that the matter of biology versus environment became central by the middle of the nineteenth century, when it was widely believed that Jews shared a common "racial nature." Mitchell B. Hart, "Jews and Race: An Introductory Essay," in *Jews and Race: Writings on Identity and Difference, 1880–1940*, ed. Mitchell B. Hart (Waltham, MA: Brandeis University Press, 2011), xv.

112. See John M. Efron, *Defenders of the Race: Jewish Doctors and Race Science in Fin-de-Siècle Europe* (New Haven: Yale University Press, 1994).

113. See Stefan Vogt, "Between Decay and Doom: Zionist Discourses of '*Untergang*' in Germany, 1890 to 1933," in *The German-Jewish Experience Revisited*, ed. Steven E. Aschheim and Vivian Liska (Berlin: Walter de Gruyter, 2015), 75–102. See also the pieces by Ruppin and Theilhaber in Hart, *Jews and Race*; Steven M. Lowenstein, "Religious Life," in Meyer and Brenner, *German-Jewish History*, vol. 3, 103–24; here 122; and Mitchell B. Hart, *Social Science and the Politics of Modern Jewish Identity* (Stanford: Stanford University Press, 2000).

114. Auslander, "Boundaries of Jewishness," 49.

115. On non-Jewish German literary figures that passed for Jews, see Thurn, *Falsche Juden*, 69–97. Elliot Ratzman writes about this general phenomenon, which he has termed *downpassing*, in his current book project, "Becoming the Other: The Religious and Ethical Dimensions of Downpassing." In American culture, perhaps the best-known example of a non-Jew who attempts to pass for a Jew is Phil Green in the film *Gentle-*

*man's Agreement* (Kazan, 1947), based on Laura Z. Hobson's novel. See Jacobson, *Whiteness*, 125–31. Another well-known and more recent example of someone who engaged in reverse passing is Rachel Dolezal, an activist who resigned from her position as a chapter president of the NAACP in 2015, when it was alleged that she misrepresented herself as African American.

116. "Ihre Erscheinung bestimmt Ihr Leben," advertisement for Bihlmaier's Institut, *C.V.-Zeitung* 11, no. 18 (April 29, 1932): 177. Recurring advertisements for Bihlmaier's Institute in Berlin appeared in the *C.V.-Zeitung* and *Das jüdische Magazin* from 1929 to 1932; ads for a different Munich clinic appeared in *Das Jüdische Echo*. See Annelie Ramsbrock, *The Science of Beauty: Culture and Cosmetics in Modern Germany, 1750–1930*, trans. David Burnett (New York: Palgrave Macmillan, 2015), 137–39; Katharina von Ankum, "Karriere—Konsum—Kosmetik. Zur Ästhetik des weiblichen Gesichts," in *Gesichter der Weimarer Republik. Eine Physiognomische Kulturgeschichte*, ed. Claudia Schmölders and Sander L. Gilman (Bonn: VG Bild-Kunst, 1999), 175–90; and Gilman, *Making the Body Beautiful*.

117. Marion Kaplan, among others, has pointed to the growing importance of biology for Jewish women in light of the antisemitism prevalent during the first half of the twentieth century. I do not contest this argument; rather, my claim deals with responses to antisemitism in the form of concealing or revealing Jewishness. See Marion A. Kaplan, "Sisterhood under Siege: Feminism and Anti-Semitism in Germany, 1904–1938," in *When Biology Became Destiny: Women in Weimar and Nazi Germany*, ed. Renate Bridenthal, Atina Grossmann, and Marion A. Kaplan (New York: Monthly Review Press, 1984), 174–96.

118. Liz Conor, *The Spectacular Modern Woman: Feminine Visibility in the 1920s* (Bloomington: Indiana University Press, 2004), 29. On the changing roles of women, see Julia Sneeringer, *Winning Women's Votes: Propaganda and Politics in Weimar Germany* (Chapel Hill: University of North Carolina Press, 2002).

119. On the New Woman, see Katharina von Ankum, ed., *Women in the Metropolis: Gender and Modernity in Weimar Culture* (Berkeley: University of California Press, 1997); Patrice Petro, *Joyless Streets: Women and Melodramatic Representation in Weimar Germany* (Princeton: Princeton University Press, 1989); Richard W. McCormick, *Gender and Sexuality in Weimar Modernity: Film, Literature, and "New Objectivity"* (New York: Palgrave, 2001); Christiane Schönfeld, ed., *Practicing Modernity: Female Creativity in the Weimar Republic* (Würzberg: Königshausen & Neumann, 2006); Janet Ward, *Weimar Surfaces: Urban Visual Culture in 1920s Germany* (Berkeley: University of California Press, 2001), 81–90; and Otto and Rocco, *New Woman International*.

120. Figure 3 depicts Luzie Hatch (1912–2001, born Hecht) with her stepmother Helene in Berlin in the 1930s. See Charlotte R. Bonelli, *Exit Berlin: How One Woman Saved Her Family from Nazi Germany* (New Haven: Yale University Press, 2014).

121. Mary Ann Doane explains that Weimar society continually tested the limits of sexuality through experimentation with transgression and exhibitionism. Mary Ann Doane, *Femmes Fatales: Feminism, Film Theory, Psychoanalysis* (New York: Routledge, 1991), 142–43.

122. On the New Jewish Woman, see Claudia T. Prestel, "The 'New Jewish Woman' in Weimar Germany," in *Jüdisches Leben in der Weimarer Republik/Jews in the Weimar*

*Republic*, ed. Wolfgang Benz, Arnold Paucker, and Peter Pulzer (Tübingen: Mohr Siebeck, 1998), 135–56; Claudia T. Prestel, "Die deutsch-jüdische Presse und die weibliche Sexualität: 'Freie Liebe' oder die Rückkehr zu traditionellem jüdischem Familienleben?" in *Frauen und Frauenbilder in der europäisch-jüdischen Presse von der Aufklärung bis 1945*, ed. Eleonore Lappin and Michael Nagel (Bremen: edition lumière bremen, 2007), 123–41; Harriet Pass Freidenreich, "Jewish Identity and the 'New Woman': Central European Jewish University Women in the Early Twentieth Century," in *Gender and Judaism: The Transformation of Tradition*, ed. Tamar M. Rudavsky (New York: New York University Press, 1995), 113–22; Harriet Pass Freidenreich, "Die jüdische 'Neue Frau' des frühen 20. Jahrhunderts," in *Deutsch-jüdische Geschichte als Geschlechtergeschichte: Studien zum 19. und 20. Jahrhundert*, ed. Kirsten Heinsohn and Stefanie Schüler-Springorum (Göttingen: Wallstein Verlag, 2006), 123–32; Harriet Pass Freidenreich, "How Central European Jewish Women Confronted Modernity," in *Women and Judaism: New Insights and Scholarship*, ed. Frederick E. Greenspahn (New York: New York University Press, 2009), 131–52; and Atina Grossmann, "Die Sexualreform und die 'Neue Frau': Wie jüdisch waren sie?," in Braun, *Was war deutsches Judentum*, 262–74.

## CHAPTER 1

1. Sammy Gronemann, *Schalet. Beiträge zur Philosophie des "Wenn schon"*, afterword by Joachim Schlör, 2nd ed. (Leipzig: Reclam Verlag, 1998), 48. At least 5,000 copies of *Schalet* were published by Jüdischer Verlag in 1927, and it was serialized in the "Jüdische Bibliothek" supplement of *Israelitisches Familienblatt* in February–April 1928, suggesting that as many as 100,000 readers had access to it within a year of its publication. Many anecdotes seem to be autobiographical; there is some overlap between the stories in *Schalet* and those in Gronemann's memoirs. See Sammy Gronemann, *Erinnerungen an meine Jahre in Berlin*, ed. Joachim Schlör (Berlin: Philo Verlag, 2004).

2. One historian's travelogue relates a similar situation in Rome, in which the word *shalom* resulted in a supposedly unprecedented mutual recognition between Jews (*Stammesgenossen*) not far from the Arch of Titus, which Italian Jews had traditionally avoided. Ermanno Loevinson, *Roma Israelitica. Wanderungen eines Juden durch die Kunststätten Roms* (Frankfurt am Main: J. Kauffmann Verlag, 1927), 5.

3. Gronemann, *Schalet*, 126–35; here 135.

4. John Efron explores intersections of the categories "Oriental" and "Sephardic," other valences of the term "Eastern" that were at times relevant for idealized beauty, and particularly that of Jewish women. See Efron, *German Jewry*, 94–95, 100–101. On constructions of Jewish women as "Oriental," see also Hahn, *Jewess Pallas Athena*, 30–41; and Ulrike Brunotte, Anna-Dorothea Ludewig, and Axel Stähler, eds., *Orientalism, Gender, and the Jews: Literary and Artistic Transformations of European National Discourses* (Berlin: De Gruyter Oldenbourg, 2015).

5. Darcy Buerkle, "Gendered Spectatorship, Jewish Women and Psychological Advertising in Weimar Germany," *Women's History Review* 15, no. 4 (2006): 625–36; here 631.

6. See, for example, Gilman, *Freud, Race, and Gender*; Daniel Boyarin, *Unheroic Conduct: The Rise of Heterosexuality and the Invention of the Jewish Man* (Berkeley: University of California Press, 1997); Benjamin Maria Baader, *Gender, Judaism, and Bourgeois Culture in Germany, 1800–1870* (Bloomington: Indiana University Press, 2006); and Benjamin Maria Baader, "Jewish Difference and the Feminine Spirit of Judaism in Mid-Nineteenth-Century Germany," in *Jewish Masculinities: German Jews, Gender, and History*, ed. Benjamin Maria Baader, Sharon Gillerman, and Paul Lerner (Bloomington: Indiana University Press, 2012), 50–71.

7. See discussions below of anthropologists Arkadius Elkind and Maurice Fishberg.

8. For example, Jewish art historian Aby Warburg (1866–1929) experienced outsider status partly due to his dark complexion and short stature. On Warburg and Jewish life in Hamburg more broadly, see Emily J. Levine, *Dreamland of Humanists: Warburg, Cassirer, Panofsky, and the Hamburg School* (Chicago: University of Chicago Press, 2013), 35.

9. Writing in 1947, philosopher Jean-Paul Sartre summarized how antisemites perceived Jews, implying that personal identification is shaped in part by how one is seen: "He is a Jew, the son of Jews, recognizable by his physique, by the color of his hair, by his clothing perhaps, and, so they say, by his character." Jean-Paul Sartre, *Anti-Semite and Jew: An Exploration of the Etiology of Hate*, trans. George J. Becker (New York: Schocken Books, 1995), 10. See also Stratton, *Coming Out Jewish*, 11.

10. On the ways Jewish communities were constituted, including distinctions between the concepts of *Gesellschaft*, *Gemeinschaft*, and *Gemeinde*, see Brenner and Penslar, *In Search of Jewish Community*.

11. Gay, *Freud, Jews and Other Germans*, 181–83.

12. Ginsberg, "Introduction," *Passing and the Fictions of Identity*, 4.

13. On Lavater, see Ellis Shookman, ed., *The Faces of Physiognomy: Interdisciplinary Approaches to Johann Caspar Lavater* (Columbia, SC: Camden House, 1993); Geller, *Other Jewish Question*, 21–23; and Jonathan M. Hess, *Germans, Jews and the Claims of Modernity* (New Haven: Yale University Press, 2002).

14. Jonathan M. Hess, "Jewish Emancipation and the Politics of Race," in *The German Invention of Race*, ed. Sara Eigen and Mark Larrimore (Albany: State University of New York Press, 2006), 203–12; and Hess, *Germans, Jews*, 25–49.

15. Idelson-Shein, *Difference*, 110.

16. Cited in Hess, *Germans, Jews*, 83. See also Jonathan M. Hess, "Johann David Michaelis and the Colonial Imaginary: Orientalism and the Emergence of Racial Antisemitism in Eighteenth-Century Germany," *Jewish Social Studies* 6, no. 2 (2000): 56–101.

17. This was not a new phenomenon; Elisheva Carlebach has documented the suspicions raised against Jewish converts in the early modern period, which arose partly because many convicted criminals were offered conversion to mitigate their punishment. Elisheva Carlebach, *Divided Souls: Converts from Judaism in Germany, 1500–1750* (New Haven: Yale University Press, 2001), 33–46.

18. See Endelman, *Leaving the Jewish Fold*, 312.

19. Idelson-Shein, *Difference*, 137.

20. Valerie Weinstein, "'White Jews' and Dark Continents: Capitalist Critique and its Racial Undercurrents in Detlef Sierck's *April! April!* (1935)," in *Continuity and Crisis in German Cinema, 1928–1936*, ed. Barbara Hales, Mihaela Petrescu, and Valerie Weinstein (Rochester, NY: Camden House, 2016), 132–48.

21. Gilman, *Jew's Body*, 171–76. See also Geller, *Other Jewish Question*, 219.

22. Gilman, *Freud, Race, and Gender*, 20–22, 33; and Gilman, "Salome, Syphilis," 104.

23. On *The City without Jews*, see Lisa Silverman, *Becoming Austrians*, 66–102; here 69.

24. Artur Landsberger, *Berlin ohne Juden* (Hannover: Paul Steegemann Verlag, 1925), 16. This novel was also serialized in *Israelitisches Familienblatt* 27, no. 43–50 (October–December 1925). On Bettauer, see Beth Simone Noveck, "1925: Hugo Bettauer's Assassination by Otto Rothstock in Vienna Marks the First Political Murder by the Nazis in Austria," in Sander L. Gilman and Jack Zipes, eds., *Yale Companion to Jewish Writing and Thought in German Culture, 1096–1996* (New Haven: Yale University Press, 1997), 440–47.

25. See Geller, *Other Jewish Question*, 243.

26. Jack Zipes, *The Operated Jew: Two Tales of Anti-Semitism* (New York: Routledge, 1991), 48. See also Aschheim, "Reflections on Theatricality," 25–26; and Joela Jacobs, "Assimilating Aliens: Imagining National Identity in Oskar Panizza's *Operated Jew* and Salomo Friedlaender's *Operated Goy*," in *Alien Imaginations: Science Fiction and Tales of Transnationalism*, ed. Ulrike Küchler, Silja Maehl, and Graeme Stout (New York: Bloomsbury Academic, 2015), 57–72.

27. This is also the topic of American writer Jess Row's novel *Your Face in Mine* (2014).

28. George Schuyler, *Black No More* (Boston: Northeastern University Press, 1989), 154. See also Mar Gallego, *Passing Novels in the Harlem Renaissance: Identity Politics and Textual Strategies* (Münster: LIT Verlag, 2003), 100.

29. Schuyler, *Black No More*, 24.

30. See David M. Goldenberg, *The Curse of Ham: Race and Slavery in Early Judaism, Christianity, and Islam* (Princeton: Princeton University Press, 2003), 178–82.

31. Joseph Roth, *The Wandering Jews*, trans. Michael Hofmann (New York: W. W. Norton, 2001), 19; and Joseph Roth, *Juden auf Wanderschaft* (Munich: Deutscher Taschenbuch Verlag, 2006), 20.

32. Ruth Mellinkoff, *The Mark of Cain* (Eugene, OR: Wipf and Stock, 1981), 27–29.

33. "The Princess and the Seven Geese (1714–22)," in *No Star Too Beautiful: Yiddish Stories from 1382 to the Present*, ed. and trans. Joachim Neugroschel (New York: W. W. Norton, 2002), 84–91.

34. Ossip Dymow, "Das Zeichen," *Jüdische Rundschau* 33, no. 68 (August 28, 1928): 487. From 1927 to 1932, Dymow spent time in Berlin and worked with Max Reinhardt. On Dymow, see Kay Weniger, *"Es wird im Leben dir mehr genommen als gegeben . . .". Lexikon der aus Deutschland und Österreich emigrierten Filmschaffenden 1933 bis 1945* (Hamburg: ACABUS Verlag, 2011), 569–70.

35. See, for example, Lasker-Schüler's poem "Gebet" (Prayer) from 1917, in *Star in*

*My Forehead: Selected Poems by Else Lasker-Schüler*, trans. Janine Canan (Duluth, MN: Holy Cow! Press, 2000), 93.

36. John Höxter, "Die Dichterin Else Lasker-Schüler," *Schlemiel. Jüdische Blätter für Humor und Kunst*, no. 8 (1919): 119. Under Nazi rule, some Polish Jews were branded with a Star of David on their foreheads. One notable example of branding in twenty-first-century popular culture, Quentin Tarantino's film *Inglourious Basterds* (2009), envisions a reversal of this practice in the form of Jews who carve swastikas into the foreheads of captured Nazis. In a different assessment of Weimar-era branding, Todd Herzog has drawn a parallel between the Star of David that the Nazis required Jews to wear and the chalk letter "M" that brands child-murderer Beckert at the end of Fritz Lang's film *M* (1930), suggesting that stigmatized markers of Jewishness followed in a line of markers of criminality. Todd Herzog, *Crime Stories: Criminalistic Fantasy and the Culture of Crisis in Weimar Germany* (New York: Berghahn Books, 2009), 133, 138. See also Doran, *Culture of Yellow*, 159–60.

37. Andrew Zimmerman, "Anti-Semitism as Skill: Rudolf Virchow's 'Schulstatis-tik' and the Racial Composition of Germany," *Central European History* 32, no. 4 (1999): 409–29; here 413.

38. Andrew Zimmerman, "Anti-Semitism as Skill," 423.

39. Gilman, *Jew's Body*, 177; and Andrew Zimmerman, "Anti-Semitism as Skill," 409.

40. Arkadius Elkind, "Anthropological Research on the Russian-Polish Jews, and the Value of This Research for the Anthropology of the Jews in General," in Hart, *Jews and Race*, 81–86. Elkind's essay first appeared in the *Zeitschrift für Demographie und Statistik der Juden* 2, no. 4 (1906): 49–54, and 2, no. 5 (1906): 65–69. Elkind, a Russian physician and anthropologist, compiled statistics about hair and eye color among Jews in Eastern Europe, concluding that Polish Jews were most likely to have both dark hair and dark eyes.

41. On Maurice Fishberg's study, *The Jews: A Study of Race and Environment* (1911; German translation published in 1913), see Efron, *German Jewry*, 100; and Amos Morris-Reich, *Race and Photography: Racial Photography as Scientific Evidence, 1876–1980* (Chicago: University of Chicago Press, 2016), 101–7.

42. On constructions of race and fantasies about Jews in the psychoanalytic movement, see Veronika Fuechtner, *Berlin Psychoanalytic: Psychoanalysis and Culture in Weimar Republic Germany* (Berkeley: University of California Press, 2011).

43. See Boyarin, *Unheroic Conduct*.

44. Weininger's *Geschlecht und Charakter* was published only a few months before his suicide in 1903. On Weininger and self-hatred, see Gilman, *Jewish Self-Hatred*, 293–94; and Paul Reitter, *On the Origins of Jewish Self-Hatred* (Princeton: Princeton University Press, 2012), 10–11.

45. Pellegrini, "Whiteface Performances," in Boyarin and Boyarin, *Jews and Other Differences*, 112–13; Pellegrini, *Performance Anxieties*, 17–38; Gilman, *Jew's Body*, 81; and Gilman, *Freud, Race, and Gender*, 44.

46. Walter Rathenau, "Hear, O Israel!," in *The Jew in the Modern World: A Documentary History*, 3rd ed., ed. Paul Mendes-Flohr and Jehuda Reinharz (New York: Oxford University Press, 2010), 814–17. First published as Walter Hartenau, "Hoere, Is-

rael!," *Zukunft* 18 (March 16, 1897): 454–62. Rathenau later removed this text from his collected works. See also Shulamit Volkov, *Walther Rathenau: Weimar's Fallen Statesman* (New Haven: Yale University Press, 2012), 45–59.

47. Michael Brenner has suggested that even liberal Jews who were opposed to the concept of a racialized Jewish nation referred to themselves as a *Stammesgemeinschaft* or *Abstammungsgemeinschaft*, a collective ethnic group of common descent. The term *Schicksalsgemeinschaft* (community of common fate) was also used. Michael Brenner, *Renaissance*, 37, 49; and Brenner and Penslar, introduction to Brenner and Penslar, *In Search of Jewish Community*, x. On German Jews and ethnicity, see also David A. Brenner, *Marketing Identities: The Invention of Jewish Ethnicity in Ost und West* (Detroit: Wayne State University Press, 1998), 54–56; Shulamit Volkov, "Talking of Jews, Thinking of Germans—The Ethnic Discourse in 19th Century Germany," *Tel Aviver Jahrbuch für deutsche Geschichte* 30 (2002): 37–49; and Rahden, *Jews and Other Germans*, 9–11. Marsha Rozenblit's work also treats Jewish ethnic identity in Austria. See, for example, Marsha L. Rozenblit, *Reconstructing a National Identity: The Jews of Habsburg Austria during World War I* (Oxford: Oxford University Press, 2001).

48. See Fritz Kahn excerpt in Hart, *Jews and Race*, 24–29. See also John Efron, "Scientific Racism and the Mystique of Sephardic Racial Superiority," *Leo Baeck Institute Year Book* 38 (1993): 75–96; here 91; and Michael Brenner, *Renaissance*, 48–49. Kahn also contributed to Jewish periodicals including the Berlin *Gemeindeblatt*.

49. Sammy Gronemann, *Remembrances*, undated manuscript written before 1947; excerpted in Monika Richarz, ed., *Jewish Life in Germany: Memoirs from Three Centuries*, trans. Stella P. Rosenfeld and Sidney Rosenfeld (Bloomington: Indiana University Press, 1991), 258–66; here 260.

50. See H. Unikower, "Die jüdische Nase," *Israelitisches Familienblatt* 27, no. 7 (February 12, 1925): 14–15. Unikower complained that the wanted poster issued by a Berlin court for the *Berliner Tageblatt* described suspect Heinrich David's nose as a Jewish nose.

51. On noses and nose jobs, see Gilman, *Jew's Body*, 169–93; and Gilman, *Making the Body Beautiful*. On gendered accusations of bodily excess with respect to noses and other features, see Tahneer Oksman, *"How Come Boys Get to Keep Their Noses?" Women and Jewish American Identity in Contemporary Graphic Memoirs* (New York: Columbia University Press, 2016).

52. The Zionist notion of a "community of blood" can be traced to Martin Buber's 1909 speech, "Judaism and the Jews." David Biale, *Blood and Belief: The Circulation of a Symbol between Jews and Christians* (Berkeley: University of California Press, 2007), 184–85. On *Muskeljudentum*, see Michael Stanislawski, *Zionism and the Fin de Siècle: Cosmopolitanism and Nationalism from Nordau to Jabotinsky* (Berkeley: University of California Press, 2001), 91–100; and Michael Brenner and Gideon Reuveni, eds., *Emancipation through Muscles: Jews and Sports in Europe* (Lincoln: University of Nebraska Press, 2006). On the *Volkskörper*, see Gillerman, *Germans into Jews*, 53–54. For an example of a liberal text in favor of using agriculture, gardening, and sports to counteract stereotypes about weak Jewish bodies, see Jakob Lederman, "Land!," *Der Schild* 4, no. 4 (February 15, 1925): 69–70.

53. See Hart, *Social Science,* 86; and Gillerman, *Germans into Jews,* 57, 60–63, 68–69. See also the writings of Ruppin and Theilhaber in Hart, *Jews and Race.*

54. On Zionism and gender, see Boyarin, *Unheroic Conduct,* 271–312. On antisemitic perceptions of the Jewish body, see Gilman, *Jew's Body;* Geller, *Other Jewish Question;* and Eric D. Weitz, *Weimar Germany: Promise and Tragedy* (Princeton: Princeton University Press, 2007), 320–21.

55. This question was posed in many different forums, both for Jewish audiences and for much broader audiences. See, for example, Sigmund Feist, "Sind die Juden eine Rasse?," *Zeitschrift für Demographie und Statistik der Juden* 4, nos. 1–2 (1927): 6–11; and Feist, "Are the Jews a Race?" in Hart, *Jews and Race,* 87–94. On Feist, see Morris-Reich, *Race and Photography,* 107–13. See also the discussion of Karl Kautsky's book, *Are the Jews a Race?* (1926), in Biale, *Blood and Belief,* 187.

56. Maurice Fishberg put forth one popular scientific argument that Jews in different lands came to resemble their neighbors. See the preface to Fishberg's study in Hart, *Jews and Race,* 21–23; and Biale, *Blood and Belief,* 187.

57. "Gibt es eine 'jüdische Rasse'?," *Israelitisches Familienblatt* 26, no. 22 (May 29, 1924): 11.

58. Constantin Brunner as cited in Julius Michelson, "Die Wertung der Juden in der modernen Rassenforschung," *Israelitisches Familienblatt* 30, no. 48 (November 29, 1928): 1. This passage also appears in Constantin Brunner, *Der Judenhass und die Juden* (Berlin: Oesterheld, 1918), 52.

59. Constantin Brunner, *Von den Pflichten der Juden und von den Pflichten des Staates* (Berlin: Gustav Kiepenheuer, 1930), 161. See also Andreas Kilcher, "'Das Gebot der Anpassung': Constantin Brunners Ausweg aus dem Judentum," in *Constantin Brunner im Kontext: Ein Intellektueller zwischen Kaiserreich und Exil,* ed. Irene Aue-Ben-David, Gerhard Lauer, and Jürgen Stenzel (Berlin: De Gruyter Oldenbourg, 2014), 269–90.

60. This article appeared in *Preußische Jahrbücher* in August 1931; a response was published in the *C.V.-Zeitung* shortly thereafter. See Eva Reichmann-Jungmann, "Leben oder Untergang? Eine Antwort an Constantin Brunner," *C.V.-Zeitung* 10, no. 42 (October 16, 1931): 495–96. See also Barkai, *Wehr dich,* 238–45.

61. Brunner, *Der Judenhass und die Juden,* 39.

62. See, for example, Rudolf Wertheimer, "Rasse und Recht," *Israelitisches Familienblatt* 33, no. 23 (June 4, 1931): 1.

63. Ludwig Ferdinand Clauß, *Von Seele und Antlitz der Rassen und Völker. Eine Einführung in die vergleichende Ausdrucksforschung* (Munich: J. F. Lehmanns Verlag, 1929). On editor Heinz Caspari's reception of Clauß, see Peter Weingart, *Doppel-Leben: Ludwig Ferdinand Clauss—Zwischen Rassenforschung und Widerstand* (Frankfurt am Main: Campus Verlag, 1995), 34.

64. "Einleitung der Redaktion: Von Seele und Antlitz der Juden," *Israelitisches Familienblatt* 31, no. 24 (June 13, 1929): 348. The final installment from Ludwig Ferdinand Clauß's work appeared in no. 38 (September 19, 1929): 406. Clauß's terms here are *wüstenländisch* (Oriental), *vorderasiatisch* (Near Eastern), and *mittelländisch* (Central European). In 1941, Clauß wrote that Jews had become increasingly difficult to recognize, a position that was not well received in Nazi Germany. See Morris-Reich, *Race and Photography,* 162.

65. On Hans F. K. Günther (1891–1968), see Morris-Reich, *Race and Photography*, 117–55; and Christopher M. Hutton, *Race and the Third Reich: Linguistics, Racial Anthropology and Genetics in the Dialectic of* Volk (Malden, MA: Polity Press, 2005), 35–63. Hans Günther was cited in the Jewish press already in 1925, but references to his work became more frequent in the late 1920s and early 1930s. See, for example, the special issue on the "race question" in the *C.V.-Zeitung*, especially Dr. med. Immerwahr, "Zur Geschichte der Rassentheorien," *C.V.-Zeitung* 4, no. 37 (September 11, 1925): 611–13.

66. "Unser neues Preisausschreiben: Das schöne jüdische Kind," *Israelitisches Familienblatt* 32, no. 37 (September 11, 1930): 13. Edith Stein, the German-Jewish philosopher who converted to Catholicism and became a nun, used similar terms in her descriptions of family portraits, praising the "nobility of spirit" perceptible in her grandmother's portrait. See Scott Spector, "Edith Stein's Passing Gestures: Intimate Histories, Empathetic Portraits," *New German Critique* 75 (1998): 28–56; here 48. On Stein, see also Endelman, *Leaving the Jewish Fold*, 265–68.

67. "Preisausschreiben: Das schöne jüdische Kind," *Israelitisches Familienblatt* 32, no. 47 (November 19, 1930): 180–81; and "Das Ergebnis unseres Preisausschreibens: 'Das schöne jüdische Kind,'" *Israelitisches Familienblatt* 32, no. 50 (December 11, 1930): 14. The first, second, and third prizes went to numbers 17, 6, and 4, respectively. See also Kerry Wallach, "Was auf dem (jüdischen) Spiel stand. Die Preisausschreiben der jüdischen Presse in der Weimarer Republik," in *Nicht nur Bildung, nicht nur Bürger: Juden in der Populärkultur*, ed. Klaus Hödl (Innsbruck: StudienVerlag, 2013), 45–62.

68. Michael Berkowitz has demonstrated that Jews had long praised the "handsomeness of their leaders" and that the dissemination of images of Jews shaped various Jewish initiatives. Berkowitz, *Jewish Self-Image*, 16.

69. On the Centralverein's Weimar-era agenda, see Barkai, *Wehr dich*, chapters 3–5. The hundreds of books, brochures, and pamphlets published by the CV during the Weimar Republic explicitly took on the task of defending German Jews against antisemitic accusations. See Arnold Paucker, *Der jüdische Abwehrkampf gegen Antisemitismus und Nationalsozialismus in den letzten Jahren der Weimarer Republik*, 2nd ed. (Hamburg: Leibniz-Verlag, 1968), 45–61.

70. Barkai, *Wehr dich*, 188–90.

71. Julius Goldstein, *Rasse und Politik*, 2nd ed. (Schlüchtern: Neuwerk-Verlag, 1921), 74–130.

72. "Festansprache gehalten bei der Wormser Tagung des R.j.F. am 5. September 1925 von Kam. Professor Julius Goldstein," *Der Schild* 4, no. 27 (October 9, 1925): 375–76; italics in original.

73. This was a common objection to the use of zoological classifications by some race theorists. Constantin Brunner similarly argued against using animal breed or racial classifications for the purpose of understanding humans. See Brunner, *Der Judenhass und die Juden*, 29. On the other hand, Fritz Kahn, who objected to the notion of "pure" races among humans, did not object to the notion of applying zoological classifications to human groups. See Kahn excerpt in Hart, *Jews and Race*, 24.

74. However, at least one article in *Der Schild* conceded that Jewish Germans possessed certain unique characteristics. See B. Hirschfeld, "Gibt es eine jüdische Rasse?," *Der Schild* 4, no. 34 (November 27, 1925): 434–35. See also Ruth Pierson, "Embattled

Veterans: The Reichsbund jüdischer Frontsoldaten," *Leo Baeck Institute Year Book* 19 (1974): 139–54; here 151.

75. Rechtsanwalt Foerder, "Die Rassenfrage," *Jüdisch-liberale Zeitung* 2, no. 7 (February 17, 1922): 1–2.

76. Ludwig Foerder, *Die Stellung des Centralvereins zu den innerjüdischen Fragen in den Jahren 1919–1926. Eine Denkschrift für die Vereinsmitglieder* (Breslau: Volkswacht, 1927), 5–8.

77. Friedrich Brodnitz, Kurt Cohn, and Ludwig Tietz, *Der Central-Verein der Zukunft. Eine Denkschrift zur Hauptversammlung 1928 des Central-Vereins deutscher Staatsbürger jüdischen Glaubens E.V.* (Berlin: Lichtwitz, 1928), 16. Microfilm from the Wiener Library at the Leo Baeck Institute, New York. W333–374/365. See also Paucker, *Der jüdische Abwehrkampf*, 30; and Avraham Barkai, "Between *Deutschtum* and *Judentum*: Ideological Controversies inside the Centralverein," in Brenner and Penslar, *In Search of Jewish Community*, 74–91; here 81.

78. Werner Cahnmann, *Völkische Rassenlehre: Darstellung, Kritik und Folgerungen* (Berlin: Philo Verlag, 1932), 19–24. Cahnmann notes that, according to Günther, most Sephardic Jews could be classified as "Oriental," whereas Ashkenazic Jews were more likely to be "Near Eastern" (*vorderasiatisch*) or "Eastern" (*östisch*) types. The booklet had its origins in a lecture given by Cahnmann in 1930 to division heads of the Centralverein, and also received mention in the Jewish press. See L. N., "Bücherschau: Dr. Werner Cahnmann: "Völkische Rassenlehre," *Jüdisch-liberale Zeitung* 12, no. 19 (January 1, 1933): 6.

79. Flugblatt der C.V.-Ortsgruppe Hamburg, April 1932. Reproduced in German in Paucker, *Der jüdische Abwehrkampf*, 206; and in English in *The Weimar Republic Sourcebook*, ed. Anton Kaes, Martin Jay, and Edward Dimendberg (Berkeley: University of California Press, 1994), 272–75; here 273.

80. In other cases, dark coloring was interpreted as a sign of the femme fatale. Gilman, "Salome, Syphilis," 108.

81. See Paula Hyman, "East European Jewish Women in an Age of Transition, 1880–1930," in *Jewish Women in Historical Perspective*, 2nd ed., ed. Judith R. Baskin (Detroit: Wayne State University Press, 1998), 270–86.

82. Trude Maurer, *Ostjuden in Deutschland, 1918–1933* (Hamburg: H. Christians Verlag, 1986), 65. On the absorption of East European Jews in Germany, see Schalom Adler-Rudel, *Ostjuden in Deutschland 1880–1940* (Tübingen: Mohr, 1959), 165; Aschheim, *Brothers and Strangers*, 37, 42; Sharon Gillerman, "Producing Jews: Maternity, Eugenics, and the Embodiment of the Jewish Subject," and Annemarie Sammartino, "Defining the Nation in Crisis: Citizenship Policy in the Early Weimar Republic," in *Weimar Publics/Weimar Subjects: Rethinking the Political Culture of Germany in the 1920s*, ed. Kathleen Canning, Kerstin Barndt, and Kristin McGuire (New York: Berghahn Books, 2010), 153–72 and 321–38.

83. See Verena Dohrn and Gertrud Pickhan, eds., *Transit und Transformation: Osteuropäisch-jüdische Migranten in Berlin 1918–1939* (Göttingen: Wallstein, 2010); Gennady Estraikh and Mikhail Krutikov, eds., *Yiddish in Weimar Berlin: At the Crossroads of Diaspora Politics and Culture* (London: Modern Humanities Research Association, 2010); and Seelig, *Strangers in Berlin*.

84. Wertheimer, *Unwelcome Strangers*, 81.

85. On the origins of the "cult of the Ostjuden," see Aschheim, *Brothers and Strangers*, 139–214. On tensions between Yiddish and German-speaking Jews, see Jeffrey A. Grossman, *The Discourse on Yiddish in Germany from the Enlightenment to the Second Empire* (Rochester, NY: Camden House, 2000), 209–22.

86. Solomon Maimon, *An Autobiography*, trans. J. Clark Murray (Chicago: University of Illinois Press, 2001), 189.

87. Heinrich Heine, *Über Polen*, ed. Michael Holzinger (Berlin: Hofenberg, 2014), 7–8. See also Aschheim, *Brothers and Strangers*, 185–87.

88. On primitivism in German-Jewish writing by such authors as Franz Kafka, Alfred Döblin, and Joseph Roth, see Samuel Spinner, "Plausible Primitives: Kafka and Jewish Primitivism," *German Quarterly* 89, no. 1 (2016): 17–35.

89. Gillerman, *Germans into Jews*, 66–67.

90. See Sartre, *Anti-Semite and Jew*, 48–49; and Gilman, "Salome, Syphilis," 108. On literary representations, see Florian Krobb, *Die schöne Jüdin: Jüdische Frauengestalten in der deutschsprachigen Erzählliteratur vom 17. Jahrhundert bis zum Ersten Weltkrieg* (Tübingen: Niemeyer, 1993); and Nadia Valman, *The Jewess in Nineteenth-Century British Literary Culture* (New York: Cambridge University Press, 2007).

91. On distinctions between Western and Eastern Jewish women, particularly in the works of Viennese authors such as Arthur Schnitzler, see Alison Rose, *Jewish Women in Fin de Siècle Vienna* (Austin: University of Texas Press, 2008), 203–11.

92. Franz Sachs, "Von deutschen Jüdinnen," *Der Jude* 1, no. 10 (January 1917): 662–64.

93. These same tropes occasionally appeared in memoirs; for example, Edith Stein depicted her sister Erna as having a dark complexion, whereas her own blondness placed her into the category of marginally Jewish. Spector, "Edith Stein's Passing Gestures," 51.

94. Adrienne Thomas, *Katrin Becomes a Soldier*, trans. Margaret Goldsmith (Boston: Little, Brown, 1931), 13; and Adrienne Thomas, *Die Katrin wird Soldat. Ein Roman aus Elsass-Lothringen* (Berlin: Propyläen-Verlag, 1930), 19.

95. Bertha Badt-Strauss, "Italia Judaica," *Jüdische Rundschau* 33, no. 46 (June 12, 1928): 332. Here Badt-Strauss cites Loevinson, *Roma Israelitica*.

96. Martin Freud, *Sigmund Freud: Man and Father* (New York: Vanguard Press, 1958), 101, 114. See also Ritchie Robertson, *The 'Jewish Question' in German Literature 1749–1939: Emancipation and Its Discontents* (New York: Oxford University Press, 1999), 293.

97. Arnold Zweig, *The Face of East European Jewry*, trans. Noah Isenberg (Berkeley: University of California Press, 2004), 87; and Arnold Zweig, *Das ostjüdische Antlitz zu zweiundfünfzig Zeichnungen von Hermann Struck* (Berlin: Welt-Verlag, 1922), 106–07. On Zweig, see also Leslie Morris, "Reading the Face of the Other: Arnold Zweig's and Hermann Struck's *Das ostjüdische Antlitz*," in *The Imperialist Imagination: German Colonialism and Its Legacy*, ed. Sara Friedrichsmeyer, Sara Lennox, and Susanne Zantop (Ann Arbor: University of Michigan, 1998), 189–203; and Carol Zemel, *Looking Jewish: Visual Culture and Modern Diaspora* (Bloomington: Indiana University Press, 2015), 92–94.

98. Arnold Zweig, *Juden auf der deutschen Bühne* (Berlin: Welt-Verlag, 1928), 21–26, 137–42, 193–94.

99. Rudolf Bernauer, *Das Theater meines Lebens. Erinnerungen* (Berlin: Lothar Blanvalet Verlag, 1955), 310–14, 323–24.

100. In *Der Geiger von Florenz* (*Impetuous Youth*; Czinner, 1926), Bergner starred as a defiant girl who swapped clothes with a local boy in order to escape from her Swiss boarding school over the border to Italy. In *Ariane* (Czinner, 1931) and *The Rise of Catherine the Great* (Czinner, 1934), she played a Russian schoolgirl and empress. See also the discussions of Bergner in chapters 2 and 3.

101. On the appeal of Jewish entertainers in Imperial and Weimar Germany, see Marline Otte, *Jewish Identities in German Popular Entertainment, 1890–1933* (New York: Cambridge University Press, 2006).

102. On Jewish men and hair, see Jay Geller, *Other Jewish Question*, 50–87.

103. "Die neuesten Frisuren bei Franz Daniger," advertisement, *Der Schild* 4, no. 9 (May 1, 1925): 16.

104. See, for example, "Aureol," advertisement, *C.V.-Zeitung* 8, no. 27 (July 5, 1929): 360. This Aureol hair dye was distributed by Berlin perfume manufacturer J. F. Schwarzlose Söhne beginning in 1896. It may have been connected to the French Aureole hair dye developed around 1907, which later served as an inspiration for the name of L'Oréal cosmetic company. See Steven Zdatny, "The Boyish Look and the Liberated Woman: The Politics and Aesthetics of Women's Hairstyles," *Fashion Theory* 1, no. 4 (1997): 367–98; here 373.

105. See, for example, "Kosma Locken-Kamm," advertisement, *C.V.-Zeitung* 10, no. 31 (July 31, 1931): 390; and "Haarkräusel-Lotion," advertisement, *Yidishe ilustrirte tsaytung* 1, no. 6 (June 27, 1924): 93.

106. "Das Geheimnis der Onda-Wellen," advertisement, *Die jüdische Frau* 2, nos. 11–12 (August 15, 1926): inside front cover; and 2, nos. 13–14 (September 6, 1926): inside back cover.

107. On American Jewish women's use of African American hair straightening techniques, see Kathy Peiss, *Hope in a Jar: The Making of America's Beauty Culture* (New York: Metropolitan Books, 1998), 224.

108. The term "Jewfro," a wordplay on the "Afro" hairstyle that was popularized in the 1960s, gestures toward taking pride in similarly stereotypical Jewish and Black hair types. See Eric Silverman, *A Cultural History of Jewish Dress* (New York: Bloomsbury Academic, 2013), 193–94; and Lori Harrison-Kahan, "Passing for Black, White, and Jewish: Mixed Race Identity in Rebecca Walker and Danzy Senna," in *Passing Interest: Racial Passing in US Novels, Memoirs, Television, and Film, 1990–2010*, ed. Julie Cary Nerad (Albany: State University of New York Press, 2014), 229–53; here 230, 236.

109. When Pola Negri (1897–1987) was filming *Der gelbe Schein* (1918) in Warsaw, one Jewish woman mistook Negri for a Jew due to Negri's familiarity with gefilte fish. Pola Negri, *Leben eines Stars*, ed. Axel von Cossart (Cologne: Voco-Edition, 1988), 74–75.

110. Pola Negri, "Wenn ich blond wäre . . . ," *Die Dame* 54, no. 11 (February 1927): 14–15, 32.

111. Irmgard Keun, *The Artificial Silk Girl*, trans. Kathie von Ankum (New York:

Other Press, 2002), 37; and Irmgard Keun, *Das kunstseidene Mädchen. Roman mit Materialien* (Leipzig: Ernst Klett Schulbuchverlag, 2004), 27. Keun was not Jewish, but her works were banned in Nazi Germany.

112. For biographical information on Szalit, see David Ewen, "A Great Painter of the Jew," *B'nai B'rith Magazine* 45 (1930): 267–68; Hersh Fenster, *Undzere farpaynikte kinstler. Nos artistes martyrs* (Paris: H. Fenster, 1951), 231–35; Nadine Nieszawer, ed., *Jewish Artists of the School of Paris, 1905–1939*, trans. Deborah Princ (Paris: Somogy éditions d'art, 2015), 322, 453; Hedwig Brenner, *Jüdische Frauen in der bildenden Kunst II. Ein biographisches Verzeichnis*, ed. Erhard Roy Wiehn (Constance: Hartung-Gorre Verlag, 2004), 331–32; and Serge Klarsfeld, *Mémorial de la Déportation des Juifs de France* (Paris: FFDJF Fils et Filles des Déportés Juifs de France, 2012), 583.

113. Walter Kauders, "Rahel Szalit," *Menorah* 4, no. 2 (February 1926): 87–88.

114. Rahel Szalit, "Ich bin eine jüdische Künstlerin," *Blätter des jüdischen Frauenbundes* 6, no. 9 (September 1930): 2–3.

115. On hyperbolic depictions in Szalit's illustrations, see Sabine Koller, "*Mentshelekh un stsenes*: Rahel Szalit-Marcus illustriert Sholem Aleichem," in *Leket: Jiddistik heute/Yiddish Studies Today*, ed. Marion Aptroot, Efrat Gal-Ed, Roland Gruschka, and Simon Neuberg (Düsseldorf: Düsseldorf University Press, 2012), 207–31; here 225.

116. Eduard Fuchs, *Die Juden in der Karikatur. Ein Beitrag zur Kulturgeschichte* (Munich: Albert Langen, 1921), 266–67, 310. Rahel Szalit-Marcus, *Menshelakh un stsenes: Zekhtsen tseykhenungen tsu Sholem Aleykhems verk 'Motl Peysi dem hazens yingel'* (Berlin: Klal Farlag, 1922).

117. In "Das Zion der jüdischen Frau" (first published in *Die Welt* 5, no. 17 (April 26, 1901): 3–5, Buber blamed Jewish women for the demise of Jewish community and charged them with the task of creating Jewish culture. Martin Buber, "The Jewish Woman's Zion," in *The First Buber: Youthful Zionist Writings of Martin Buber*, ed. and trans. Gilya G. Schmidt (Syracuse, NY: Syracuse University Press, 1999), 117.

118. Ger Trud, "Rahel Szalit. Eine jüdische Malerin," *Die jüdische Frau* 2, nos. 11–12 (August 15, 1926): 1.

119. Such head coverings also can indicate different affiliations of Jews. On visual representations of head coverings, see Nick Block, "Ex Libris and Exchange: Immigrant Interventions in the German-Jewish Renaissance," *German Quarterly* 86, no. 3 (2013): 334–53; here 341.

120. On the founding of the K.C., see Keith H. Pickus, *Constructing Modern Identities: Jewish University Students in Germany, 1815–1914* (Detroit: Wayne State University Press, 1999), 94–104; and Adolph Asch and Johanna Philippson, "Self-Defence at the Turn of the Century: The Emergence of the K.C.," *Leo Baeck Institute Year Book* 3 (1958): 122–39. Miriam Rürup's work confirms that there was an explicit discussion of the uses of the color yellow by student groups. Miriam Rürup, *Ehrensache. Jüdische Studentenverbindungen an deutschen Universitäten, 1886–1937* (Göttingen: Wallstein Verlag, 2008), 251. On Jewish students and student groups, see Lisa Fetheringill Zwicker, *Dueling Students: Conflict, Masculinity, and Politics in German Universities* (Ann Arbor: University of Michigan Press, 2011), 103–17; and Lisa Fetheringill Zwicker, "Performing Masculinity: Jewish Students and the Honor Code at German Universities," in Baader, Gillerman, and Lerner, *Jewish Masculinities*, 114–37.

121. The line cited here ("was Schandfleck war, ward unser Ehrenzeichen") is taken from the "Bundeslied" or "Farbenlied" of the Berlin K.C. group Sprevia. Kurt U. Bertrams, *Der Kartell-Convent und seine Verbindungen* (Hilden: WJK-Verlag, 2009), 122, 170. See also Asch and Philippson, "Self-Defence," 136.

122. On *Trotzjudentum*, see Kurt Loewenstein, "Die innerjüdische Reaktion auf die Krise der deutschen Demokratie," in Mosse und Paucker, *Entscheidungsjahr 1932*, 349–403; here 390; and Mendes-Flohr, *German Jews*, 56.

123. Volkov, *Walther Rathenau*, 49–50.

124. The yellow-like color worn by Badenia Heidelberg was actually orange. Bertrams, *Kartell-Convent*, 120–22.

125. Rahel Straus, *Wir lebten in Deutschland. Erinnerungen einer deutschen Jüdin, 1880–1933*, ed. Max Kreutzberger (Stuttgart: Deutsche Verlags-Anstalt, 1961), 92. On Rahel Straus, whom scholars have declared an exemplary new Jewish woman, see Prestel, "New Jewish Woman," in Benz, Paucker, and Pulzer, *Jüdisches Leben in der Weimar Republik*, 138–47; Freidenreich, "Die jüdische 'Neue Frau,'" in Heinsohn and Schüler-Springorum, *Deutsch-jüdische Geschichte als Geschlechtergeschichte*, 123–32; and Harriet Pass Freidenreich, *Female, Jewish and Educated: The Lives of Central European University Women* (Bloomington: Indiana University Press, 2002).

126. On the use of blue and white by Zionist groups, see Jehuda Reinharz, *Dokumente zur Geschichte des deutschen Zionismus, 1882–1993* (Tübingen: Mohr, 1981), xxxix–xl. On the history of the Star of David emblem, see Don Handelman and Lea Shamgar-Handelman, "Shaping Time: The Choice of the National Emblem of Israel," in *Culture through Time: Anthropological Approaches*, ed. Emiko Ohnuki-Tierney (Stanford: Stanford University Press, 1990), 193–226.

127. Gronemann, *Schalet*, 120.

128. Gershom Scholem, "The Star of David: History of a Symbol," in Gershom Scholem, *The Messianic Idea in Judaism and Other Essays on Jewish Spirituality* (New York: Schocken Books, 1995), 257–81; here 81. This essay was first published in 1948 and expanded in 1963. Philosopher Franz Rosenzweig (1886–1929), too, referenced the Star of David in his major work, *Der Stern der Erlösung* (The Star of Redemption, 1921).

129. Bertrams, *Kartell-Convent*, 197.

130. See Henry Buxhaum, *Recollections* (1979); excerpted in Richarz, *Jewish Life in Germany*, 301–6; here 304.

131. Edgar Marx, "Ideological Self-Determination of Bar Kochba: The New Year of the Jewish Gymnastics and Sports Association Bar Kochba," in Kaes, Jay, and Dimendberg, *Weimar Republic Sourcebook*, 262–63; here 263.

132. The notice "Tragt Euer Abzeichen überall!" appears in at least five issues of *Der Schild* beginning with 4, no. 3 (February 1, 1925): 59. "Tragt und grüßt unser Abzeichen!" appears in several forms; see, for example, 4, no. 35 (December 4, 1925): 443; and 5, no. 5 (February 1, 1926): 37: "Sportkameraden, tragt und grüßt unser Sportabzeichen!"

133. Pierson, "Embattled Veterans," 148; and Paucker, *Der jüdische Abwehrkampf*, 34.

134. "Tragt eure Kriegsauszeichnungen!," *Der Schild* 11, no. 13 (July 14, 1932): 100.

On war decorations worn by members of the RjF after January 1933, see Tim Grady, "Fighting a Lost Battle: The *Reichsbund jüdischer Frontsoldaten* and the Rise of National Socialism," *German History* 28, no. 1 (2010): 1–20; here 13; and Grady, *German-Jewish Soldiers*.

135. Max Reiner, *Mein Leben in Deutschland vor und nach dem Jahre 1933* (1940), 185, ME 517, Leo Baeck Institute, New York. See also Landau, *My Life*, in Richarz, *Jewish Life in Germany*, 310–12; and "Edwin Landau" and "Max Reiner" in *Jüdisches Leben in Deutschland. Selbstzeugnisse zur Sozialgeschichte 1918–1945*, ed. Monika Richarz (Stuttgart: Deutsche Verlags-Anstalt, 1982), 99–108 and 109–19; here 104, 115. See also Trude Maurer, "From Everyday Life to a State of Emergency: Jews in Weimar and Nazi Germany," in *Jewish Daily Life in Germany, 1618–1945*, ed. Marion A. Kaplan (New York: Oxford University Press, 2005), 314.

136. Robert Weltsch, "Tragt ihn mit Stolz, den gelben Fleck," *Jüdische Rundschau* 38, no. 27 (April 4, 1933): 131–32.

137. See Edwin Landau, *My Life before and after Hitler* (1940); excerpted in Richarz, *Jewish Life in Germany*, 306–15; here 313.

138. Some felt that being perpetually marked as Jews transformed them into objects. See Sartre, *Anti-Semite and Jew*, 76–77. Cf. Alan T. Levenson, *Between Philosemitism and Antisemitism: Defenses of Jews and Judaism in Germany, 1871–1932* (Lincoln: University of Nebraska Press, 2004), 5–10.

139. See Gronemann's memoirs at the Leo Baeck Institute, New York, and in two published volumes: Sammy Gronemann, *Erinnerungen*, ed. Joachim Schlör (Berlin: Philo Verlag, 2002); and Gronemann, *Erinnerungen an meine Jahre in Berlin*. On Gronemann's participation in *Schlemiel*, see David A. Brenner, *German-Jewish Popular Culture before the Holocaust: Kafka's Kitsch* (New York: Routledge, 2008), 34–35.

140. Michael Brenner, *Renaissance*, 143–46.

141. See Joachim Schlör, foreword to Sammy Gronemann, *Utter Chaos*, trans. Penny Milbouer (Bloomington: Indiana University Press, 2016), xii.

142. Hanni Mittelmann has suggested that one of Gronemann's accomplishments in *Schalet* was the depiction of breaks with tradition as a part of the continuity of Jewish society through the ages. Hanni Mittelmann, "Vom Essen und von Zionismus: Sammy Gronemanns National-Jüdisches Anekdotenbuch *Schalet. Beiträge zur Philosophie des 'Wenn schon,'"* *New German Review* 19 (2003–04): 30–39; here 35; and Hanni Mittelmann, *Sammy Gronemann (1875–1952): Zionist, Schriftsteller und Satiriker in Deutschland und Palästina* (Frankfurt am Main: Campus Verlag, 2004), 90–102.

143. Gronemann, *Schalet*, 120.

144. Gronemann, *Schalet*, 115.

145. On New Women and fashion, see Irene Guenther, *Nazi Chic? Fashioning Women in the Third Reich* (Oxford: Berg, 2004), 53–58; and Mila Ganeva, *Women in Weimar Fashion: Discourses and Displays in German Culture, 1918–1933* (Rochester, NY: Camden House, 2008), 3–4.

146. One anecdote in *Die jüdische Frau* reveals another "Jewish" perspective on short hair, namely that the cost of the frequent haircuts to maintain a bob would be better allocated as a donation to a charity for orphans. This appeared above an article about rabbis campaigning for women to restore propriety to their appearance. See Susi Würz-

burg, "Gespräch: Der Bubikopf" and "Gegen Entartungen der Mode," *Die jüdische Frau* 2, nos. 9–10 (June 15, 1926): 8.

147. See, for example, ads for *Bubikopf* wigs made by Fischer's Special Hair House in *Der Israelit* from March 1929 to 1931; here 70, no. 10 (March 7, 1929): 8; and ads for Franz Daniger hair pieces in all colors that appeared in the Berlin *Gemeindeblatt* in 1925 and 1926.

148. "Florian Elzer Eleganter Schönheitssalon," advertisement, *Der Israelit* 73, no. 29 (July 14, 1932): 12.

## CHAPTER 2

1. "Jüdische Kinder in der Schule. Eine Schlußbetrachtung zu unserer Rundfrage," *C.V.-Zeitung* 11, no. 3 (January 15, 1932): 19.

2. "Das C.V.-Kind in der Schule," cited in *Jüdische Rundschau* 37, no. 5 (January 19, 1932): 22. See also Kurt Loewenstein, "Die innerjüdische Reaktion auf die Krise der deutschen Demokratie," in Mosse and Paucker, *Entscheidungsjahr 1932*, 400.

3. Gronemann, *Schalet*, 48.

4. "Uns fällt auf . . . Man 'trägt' wieder Judentum," *Israelitisches Familienblatt* 34, no. 47 (November 24, 1932): 4.

5. Cf. Sedgwick, *Epistemology*, 22, 75–82.

6. See Michael Warner, "Publics and Counterpublics (Abbreviated Version)," *Quarterly Journal of Speech* 88, no. 4 (2002): 413–25.

7. Bial, *Acting Jewish*, 16–20. See also note 6 to the introduction.

8. As Sarah Wobick-Segev has argued with respect to the first decade of the twentieth century, certain spaces in Germany (cafés, specific hotels, and even spas) became "places of Jewish socialization and culture due to, in part, the sheer number of Jews who visited." Sarah E. Wobick-Segev, "German-Jewish Spatial Cultures: Consuming and Refashioning Jewish Belonging in Berlin, 1890–1910," in *Longing, Belonging, and the Making of Jewish Consumer Culture*, ed. Gideon Reuveni and Nils H. Roemer (Boston: Brill, 2010), 39–60; here 47. On Jews and urban spaces, see also Joachim Schlör, *Das Ich der Stadt. Debatten über Judentum und Urbanität 1822–1938* (Göttingen: Vandenhoeck & Ruprecht, 2005).

9. Upon reading a volume of Buber's Hasidic stories in 1912, philosopher Ernst Bloch exclaimed: "The pride of being Jewish is reawakened!" (*Neu erwacht der Stolz, jüdisch zu sein!*). Translation cited in Mendes-Flohr, *German Jews*, 57. On the pride with which Jews participated in and were co-constitutive of German culture, see Frank Trommler, *Kulturmacht ohne Kompass: Deutsche Auswärtige Kulturbeziehungen im 20. Jahrhundert* (Cologne: Böhlau Verlag, 2014), 173–84.

10. Kurt Pinczower, "Marta Jacob," *Das jüdische Magazin* 1, no. 3 (September–October 1929): 52–54.

11. "Die schönste Frau Europas—eine Jüdin," *Israelitisches Familienblatt* 31, no. 8 (February 21, 1929): 15. See also chapter 3; and Kerry Wallach, "Recognition for the 'Beautiful Jewess': Beauty Queens Crowned by Modern Jewish Print Media," in *Globalizing Beauty: Consumerism and Body Aesthetics in the Twentieth Century*, ed. Hartmut Berghoff and Thomas Kühne (New York: Palgrave Macmillan, 2013), 131–50.

12. Ida Levy, "Juden-Frauen," *Die jüdische Frau* 2, nos. 11–12 (August 15, 1926): 10.

13. Buber's journal explicitly referenced Gabriel Riesser's journal, *Der Jude: Ein Journal für Gewissens-Freiheit* (1830s). See Arthur A. Cohen, introduction to *The Jew: Essays from Martin Buber's Journal* Der Jude, *1916–1928*, ed. Arthur A. Cohen and trans. Joachim Neugroschel (Tuscaloosa: University of Alabama Press, 1980), 3–14; here 3; and Eleonore Lappin, *Der Jude. 1916–1928. Jüdische Moderne zwischen Universalismus und Partikularismus* (Tübingen: Mohr Siebeck, 2000), 4.

14. Joseph Roth, *Wandering Jews*, 22; Joseph Roth, *Juden auf Wanderschaft*, 23.

15. See Gideon Reuveni, *Reading Germany: Literature and Consumer Culture in Germany before 1933*, trans. Ruth Morris (New York: Berghahn Books, 2006), 105–9; and Peter Fritzsche, *Reading Berlin 1900* (Cambridge: Harvard University Press, 1996).

16. "Die Tribüne der Frau," *Die jüdische Frau* 1, no. 2 (May 22, 1925): 14.

17. "Die Tribüne der Frau," *Die jüdische Frau* 1, no. 3 (June 7, 1925): 14.

18. Newspapers and books that were coded Jewish were not the only ones kept out of view; those aligned with the politics of the extreme right also were hidden. For example, journalist Max Reiner noted that he never observed a single person reading Hitler's *Mein Kampf* on a train before 1933, and that people regarded Reiner with great suspicion when he once read a book by Nazi ideologist Alfred Rosenberg in the Berlin subway. Reiner, *Mein Leben*, unpublished manuscript, Leo Baeck Institute, 147.

19. *Die jüdische Frau*, for example, featured ads stating that the magazine was available at various resorts. "Die Zeitschrift 'Die jüdische Frau' liegt in den Lesesälen der Badeorte aus," advertisement, *Die jüdische Frau* 2, nos. 9–10 (June 15, 1926): 8.

20. Gronemann, *Schalet*, 187–88.

21. On communities brought together by newspapers, see Benedict Anderson, *Imagined Communities: Reflections on the Origin and Spread of Nationalism*, rev. ed. (London: Verso, 2006).

22. Corey Ross, *Media and the Making of Modern Germany: Mass Communications, Society, and Politics from the Empire to the Third Reich* (New York: Oxford University Press, 2008), 147.

23. Katrin Diehl, *Die jüdische Presse im Dritten Reich. Zwischen Selbstbehauptung und Fremdbestimmung* (Tübingen: Max Niemeyer Verlag, 1997), 18; and Trude Maurer, "Die Juden in der Weimarer Republik," in *Zerbrochene Geschichte: Leben und Selbstverständnis der Juden in Deutschland*, ed. Dirk Blasius and Dan Diner (Frankfurt am Main: Fischer Taschenbuch Verlag, 1991), 102–20.

24. See circulation data in *Sperlings Zeitschriften- u. Zeitungs-Adreßbuch. Die wichtigsten deutschen Zeitschriften und politischen Zeitungen Deutschlands, Österreichs und des Auslandes*, 55th ed. (Leipzig: Verlag des Börsenvereins der Deutschen Buchhändler zu Leipzig, 1929), 369. The *Wiener Morgenzeitung*, the first German-language daily Jewish newspaper, appeared in Vienna from January 1919 to September 1927. In Germany, the best-selling *Israelitisches Familienblatt* had a circulation of 35,000 and may have reached as many as 90,000 readers, or roughly 15 percent of the potential market. The *C.V.-Zeitung* was delivered to every member of the Centralverein and thus boasted a circulation of over 70,000. The official organ of the Zionistische Vereinigung für Deutschland, the twice weekly *Jüdische Rundschau*, appeared most frequently during the Weimar period. It maintained 10,000 to 15,000 subscribers until

1932, and its circulation rose to 40,000 in 1933. On the Weimar Jewish press, see Kerry Wallach, "Observable Type: Jewish Women and the Jewish Press in Weimar Germany" (PhD diss., University of Pennsylvania, 2011); and Marion Neiss, *Presse im Transit: Jiddische Zeitungen und Zeitschriften in Berlin von 1919 bis 1925* (Berlin: Metropol Verlag, 2002). On the Jewish press in the 1930s, see Herbert Freeden, *The Jewish Press in the Third Reich*, trans. William Templer (Providence, RI: Berg Publishers, 1993); and Diehl, *Die jüdische Presse*.

25. Historian Peter Pulzer has described journalism as the profession most "completely dominated by Jews." Peter Pulzer, *The Rise of Political Anti-Semitism in Germany and Austria* (London: Peter Halban, 1988), 13. See also Paul Reitter, *The Anti-Journalist: Karl-Kraus and Jewish Self-Fashioning in Fin-de-Siècle Europe* (Chicago: University of Chicago Press, 2008), 61. Jewish participation in the mainstream liberal and left-wing press led many slanderously to term this print sector the "*Judenpresse*"; such accusations of Jewish domination also led to the defamatory label "*Judenrepublik*" for the Weimar Republic. See Jost Hermand, "Juden in der Kultur der Weimarer Republik," in *Juden in der Weimarer Republik*, ed. Walter Grab and Julius Schoeps (Stuttgart: Burg Verlag, 1986), 9–37; and Weitz, *Weimar Germany*, 333.

26. Werner T. Angress, *Witness to the Storm: A Jewish Journey from Nazi Berlin to the 82nd Airborne, 1920–1945* (Durham, NC: CreateSpace Independent Publishing Platform, 2012), 77–78; and Werner T. Angress, *. . . immer etwas abseits: Jugenderinnerungen eines jüdischen Berliners, 1920–1945* (Berlin: Edition Hentrich, 2005), 80.

27. English Transcript of Maya Zack's Interview with Manfred Nomburg (who later took the name Yair Noam), Israel, 2009. Transcript provided as part of the exhibition "Maya Zack: Living Room," Jewish Museum, New York, July–October 2011.

28. Joachim Prinz, "Mechanischer Gottesdienst," *Berliner jüdische Zeitung* 1, no. 11 (November 24, 1929): 4.

29. See letter (likely from Leo Kreindler) to "Redaktion der B.Z. am Mittag," February 2, 1932, and other lecture publicity. Stiftung Neue Synagoge Berlin—Centrum Judaicum, Archiv (CJA), 1 (Gesamtarchiv der deutschen Juden), 75A Be2, Nr. 20 (Ident.-Nr. 245). See also Loewenstein, "Die innerjüdische Reaktion," 358; Lotte Pulvermacher, "Die neue Synagoge Prinzregentenstraße in Berlin," *Bayerische Israelitische Gemeindezeitung* 6, no. 19 (October 1, 1930): 304; and Michael A. Meyer, "Women in the European Jewish Reform Movement," in Kaplan and Dash Moore, *Gender and Jewish History*, 139–57; here 141.

30. Lotte Hirschberg (1898–1993), *Mein Leben: Geschrieben 1982–1985*, 7, ME 1531, Leo Baeck Institute, New York. On the social structures of Jews in Breslau more broadly, see Rahden, *Jews and Other Germans*.

31. Kaplan, "Sisterhood under Siege," in Bridenthal, Grossmann, and Kaplan, *When Biology Became Destiny*, 187; this page includes the translation of the citation from Hannah Karminski, "Forderungen der Gegenwart," *Blätter des Jüdischen Frauenbundes* 7, no. 12 (December 1930): 5–6. Kaplan has also written about the fact that the Jüdischer Frauenbund joined the Bund deutscher Frauenvereine and Nationaler Frauendienst during the First World War as a specifically Jewish organization. See Kaplan, *Making of the Jewish Middle Class*, 221–25; and Marion A. Kaplan, *The Jewish Feminist Movement in Germany: The Campaigns of the Jüdischer Frauenbund, 1904–1938* (Westport, CT: Greenwood Press, 1979).

32. See "Das geistige Judenproblem in Amerika," *Jüdische Rundschau* 32, no. 16 (February 25, 1927): 112. See also the following article, from which I have taken the English translation of this quote: "Plea for Reorganization of Jewish Life Made before Menorah Conference," *Jewish Telegraphic Agency*, February 1, 1927.

33. "Unsere Inserenten," *Der Schild* 5, no. 37 (September 13, 1926): 291.

34. Die Redaktion, "Zum Beginn des 5. Jahrgangs," *Blätter des Jüdischen Frauenbundes* 5, no. 1 (January 1929): 1.

35. Wallach, "Was auf dem (jüdischen) Spiel stand," in Hödl, *Nicht nur Bildung, nicht nur Bürger*, 56.

36. For an example of an advertisement for soap that was marketed as kosher for Passover, see "Seife—Alfred Blochert," *C.V.-Zeitung* 3, no. 14 (April 3, 1924): 171.

37. See Buerkle, "Gendered Spectatorship," 626; Ward, *Weimar Surfaces*, 231–33; and Erica Carter, "Frauen und die Öffentlichkeit des Konsums," in *Die Konsumgesellschaft in Deutschland 1890–1990. Ein Handbuch*, ed. Heinz-Gerhard Haupt and Claudius Torp (Frankfurt am Main: Campus Verlag, 2009), 154–71; here 158.

38. See Paul Lerner, *The Consuming Temple: Jews, Department Stores, and the Consumer Revolution in Germany, 1880–1940* (Ithaca: Cornell University Press, 2015); Paul Lerner, "Consuming Powers: The 'Jewish Department Store' in German Politics and Culture," in *The Economy in Jewish History: New Perspectives on the Interrelationship between Ethnicity and Economic Life*, ed. Gideon Reuveni and Sarah Wobick-Segev (New York: Berghahn Books, 2011), 135–54; and Michael Brenner, *Renaissance*, 92.

39. The Tietz family was known for strong affiliations with the liberal faction of the Berlin Jewish community, and was even religiously observant to a point: supposedly the Tietz stores closed on the High Holidays, though they remained open on Saturdays. On the Tietz family, see Doris Wittner, "Jüdische Köpfe. Familie Tietz," *Jüdisch-liberale Zeitung* 8, no. 21 (May 24, 1928): 5–6; and Lerner, *Consuming Temple*, 39–41.

40. Lerner, *Consuming Temple*, 6.

41. Gideon Reuveni, "Advertising, Jewish Ethnic Marketing, and Consumer Ambivalence in Weimar Germany," in Reuveni and Roemer, *Longing, Belonging*, 113–38; here 118.

42. On the marketing of Jewish-owned department stores, see Lerner, *Consuming Temple*; and Kerry Wallach, "Kosher Seductions: Jewish Women as Employees and Consumers in German Department Stores," in *Das Berliner Warenhaus: Geschichte und Diskurse/The Berlin Department Store: History and Discourse*, ed. Godela Weiss-Sussex and Ulrike Zitzlsperger (Frankfurt am Main: Peter Lang, 2013), 117–37.

43. Malkin, "Transforming in Public," in Malkin and Rokem, *Jews and the Making of Modern German Theatre*, 165–66. Sara Hall has written about how criminal investigators relied on the medium of film to capture gestures and other "nuanced qualities of human appearance that were believed to constitute unique identifiability." Sara F. Hall, "Making the Case for German Police Films," *Historical Journal of Film, Radio and Television* 27, no. 4 (2007): 497–511; here 501.

44. See the discussion of Jews as chameleons in chapter 4.

45. See, for example, Aschheim, "Reflections on Theatricality," in Malkin and Rokem, *Jews and the Making of Modern German Theatre*, 21.

46. In this book, I do not consider theatrical performances designed exclusively for

Jewish audiences, for example Yiddish and Hebrew-language performances and Jewish theater troupes. On the history of Jewish theater, see Heidelore Riss, *Ansätze zu einer Geschichte des jüdischen Theaters in Berlin 1889–1936* (Frankfurt am Main: Peter Lang, 2000); and Peter Sprengel, *Populäres Jüdisches Theater in Berlin von 1877 bis 1933* (Berlin: Haude und Spener, 1997).

47. See Peter Jelavich, "How 'Jewish' Was Theatre in Imperial Berlin?," in Malkin and Rokem, *Jews and the Making of Modern German Theatre*, 39–58; and Peter Jelavich, "Performing High and Low: Jews in Modern Theater, Cabaret, Revue, and Film," in *Berlin Metropolis: Jews and the New Culture, 1890–1918*, ed. Emily D. Bilski (Berkeley: University of California Press, 1999), 209–34.

48. Otte, *Jewish Identities*, 17, 133, 239.

49. Zweig, *Juden auf der deutschen Bühne*, 141. On Zweig, see Malkin, "Transforming in Public," in Malkin and Rokem, *Jews and the Making of Modern German Theatre*, 165–66; Peter W. Marx, "Arnold Zweig and the Critics: Reconsidering the Jewish 'Contribution' to German Theatre," in Malkin and Rokem, *Jews and the Making of Modern German Theatre*, 116–31; Galili Shahar, "The Jewish Actor and the Theatre of Modernism in Germany," *Theatre Research International* 29, no. 3 (2004): 216–31; and Galili Shahar, *Theatrum judaicum. Denkspiele im deutsch-jüdischen Diskurs der Moderne* (Bielefeld: Aisthesis Verlag, 2007).

50. Julius Bab, *Schauspieler und Schaukunst* (Berlin: Oesterheld & Co. Verlag, 1926), 121, 189–90.

51. On Bergner's relationship to Jewishness, see Kerry Wallach, "Escape Artistry: Elisabeth Bergner and Jewish Disappearance in *Der träumende Mund* (Czinner, 1932)," *German Studies Review* 38, no. 1 (2015): 17–34.

52. Doris Wittner, "Die theatralische Sendung der Juden," *Jüdisch-liberale Zeitung* 5, no. 31 (July 31, 1925): 525. On Wittner, see Ruth Pierson, "German Jewish Identity in the Weimar Republic" (PhD diss., Yale University, 1970), 83–86; and Kerry Wallach, "Front-Page Jews: Doris Wittner's (1880–1937) Berlin Feuilletons," in *Discovering Women's History: German-Speaking Journalists (1900–1950)*, ed. Christa Spreizer (Oxford: Peter Lang, 2014), 123–45.

53. Doris Wittner, "Die dichterische Begabung des Judentums," *Gemeindeblatt der jüdischen Gemeinde zu Berlin* 13, nos. 11–12 (December 1, 1923): 69–70.

54. Arnold Zweig included several pages on Irene Triesch in his study of Jews and German theater. Zweig, *Juden auf der deutschen Bühne*, 174–76. She is also mentioned in some lexicons, including Jutta Dick and Marina Sassenberg, eds., *Jüdische Frauen im 19. und 20. Jahrhundert. Lexikon zu Leben und Werk* (Reinbek bei Hamburg: Rowohlt, 1993), 372–74.

55. Frederick J. Marker and Lise-Lone Marker, *Ibsen's Lively Art: A Performance Study of the Major Plays* (Cambridge: Cambridge University Press, 1989), 57.

56. Doris Wittner, "Irene Triesch als Vorleserin," *Jüdisch-liberale Zeitung* 7, no. 7 (February 18, 1927): 3.

57. On actors who "passed" by performing non-Jewish roles, see Bial, *Acting Jewish*, 17.

58. Bernauer, *Theater meines Lebens*, 255.

59. Irene Triesch Lamond, postscript to *The Memoirs of Frederic Lamond* (Glasgow: William MacLellan, 1949), 124–26.

60. "'Rosmersholm' Revived. Mme. Triesch Gives an Admirable Performance of Ibsen Role," *New York Times*, February 8, 1924, 22.

61. See Kirsten Fermaglich, "'What's Uncle Sam's Last Name?' Jews and Name Changing in New York City during the World War II Era," *Journal of American History* 102, no. 3 (2015): 719–45.

62. Bernauer later criticized Triesch's performance of Goethe's Iphigenie as "too Greek and not Germanic enough." Bernauer, *Theater meines Lebens*, 352.

63. Bertha Badt-Strauss, "Irene Triesch liest zum Besten der 'Jüdischen Altershilfe,'" *Jüdische Rundschau* 32, no. 13 (February 15, 1927): 90.

64. On Pinschewer's advertising films, see Julius Pinschewer, "Film Advertising," in *The Promise of Cinema: German Film Theory, 1907–1933*, ed. Anton Kaes, Nicholas Baer, and Michael Cowan (Berkeley: University of California Press, 2016), 240–42. Another Pinschewer film with visible Jewish symbols is *Die Zauberflasche* (1918), in which a man receives a magical bottle with a Star of David on it.

65. Jeanpaul Goergen, "Julius Pinschewer. Künstler und Kaufmann, Pionier des Werbefilms," *epd Film* 3 (1992): 16–22; here 22.

66. André Amsler, *"Wer dem Werbefilm verfällt, ist verloren für die Welt": Das Werk von Julius Pinschewer, 1883–1961* (Zurich: Chronos Verlag, 1997), 281–82.

67. "Hebräisch im Film," *Berliner jüdische Zeitung* 1, no. 6 (October 20, 1929): 2.

68. The Film-Prüfstelle Berlin card (no. 25980) is dated May 17, 1930. See also Fritz Olimsky, "Marionetten-Tonfilm. Sondervorführung," folder 13501, Stiftung Deutsche Kinemathek, Schriftgutarchiv, Berlin.

69. The father in the frame story is played by an actual German rabbi; the mother is played by Pinschewer's wife, Charlotte; and the young boy is played by a family nephew. It is uncertain who plays the other two children. Amsler, *Wer dem Werbefilm verfällt*, 43, 282–88. See also Martin Loiperdinger, ed., "Julius Pinschewer: Klassiker des Werbefilms" (Berlin: ARTE edition, absolut MEDIEN, 2010), DVD liner notes, 26. The DVD contains only the German version of *Chad Gadjo*.

70. S. S. Prawer suggests that director G. W. Pabst does this in a scene featuring Fritz Kortner in *Die Büchse der Pandora* (1929). See S. S. Prawer, *Between Two Worlds: The Jewish Presence in German and Austrian Film, 1910–1933* (New York: Berghahn Books, 2005), 84.

71. On the power of animated objects in film, see Brook Henkel, "Objects in Motion: Hans Richter's *Vormitagsspuk* (1928) and the Crisis of Avant-Garde Film," in Hales, Petrescu, and Weinstein, *Continuity and Crisis*, 233–50.

72. On Pinschewer's work, see Michael Cowan, "Fidelity, Capture and the Sound Advertisement. Julius Pinschewer and Rudi Klemm's *Die chinesische Nachtigall*," *Zeitgeschichte* 41, no. 2 (2014): 77–88; Michael Cowan, "The Ambivalence of Ornament: Silhouette Advertisements in Print and Film in Early Twentieth-Century Germany," *Art History* 36, no. 4 (2013): 784–809; and Michael Cowan, "Advertising, Rhythm, and the Filmic Avant-Garde in Weimar: Guido Seeber and Julius Pinschewer's *Kipho* Film," *October* 131 (Winter 2010): 23–50. See also El Lissitzky, *Had Gadya: The Only Kid. Facsimile of El Lissitzky's Edition of 1919*, ed. Arnold J. Band (Los Angeles: Getty Research Institute, 2004).

73. As a child, Julius Pinschewer received a pet sheep from his father. Amsler, *Wer dem Werbefilm verfällt*, 18.

74. "Irene Triesch auf der Kanzel. Freitagabend-Gottesdienste der Reformgemeinde," *Jüdisch-liberale Zeitung* 12, no. 16 (November 14, 1932): 1; and "Die Einrichtung eines Freitag-Abend-Gottesdienstes," *Mitteilungen der jüdischen Reformgemeinde zu Berlin* 15, no. 6 (November 1, 1932): 12. This image of Triesch also appeared on page 12 of the *Mitteilungen*; it likely depicts Triesch circa 1905 in the title role of Gerhart Hauptmann's *Elga*. On broader debates about women's leadership, see Michael A. Meyer, "Women in the European Jewish Reform Movement," in Kaplan and Dash Moore, *Gender and Jewish History*, 139–57.

75. George Goetz, "Kunst und Kanzel. Irene Triesch als Bibelleserin im Reform-Gottesdienst," *Jüdisch-liberale Zeitung* 12, no. 18 (December 15, 1932): 8.

76. Max Brod, "Bemerkung zu einigen Berliner Kabaretts," *Jüdische Rundschau* 37, monthly issue no. 4 (April 1932): 8.

77. On Jewish theatrical performances after 1933, see Rebecca Rovit, *The Jewish Kulturbund Theatre Company in Nazi Berlin* (Iowa City: University of Iowa Press, 2012).

78. On Lubitsch, see Valerie Weinstein, "Anti-Semitism or Jewish 'Camp'? Ernst Lubitsch's *Schuhpalast Pinkus* (1916) and *Meyer aus Berlin* (1918)," *German Life & Letters* 59, no. 1 (2006): 101–21; Valerie Weinstein, "(Un)Fashioning Identities: Ernst Lubitsch's Early Comedies of Mistaken Identities," in *Visual Culture in Twentieth-Century Germany: Text as Spectacle*, ed. Gail Finney (Bloomington: Indiana University Press, 2006), 120–33; Richard W. McCormick, "Transnational Jewish Comedy: Sex and Politics in the Films of Ernst Lubitsch—From Berlin to Hollywood," in *Three-Way Street: Germans, Jews, and the Transnational*, ed. Jay Howard Geller and Leslie Morris (Ann Arbor: University of Michigan Press, 2016), 169–96 (and Richard McCormick's book-in-progress on Lubitsch); Ashkenazi, *Weimar Film*, 21–34, 51–57; Prawer, *Between Two Worlds*, 42–53; and Sabine Hake, *Passions and Deceptions: The Early Films of Ernst Lubitsch* (Princeton: Princeton University Press, 1992).

79. Ruth Morold, "Jüdische Filme," *Jüdische Rundschau* 31, no. 36 (May 11, 1926): 275; and R. M., "Das alte Gesetz," *Jüdische Rundschau* 34, no. 16 (February 26, 1929): 101. On *Das alte Gesetz*, see Cynthia Walk, "Romeo with Sidelocks: Jewish-Gentile Romance in E. A. Dupont's *Das alte Gesetz* (1923) and Other Early Weimar Assimilation Films," in *The Many Faces of Weimar Cinema: Rediscovering Germany's Filmic Legacy*, ed. Christian Rogowski (Rochester, NY: Camden House, 2010), 84–101; Darcy Buerkle, "Caught in the Act: Norbert Elias, Emotion, and *The Ancient Law*," *Journal of Modern Jewish Studies* 8, no. 1 (2009): 83–102; Valerie Weinstein, "Dissolving Boundaries: Assimilation and Allosemitism in E. A. Dupont's *Das alte Gesetz* (1923) and Veit Harlan's *Jud Süss* (1940)," *German Quarterly* 78, no. 4 (2005): 496–516; here 507; and Peter Jelavich, "Popular Entertainment and Mass Media: The Central Arenas of German-Jewish Cultural Engagement," in Aschheim and Liska, *German-Jewish Experience Revisited*, 103–16; here 110–11. A new restoration of *Das alte Gesetz* is currently in progress and will be completed in 2018.

80. See Peter Jelavich, *Berlin Cabaret* (Cambridge: Harvard University Press, 1993), 201–2.

81. On Jews in the German film industry, see Irene Stratenwerth and Hermann Simon, eds., *Pioniere in Celluloid: Juden in der frühen Filmwelt* (Berlin: Henschel, 2004); and Ashkenazi, *Weimar Film*, 5–15.

82. Harley Erdman has identified a trend toward less visible Jewish characters in American theater in the early twentieth century. Harley Erdman, *Staging the Jew: The Performance of an American Ethnicity, 1860–1920* (New Brunswick, NJ: Rutgers University Press, 1997), 144–61.

83. Valerie Weinstein is currently completing a book on film comedy and antisemitism in Nazi Germany, in which she argues that many antisemitic portrayals in these films represent continuations of trends in the Weimar era.

84. Hans Wollenberg experienced antisemitism as a soldier in the First World War. After 1933, Wollenberg focused his efforts on Jewish self-defense; he served as an editor of *Der Schild* from 1934 to 1938. Max Kolpenitzky (also Max Colpet or Colpe), who later collaborated with Billy Wilder, experienced antisemitism as the son of Russian immigrants growing up in Hamburg. Ulrich Döge, ed., *Hans Wollenberg. Filmpublizist. Mit Kritiken und Aufsätzen von Hans Wollenberg* (Munich: edition text + kritik, 2013); and Max Colpet, *Sag mir wo die Jahre sind. Erinnerungen eines unverbesserlichen Optimisten* (Gütersloh: Mohndruck Reinhard Mohn, 1976).

85. Julius Rosenbaum, "Antisemitische Darstellung im Film," *Israelitisches Familienblatt* 28, no. 46 (November 18, 1926): 12. This article also mentions *Im weißen Rößl* (Oswald, 1926) and *Der Feldherrnhügel* (Schönfelder/Löwenstein, 1926).

86. Wim., "Die Stadt ohne Juden. Ein neuer Schundfilm," *C.V.-Zeitung* 5, no. 30 (July 23, 1926): 399–400. See also "An den Pranger! Uraufführung eines Schundfilms," *Der Schild* 5, no. 30 (July 26, 1926): 237. In her analysis of *Die Stadt ohne Juden*, Lisa Silverman has noted that the Jewish affect and exaggerated gestures of actress Gisela Werbezirk (1875–1956) marked Werbezirk's Christian character as a thinly disguised "Yiddishe Mama," possibly "to reassure audiences that Jewish women could not really 'pass' as non-Jews." Lisa Silverman, *Becoming Austrians*, 71, 233.

87. See Hans Wollenberg, "Die Fabel vom 'verjudeten' Film. Eine sachliche Widerlegung," *C.V.-Zeitung* 6, no. 49 (December 9, 1927): 681; and Hans Wollenberg, "Der Film und seine Beherrscher," *C.V.-Zeitung* 9, no. 19 (May 9, 1930): 248.

88. Hans Wollenberg, "Der Jude im Film," *C.V.-Zeitung* 6, no. 37 (September 16, 1927): 523. On earlier debates in the *C.V.-Zeitung* about theater and the distortion of Jewish characters in cabaret, see Anat Feinberg, "The Unknown Leopold Jessner: German Theatre and Jewish Identity," in Malkin and Rokem, *Jews and the Making of Modern German Theatre*, 232–60; here 238; and Otte, *Jewish Identities*, 255.

89. Wollenberg, "Der Jude im Film," 523.

90. Wollenberg, "Der Jude im Film," 523.

91. "Selbstachtung oder Selbstverhöhnung: Der Jude als Typ im Film, Kabarett und auf der Bühne," *C.V.-Zeitung* 10, no. 49 (December 4, 1931): 558. See also Horst Claus, "Komische Juden oder komische Typen? Hans Steinhoffs *Familientag im Hause Prellstein*," in *Spaß beiseite, Film ab. Jüdischer Humor oder verdrängendes Lachen in der Filmkomödie bis 1945*, ed. Jan Distelmeyer (Hamburg: edition text + kritik, 2006), 21–32; here 29.

92. Max Kolpenitzky, "Der Jude im Film," *Israelitisches Familienblatt* 29, no. 31 (August 4, 1927): 9–10.

93. David Arjeh, "Der Jude im Film," *Jüdische Rundschau* 32, no. 28 (April 8, 1927): 207.

94. C. A. Bratter, "Der amerikanische Jude," *C.V.-Zeitung* 1, no. 14 (August 10,

1922): 179–82; here 181. Bratter further suggested that seeing a performance of this work in Berlin did not provide enough insight into its significance in the United States. On the U.S. reception of the play *Potash and Perlmutter*, see Erdman, *Staging the Jew*, 153–56.

95. A Berlin theatrical performance of this same work prompted one critic to praise its authentic Jewish elements, specifically the "true intersection of Talmud Jew and merchant Jew" enacted by cabaret performer Paul Graetz (1880–1937). See Botho Laserstein, "Potasch und Perlmutter," *Jüdisch-liberale Zeitung* 5, no. 45 (November 6, 1925): 2.

96. See "Fun film: Potash un Perlmutter," *Yidishe ilustrirte tsaytung* 1, no. 17 (July 12, 1924): 266; and "Potasch und Perlmutter," advertisement, *Yidishe ilustrirte tsaytung* 1, no. 19 (September 26, 1924): 302. Among the participating Berlin fashion houses was the Jewish-owned house, Max Becker.

97. On fashion shows and film, see Ganeva, *Women in Weimar Fashion*, 113–41.

98. Yva's *Charleston* appeared on the cover of the *Berliner Illustrirte Zeitung* to celebrate the New Year 1927/1928. See Marion Beckers and Elisabeth Moortgat, eds., *Yva: Photographien 1925–1938* (Berlin: Das Verborgene Museum, 2001), 44–46; and Carmel Finnan, "Between Challenge and Conformity: Yva's Photographic Career and Œuvre," in Schönfeld, *Practicing Modernity*, 120–38; here 127. On Yva, see also Mila Ganeva, "Fashion Photography and Women's Modernity in Weimar Germany: The Case of Yva," *NWSA Journal* 15, no. 3 (2003): 1–25.

99. "Der Jazzsänger," advertisement, *Der Israelit* 69, no. 43 (October 25, 1928): 9. See also "Al Jolson in Der Jazzsänger," advertisement, *C.V.-Zeitung* 7, no. 37 (September 14, 1928): 527. The rerelease of the film in Germany on November 26, 1929 was the synchronized sound version. On the film's release dates, see Gero Gandert, ed., *Der Film der Weimarer Republik, 1929. Ein Handbuch der zeitgenössischen Kritik* (Berlin: Walter de Gruyter, 1993), 869.

100. B. F., "Ein jüdischer Film ('Der Jazzsänger,' Gloria-Palast, Berlin)," *Jüdische Rundschau* 33, nos. 76–77 (September 28, 1928): 544.

101. See Uta G. Poiger, *Jazz, Rock, and Rebels. Cold War Politics and American Culture in a Divided Germany* (Berkeley: University of California Press, 2000), 20.

102. See, for example, the discussion and image in Sundquist, *Strangers in the Land*, 184–85.

103. "Der Jazzsänger," *C.V.-Zeitung* 7, no. 39 (September 28, 1928): 550.

104. See Lutz Koepnick, "3 June 1929: Lloyd Bacon's *The Singing Fool* Triggers Debate about Sound Film," in *A New History of German Cinema*, ed. Jennifer Kapczynski and Michael D. Richardson (Rochester, NY: Camden House, 2012), 197–201.

105. Prawer, *Between Two Worlds*, 98.

106. "Die Begleitmusik," *Israelitisches Familienblatt* 32, no. 4 (January 23, 1930): 63. This cartoon references the line "Siegreich woll'n wir Frankreich schlagen," which is taken from a German military marching song.

107. "Wieder ein Tonfilm mit AL JOLSON!," advertisement, *Berliner jüdische Zeitung* 1, no. 13 (December 8, 1929): 7.

108. "Wieder spielt, singt und spricht Al Jolson in Der Jazzsänger," advertisement, *Gemeindeblatt der Jüdischen Gemeinde zu Berlin* 19, no. 11 (November 1929): 605.

109. Michael Rogin, *Blackface, White Noise: Jewish Immigrants in the Hollywood Melting Pot* (Berkeley: University of California Press, 1996), 12–13, 79–90. Michael Rogin reads *The Jazz Singer* as having used blackface to "screen out" or excise "subversive historical alternatives" to Americanization including Jewishness.

110. On conflations of jazz with Blackness in Weimar culture, see Theodore F. Rippey, "Rationalisation, Race, and the Weimar Response to Jazz," *German Life & Letters* 60, no. 1 (2007): 75–97. On American jazz and entertainment forms in Weimar culture more broadly, see Jost Hermand and Frank Trommler, *Die Kultur der Weimarer Republik* (Munich: Nymphenburger Verlagshandlung, 1978), 49–57, 313–22.

111. *Moritz macht sein Glück* can be viewed at the Bundesarchiv-Filmarchiv, Berlin. On other films starring Siegfried Arno, see Prawer, *Between Two Worlds*, 123–29; and Daniel H. Magilow, "16 December 1927: Debut of *Familientag im Hause Prellstein* Provokes Debate about Jewish Identity in Popular Cinema," in Kapczynski and Richardson, *New History of German Cinema*, 178–84.

112. I borrow the term "screen passing" from Yiman Wang. See Yiman Wang, "The Art of Screen Passing: Anna May Wong's Yellow Yellowface Performance in the Art Deco Era," *Camera Obscura* 20, no. 3 (2005): 159–91; here 160–61.

113. On Jewface, see Erdman, *Staging the Jew*, 102; Harrison-Kahan, *White Negress*, 21; and Jon Stratton, "Television Blackface: Jews, Race, and Comedy in the UK and Australia," in *The Routledge Handbook of Contemporary Jewish Cultures*, ed. Laurence Roth and Nadia Valman (New York: Routledge, 2015), 224–35; here 228.

114. Gotthelf Jacoby, "Jüdisches von Film und Bühne," *Israelitisches Familienblatt* 32, no. 2 (January 9, 1930): 50–51.

115. Harley Erdman has argued that the representation of this same historical role model in the popular play *Disraeli* brought the "exemplary, upstanding Jewish male protagonist" to American stages in the 1910s. Erdman, *Staging the Jew*, 145–49.

116. "Jüdischer Wohlfahrtsfilm 'Ein Freitag-Abend,'" *Bayerische Israelitische Gemeindezeitung* 1, no. 11 (November 11, 1927): 339.

117. "Neue jüdische Bühnen- und Filmwerke," *Israelitisches Familienblatt* 28, no. 50 (December 16, 1926): 509. See also Betty Heimann, "Freitagabend," *Israelitisches Familienblatt* 29, no. 34 (1927).

118. Regina Isaacsohn, "Ein Freitag Abend," *Die jüdische Frau* 2, nos. 13–14 (September 6, 1926): 8.

119. On Jewish charity and social welfare efforts, see Kaplan, *Making of the Jewish Middle Class*, 199–211; and Gillerman, *Germans into Jews*.

120. On early films about Israel/Palestine, see Hillel Tryster, *Israel before Israel: Silent Cinema in the Holy Land* (Jerusalem: Steven Spielberg Jewish Film Archive of the Avraham Harman Institute of Contemporary Jewry, Hebrew University of Jerusalem and the Central Zionist Archives, 1995).

121. Anat Feinberg, "'Wir laden Sie höflich ein'—The Grüngard Salon and Jewish-Zionist Sociability in Berlin in the 1920s," in Dohrn and Pickhan, *Transit und Transformation*, 234–53; here 244. See also "Berliner Kalendar," *Jüdische Rundschau* 30, no. 95 (December 4, 1925): 796.

122. C. A., "Ein Palästina-Film," *Jüdische Rundschau* 33, no. 67 (August 24, 1928): 478.

123. *Frühling in Palästina* can be viewed at the Bundesarchiv-Filmarchiv, Berlin. See "Der neue Palästina-Film," *Jüdische Rundschau* 33, no. 90 (November 13, 1928): 632.

124. "Der neue große Kulturfilm: 'Frühling in Palästina'," *Jüdische Rundschau* 33, no. 91 (November 16, 1928): 640; "Frühling in Palästina," *Jüdische Rundschau* 33, no. 93 (November 23, 1928): 654; and "Frühling in Palästina," *Jüdische Rundschau* 33, no. 101 (December 21, 1928): 716.

125. *Makkabäer* can be viewed at the Bundesarchiv-Filmarchiv, Berlin. It was at this 1929 sports festival in Czechoslovakia that a Jewish Olympics was formally proposed and approved; the first official Maccabiah Games took place in Tel Aviv in 1932.

126. A. Rosenfeld, "Der Makkabi-Film," *Jüdische Rundschau* 35, no. 5 (January 17, 1930): 38.

127. Sociologist Emilie Altenloh argued in her 1914 dissertation that early German cinema was particularly aware of its female audiences. See "On the Sociology of the Cinema" in *German Essays on Film*, ed. Richard W. McCormick and Alison Guenther-Pal (New York: Continuum, 2004), 29–47; and Thomas Elsaesser, "General Introduction," in *A Second Life: German Cinema's First Decades*, ed. Thomas Elsaesser and Michael Wedel (Amsterdam: Amsterdam University Press, 1996), 22.

128. Heinz Ludwigg, "Die Frau und der Film—Eine improvosierte Plauderei," *Die jüdische Frau* 1, no. 1 (May 5, 1925): 12.

129. Siegfried Kracauer, "The Little Shopgirls Go to the Movies," in *The Mass Ornament: Weimar Essays*, trans. and ed. Thomas Y. Levin (Cambridge: Harvard University Press, 1995), 291–304; here 292.

130. Mary Ann Doane, "Film and the Masquerade: Theorising the Female Spectator," in *Feminist Film Theory: A Reader*, ed. Sue Thornham (New York: New York University Press, 1999), 131–45.

131. Because no copy of *Leichte Kavallerie* is available in film archives, I have drawn information about the film's content from the intertitles and other print materials, folder 1361, Stiftung Deutsche Kinemathek, Schriftgutarchiv, Berlin. The Film-Prüfstelle Berlin card (no. 16777) is dated September 28, 1927.

132. On the reception of *Leichte Kavallerie* in the general press, see Philipp Stiasny, "Filme über den Ersten Weltkrieg und ihre Presserezeption in der Weimarer Republik" (master's thesis, Humboldt-Universität zu Berlin, 1999), 167–68.

133. Kracauer, "Film 1928," in *Mass Ornament*, 307–30; here 309.

134. The press mentioned little about the film's director, Rolf Randolf (1878–1941, born Rudolf Zanbauer), a non-Jew who continued making films in Germany until his death in 1941.

135. "Jüdisches in einem neuen Großfilm," *Israelitisches Familienblatt* 29, no. 40 (October 5, 1927): 13. The film was also advertised in *Jüdische Rundschau*: "Spielplan der Ufa-Theater," *Jüdische Rundschau* 32, no. 97 (December 6, 1927): 692.

136. Though not Jewish, Elizza La Porta (1902–97, born Eliza Streinu) was married to a Jewish man (Siegfried Pinkus); they left Berlin for Los Angeles in the late 1930s. See "Elizza La Porta" in Weniger, *Es wird im Leben*, 290–91.

137. On Wegener's *Der Golem*, see Noah Isenberg, *Between Redemption and Doom: The Strains of German-Jewish Modernism* (Lincoln: University of Nebraska Press,

1999), 77–104; Noah Isenberg, "Of Monsters and Magicians: Paul Wegener's *The Golem: How He Came into the World* (1920)," in *Weimar Cinema: An Essential Guide to the Classic Films of the Era*, ed. Noah Isenberg (New York: Columbia University Press, 2009), 33–54; Cathy S. Gelbin, *The Golem Returns: From German Romantic Literature to Global Jewish Culture, 1808–2008* (Ann Arbor: University of Michigan Press, 2011), 115–23; and Maya Barzilai, *Golem: Modern Wars and Their Monsters* (New York: New York University Press, 2016).

138. Among other works, see Petro, *Joyless Streets*; and Heide Schlüpmann, "Highway through the Void: The Film Theorist and the Film Actress," in *Culture in the Anteroom: The Legacies of Siegfried Kracauer*, ed. Gerd Gemünden and Johannes von Moltke (Ann Arbor: University of Michigan Press, 2012), 76–89.

139. Georg Herzberg, "Leichte Kavallerie (Marmorhaus)," *Film-Kurier*, October 14, 1927, folder 1361, Stiftung Deutsche Kinemathek, Schriftgutarchiv, Berlin.

140. Oswald's *Dreyfus* was reviewed or publicized in all of the major German-Jewish newspapers; see below and the advertisement in *Jüdische Rundschau* 35, no. 66 (August 22, 1930): 438.

141. See, for example, Jill Suzanne Smith, "Richard Oswald and the Social Hygiene Film: Promoting Public Health or Promiscuity?," in Rogowski, *Many Faces of Weimar Cinema*, 13–30; and Ashkenazi, *Weimar Film*, 97–110, 133–37.

142. Prawer, *Between Two Worlds*, 149; and Ashkenazi, *Weimar Film*, 99–101.

143. Kortner performed the role of Shylock hundreds of times from 1916 until 1968. See Klaus Völker, *Fritz Kortner: Schauspieler und Regisseur* (Berlin: Hentrich, 1987), 93.

144. On Kortner's appearance, see Richard Critchfield, *From Shakespeare to Frisch: The Provocative Fritz Kortner* (Heidelberg: Synchron, 2008), 32. See also Robert Shandley, "Fritz Kortner's Last Illusion," in *Unlikely History: The Changing German-Jewish Symbiosis, 1945–2000*, ed. Leslie Morris and Jack Zipes (New York: Palgrave, 2002), 251–61; and Prawer, *Between Two Worlds*, x–xi.

145. Doris Wittner, "Dreyfus im Film," *Jüdisch-liberale Zeitung* 10, no. 37 (September 10, 1930): 2.

146. Will Pleß, "Dreyfus. Zum neuen Oswald-Tonfilm," *Israelitisches Familienblatt* 32, no. 41 (October 9, 1930): 164–65. Of this same cry of Kortner's, critic Hans Feld later wrote that it "had the sound of a trumpet summoning to the Last Judgment." Hans Feld, "Jews in the Development of the German Film Industry. Notes from the Recollections of a Berlin Film Critic," *Leo Baeck Institute Year Book* 27 (1982): 337–65; here 358.

147. Richard Oswald to Siegfried Kracauer, undated letter probably written in June 1947. Helmut G. Asper, "'Für Ihre Files will ich Ihnen ein paar Facts geben'. Richard Oswald an Siegfried Kracauer über seine Filmarbeit in der Weimarer Republik und im amerikanischen Exil," *Filmblatt* 5, no. 14 (2000): 22–27; here 25.

148. Joseph Goebbels supposedly interpreted the film *Dreyfus* as a strategic anti-NSDAP (National Socialist German Workers' Party, or Nazi Party) election maneuver. See William Grange, *Historical Dictionary of German Theater* (Lanham, MD: Scarecrow Press, 2006), 125. In the United States, too, the film was screened as an anti-Nazi act: it was shown at the Thalia Theatre in New York in late 1940 when two Jewish

groups that opposed the screening of Nazi films in America, the Joint Boycott Council and the Non-Sectarian Anti-Nazi League, supported its release. See Harry Waldman, *Nazi Films in America, 1933–1942* (Jefferson, NC: McFarland, 2008), 259–60.

149. Kortner's autobiography also briefly notes that he toured Germany with *Dreyfus* as a triumphant Jew in the fight against antisemitism. Fritz Kortner, *Aller Tage Abend* (Munich: Kindler Verlag, 1959), 415.

150. See, for example, Dr. M[argarete] E[delheim], "Die Dreyfus-Tragödie als Film," *C.V.-Zeitung* 9, no. 34 (August 22, 1930): 447; and I[gnaz] E[mrich], "Dreyfus im Film," *Das Jüdische Echo* 17, no. 35 (August 29, 1930): 493–94.

151. Pleß, "Dreyfus," 164–65.

152. On Mosheim's biography, see the transcript of oral history interviews with Grete Mosheim conducted by Armin Eichholz, Grete Mosheim Collection, No. 211, Box 6.5–6.8; here 6.5: 8, 72 and 6.6: 109, USC Special Collections, Los Angeles. This lengthy transcription (335 typed pages; hereinafter "GM Interview") reflects interviews most likely conducted in 1985 in preparation for a biography of Mosheim that never came to fruition; one letter suggests that Mosheim's failing memory was to blame for the termination of the project. Mosheim was not alone in having learned at a relatively late age about her family's connections to Jewishness. Political theorist Hannah Arendt (1906–75), too, maintained that her family never uttered the word "Jew" at home, and that she learned about her Jewishness through antisemitic remarks. See Hannah Arendt, "Zur Person," interview by Günter Gaus, ZDF television, West Germany, October 28, 1964 (https://www.youtube.com/watch?v=J9SyTEUi6Kw).

153. Kortner, *Aller Tage Abend*, 401.

154. "Eine Schauspielerin von Format," *Die junge Dame*, 1934, no. 8, Grete Mosheim Collection, Box 2.24, USC Special Collections, Los Angeles.

155. Rudolf Arnheim, *Film Essays and Criticism* (Madison: University of Wisconsin Press, 1997), 217. Hubert von Meyerinck, *Meine berühmten Freundinnen. Erinnerungen* (Düsseldorf: Econ-Verlag, 1967), 140.

156. GM Interview 6.5, 39.

157. Mosheim recalled that she took the role of Lucie Dreyfus mainly because her then husband, Oskar Homolka, stood a better chance of landing the role of Esterhazy if she agreed to bring her "power of attraction" (*Anziehungskraft*) to the film. GM Interview 6.5, 49.

158. Prawer, *Between Two Worlds*, 154.

## CHAPTER 3

1. See, for example, Hans Guggenheimer, "Bayerische Sommerfrischen! Ein Mahnwort an jüdische Reisende," *C.V.- Zeitung* 1, no. 4 (May 26, 1922): 49. On resort antisemitism, see Frank Bajohr, *"Unser Hotel ist judenfrei". Bäder-Antisemitismus im 19. und 20. Jahrhundert* (Frankfurt am Main: Fischer Taschenbuch Verlag, 2003), 53–115; and Inbal Steinitz, *Der Kampf jüdischer Anwälte gegen den Antisemitismus: Rechtsschutz durch den Centralverein deutscher Staatsbürger jüdischen Glaubens (1893–1933)* (Berlin: Metropol-Verlag, 2007). See also the discussion in *Der Schild* 4, nos. 23, 25, 33 (1925).

2. On representations of wealthy German Jews, see David Brenner, *Marketing Identities*, 92. On American Jewish women and excess, see Jenna Weissman Joselit, *A Perfect Fit: Clothes, Character, and the Promise of America* (New York: Metropolitan Books, 2001), 181–87; and Riv-Ellen Prell, *Fighting to Become Americans: Assimilation and the Trouble between Jewish Women and Jewish Men* (Boston: Beacon Press, 1999), 43, 163. On the stereotype of the JAP (Jewish American Princess), see also Zemel, *Looking Jewish*, 107, 124–26. In American Jewish culture, see Abraham Cahan's novel, *The Rise of David Levinsky* (1917), in which Cahan describes the figure of Auntie Yetta, "whose fingers were a veritable jewelry store," and as someone who went out of her way to exhibit her "flaming rings." Abraham Cahan, *The Rise of David Levinsky*, introduction by John Higham (New York: Harper and Row, 1960), 367.

3. "Die Blonde und die Brünette," *Israelitisches Familienblatt* 27, no. 29 (July 16, 1925): 9.

4. Anita Loos's Lorelei stories were serialized in *Harper's Bazaar* beginning in March 1925. See Lisa Mendelman, "Sentimental Satire in Anita Loos's *Gentlemen Prefer Blondes*," in *The Sentimental Mode: Essays in Literature, Film and Television*, ed. Jennifer A. Williamson, Jennifer Larson, and Ashley Reed (Jefferson, NC: McFarland and Company, 2014), 36–56. *Gentlemen Prefer Blondes* also appeared in German magazines under the title *Blondinen bevorzugt*; see *Die Dame* 54, no. 23 (August 1927), 28.

5. Kleinol Henna Shampoo, advertisement, *Gemeindeblatt der Jüdischen Gemeinde zu Berlin* 21, no. 12 (December 1931): 369.

6. See Buerkle, "Gendered Spectatorship," 631; and Guenther, *Nazi Chic*, 91–92, 98–109. The *Jüdische Rundschau* advertised such films as *Blonde or Brunette* (Rosson, 1927) that referenced larger debates about appearance. See "Blond oder Braun," *Jüdische Rundschau* 33, nos. 38–39 (May 16, 1928): 283.

7. On passing in Nazi Germany, see Marion A. Kaplan, *Between Dignity and Despair: Jewish Life in Nazi Germany* (New York: Oxford University Press, 1998), 35–36.

8. Wendy Brown, *Regulating Aversion: Tolerance in the Age of Identity and Empire* (Princeton: Princeton University Press, 2006), 7. On self-policing, see also Foucault, *Discipline and Punish*.

9. On hidden Jewishness in other contexts, such as the crypto-Jews in Spain, see Janet Jacobs, *Hidden Heritage*; and Gilman, *Jewish Self-Hatred*, 270. On the legacy of marranos and conversos in German-Jewish contexts, see Skolnik, *Jewish Pasts*, 154–55.

10. For a detailed account of the attacks during the period 1924–29, see Hecht, *Deutsche Juden*, 187–205. On Leipzig, see Jon Gunnar Mølstre Simonsen, "Perfect Targets—Antisemitism and Eastern Jews in Leipzig, 1919–1923," *Leo Baeck Institute Year Book* 51 (2006): 79–101.

11. On violence against street hawkers, see Molly Loberg, "The Streetscape of Economic Crisis: Commerce, Politics, and Urban Space in Interwar Berlin," *Journal of Modern History* 85, no. 2 (2013): 364–402.

12. See "Die judenfeindlichen Ausschreitungen in Berlin," *Jüdische Rundschau* 28, no. 96 (November 9, 1923): 557–59. See also Large, "Out with the Ostjuden," in Hoffmann, Bergmann, and Smith, *Exclusionary Violence*; and Maurer, *Ostjuden in Deutschland*.

13. See Aschheim, *Brothers and Strangers*, 44–45.

14. See Sonja Miltenberger, *Jüdisches Leben am Kurfürstendamm*, ed. Birgit Jochens (Berlin: Text Verlag Edition Berlin, 2011), 14.

15. Kurt Zielenziger, "Kurfürstendamm und Alexanderplatz. Eine zeitgemäße Betrachtung," *C.V.-Zeitung* 4, no. 48 (November 27, 1925): 755. Cf. Gabriel Eikenberg, *Der Mythos deutscher Kultur im Spiegel jüdischer Presse in Deutschland und Österreich von 1918 bis 1938* (Hildesheim: Georg Olms Verlag, 2010), 127.

16. See Kreutzmüller, *Final Sale*, 101, 138n20.

17. On the 1927 attacks, see Thomas Friedrich, *Hitler's Berlin: Abused City*, trans. Stewart Spencer (New Haven: Yale University Press, 2012), 103–6; and Hecht, *Deutsche Juden*, 196–97.

18. "Nastätten—Köln—Berlin. Der nationalsozialistische Terror wählt an," *C.V.-Zeitung* 6, no. 12 (March 25, 1927): 151.

19. Also around this time, in 1928, the Centralverein founded its "Office Wilhelmstraße," a (nonsecret) organization designed to develop new forms of propaganda to counter antisemitic propaganda. See Isabel Enzenbach, "'Kennwort: Gummi': Der Centralverein deutscher Staatsbürger jüdischen Glaubens im Kampf um den öffentlichen Raum von 1892 bis zum Ende der Weimarer Republik," in Braun, *Was war deutsches Judentum*, 203–20.

20. On the Jewish Defense Service, see Avraham Barkai, "Political Orientations and Crisis Consciousness," in Meyer and Brenner, *German-Jewish History*, vol. 4, 121–24; Donald L. Niewyk, *The Jews in Weimar Germany*, with a new introduction by the author (New Brunswick, NJ: Transaction Publishers, 2001), 91; and Dunker, *Reichsbund*, 63–66, 262–64. In 1973, Dunker interviewed a former member of the JAD, Fritz Lewinson, who claimed that the JAD had been involved in mitigating the damage of the 1931 attacks.

21. "Die Ausschreitungen am Kurfürstendamm," *C.V.-Zeitung* 10, no. 38 (September 18, 1931): 457–58. On the so-called Kurfürstendamm pogrom, see Hecht, *Deutsche Juden*, 240–53; Kreutzmüller, *Final Sale*, 101; Jelavich, *Berlin Cabaret*, 202–3; and Amos Elon, *The Pity of It All: A History of Jews in Germany, 1743–1933* (New York: Metropolitan Books, 2002), 387.

22. Reiner, *Mein Leben*, 155; and "Max Reiner," in Richarz, *Jüdisches Leben*, 113–14.

23. "Kritischer Rückblick. Nachwort zu den Ausschreitungen im Berliner Westen," *Der Schild* 10, no. 19 (October 8, 1931): 149.

24. The feud occurred in newspapers including *Alarm*, which was nominally affiliated with the Centralverein. On *Alarm*, a newspaper distributed by journalist Artur Schweriner, see Jacob Toury, "Die Judenfrage in der Entstehungsphase des Reichsbanners Schwarz-Rot-Gold," in *Juden und deutsche Arbeiterbewegung bis 1933: Soziale Utopien und religiös-kulturelle Traditionen*, ed. Ludger Heid and Arnold Paucker (Tübingen: Mohr, 1992), 215–36; here 229.

25. Letter to Wilhelm Graetz, November 6, 1931, Centrum Judaicum Archival Materials, 1,75D Gr 1, Nr. 7, #13319, Bl. 196–198. The signatures on this letter are nearly illegible; it appears that two people signed the letter whose last names were "Zwirn" and "Callmann." Zwirn might be Zionist Isaak Zwirn; Callmann might be either Walter Callmann, an active member of the RjF, or Rudolf Callmann of the Centralverein. Graetz was part of the executive board of the Centralverein; he also was a member of the board of the Berlin Jewish community from 1931 to 1936. See Wilhelm Graetz, "Jüdische Jugend in der Grossstadt," *C.V.-Zeitung* 12, no. 2 (January 12, 1933): 13.

26. Gay, *Freud, Jews and Other Germans*, 199–200, 187.

27. On inner-Jewish critiques of Austrian Jewish women and luxury, see Rose, *Jewish Women*, 65–66, 72.

28. On debates about Jewish women and fashion, see Kerry Wallach, "Weimar Jewish Chic: Jewish Women and Fashion in 1920s Germany," in Greenspoon, *Fashioning Jews*, 113–35.

29. On representations of Jews as wealthy, including as bankers and moneylenders, see Fritz Backhaus, Raphael Gross, and Liliane Weissberg, eds., *Juden. Geld. Eine Vorstellung* (Frankfurt am Main: Campus Verlag, 2013).

30. Arnim, "Über die Kennzeichen," in Arnim, *Texte der deutschen Tischgesellschaft*, 124.

31. On similar antisemitic caricatures in Nazi Germany, see Weinstein, "White Jews," in Hales, Petrescu, and Weinstein, *Continuity and Crisis in German Cinema*, xx.

32. On depictions of Jews in *Fliegende Blätter*, see Henry Wassermann, "Caricature, Anti-Jewish (Modern)" and "*Fliegende Blätter*," in *Antisemitism: A Historical Encyclopedia of Prejudice and Persecution*, vol. 1, ed. Richard S. Levy (Santa Barbara, CA: ABC-CLIO, 2005), 102–7, 230–31; and Henry Wassermann, "The Fliegende Blätter as a Source for the Social History of German Jewry," *Leo Baeck Institute Year Book* 28 (1983): 93–138.

33. "Der theure Schmuck," *Fliegende Blätter* 11, no. 251 (1850): 88, http://dx.doi.org/doi:10.11588/diglit.2113.11. See also Fuchs, *Die Juden in der Karikatur*, 153.

34. See Andrew R. Heinze, *Adapting to Abundance: Jewish Immigrants, Mass Consumption, and the Search for American Identity* (New York: Columbia University Press, 1990).

35. The "Jew-els" caricature appeared in *Beckett's Budget*, April 10, 1929; reprinted in Conor, *Spectacular Modern Woman*, 194.

36. Drawing by Fritz Julian Levi in *Schlemiel. Jüdische Blätter für Humor und Kunst*, no. 14 (1920): 196.

37. Rathenau, "Hear, O Israel!," 816. See also chapter 1.

38. On the reception of Rathenau in the German-Jewish press, see Eikenberg, *Mythos deutscher Kultur*, 107–8; and Volkov, *Walther Rathenau*.

39. "Walter Rathenau über die Frau," *Die jüdische Frau* 1, no. 2 (May 22, 1925): 6.

40. E. M. "Berlin," *Allgemeine Zeitung des Judentums* 85, no. 19 (September 16, 1921): supplement p. 2; and Ernst Schäffer, "Selbstzucht!," *Der Schild* 5, no. 20 (May 17, 1926): 153. See also Adolph Asch, "Fight for German Jewry's Honour: Reminiscences about the R.J.F.," *AJR Information* 16, no. 8 (1961): 9.

41. See Otte, *Jewish Identities*, 255.

42. "Der RjF tritt ein für straffe Selbstzucht und Einfachheit der Lebensführung!," undated pamphlet, Centrum Judaicum Archival Materials, 1,75A Be2, Nr. 9 (Ident.-Nr.233) [236].

43. Undated brochure, possibly circa 1921. Cited in Niewyk, *Jews in Weimar Germany*, 92; see also Dunker, *Reichsbund*, 49.

44. Niewyk, *Jews in Weimar Germany*, 91–95.

45. "Jüdische Frauen!," *Der Schild* 1, no. 10 (October 1922): 4; italics in original.

46. In his memoirs, Asch wrote that he was a cofounder of the Berlin branch of the Self-discipline Organization, together with Alfred Wiener, who served as a representa-

tive of the Centralverein. Ulrich Dunker suggests this is a problematic assertion because Asch was not listed as one of the attendees of the meeting at which the *Selbstzuchtaktion* was first discussed. Rather, Dunker suggests that Rabbi Klein of Düsseldorf, teacher Arnold Stein, and attorney Samoje first discussed this project, as recorded in *Der Schild* in 1921. Dunker notes that Asch was the chairman of the "Zoo District" (Bezirk Zoo) in 1922, and that he led the Propaganda and Entertainment Committee beginning in 1923. Dunker, *Reichsbund*, 253. See also "Aus den Ortsgruppen," *Der Schild* 11, no. 14 (December 1922/January 1923): 3–4. It is also possible that RjF founder Leo Löwenstein (1877–1956) headed up the self-discipline efforts on a national level; Walter Callmann (1885–1960; formerly Wilhelm Schmidt) was supposedly later active in the Berlin local division. See Ernst Schäffer, "Selbstzucht!," *Der Schild* 5, no. 20 (May 17, 1926): 153.

47. Adolf Asch, *Auszug aus Memoiren von Dr. Adolf Asch (Die Inflationsjahre 1919–1928)*, 3, file no. 2 (Adolph Asch), Leo Baeck Institute, Jerusalem. Translation cited in Gay, *Freud, Jews and Other Germans*, 183. Because Asch's first name is spelled with a "ph" in English-language publications from after the Second World War, I retain that spelling here.

48. Asch, *Memoiren (Die Inflationsjahre)*, unpublished manuscript, Leo Baeck Institute, 4.

49. See Asch, "Fight for German Jewry's Honour," 9.

50. Historian Lisa Fetheringill Zwicker points out that Asch's response to this attack was to argue for the effectiveness of Jewish organizations in combating antisemitism, though she rightly challenges the validity of Asch's claims of the success of these organizations. Zwicker, "Performing Masculinity," in Baader, Gillerman, and Lerner, *Jewish Masculinities*, 129.

51. Avraham Barkai, "The Organized Jewish Community," in Meyer and Brenner, *German-Jewish History*, vol. 4, 87; and Barkai, *Wehr dich*.

52. Der Vorstand des Allgemeinen Rabbinerverbandes in Deutschland, "Ein Mahnwort an Alle!," *C.V.-Zeitung* 1, no. 7 (June 15, 1922): 85.

53. Ludwig Holländer, "Selbstwürde," *C.V.-Zeitung* 1, no. 14 (August 10, 1922): 173. See also Barkai, *Wehr dich*, 108–09.

54. "Frauenmoden," *Der Israelit* 66, no. 3 (January 15, 1925): 1–2.

55. Kaplan, "Sisterhood under Siege," in Bridenthal, Grossmann, and Kaplan, *When Biology Became Destiny*, 190–91. On the politicization of German women's fashion, see Maria Makela, "The Rise and Fall of the Flapper Dress: Nationalism and Anti-Semitism in Early-Twentieth Century Discourses on German Fashion," *Journal of Popular Culture* 34, no. 3 (2000): 183–208.

56. Else Fuchs-Hes, "Frauenpsyche und Mode," *Israelitisches Familienblatt* 27, no. 26 (June 25, 1925): 17. On Else Fuchs-Hes (born Hes, later Else Rabin), see Claudia Prestel, "Frauenpolitik oder Parteipolitik? Jüdische Frauen in innerjüdischer Politik in der Weimarer Republik," *Archiv für Sozialgeschichte* 37 (1997): 121–55.

57. Doris Wittner, "Frauenmode," *C.V.-Zeitung* 5, no. 28 (July 9, 1926): 373–74. See also the short article to which this piece was a response: "Gegen die Auswüchse der Frauenmode," *C.V.-Zeitung* 5, no. 26 (June 25, 1926): 350.

58. Regina Isaacsohn, "Die deutsch-jüdische Frau in ihrem Vaterland," *Jüdisch-liberale Zeitung* 11, nos. 32–33 (August 19, 1931): 11.

59. [Leo] Baeck, ". . . alles wahre Ideale erstorben," *C.V.-Zeitung* 10, no. 38 (September 18, 1931): 457. See also Hecht, *Deutsche Juden*, 247.

60. Regina Isaacsohn, "Es ist wichtig . . . Eine Frauenstimme über die Möglichkeit der Aufklärungsarbeit," *Der Schild* 10, no. 22 (November 26, 1931): 175.

61. On the regulation of Jews by the state, see Brown, *Regulating Aversion*, 69; and Pulzer, *Jews and the German State*.

62. See Mirjam Zadoff, *Next Year in Marienbad: The Lost Worlds of Jewish Spa Culture* (Philadelphia: University of Pennsylvania Press, 2012), 33. See also Kaplan, *Making of the Jewish Middle Class*, 124–25.

63. Zadoff, *Next Year*, 83; see also Garber, *Vested Interests*, 130.

64. Bajohr, *Unser Hotel ist judenfrei*, 11–16.

65. Prediger Goldmann-Herford, "Vor der Sommerreise. Ein Mahnwort an die deutschen Juden," *C.V.-Zeitung* 3, no. 21 (May 22, 1924): 306. Although it is coincidental that "genteel," here a translation of the word *vornehm* (also elegant, posh, or noble), bears some resemblance to the word "gentile," I would suggest that instructing Jews to strive for genteel restraint was akin to instructing them to appear non-Jewish.

66. Hirschberg, *Mein Leben*, unpublished manuscript, Leo Baeck Institute, 17–18. Today Altheide is located in southwestern Poland.

67. Zadoff, *Next Year*, 95, 76–78.

68. See, for example, Philipp Löwenfeld, *Memoirs*, undated manuscript written between 1940 and 1945, excerpted in Richarz, *Jewish Life in Germany*, 234–46. David Clay Large also discusses the surprise Western Jews experienced upon confronting Eastern Jews who exhibited material opulence. See David Clay Large, *The Grand Spas of Central Europe: A History of Intrigue, Politics, Art, and Healing* (Lanham, MD: Rowman and Littlefield, 2015), 252–53.

69. Zadoff, *Next Year*, 85–86.

70. Notable contributions by Brod appeared in the Jewish magazines *Der Jude* and *Neue jüdische Monatshefte*, as well as the Prague Zionist weekly, *Selbstwehr*; he was also head feuilleton editor of the *Prager Tagblatt* beginning in 1918.

71. Brod first encountered Buber while attending the first of his three speeches about Judaism, which Buber delivered in Prague in 1909. See Margarita Pazi, *Max Brod. Werk und Persönlichkeit* (Bonn: H. Bouvier u. Co. Verlag, 1970), 57–58; and Max Brod, *Streitbares Leben. Autobiographie* (Munich: Kindler Verlag, 1960), 79. On Buber's Zionist antimaterialism, see David Biale, *Eros and the Jews: From Biblical Israel to Contemporary America* (Berkeley: University of California Press, 1997), 180–82.

72. See, for example, the following articles about types of Jewish women: Franz Sachs, "Von deutschen Jüdinnen," *Der Jude* 1, no. 10 (January 1917): 662–64; Hildegard Krohn, Martha Epstein, and Johanna Simon-Friedberg, "Von deutschen Jüdinnen," *Der Jude* 1, no. 12 (March 1917): 849–51; Max Brod, "Jüdinnen," *Neue jüdische Monatshefte* 2, no. 20 (July 25, 1918): 481; Abraham Schwadron, "Die Jüdin als Assimilantin," *Neue jüdische Monatshefte* 2, no. 20 (July 25, 1918): 515; and Ernst Emil Schweitzer, "Eine Beschimpfung der jüdischen Frau. Ein Protest," *Allgemeine Zeitung des Judentums* 83, no. 1 (January 3, 1919): 7–9.

73. For a complete bibliography of Brod's published work, see Gaëlle Vassogne, *Max Brod in Prag. Identität und Vermittlung* (Tübingen: Max Niemeyer Verlag, 2009).

74. Friedrich Weihs, *Aus Geschichte und Leben der Teplitzer Judengemeinde*

*(1782–1932)* (Prague: Jüdischer Buch- und Kunstverlag, 1932), 40–41. In 1811, Rahel Varnhagen described her anticipation of a trip to Teplitz. See Heidi Thomann Tewarson, "Jüdisches—Weibliches: Rahel Levin Varnhagens Reisen als Überschreitungen," *German Quarterly* 66, no. 2 (1993): 145–59; here 150. On Teplitz, see also Simone Lässig, *Jüdische Wege ins Bürgertum. Kulturelles Kapital und sozialer Aufstieg im 19. Jahrhundert* (Göttingen: Vandenhoeck & Ruprecht, 2004).

75. See Hans Dieter Zimmermann, afterword to Max Brod, *Jüdinnen. Roman und andere Prosa aus den Jahren 1906–1916*, with a foreword by Alena Wagnerová (Göttingen: Wallstein Verlag, 2013), 331–41; here 338.

76. See Spector, *Prague Territories*, 186–87; and Vassogne, *Max Brod in Prag*, 51.

77. Max Brod, *Jüdinnen. Ein Roman* (1911; repr., Leipzig: Kurt Wolff Verlag, 1915), 43–44. Citations refer to the 1915 edition.

78. Brod, *Jüdinnen*, 69. See also Robertson, *Jewish Question*, 282.

79. Brod, *Jüdinnen*, 306.

80. Brod defended the types he established in *Jüdinnen* shortly after their creation. See Vassogne, *Max Brod in Prag*, 55–56, 255.

81. On the hotel setting of *Fräulein Else*, see Bettina Matthias, *The Hotel as Setting in Early 20th-Century German and Austrian Literature: Checking In to Tell a Story* (Rochester, NY: Camden House, 2006), 67–103.

82. On earlier works of Schnitzler's with Jewish content that was more explicit, including *Der Weg ins Freie* (The Road into the Open, 1908) and *Professor Bernhardi* (1912), see Gillman, *Viennese Jewish Modernism*, 101–26.

83. On the ways in which Dorsday is coded as an East European Jew and the significance of Jewishness for understanding *Fraülein Else*, see Andrew Barker, *Fictions from an Orphan State: Literary Reflections of Austria between Habsburg and Hitler* (Rochester, NY: Camden House, 2012), 51.

84. Arthur Schnitzler, *Fräulein Else*, trans. F. H. Lyon (London: Pushkin Press, 2012), 22.

85. Sander Gilman has argued that this unspecified *it* signifies the "visible invisibility of the Jewishness of her parents" as embedded in Else's mother's language through accent and word choice. Sander L. Gilman, *Franz Kafka: The Jewish Patient* (New York: Routledge, 1995), 25. See also Robertson, *Jewish Question*, 283–85.

86. See Wallach, "Escape Artistry."

87. Schnitzler, *Fräulein Else*, 12.

88. Critic Siegfried Kracauer famously characterized the bodies of such women as key to understanding mechanized modernity: the legs of the dancers mesmerized the German masses with a radical, even hypnotic mass ornament. Kracauer, "The Mass Ornament," in *Mass Ornament*, 75–86.

89. Ritchie Robertson has suggested the arrival of relatives was a recurring theme in Jewish literature of this time. See Robertson, *Jewish Question*, 274.

90. The fictional town of Haiderstadt bears some similarities to the actual town of Halberstadt, a center of Orthodox Jewish learning near Hannover.

91. Kate Elswit, who highlights the centrality of public dance performances in Weimar culture, points out that especially the performances of many women could be purchased. Kate Elswit, *Watching Weimar Dance* (New York: Oxford University Press, 2014), 63–64.

92. *Esther* was published in the *Allgemeine Zeitung des Judentums* from April to June 1920, and a slightly modified version appeared as *Die Tänzerin* in the *Israelitisches Familienblatt* from September to November 1920. All citations refer to the version first published in *Allgemeine Zeitung des Judentums*. In 1920, the combined circulations of these two periodicals approached 34,000, which suggests they had approximately 100,000 total readers. See circulation data in *Sperlings*, 369. See also chapter 2, note 24.

93. A third version of the novel, a 52-page typed manuscript with notes handwritten by Krämer, can be found among Krämer's papers. See "Esther," Clementine Krämer Papers, microfilm 790, reel no. 1, folder 28, Leo Baeck Institute, New York and Berlin. Krämer's notes reflect some of the minor changes she made when revising the text for its publication in the *Familienblatt*. That Krämer's revised draft still bears the title *Esther* suggests that the editors of the *Familienblatt* may have changed the title. Other modifications, too, indicate that the second version had been copyedited and streamlined so as to appeal to a more mainstream audience; slight linguistic modifications suggest a move away from Yiddishized terms and expressions (for example: "*als*" instead of "*wie*").

94. Jonathan Hess, *Middlebrow Literature and the Making of German-Jewish Identity* (Stanford: Stanford University Press, 2010), 11, 23; and Skolnik, *Jewish Pasts*. Jonathan Hess has suggested that the creation of Jewish fiction played a major role in shaping German-Jewish nineteenth-century identity, and that the 1920s saw a continuation of earlier trends.

95. Clementine Krämer's parents moved from Rheinbischofsheim, near Alsace, to Karlsruhe when she was seven years old; she spent her vacations visiting relatives in Rheinbischofsheim and in Mühringen, a small town in the Black Forest. Depictions of Jewish life in rural German villages can be found in several of Krämer's works that were serialized in the Jewish press, including *Der Weg des jungen Hermann Kahn* (The Path of Young Hermann Kahn; serialized in *Allgemeine Zeitung des Judentums* in 1918, nos. 5–16); *Erinnerungen* (Memories; sketches published in the *Jüdisch-liberale Zeitung* in September–October 1924); and *Esther*.

96. Elizabeth Loentz, "'The Most Famous Jewish Pacifist was Jesus of Nazareth': German-Jewish Pacifist Clementine Krämer's Stories of War and Visions for Peace," *Women in German Yearbook* 23 (2007): 126–55; here 128. Other women journalists who made significant contributions to the Jewish press, such as Doris Wittner and Bertha Badt-Strauss, similarly saved articles on Jewish topics for Jewish publications.

97. On Krämer's biography, see Werner J. Cahnman, "The Life of Clementine Kraemer," *Leo Baeck Institute Year Book* 9 (1964): 267–92; here 268.

98. Krämer's only two novels were both published exclusively in Jewish periodicals. Krämer's nephew, Werner Cahnman, suggests that *Esther* can be read as a companion piece to Krämer's first novel, *Der Weg des jungen Hermann Kahn*. Cahnman further suggests that parts of *Hermann Kahn* are based on elements from Krämer's life and the lives of people in her family. Cahnman, "Life of Clementine Kraemer," 276–78.

99. In a different article, Krämer proclaims the biblical Queen Esther a model for contemporary Jewish women. Clementine Krämer, "Biblische und moderne Frauen: Esther," *Jüdisch-liberale Zeitung* 5, no. 44 (October 30, 1925): 1–2.

100. Sonia Gollance argues that Krämer's Esther uses dance as a way of gaining

agency after a childhood trauma. See Sonia Gollance, "Harmonious Instability: (Mixed) Dancing and Partner Choice in German-Jewish and Yiddish Literature" (PhD diss., University of Pennsylvania, 2017). On literary images of Jews as parvenus, see David Brenner, *Marketing Identities*, 85–86.

101. See the first three installments of *Esther* in *Allgemeine Zeitung des Judentums* 84, nos. 14, 15, 16 (April 1920), pages 156, 166, 178, respectively.

102. Eve Sedgwick has pointed out that other works with similarities to the biblical Book of Esther, such as French playwright Racine's *Esther* (1689), also incorporate the moment of surprise when Ahashuerus discovers that Esther is Jewish. Sedgwick, *Epistemology*, 75–80.

103. Ritchie Robertson has suggested this was a recurring theme in Jewish literature of this time. Robertson, *Jewish Question*, 274.

104. Krämer, "Esther," *Allgemeine Zeitung des Judentums* 84, no. 19 (May 7, 1920): 214–16; here 215.

105. Historically, most inner-Jewish complaints about and criticisms of Jewish cabaret performers were aimed at those who explicitly made fun of Jews or used numerous Yiddish references. See Jelavich, *Berlin Cabaret*, 123–34; and Otte, *Jewish Identities*, 255–57.

106. Krämer, "Esther," *Allgemeine Zeitung des Judentums* 84, no. 23 (June 4, 1920): 263–64; here 264.

107. Klaus Mann's character Greta Valentin in *Treffpunkt im Unendlichen* (1932) bears similarities to Lena Amsel. Annemarie Schwarzenbach, in her then still unpublished *Pariser Novelle* (1929), described Lena Amsel as a "small Polish Jewess" (*kleine polnische Jüdin*). See Ruth Landshoff-Yorck, *Roman einer Tänzerin. Erstausgabe aus dem Nachlaß*, ed. and with an afterword by Walter Fähnders (Berlin: AvivA, 2002), 116. It is possible that Krämer's *Esther*, too, could have been inspired by the success of Lena Amsel, who was well known in Germany by 1920.

108. Several poems by Ruth Landshoff-Yorck with Jewish themes were published in a small volume in 1934; it is possible that some were written in 1932. See Rut Landshoff, *Gedichte* (1934), Deutsches Literaturarchiv Marbach.

109. Ursula Krechel has suggested that taking her mother's name could be interpreted as an act of disguising a recognizably Jewish name. See Ursula Krechel, "'In hartes Grau verwandelt ist das Grün'. Ruth Landshoff-Yorck: Jüdin, Deutsche, Berlinerin," in *'Not an Essence but a Positioning': German-Speaking Jewish Women Writers 1900–1938*, ed. Andrea Hammel and Godela Weiss-Sussex (Munich: Martin Meidenbauer Verlag, 2009), 233–45; here 235.

110. On associations of Jews with vampires, particularly in *Nosferatu*, see Kaes, *Shell Shock Cinema*, 110–13.

111. Landshoff-Yorck, *Roman einer Tänzerin*, 114.

112. Landshoff-Yorck, *Roman einer Tänzerin*, 157; and Walter Fähnders, "Über zwei Romane, die 1933 nicht erscheinen durften: Mela Hartwigs *Bin ich ein überflüssiger Mensch?* und Ruth Landshoff-Yorcks *Roman einer Tänzerin*," in *Chloe: Beihefte zum Daphnis, Regionaler Kulturraum und intellektuelle Kommunikation von Humanismus bis ins Zeitalter des Internet*, vol. 36, ed. Axel E. Walter (Amsterdam: Rodopi, 2005), 161–90; here 167. For details about her life, see also Ruth Landshoff-Yorck, *Klatsch,*

*Ruhm und kleine Feuer: Biographische Impressionen* (Cologne: Kiepenheuer & Witsch, 1963).

113. Landshoff-Yorck, *Roman einer Tänzerin*, 10, 11, 7.

114. Landshoff-Yorck, *Roman einer Tänzerin*, 23, 24.

115. Landshoff-Yorck, *Roman einer Tänzerin*, 29.

116. See Wallach, "Recognition for the 'Beautiful Jewess,'" in Berghoff and Kühne, *Globalizing Beauty*.

117. "Die schönste Frau Europas—eine Jüdin!," *Israelitisches Familienblatt* 30, no. 9 (February 28, 1929): illustrated supplement cover.

118. H[einz] C[aspari], "Arme Miß Europa!," *Israelitisches Familienblatt* 30, no. 14 (April 4, 1929): 2. See also "Anti-Semites Annoy 'Miss Europe,'" *New York Times*, March 31, 1929.

119. "Miß Europa möchte heiraten," *Israelitisches Familienblatt* 30, no. 11 (March 14, 1929): 15.

120. For biographical information on Lisl Goldarbeiter, see the documentary film *Miss Universe 1929—Lisl Goldarbeiter: A Queen in Wien*, directed by Péter Forgács (Budapest, 2006), DVD. See also Elisabeth Patsios, *Die Schönste der Schönen: Geschichte der Miss Austria 1929–2009* (Vienna: Molden, 2009), 57–67.

121. "Lisl Goldarbeiter als schönste Frau der Welt erklärt," *Israelitisches Familienblatt* 30, no. 25 (June 20, 1929): 16.

122. "Auch 'Miss Austria' eine Jüdin," *Israelitisches Familienblatt* 30, no. 8 (February 21, 1929): 15.

123. "'Miss Universe' Jeered in Rumania as Too Thin: Austrian Jewish Beauty Seeks Refuge in Cathedral and Police Rescue Her," *New York Times*, August 30, 1929, 2; and "Rumania: Miss Universe Mobbed," *Time*, September 9, 1929.

## CHAPTER 4

1. Deborah Cohen has suggested that the first comparison of Jews with chameleons was made in *Genius of Judaism* (1833) by Isaac d'Israeli, the father of British prime minister Benjamin Disraeli. Cohen, "Who Was Who," 478.

2. Moses Waldmann, "Der ängstliche Jude," *Jüdische Rundschau* 31, no. 33 (April 30, 1926): 245. Elsewhere, Waldmann claimed that appearance was not a reliable indicator of Jewishness because Jews possessed a kind of indelible essence. See Moses Waldmann, "Pogromangst," *Jüdische Rundschau* 35, nos. 77–78 (October 1, 1930): 503–4. On Waldmann, see Warren Rosenblum, "Jews, Justice, and the Power of 'Sensation' in the Weimar Republic," *Leo Baeck Institute Year Book* 58 (2013): 35–52; here 35.

3. On accusations of Jewish mimicry and camouflage, see Aschheim, "Reflections on Theatricality," in Malkin and Rokem, *Jews and the Making of Modern German Theatre*, 26–27; and Itzkovitz, "Passing Like Me," 38–39.

4. Waldmann, "Der ängstliche Jude," 245.

5. Ernst L. Loewenberg, "Jakob Loewenberg: Excerpts from his Diaries and Letters," *Leo Baeck Institute Year Book* 15 (1970): 183–209. Ernst mentions only perfor-

mances of his father's historical drama *Aelfrida* (1919) and his pacifist play *Vor dem Feind* (1895). Ludwig Davidsohn's obituary for Jakob Loewenberg states that the Hamburg Stadttheater performed two of his *Trauerspiele* and one *Märchenspiel*, which is consistent with Ernst's account. Ludwig Davidsohn, "Zwei Tote: Hugo Salus, Jacob Loewenberg," *Jüdisch-liberale Zeitung* 9, no. 7 (February 15, 1929): 1–2.

6. Jakob Loewenberg, *Der gelbe Fleck, ein Drama* in *Der gelbe Fleck* (Berlin: Philo Verlag, 1924), 119–43; here 139.

7. On Loewenberg, see Itta Shedletzky, "Ludwig Jacobowski (1868–1900) und Jakob Loewenberg (1856–1929). Literarisches Leben und Schaffen 'aus deutscher und aus jüdischer Seele'," in *Juden in der deutschen Literatur. Ein deutsch-israelisches Symposion*, ed. Stéphane Mosès and Albrecht Schöne (Frankfurt am Main: Suhrkamp, 1986), 194–209; and Petra Renneke, "Jakob Loewenberg und die '*Kunstwart*-Debatte,'" in *Jüdische Literatur in Westfalen. Spuren jüdischen Lebens in der westfälischen Literatur*, ed. Hartmut Steinecke, Iris Nölle-Hornkamp, and Günter Tiggesbäumker (Bielefeld: Aisthesis, 2004), 64–98.

8. See Ernst Loewenberg, "Jakob Loewenberg. Excerpts"; and Ernst Loewenberg, "Jakob Loewenberg. Lebensbild eines deutschen Juden," *Jahrbuch für jüdische Geschichte und Literatur* 29, no. 1 (1931): 99–151.

9. Today, Jakob Loewenberg is also remembered for his commentary on Moritz Goldstein's article in the "*Kunstwart*-Debatte" of 1912. In this text, Loewenberg recalls the childhood experience of having been recognized and called a Jew while walking in a village where no Jews lived. See Jakob Loewenberg, "[Sprechsaal]," *Kunstwart* 25, no. 22 (1912): 245–49, cited in Renneke, "Jakob Loewenberg," 80. See also note 55 to the introduction.

10. "Das Jüdische in meinem Wesen und Schaffen. Antworten auf eine Rundfrage," *Jüdisch-liberale Zeitung* 5, no. 42 (October 16, 1925): 1.

11. "Jakob Loewenberg," *Jüdische Rundschau* 34, no. 14 (February 19, 1929): 86.

12. Ernst Loewenberg, "Jakob Loewenberg. Excerpts," 198, 208. See also Ernst Loewenberg, "Jakob Loewenberg. Lebensbild," 146.

13. It is possible that Zionist criticism of Loewenberg's earlier writings (such as his novel *Aus zwei Quellen*) caused him to wait before publishing this provocative drama. See Shedletzky, "Ludwig Jacobowski," in Mosès and Schöne, *Juden in der deutschen*, 199–200.

14. "Das Abzeichen der Juden im Mittelalter war Der gelbe Fleck," advertisement, *C.V.-Zeitung* 4, no. 10 (March 6, 1925): 185. See also "Überall spricht man von . . . ," advertisement, *C.V.-Zeitung* 5, no. 29 (July 16, 1926): 389.

15. Harry Epstein, "Der gelbe Fleck," *Jüdische Rundschau* 31, no. 94 (November 30, 1926): 677.

16. Robert Weltsch, "Tragt ihn mit Stolz, den gelben Fleck," *Jüdische Rundschau* 38, no. 27 (April 4, 1933): 131–32. See also chapter 1.

17. Loewenberg, *Der gelbe Fleck*, 135, 127, 136.

18. Loewenberg, *Der gelbe Fleck*, 141.

19. Fritz Julian Levi, "Fasching," *Schlemiel. Jüdische Blätter für Humor und Kunst*, no. 15 (1920): 197. In this cartoon, the use of the Polish word *Panie* hints that the mask being removed is that of an East European Jew in disguise. On masks as a popular trope in the United States, see Alys Eve Weinbaum, "Racial Masquerade: Consumption and

Contestation of American Modernity," in *The Modern Girl around the World: Consumption, Modernity, and Globalization*, ed. Alys Eve Weinbaum, Lynn M. Thomas, Priti Ramamurthy, Uta G. Poiger, Madeleine Yue Dong, and Tani E. Barlow (Durham, NC: Duke University Press, 2008), 120–46.

20. Loewenberg, *Der gelbe Fleck*, 127.

21. Hans's plight stands in opposition to that of Daniel Deronda, the eponymous protagonist of British-Jewish writer George Eliot's popular novel from 1876. Unlike Daniel, whose discovery that his mother is Jewish enables him to marry the Jewish woman he loves—and whose situation parallels Martha's in several ways—Hans's Jewishness will separate him from all that he has come to value. *Daniel Deronda* was especially popular among Jews in Weimar Germany and into the later 1930s; a German translation was serialized in the *Israelitisches Familienblatt* (1925, no. 33 through 1926, no. 14). Jonathan Hess has noted the novel's popularity among nineteenth-century German-Jewish audiences. See Hess, *Middlebrow Literature*, 193–97.

22. On antisemitism in German student groups, see Zwicker, *Dueling Students*, 94–95, 112–16, 118–32; and Pickus, *Constructing Modern Identities*, 73–88.

23. See Kaplan, *Making of the Jewish Middle Class*, 149. In the United States, Jewish fraternities and sororities also emerged in response to the exclusion of Jews from other student groups. See Shira Kohn, "A Gentlewoman's Agreement: Jewish Sororities in Postwar America, 1947–1964" (PhD diss., New York University, 2013).

24. Josef Feiner, "Jakob Loewenberg," *Israelitisches Familienblatt* 31, no. 7 (February 14, 1929).

25. Kenji Yoshino has suggested (with specific reference to the history of homosexuality) that conversion is the first and most extreme stage in a population's or individual's attempt to come to term with difference; passing and covering constitute the progressively less extreme later stages. Yoshino, *Covering*, 18–19.

26. Endelman, *Leaving the Jewish Fold*, 7.

27. See Dieter Schmauss and Georg Schirmers, eds., *Menachem Birnbaum. Leben und Werk eines jüdischen Künstlers. Eine Ausstellung der Universitätsbibliothek Hagen, 9. November bis 20. Dezember 1999* (Hagen: Fernuniversität Hagen and AVZ/Bibliothek, 1999).

28. Menachem Birnbaum, cartoon, *Schlemiel. Jüdische Blätter für Humor und Kunst*, no. 10 (1919): 137.

29. It is possible that this cartoon references earlier satirical representations of Berlin Jews who desired upward mobility. See David Brenner, *Marketing Identities*, 92–93.

30. Ernst Loewenberg, "Jakob Loewenberg. Excerpts," 201.

31. The poem "Getauft" was originally part of Loewenberg's poetry cycle "Lieder eines Semiten." See Jakob Loewenberg, *Aus jüdischer Seele. Ausgewählte Werke*, ed. Winfried Kempf (Hamburg: IGEL Verlag Literatur & Wissenschaft, 2011), 21–22.

32. Ernst Loewenberg, "Jakob Loewenberg. Excerpts," 201.

33. Jakob Loewenberg, "Der Herr Professor," in *Der gelbe Fleck* (Berlin: Philo Verlag, 1924), 59–74; here 69. See also Jakob Loewenberg, "Der Herr Professor," *Israelitisches Familienblatt* 27, no. 11–12.

34. Alice Lieberg, *Remembrance of Things Past* (Dedham, MA: Sylvester Press, 1993), 40. Alice Lieberg was born Alice Halberstam in Leipzig in 1904.

35. See Jonathan M. Hess, "Fictions of a German-Jewish Public: Ludwig Jaco-

bowski's *Werther the Jew* and Its Readers," *Jewish Social Studies* 11, no. 2 (2005): 202–30.

36. Psychiatrist Richard Detlev Loewenberg, another son of Jakob Loewenberg, published a broader study of suicide in Hamburg in 1932, *Über den Selbstmord in Hamburg in den letzten fünfzig Jahren (1880–1930).* See Niewyk, *Jews in Weimar Germany,* 20.

37. Darcy Buerkle demonstrates that the Berlin census of 1925–26 led the Jewish community to initiate preventative campaigns against suicide. Buerkle, *Nothing Happened,* 167–72.

38. "Die Vergangenheit des Herrn Woldemaras. Ein Beitrag zum Kapitel von Heimatrecht," *C.V.-Zeitung* 7, no. 4 (January 27, 1928): 38.

39. Politicus, "Eingesandt: Vorbildliche Assimilationsfähigkeit," *Jüdische Rundschau* 33, no. 10 (February 3, 1928): 72.

40. See Dr. B. C., "Der jüdische Name," *Der Israelit* 65, no. 2 (January 10, 1924): 1; "Rabb. Dr. M. Weinberg, "Der jüdische Name. Eine geschichtliche Betrachtung," *Der Israelit* 65, no. 5 (January 31, 1924): 12; and subsequent responses in issues nos. 7 and 12.

41. In 1920, *Der Israelit* published a two-part article about the history of German-Jewish surnames as told by Professor L. Günther. "Die Familiennamen der deutschen Juden," *Der Israelit* 61, nos. 42 and 46 (October 21, 1920 and November 18, 1920): 10. In 1924, Arthur Czellitzer founded the Gesellschaft für jüdische Familien-Forschung, as well as its magazine, *Jüdische Familien-Forschung,* which published Heinrich Loewe's research on the history of Jewish names. See Heinrich Loewe, "Geschichten von jüdischen Namen," *Jüdische Familien-Forschung* 3, no. 12 (December 1927): 274–80; and a reprinted version of this article in *Das jüdische Echo* 15, no. 10.

42. Elias Canetti, *The Torch in My Ear,* trans. Joachim Neugroschel (New York: Farrar, Straus and Giroux, 1982), 24.

43. Dietz Bering, *The Stigma of Names: Antisemitism in German Daily Life, 1812–1933,* trans. Neville Plaice (Ann Arbor: University of Michigan, 1992), 124–26, 137, 141, 149–80.

44. Kirsten Fermaglich, "'Too Long, Too Foreign . . . Too Jewish': Jews, Name Changing, and Family Mobility in New York City, 1917–1942," *Journal of American Ethnic History* 34, no. 3 (2015): 34–57; here 46, 48–49.

45. Kerry Wallach, "Mascha Kaléko Advertises the New Jewish Woman," in *'Not an Essence but a Positioning': German-Speaking Jewish Women Writers 1900–1938,* ed. Andrea Hammel and Godela Weiss-Sussex (Munich: Martin Meidenbauer Verlag, 2009), 211–31; here 214.

46. Ganeva, "Fashion Photography," 6.

47. "Der Name ist 'verdächtig,'" *Israelitisches Familienblatt* 35, no. 3 (January 9, 1933): 3.

48. On Bondy's Jewishness, see Werner T. Angress, *Between Fear and Hope: Jewish Youth in the Third Reich,* trans. Werner T. Angress and Christine Granger (New York: Columbia University Press, 1988), 57–58.

49. Bruce Murray, *Film and the German Left in the Weimar Republic: From* Caligari *to* Kuhle Wampe (Austin: University of Texas Press, 1990), 121–24.

50. The televised version of *Überflüssige Menschen* is the only surviving version accessible today, on VHS at the Bundesarchiv-Filmarchiv in Berlin. This recording is of a screening at the Filmtheater Metropol in Bonn in September 1978; it includes a live orchestra accompaniment conducted by Werner Schmidt-Boelcke and was broadcast by ZDF on June 6, 1985. See also Heiko Bockstiegel, *"Schmidt-Boelcke dirigiert": Ein Musikerleben zwischen Kunst und Medienlandschaft* (Wolfratshausen: J. L. G. Grimm, 1994), 236–41.

51. An earlier Russian short film adaptation, *Romance with a Double Bass* (Hansen, 1911), was the first film adaptation of Chekhov's works.

52. Elza Temary (1905–68, also Elza K. Splane) was born in Germany and acted in over 30 films between 1926 and 1932, after which she left Germany for the United States.

53. On Jewishness in Chekhov's story "Rothschild's Fiddle," see Leonid Livak, *The Jewish Persona in the European Imagination: A Case of Russian Literature* (Stanford: Stanford University Press, 2010), 258–71.

54. "Neue jüdische Bühnen- und Filmwerke," *Israelitisches Familienblatt* 28, no. 50 (December 16, 1926): 508–9.

55. The intertitles can be found in the Film-Prüfstelle Berlin card (no. 13994), which is dated October 27, 1926.

56. Hans Wollenberg, "Überflüssige Menschen," *Lichtbild-Bühne*, no. 262, November 3, 1927. Both Wollenberg reviews are reprinted in full in Oksana Bulgakowa, ed., *Die ungewöhnlichen Abenteuer des Dr. Mabuse im Lande der Bolschewiki. Das Buch zur Filmreihe "Moskau—Berlin"* (Berlin: Freunde der Deutschen Kinemathek, 1995), 135–36.

57. [r.], "Film-Kritik: Überflüssige Menschen," November 3, 1926, folder 453, Stiftung Deutsche Kinemathek, Schriftgutarchiv, Berlin. See also the review by G. G. in *Kino*, no. 167, 1928; cited in Bulgakowa, *Die ungewöhnlichen Abenteuer*, 136–37.

58. Herbert Ihering, "Überflüssige Menschen," Herbert Ihering Archive, no. 4729, Akademie der Künste, Berlin.

59. Ernst Blass, "Elisabeth Bergner," *Das jüdische Magazin* 1, no. 4 (November 1929): 22.

60. Dr. Bessels Verwandlung can be viewed at the Bundesarchiv-Filmarchiv in Berlin. Another well-known film in this genre was *Heimkehr* (Homecoming, 1928), directed by Joe May and produced by Erich Pommer, also for Ufa. See Philipp Stiasny, "4 March 1921: With *Das Floss der Toten*, the Dead Come Back to Town," in Kapczynski and Richardson, *New History of German Cinema*, 93–97; Philipp Stiasny, *Das Kino und der Krieg. Deutschland 1914–1929* (Munich: edition text + kritik, 2009); and Ashkenazi, *Weimar Film*, 133–47.

61. Another non-Jewish actor whose performances of wandering coded him Jewish was Charlie Chaplin, who was more closely associated with East European Jewry. See Liliane Weissberg, *Hannah Arendt, Charlie Chaplin und die verborgene jüdische Tradition* (Graz: Leykam, 2009).

62. Herbert Ihering, "Mensch ohne Namen," Herbert Ihering Archive, no. 5513, Akademie der Künste, Berlin. This review was likely published in the *Berliner Börsen-Courier* on July 2, 1932. See also two reviews in folder 5385, Stiftung Deutsche Kine-

mathek, Schriftgutarchiv, Berlin: Fritz Olimsky, "Werner Krauß in 'Mensch ohne Namen'," *Berliner Börsen-Zeitung*, July 2, 1932; and H. H. Bormann, "'Mensch ohne
Namen'. Der neue Werner-Krauß-Film der Ufa," *Kölnische Volkszeitung*, July 15, 1932.

63. Letter from Werner Krauss to Wolfgang Goetz, June 28, 1932. Wolfgang Goetz
Archive, no. 534, Akademie der Künste, Berlin. It is possible that actress Helene Thimig also was not present at the film's premiere; a diary entry suggests that she and her
husband, Max Reinhardt, visited journalist Max Reiner in Schloss Leopoldskron in
Austria on July 8, 1932. Reiner, *Mein Leben*, 162.

64. Werner Krauss, *Das Schauspiel meines Lebens, einem Freund erzählt*, introduction by Carl Zuckmayer (Stuttgart: Henry Goverts Verlag, 1958), 155. Siegfried Kracauer's generally unfavorable review of the film also faults Robert Liebmann's screenplay for not having done justice to Balzac's text. Siegfried Kracauer, "Film-Sommer.
Filmrez.: Mensch ohne Namen," *Frankfurter Zeitung*, July 8, 1932; reprinted in Siegfried Kracauer, *Kleine Schriften zum Film, Werke* 6, no. 3, 1932–1961, ed. Inka Mülder-
Bach, Mirjam Wenzel, and Sabine Biebl (Frankfurt am Main: Suhrkamp Verlag, 2004),
73–76.

65. See H. T. S., "Mensch Ohne Namen (1932)—'The Man Without a Name,'" *New
York Times*, November 7, 1932; and Ulrike Heikaus, *Deutschsprachige Filme als Kulturinsel. Zur kulturellen Integration der deutschsprachigen Juden in Palästina, 1933–
1945* (Potsdam: Universitätsverlag Potsdam, 2009), 54, 81. Gustav Ucicky's 1931 film,
*Im Geheimdienst*, also showed in Jerusalem in 1932.

66. I use the translation "shyster lawyer" for *Winkeladvokat* in part because of its
overtly Jewish connotations as an English slang term or slur. The term *shyster* was also
used in several English-language films and radio shows in the early 1930s. See, for
example, the Marx Brothers' film, *Monkey Business* (McLeod, 1931), and their radio
show, *Flywheel, Shyster, and Flywheel*, which was broadcast in late 1932 and 1933.

67. See L. Mischkowski, "Kino in der Kleinstadt," *Jüdische Rundschau* 37, monthly
issue no. 8 (November 1932): 6.

68. Mischkowski, "Kino in der Kleinstadt," 6.

69. "Mißton im Tonfilm," *C.V.-Zeitung* 9, no. 49 (December 5, 1930): 628.

70. On Falkenstein's roles in Ufa films, see Klaus Kreimeier, *The Ufa Story: A History of Germany's Greatest Film Company, 1918–1945*, trans. Robert and Rita Kimber
(Berkeley: University of California Press, 1996), 212.

71. Kay Weniger, *Zwischen Bühne und Baracke. Lexikon der verfolgten Theater-,
Film- und Musikkünstler 1933–1945* (Berlin: Metropol, 2008), 108–10.

72. On Gustav Ucicky's biography, see Christoph Brecht, Armin Loacker, and Ines
Steiner, *Professionalist und Propagandist: Der Kameramann und Regisseur Gustav
Ucicky* (Vienna: Verlag Filmarchiv Austria, 2014). Ucicky still makes the news today,
but even more than his films one is likely to hear about his legacy as a controversial
collector of art, including the purchase of numerous stolen artworks by Gustav Klimt.

73. Both *Flüchtlinge* and *Heimkehr* were based on screenplays written by fervent
nationalist Gerhard Menzel. *Flüchtlinge* won the first Nazi National Film Prize in 1934,
and *Heimkehr*, along with only four other films, received the honor "Film of the Nation." See Eric Rentschler, *The Ministry of Illusion: Nazi Cinema and Its Afterlife*
(Cambridge: Harvard University Press, 1996), 132, 255.

74. Rentschler, *Ministry of Illusion*, 176, 5.

75. Mischkowski, "Kino in der Kleinstadt," 6. Herbert Ihering called Krauss's role in *Mensch ohne Namen* "a Yorck of the automobile industry." Ihering, "Mensch ohne Namen," in Herbert Ihering Archive, Akademie der Künste.

76. Honoré de Balzac, *Colonel Chabert*, trans. Carol Cosman (New York: New Directions, 1997). In German, the title is translated as "Oberst Chabert." A French period film also based on Balzac's novella was made in 1994; titled *Le colonel Chabert*, it stars Gérard Depardieu and Fanny Ardant.

77. Krauss, *Schauspiel meines Lebens*, 155.

78. Balzac, *Chabert*, 74–75, 77, 27, 35. Christoph Brecht has argued that Balzac's attorney is the only person of integrity in a dismal landscape of scheming characters, whereas the characters in Ucicky's film tend to be full of good intentions. See Brecht, Loacker, and Steiner, *Professionalist und Propagandist*, 204.

79. On constructions of the Jewish *"Witz,"* see Valerie Weinstein's work on film comedy and antisemitism in Nazi Germany. For further biographical information about Franz Friedrich Grünbaum, see Thomas Soxberger, "'Will the Real Fritz Grünbaum Please Stand Up?' Die biographische Forschung zu Fritz Grünbaum und ihre Probleme," in *Gute Unterhaltung. Fritz Grünbaum und die Vergnügungskultur im Wien der 1920er und 1930er Jahre*, ed. Brigitte Dalinger, Kurt Ifkovits, and Andrea B. Braidt (Frankfurt am Main: Peter Lang, 2008), 9–23; here 18, 22; Christoph Wagner-Trenkwitz and Marie Th. Arnbom, eds., *Grüß mich Gott! Fritz Grünbaum (1880–1941). Eine Biographie* (Vienna: Brandstätter Verlag, 2005), 179–91; and Hans Veigl, *Lachen im Keller. Kabarett und Kleinkunst in Wien 1900 bis 1945* (Graz: Österreichisches Kabarettarchiv, 2013).

80. See Georg Markus, *Das große Karl Farkas Buch. Sein Leben, seine besten Texte, Conférencen und Doppelconférencen* (Vienna: Amalthea, 1993), 56–58.

81. Georg Markus, *Wenn man trotzdem lacht: Geschichte und Geschichten des österreichischen Humors* (Vienna: Amalthea, 2012), 29.

82. See Peter Gölz, "Haha Hitler! Coming to Terms with Dani Levy," in *Cinema and Social Change in Germany and Austria*, ed. Gabriele Mueller and James M. Skidmore (Waterloo, ON: Wilfrid Laurier University Press, 2012), 173–88; here 178.

83. Wollenberg, for example, poses the question, "Who doesn't know the Jewish lawyer-type of Paul Morgan, with bad manners and scheming (*mauschelnd*)." Hans Wollenberg, "Der Jude im Film," *C.V.-Zeitung* 6, no. 37 (September 16, 1927): 523.

84. As Avraham Barkai notes, even after several thousand Jews were forced to stop practicing law in early 1933, there were still nearly 4,000 Jewish lawyers, or over 16 percent of all lawyers in Germany, in June 1933. In Vienna circa 1925, Jews constituted 62 percent of all lawyers in private practice. See Avraham Barkai, "Population Decline and Economic Stagnation," in Meyer and Brenner, *German-Jewish History*, vol. 4, 30–44; here 36–37.

85. Hans-Peter Bayerdörfer has suggested that this seemingly antisemitic line from *Die Verbrecher* reflects the actual phenomenon of a disproportionate number of Jewish attorneys fighting for the justice regularly denied them. Hans-Peter Bayerdörfer, "'Die Advokaten sind alle Juden'—Juztizdebatte und Zeitstück auf der Bühne der Weimarer Republik," in *Handbuch zur deutsch-jüdischen Literatur des 20. Jahrhunderts*, ed. Daniel Hoffmann (Paderborn: Ferdinand Schöningh, 2002), 219–34.

86. Adolf Asch, *Auszug aus Memoiren von Dr. Adolf Asch (Rechtsanwalt am A.G.*

*Berlin-Schöneberg, 1908–1914)*, 3, file no. 2 (Adolph Asch), Leo Baeck Institute, Jerusalem, 3.

87. Grünbaum states this in a newspaper article dated January 21, 1933. Cited in Soxberger, "Will the Real," in Dalinger, Ifkovits, and Braidt, *Gute Unterhaltung*, 11.

88. Fritz Grünbaum, letter to the editor of *Die neue Welt*, no. 257 (August 19, 1932), 8. Cited in Günter Krenn, "'Aus dem Geiste der Operette?' Der Unterhaltungstonfilm als Politikum in den 1930er und 1940er Jahren," in Dalinger, Ifkovits, and Braidt, *Gute Unterhaltung*, 97–107; here 98.

89. Krenn, "Aus dem Geiste," in Dalinger, Ifkovits, and Braidt, *Gute Unterhaltung*, 99.

90. On height as an indicator of Jewishness in Weimar culture, see Julia Schäfer, "'Der wahre Jacob' und 'Kikeriki'. Jüdische und proletarische Körper in satirischen Zeitschriften der zwanziger Jahre," in *Leibhaftige Moderne. Körper in Kunst und Massenmedien 1918 bis 1933*, ed. Michael Cowan and Kai Marcel Sicks (Bielefeld: Transcript Verlag, 2005), 322–38; here 330.

91. Other films including *Arm wie eine Kirchenmaus* use more eye-level camera angles; Grünbaum appears taller in other films than in *Mensch ohne Namen*.

92. Rentschler, *Ministry of Illusion*, 157–58.

93. Herbert Ihering, *Werner Krauss. Ein Schauspieler und das neunzehnte Jahrhundert*, ed. Sabine Zolchow and Rudolf Mast, foreword by Klaus Kreimeier (Berlin: Verlag Vorwerk 8, 1997), 59.

94. Valerie Weinstein suggests that Krauss played all Jewish roles in the film except for those of the extras and Jud Süß himself, indicating that all Jews look the same. Weinstein, "Dissolving Boundaries," 507.

95. Werner Krauss was eventually allowed to return to acting after undergoing an official de-Nazification process. Even friends who ceased to have contact with Krauss due to his change of heart during the years of Nazi rule, such as Elisabeth Bergner, resumed their relationships with him after the war. See Elisabeth Bergner, *Bewundert viel und viel gescholten. Unordentliche Erinnerungen* (Munich: C. Bertelsmann, 1978), 117–19.

96. On nose jobs, see chapter 1, note 51.

97. Noah Isenberg, introduction to *Weimar Cinema: An Essential Guide to the Classic Films of the Era*, ed. Noah Isenberg (New York: Columbia University Press, 2009), 1–12; here 5–6. Isenberg references Peter Sloterdijk's term for the Weimar Republic, namely the "German Republic of Imposters."

98. Christoph Brecht points out that the public is forbidden from attending the courtroom proceedings in *Mensch ohne Namen*, which differentiates this film from other early sound film courtroom dramas. See Brecht, Loacker, and Steiner, *Professionalist und Propagandist*, 207.

99. Weinstein, "Dissolving Boundaries," 499.

100. Cited in Max Goldschmidt, "Über Entstehung und Änderung jüdischer Namen," *Jüdisch-liberale Zeitung* 7, no. 35 (September 2, 1927): 7.

101. Interestingly, Martin's new name reappeared several years later in a novel by a different "Miller": the narrator of American writer Henry Miller's partly autobiographical *Tropic of Capricorn* (1939) randomly, and perhaps ironically, claims to be Gottlieb

Leberecht Müller, "because everyone loves a right-living man!" Henry Miller, *Tropic of Capricorn* (New York: Grove Press, 1961), 227–30; here 229. Henry Miller embedded this character in his controversial novel without ever mentioning the film; Miller's narrator states only that he recognizes himself on screen. Filmgoers reading Henry Miller could thus appreciate the transformational chain reaction of a film about visibility and adopting new names. Thomas Nesbit argues that Miller used the literal meaning of "Gottlieb Leberecht Müller" to claim he has changed his misguided ways. See Thomas Nesbit, *Henry Miller and Religion* (New York: Routledge, 2007), 65. According to Jay Martin, Henry Miller knew German and saw *Mensch ohne Namen* with two friends in 1932 at the Studio L'Étoile in Paris. See Jay Martin, *Always Merry and Bright: The Life of Henry Miller: An Unauthorized Biography* (Santa Barbara, CA: Capra, 1978), 323. It is also possible that Miller saw the French version, *Un homme sans nom*, a coproduction directed by Gustav Ucicky and Robert Le Bon, which premiered in Paris on November 1, 1932. Although the French version featured an entirely French cast, several filmmakers—Ucicky, Liebmann, and cinematographer Carl Hoffmann—are credited in both the German and French versions.

102. S. S. Prawer has suggested that Weimar directors including Ludwig Berger and G. W. Pabst marked Falkenstein as Jewish by showing him in the frame with a Jewish menorah. Prawer, *Between Two Worlds*, 178.

## CONCLUSION

1. Whereas many scholars have compared African Americans and American Jews, few have considered parallels between the experiences of African Americans and German Jews in the early twentieth century. On African Americans and American Jews, see, for example, Adam Meyer, *Black-Jewish Relations in African American and Jewish American Fiction: An Anthology* (Lanham, MD: Scarecrow Press, 2002); Adam Meyer, "Not Entirely Strange, but Not Entirely Friendly Either: Images of Jews in African American Passing Novels through the Harlem Renaissance," *African American Review* 38, no. 3 (2004): 441–50; Carol J. Batker, *Reforming Fictions: Native, African, and Jewish American Women's Literature and Journalism in the Progressive Era* (New York: Columbia University Press, 2000); Rottenberg, *Performing Americanness*; Rottenberg, *Black Harlem*; Harrison-Kahan, *White Negress*; and Glaser, *Borrowed Voices*. Additionally, recent scholarship in the field of Black German studies has expanded the study of African Americans (and the African/Black Diaspora more broadly) and Germans, though Jews are not a major focus of these studies. See, for example, Greene and Ortlepp, *Germans and African Americans*; Maria I. Diedrich and Jürgen Heinrichs, eds., *From Black to Schwarz: Cultural Crossovers between African America and Germany* (Münster: LIT Verlag, 2011); Charlotte Szilagyi, Sabrina K. Rahman, and Michael Saman, eds., *Imagining Blackness in Germany and Austria* (Newcastle upon Tyne, UK: Cambridge Scholars Publishing, 2012); and Mischa Honeck, Martin Klimke, and Anne Kuhlmann, eds., *Germany and the Black Diaspora: Points of Contact, 1250–1914* (New York: Berghahn Books, 2013). On German Jews and Blackness, see the work of Sander L. Gilman, especially *On Blackness without Blacks: Essays on the Im-*

*age of the Black in Germany* (Boston: G. K. Hall, 1982); *Difference and Pathology: Stereotypes of Sexuality, Race, and Madness* (Ithaca: Cornell University Press, 1985); *Freud, Race, and Gender*; and *Jew's Body*. See also Reinhold Grimm, "Germans, Blacks, and Jews; or Is There a German Blackness of Its Own?," in *Blacks and German Culture*, ed. Reinhold Grimm and Jost Hermand (Madison: University of Wisconsin Press, 1986), 150–84; and Birgit Haehnel, "'The Black Jew': An Afterimage of German Colonialism," in *German Colonialism, Visual Culture, and Modern Memory*, ed. Volker M. Langbehn (New York: Routledge, 2010), 239–59. In a comparative project with some parallels to this study, Marc Caplan examines African and Yiddish literatures. Marc Caplan, *How Strange the Change: Language, Temporality, and Narrative Form in Peripheral Modernisms* (Stanford: Stanford University Press, 2011).

2. See Thomas R. Pegram, *One Hundred Percent American: The Rebirth and Decline of the Ku Klux Klan in the 1920s* (Lanham, MD: Ivan R. Dee, 2011). See also Caroline E. Light, *That Pride of Race and Character: The Roots of Jewish Benevolence in the Jim Crow South* (New York: New York University, 2014), 11; and Hasia R. Diner, *In the Almost Promised Land: American Jews and Blacks, 1915–1935* (Baltimore: Johns Hopkins University Press, 1977), 74–76, 96–97.

3. Peter Pulzer, introduction to Meyer and Brenner, *German-Jewish History*, vol. 3, 1–6; here 4.

4. Peter Pulzer has suggested that, with respect to the political situation of Jews, the Weimar Republic "in many ways promised to be a Jewish Elysium." Pulzer, *Jews and the German State*, 271.

5. On Afro-Germans in the early twentieth century, see Patricia Mazón and Reinhild Steingröver, eds., *Not So Plain as Black and White: Afro-German Culture and History, 1890–2000*, foreword by Russell Berman (Rochester, NY: University of Rochester Press, 2005); and Tina M. Campt, *Other Germans: Black Germans and the Politics of Race, Gender, and Memory in the Third Reich* (Ann Arbor: University of Michigan Press, 2004).

6. Laura Browder has suggested that Jewish American literature became increasingly politicized in the 1910s and 1920s with the rise of eugenics and institutionalized antisemitism. Laura Browder, *Slippery Characters: Ethnic Impersonators and American Identities* (Chapel Hill: University of North Carolina Press, 2000), 142. On historical instances of American Jewish passing, see Endelman, *Leaving the Jewish Fold*.

7. Jennifer V. Evans, "Introduction: Why Queer German History?," *German History* 34, no. 3 (2016): 371–84; here 375.

8. Muslims, especially Muslims with Turkish heritage, constitute another minority group that is often considered with respect to visibility in postwar Germany. On constructions of racial difference after the Second World War, see Chin et al., *After the Nazi Racial State*.

9. Adam Meyer, "Not Entirely Strange," 442.

10. For example, in *Comedy: American Style* (1933), Jessie Fauset groups together Jews and people of color as "foreigners." One Black character points out that some Jews have kinkier hair than certain Blacks; another invokes Shylock's famous "Hath not a Jew eyes?" speech from Shakespeare's *Merchant of Venice* as a plea for universal acceptance of racialized difference. Jessie Redmon Fauset, *Comedy: American Style*, ed. and with an introduction by Cherene Sherrard-Johnson (New Brunswick, NJ: Rutgers

University Press, 2009), 38, 52, 70, 192, 237. See also Adam Meyer, "Not Entirely Strange," 443, and Adam Meyer, *Black-Jewish Relations*, 22.

11. Dean Franco has suggested that the proximity of African Americans and Jews seems to have enabled them to witness and learn from each other's experiences. Dean J. Franco, *Race, Rights, and Recognition: Jewish American Literature since 1969* (Ithaca: Cornell University Press, 2012), 4–5. See also Glaser, *Borrowed Voices*.

12. In many passing narratives, a great deal of responsibility is attributed to the audience, for which "persuasion [is] an effect of identification," according to Marcia Alesan Dawkins. Dawkins, *Clearly Invisible,* 19.

13. Amy Robinson's term for this figure is the "in-group clairvoyant." Amy Robinson, "It Takes One to Know One: Passing and Communities of Common Interest," *Critical Inquiry* 20, no. 4 (1994): 715–36; here 716. See also Dawkins, *Clearly Invisible*, 17.

14. See Gay, *Freud, Jews and Other Germans*, 182–83; and Endelman, *Leaving the Jewish Fold*, 181.

15. Ralph Ellison, "The World and the Jug" (1946), in *Shadow and Act* (New York: Random House, 1964), 124. Allyson Hobbs explains that Ellison's assertion led to the installment of black "spotters" to eject passers from Washington, DC, movie theaters. See Hobbs, *Chosen Exile*, 164, 268.

16. This quote is from Audre Lorde's *Zami* (1982). Cited in Robinson, "It Takes One," 720.

17. Schnitzler, *Fräulein Else*, 22; see also chapter 3.

18. Nella Larsen, *Passing: Authoritative Text, Backgrounds and Contexts, Criticism*, ed. Carla Kaplan (New York: W. W. Norton, 2007), 55. Irene makes this comment to the character modeled on Carl Van Vechten; see note 39 below.

19. See Hobbs, *Chosen Exile*, 163.

20. Robinson, "It Takes One."

21. W. E. B. Du Bois, "Passing," *The Crisis* 31, no. 36 (July 1929): 234, 248–50. Reprinted in Larsen, *Passing: Authoritative Text*, 97–98.

22. Several contributions to Kelby Harrison and Dennis Cooley's edited volume *Passing/Out: Sexual Identity Veiled and Revealed* (Burlington, VT: Ashgate, 2012) take up ethical concerns; Harrison further addresses ethical questions in *Sexual Deceit: The Ethics of Passing* (Lanham, MD: Lexington Books, 2013).

23. Kathleen Pfeiffer has argued that motivation for passing was heightened and reflected in the three decades following the *Plessy v. Ferguson* Supreme Court decision in 1896. Kathleen Pfeiffer, *Race Passing and American Individualism* (Amherst: University of Massachusetts Press, 2003), 1. On Plessy, see also Hobbs, *Chosen Exile*, 105–12.

24. James Weldon Johnson, *The Autobiography of an Ex-Colored Man* (Boston: Sherman, French & Company, 1912), 155.

25. Edith Falk, "Gedanken zur Negerfrage," *Jüdisch-liberale Zeitung* 9, no. 16 (April 19, 1929): 2. On the German translation of Johnson's novel, *Der weiße Neger*, see also A. B. Christa Schwarz, "New Negro Renaissance—'Neger-Renaissance': Crossovers between African America and Germany during the Era of the Harlem Renaissance," in Diedrich and Heinrichs, *From Black to Schwarz*, 49–74.

26. Anna Nußbaum, *Afrika singt: Eine Auslese neuer afro-amerikanischer Lyrik*

(Vienna: Speidel, 1929), 8–9. Anna Nußbaum (1887–1931), a teacher and translator in Vienna, likely hailed from a Galician Jewish family.

27. Martha Weltsch, "Afrika singt . . . ," *Jüdische Rundschau* 34, no. 16 (February 26, 1929): 101. See also Schwarz, "New Negro Renaissance," 63. Martha Weltsch (1893–1930) was the first wife of *Jüdische Rundschau* editor Robert Weltsch.

28. Aside from the articles discussed here, several other articles in the *Israelitisches Familienblatt* discussed Black Jews, for example, "Die Negersynagoge in New York," 26, no. 41 (1924); "Die Negerjuden von Harlem," 32, no. 30 (1930); and "Neger oder Juden?," 34, no. 6 (1932). Several authors of German-Jewish descent, notably Yvan Goll (1891–1950) and his wife, Claire Goll (1891–1977), wrote about Black performers in Europe and interracial relationships, respectively. See Christian Rogowski, "Staging the African American Conquest of Old Europe: Ernst Krenek's *Jonny spielt auf*," in Diedrich and Heinrichs, *From Black to Schwarz*, 97–118.

29. On the "tragic mulatta" stereotype, see Jacquelyn Y. McLendon, *The Politics of Color in the Fiction of Jessie Fauset and Nella Larsen* (Charlottesville: University Press of Virginia, 1995), 13–27; and Sollors, *Neither Black*, 220–45. On biracial identity, see Rafael Walker, "Nella Larsen Reconsidered: The Trouble with Desire in *Quicksand* and *Passing*," *MELUS* 41, no. 1 (2016): 165–92.

30. Teresa C. Zackodnik, *The Mulatta and the Politics of Race* (Jackson: University Press of Mississippi, 2004), xvii–xix. Although Jewish texts understandably do not foreground "mixed" characters in the same way, the notion that a person with one Jewish and one non-Jewish parent might be less visibly Jewish on a racialized level was fairly widespread; actress Grete Mosheim provides one such example. On mixed-race characters in German-Jewish contexts, see Todd Herzog, "Hybrids and Mischlinge: Translating Anglo-American Cultural Theory into German," *German Quarterly* 70, no. 1 (1997): 1–17.

31. On dual coding in Jewish contexts, see note 6 to the introduction.

32. Walter White wrote about his struggles with invisibility in his 1948 autobiography: "I am a Negro. My skin is white, my eyes are blue, my hair is blond. The traits of my race are nowhere visible upon me." Another chapter of White's autobiography "A Jew Is Lynched," tells of the lynching of Leo Frank in Georgia in 1915 and the parallels in mob violence incited by racism and antisemitism. Walter Francis White, *A Man Called White: The Autobiography of Walter White*, foreword by Andrew Young (Athens: University of Georgia Press, 1995), 3, 23–27. See also Sundquist, *Strangers in the Land*, 193–97, 213.

33. Fräulein Else, too, is described as a "reddish blonde." Red-haired literary characters have long represented the dangers of difference and the unknown; in fact, many portrayals of evil Jewish characters have red hair, including Shakespeare's Shylock. Beginning in the medieval period, Cain's hair was sometimes depicted as red, as was Judas's. See Ruth Mellinkoff, "Judas's Red Hair and the Jews," *Journal of Jewish Art* 9 (1982): 31–46; and Rebekka Voß, "Entangled Stories: The Red Jews in Premodern Yiddish and German Apocalyptic Lore," *AJS Review* 36, no. 1 (2012): 1–41.

34. Similar to *Flight*, Jessie Fauset's novel *Plum Bun: A Novel without a Moral* (1929) also contrasts the visibility of a light-skinned African American woman, Angela Murray, with that of a Jewish woman, Rachel Salting. Adam Meyer argues that Fauset's

novel uses the character of Rachel Salting to suggest that Jewish identity is immediately recognizable and that Jewish passing is impossible. Adam Meyer, "Not Entirely Strange," 445. Fauset (1882–1961) was born in Philadelphia but made her way to New York, where she also worked for the NAACP for several years. As a literary editor in its cultural branch, she published the works of such major writers as Jean Toomer and Langston Hughes. On Fauset, see McLendon, *Politics of Color*; and Deborah E. Mc-Dowell, introduction to *Quicksand and Passing* by Nella Larson, ed. and with an introduction by Deborah E. McDowell (New Brunswick, NJ: Rutgers University Press, 1991), x, xiii.

35. Walter White, *Flight* (Baton Rouge: Louisiana State University Press, 1998), 220.

36. White, *Flight*, 238, 274. Adam Meyer has argued that with the word "almost," Walter White here "insinuates that Mimi has a natural bond with other Blacks." Adam Meyer, "Not Entirely Strange," 448.

37. White, *Flight*, 264–65.

38. White, *Flight*, 290. See also Rogin, *Blackface, White Noise*, 12–13, 73–120. Although nothing indicates which show Mimi attends, the novel was published not long after the tremendously successful Broadway run of the 1925 play on which *The Jazz Singer* was based.

39. In Harlem, Larsen befriended other Black writers, as well as patrons of the Harlem Renaissance such as Carl Van Vechten, to whom *Passing* is dedicated and on whom a minor character is based.

40. On Irene's unreliability, see Caughie, *Passing and Pedagogy*, 125–34.

41. Also at issue is Irene's relationship with Clare; numerous allusions throughout the text hint that Irene develops a romantic or erotic attraction to Clare, suggesting that queer passing may also occur between the lines of more obvious racial passing. Mc-Dowell, introduction to Larsen, *Quicksand and Passing*, xxiv–xxx. See also Butler, *Bodies That Matter*, 170; and Berlant, *Female Complaint*, 109.

42. Larsen, *Passing: Authoritative Text*, 21, 54. On fears that cosmetics, hair dye, and other appearance-altering techniques would aid those who wished to pass, see Peiss, *Hope in a Jar*, 33–39.

43. On the stereotypical dark coloring of Jewish women, see chapter 1. On overt references to Jewishness in Larsen's *Passing*, see Rottenberg, *Performing American-ness*, 90–91; and Larsen, *Passing: Authoritative Text*, 50.

44. See Shane White and Graham White, *Stylin': African American Expressive Culture from Its Beginnings to the Zoot Suit* (Ithaca: Cornell University Press, 1998), 175.

45. Some African American writers depict women as particularly "mercurial" in nature, a term that Yuri Slezkine has applied to the adaptability and mobility of Jews. See White, *Flight*, 103, 191; and Yuri Slezkine, *The Jewish Century* (Princeton: Princeton University Press, 2004), 10, 19, 21.

46. Images of the New Negro Woman can be found in the art and literature of the Harlem Renaissance. This figure perhaps finds her counterpart in the New Jewish Woman, a type that never emerged to the same degree, but which existed insofar as Jewish women began to embrace public forms of visibility. See Cherene Sherrard-Johnson, *Portraits of the New Negro Woman: Visual and Literary Culture in the Har-*

*lem Renaissance* (New Brunswick, NJ: Rutgers University Press, 2007); and note 122 to the introduction.

47. Jill Suzanne Smith, *Berlin Coquette: Prostitution and the New German Woman, 1890–1933* (Ithaca: Cornell University Press, 2013), 149; Sutton, *Masculine Woman,* 116; and McCormick, *Gender and Sexuality.*

48. I follow Clayton Whisnant in using the term "scene" instead of "subculture." See Clayton J. Whisnant, *Queer Identities and Politics in Germany: A History, 1880–1945* (New York: Harrington Park Press, 2016), 11.

49. See Sutton, *Masculine Woman,* 34n20; Marsha Meskimmon, *We Weren't Modern Enough: Women Artists and the Limits of German Modernism* (Berkeley: University of California Press, 1999), 206; and Marti M. Lybeck, *Desiring Emancipation: New Women and Homosexuality in Germany, 1890–1933* (Albany: State University of New York Press, 2014), 11–12. On the use of similarly coded terms in interwar Britain, see Matt Houlbrook, *Queer London: Perils and Pleasures in the Sexual Metropolis, 1918–1957* (Chicago: University of Chicago Press, 2005).

50. Geertje Mak, "'Passing Women' im Sprechzimmer von Magnus Hirschfeld: Warum der Begriff 'Transvestit' nicht für Frauen in Männerkleidern eingeführt wurde," *Österreichische Zeitschrift für Geschichtswissenschaften* 9, no. 3 (1998): 390.

51. Sedgwick, *Epistemology,* 3.

52. C. Riley Snorton, for example, emphasizes the significance of racialized bodies in discussions of closetedness. C. Riley Snorton, *Nobody Is Supposed to Know: Black Sexuality on the Down Low* (Minneapolis: University of Minnesota Press, 2014), 19, 158n52.

53. Jonathan Friedman has posed similar questions with respect to the Jewish American context. See Jonathan C. Friedman, *Rainbow Jews: Jewish and Gay Identity in the Performing Arts* (Lanham, MD: Lexington Books, 2007). On other queer theatrical performances, see Robert A. Schanke and Kim Marra, eds., *Passing Performances: Queer Readings of Leading Players in American Theater History* (Ann Arbor: University of Michigan Press, 1998).

54. See Jill Suzanne Smith, "Richard Oswald and the Social Hygiene Film: Promoting Public Health or Promiscuity?," and Elizabeth Otto, "*Schaulust:* Sexuality and Trauma in Conrad Veidt's Masculine Masquerades," in Rogowski, *Many Faces of Weimar Cinema,* 13–30 and 134–52.

55. Marhoefer, *Sex and Weimar,* 124. Hirschfeld also estimated in 1904 that for every 20 homosexuals arrested in Berlin each year, there were at least 2,000 others who fell prey to blackmailers but were not arrested. Cited in James D. Steakley, "Cinema and Censorship in the Weimar Republic: The Case of *Anders als die Andern,*" *Film History* 11, no. 2 (1999): 181–203; here 186.

56. On the implications of the increased visibility of homosexuality for Oswald's later films, see Anjeana K. Hans, *Gender and the Uncanny in Films of the Weimar Republic* (Detroit: Wayne State University Press, 2014), 102.

57. Elena Mancini, *Magnus Hirschfeld and the Quest for Sexual Freedom: A History of the First International Sexual Freedom Movement* (New York: Palgrave Macmillan, 2010), 136. See also Efron, *Defenders of the Race;* and Atina Grossmann, *Reforming Sex: The German Movement for Birth Control and Abortion Reform, 1920–1950*

(Oxford: Oxford University Press, 1995), 49. While in exile after the Nazi rise to power, Hirschfeld worked on a study of racism in which he joined others in offering a scientific explanation for the lack of racial distinctiveness among Jews. See Magnus Hirschfeld, *Racism*, trans. and ed. Eden and Cedar Paul (1938; repr. Port Washington, NY: Kennikat Press, 1973), 58–68.

58. Stratenwerth and Simon, *Pioniere in Celluloid*, 223; and Buerkle, "Caught in the Act," 98n46. See also Walther Friedmann, "Homosexuality and Jewishness: The Latest Method of Agitation against 'Aufklärungsfilme,'" in Kaes, Baer, and Cowan, *Promise of Cinema*, 240–42.

59. See chapter 1 on the prize contest, "The Beautiful Jewish Child."

60. Mancini, *Magnus Hirschfeld*, 111. On Hirschfeld and his institute more generally, see also Whisnant, *Queer Identities*, 173–78.

61. Sutton, *Masculine Woman*, 111–17; and Garber, *Vested Interests*, 55, 131. Scott Spector has pointed out that major media scandals related to sex, homosexuality, and gender passing occurred beginning in the 1860s. See Scott Spector, *Violent Sensations: Sex, Crime, and Utopia in Vienna and Berlin, 1860–1914* (Chicago: University of Chicago Press, 2016).

62. Many would argue that such procedures did not aid transgender or transsexual individuals in "passing" per se, but rather in becoming their "true" selves. See, for example, Judith Halberstam, *Female Masculinity* (Durham, NC: Duke University Press, 1998), 21.

63. Gilman, *Making the Body Beautiful*, 281–82; and Sander L. Gilman, "Preface: Whose Body Is It, Anyway? Hermaphrodites, Gays, and Jews in N. O. Body's Germany," in N. O. Body, *Memoirs of a Man's Maiden Years*, trans. Deborah Simon (Philadelphia: University of Pennsylvania Press, 2006), xii–xxiv; here xix. On Baer's involvement in the Jewish community, see also David Brenner, *Kafka's Kitsch*, 41–49.

64. Marhoefer, *Sex and Weimar*, 119–23; Lybeck, *Desiring Emancipation*, 164.

65. Marhoefer, *Sex and Weimar*, 63; Sutton, "We Too," 342.

66. Marti M. Lybeck, "Writing Love, Feeling Shame: Rethinking Respectability in the Weimar Homosexual Women's Movement," in *After the History of Sexuality: German Genealogies with and beyond Foucault*, ed. Scott Spector, Helmut Puff, and Dagmar Herzog (New York: Berghahn Books, 2012), 156–68; here 158. Lybeck further notes that both prostitutes and bisexuals were excluded from the homosexual community. Lybeck, *Desiring Emancipation*, 170.

67. On Berlin's gay and lesbian bars, see Whisnant, *Queer Identities*, 92–98; here 92. On women's clubs, see also Lybeck, *Desiring Emancipation*, 151–58; and Annelie Lütgens, "The Conspiracy of Women: Images of City Life in the Work of Jeanne Mammen," in Ankum, *Women in the Metropolis*, 89–105; here 99. Artist Jeanne Mammen painted a watercolor of the wine restaurant Como in 1926, and Otto Dix painted the Eldorado in 1927. Isherwood's *Berlin Stories* (1935/39) notably served as the inspiration for the American film *Cabaret* (Fosse, 1972), which, as Noah Isenberg has pointed out, serves as one of the best-known visual representations of Weimar Berlin's nightlife for many Anglo-American viewers. Noah Isenberg, introduction to *Weimar Cinema: An Essential Guide*, 1–12; here 3.

68. Sutton, "We Too," 339, 351n25.

69. On the JAD, see chapter 3; on displaying periodicals in public, see chapter 2.

70. Alexander Doty, *Making Things Perfectly Queer: Interpreting Mass Culture* (Minneapolis: University of Minnesota, 1993), 3. See also Stratton, *Coming Out Jewish*, 271n65.

71. See Richard Dyer, *Now You See It: Studies in Lesbian and Gay Film*, 2nd ed., with Julianne Pidduck (London: Routledge, 2003), 23–62; Alice A. Kuzniar, *The Queer German Cinema* (Stanford: Stanford University Press, 2000), 37–39; Silke Arnold-de Simine and Christine Mielke, *Charleys Tanten und Astas Enkel: 100 Jahre Crossdressing in der deutschen Filmkomödie* (Trier: Wissenschaftlicher Verlag Trier, 2012); Weinstein, "(Un)Fashioning Identities," in Finney, *Visual Culture*; and McCormick, "Transnational Jewish Comedy," in Geller and Morris, *Three-Way Street*, 179, 189.

72. A well-known Yiddish film, *Yidl mitn Fidl* (*Yiddle with His Fiddle*; Green, 1936), contains a similar plotline. On *Yidl*, see Hoffman, *Passing Game*, 75–83.

73. See, for example, Jeffrey Goldberg, "Is It Time for the Jews to Leave Europe?," *Atlantic*, April 2015, cover story.

# Selected Bibliography

## LIBRARIES AND ARCHIVAL COLLECTIONS

*Germany*

Akademie der Künste, Berlin
Bundesarchiv-Filmarchiv, Berlin
Deutsches Literaturarchiv Marbach, Marbach am Neckar
Leo Baeck Institut, Jüdisches Museum, Berlin
Sammlung Modebild—Lipperheidesche Kostümbibliothek, Berlin
Staatsbibliothek zu Berlin—Preußischer Kulturbesitz, Berlin
Stiftung Deutsche Kinemathek—Museum für Film und Fernsehen, Berlin
Stiftung Neue Synagoge Berlin—Centrum Judaicum Archiv, Berlin

*Israel*

Leo Baeck Institute, Jerusalem

*United States*

Dorot Jewish Division, New York Public Library, New York
Leo Baeck Institute, Center for Jewish History, New York
Library at the Herbert D. Katz Center for Advanced Judaic Studies, Philadelphia
Library of Congress, Washington, DC
University of Southern California Libraries Special Collections, Los Angeles
YIVO Institute for Jewish Research, Center for Jewish History, New York

## UNPUBLISHED PAPERS OF INDIVIDUALS

Adolf Asch Collection. File no. 2 (Adolph Asch). Leo Baeck Institute, Jerusalem.
Bertha Badt-Strauss Collection. AR 3945 and MM4. Leo Baeck Institute, New York.
Max Brod Collection. AR 1023. Leo Baeck Institute, New York.
Wilhelm Graetz. 1,75D Gr 1. Stiftung Neue Synagoge—Centrum Judaicum Archiv, Berlin.

Sammy Gronemann. *Erinnerungen.* ME 203. Leo Baeck Institute, New York.
Lotte Hirschberg. *Mein Leben.* ME 1531. Leo Baeck Institute, New York.
Clementine Krämer Collection. AR 2402. Leo Baeck Institute, New York.
Grete Mosheim Collection. No. 211. USC Special Collections, Los Angeles.
Max Reiner. *Mein Leben in Deutschland vor und nach dem Jahre 1933* (1940). ME 517.
    Leo Baeck Institute, New York.
Joseph Roth Collection. AR 1764. Leo Baeck Institute, New York.

## JEWISH NEWSPAPERS AND PERIODICALS

*Allgemeine Zeitung des Judentums,* Berlin (1837–1922)
*Bayerische Israelitische Gemeindezeitung,* Munich (1925–37)
*Berliner jüdische Zeitung,* Berlin (1929–30)
*Blätter des jüdischen Frauenbundes,* Berlin (1924–38)
*Centralverein/C.V.-Zeitung,* Berlin (1922–38)
*Gemeindeblatt der jüdischen Gemeinde zu Berlin,* Berlin (1909–37)
*Der Israelit. Ein Centralorgan für das orthodoxe Judentum,* Frankfurt am Main (1860–
    1938)
*Israelitisches Familienblatt,* Hamburg, Berlin, and Frankfurt am Main (1898–1938)
*Jahrbuch für jüdische Geschichte und Literatur,* Berlin (1898–1938)
*Der Jude. Eine Monatsschrift,* Berlin and Vienna (1916–28)
*Jüdisch-liberale Zeitung,* Breslau and Berlin (1920–36)
*Das jüdische Echo,* Munich (1914–33)
*Jüdische Familien-Forschung,* Berlin (1924–38)
*Die jüdische Frau,* Berlin (1925–27)
*Das jüdische Magazin,* Berlin (1929–30)
*Jüdische Rundschau,* Berlin (1902–38)
*Menorah,* Vienna, Frankfurt am Main and Berlin (1923–32)
*Mitteilungen der Jüdischen Reformgemeinde zu Berlin,* Berlin (1918–38)
*Der Morgen. Zweimonatsschrift,* Berlin (1925–38)
*Neue jüdische Monatshefte,* Berlin (1916–20)
*Der Schild. Zeitschrift des Reichsbundes jüdischer Frontsoldaten,* Berlin (1922–38)
*Schlemiel. Jüdische Blätter für Humor und Kunst,* Berlin (1919–20, 1924)
*Yidishe ilustrirte tsaytung/Jüdische Illustrierte Zeitung,* Berlin (1924)

## SELECTED PUBLISHED SOURCES

Abrams, Nathan, ed. *Hidden in Plain Sight: Jews and Jewishness in British Film, Tele-
    vision, and Popular Culture.* Evanston, IL: Northwestern University Press, 2016.
Ahmed, Aischa. "'Na ja, irgendwie hat man das ja gesehen'. Passing in Deutschland–
    Überlegungen zu Repräsentation und Differenz." In *Mythen, Masken und Subjekte.
    Kritische Weißseinsforschung in Deutschland,* edited by Maureen Maisha Eggers,
    Grada Kilomba, Peggy Piesche, and Susan Arndt, 270–82. Münster: Unrast, 2005.
Ahmed, Sara. "'She'll Wake Up One of These Days and Find She's Turned into a Nig-

ger': Passing through Hybridity." *Theory, Culture & Society* 16, no. 2 (1999): 87–106.

Ahmed, Sara. *Strange Encounters: Embodied Others in Post-Coloniality.* New York: Routledge, 2000.

Amsler, André. *"Wer dem Werbefilm verfällt, ist verloren für die Welt": Das Werk von Julius Pinschewer, 1883–1961.* Zurich: Chronos Verlag, 1997.

Angress, Werner T. *Between Fear and Hope: Jewish Youth in the Third Reich.* Translated by Werner T. Angress and Christine Granger. New York: Columbia University Press, 1988.

Angress, Werner T. "The German Army's *'Judenzählung'* of 1916: Genesis–Consequences—Significance." *Leo Baeck Institute Year Book* 23 (1978): 117–38.

Angress, Werner T. *Witness to the Storm: A Jewish Journey from Nazi Berlin to the 82nd Airborne, 1920–1945.* Durham, NC: CreateSpace Independent Publishing Platform, 2012.

Ankum, Katharina von, ed. *Women in the Metropolis: Gender and Modernity in Weimar Culture.* Berkeley: University of California Press, 1997.

Arnheim, Rudolf. *Film Essays and Criticism.* Madison: University of Wisconsin Press, 1997.

Arnim, Ludwig Achim von. *Texte der deutschen Tischgesellschaft.* Edited by Stefan Nienhaus. Tübingen: Max Niemeyer Verlag, 2008.

Arnold-de Simine, Silke, and Christine Mielke. *Charleys Tanten und Astas Enkel. 100 Jahre Crossdressing in der deutschen Filmkomödie.* Trier: Wissenschaftlicher Verlag Trier, 2012.

Asch, Adolph, and Johanna Philippson. "Self-Defence at the Turn of the Century: The Emergence of the K.C." *Leo Baeck Institute Year Book* 3 (1958): 122–39.

Aschheim, Steven E. *Brothers and Strangers: The East European Jew in German and German Jewish Consciousness, 1800–1923.* Madison: University of Wisconsin Press, 1982.

Aschheim, Steven E. *In Times of Crisis: Essays on European Culture, Germans, and Jews.* Madison: University of Wisconsin Press, 2001.

Aschheim, Steven E., and Vivian Liska, eds. *The German-Jewish Experience Revisited.* Berlin: Walter de Gruyter, 2015.

Ashkenazi, Ofer. *Weimar Film and Modern Jewish Identity.* New York: Palgrave Macmillan, 2012.

Aue-Ben-David, Irene, Gerhard Lauer, and Jürgen Stenzel, eds. *Constantin Brunner im Kontext. Ein Intellektueller zwischen Kaiserreich und Exil.* Berlin: De Gruyter Oldenbourg; Jerusalem: Magnes Press, 2014.

Auslander, Leora. "The Boundaries of Jewishness, or When Is a Cultural Practice Jewish?" *Journal of Modern Jewish Studies* 8, no. 1 (2009): 47–64.

Auslander, Leora. "'Jewish Taste?': Jews and the Aesthetics of Everyday Life in Paris and Berlin, 1920–1942." In *Histories of Leisure*, edited by Rudy Koshar, 299–318. Oxford: Berg, 2002.

Baader, Benjamin Maria. *Gender, Judaism, and Bourgeois Culture in Germany, 1800–1870.* Bloomington: Indiana University Press, 2006.

Baader, Benjamin Maria, Sharon Gillerman, and Paul Lerner, eds. *Jewish Masculini-*

*ties: German Jews, Gender, and History*. Bloomington: Indiana University Press, 2012.

Bab, Julius. *Schauspieler und Schaukunst*. Berlin: Oesterheld & Co. Verlag, 1926.

Backhaus, Fritz, Raphael Gross, and Liliane Weissberg, eds. *Juden. Geld. Eine Vorstellung*. Frankfurt am Main: Campus Verlag, 2013.

Bajohr, Frank. *"Unser Hotel ist judenfrei". Bäder-Antisemitismus im 19. und 20. Jahrhundert*. Frankfurt am Main: Fischer Taschenbuch Verlag, 2003.

Barkai, Avraham. *"Wehr dich!" Der Centralverein deutscher Staatsbürger jüdischen Glaubens (C.V.) 1893–1938*. Munich: Beck, 2002.

Barker, Andrew. *Fictions from an Orphan State: Literary Reflections of Austria between Habsburg and Hitler*. Rochester, NY: Camden House, 2012.

Ben-Ur, Aviva. "Funny, You Don't Look Jewish! 'Passing' and the Elasticity of Ethnic Identity among Levantine Sephardic Immigrants in Early 20th Century America." *Kolor: Journal on Moving Communities* 2 (2002): 9–18.

Benz, Wolfgang, Arnold Paucker, and Peter Pulzer, eds. *Jüdisches Leben in der Weimarer Republik/Jews in the Weimar Republic*. Tübingen: Mohr Siebeck, 1998.

Bergner, Elisabeth. *Bewundert viel und viel gescholten. Unordentliche Erinnerungen*. Munich: C. Bertelsmann, 1978.

Bering, Dietz. *The Stigma of Names: Antisemitism in German Daily Life, 1812–1933*. Translated by Neville Plaice. Ann Arbor: University of Michigan, 1992.

Berkowitz, Michael. *The Jewish Self-Image in the West*. New York: New York University Press, 2000.

Bernauer, Rudolf. *Das Theater meines Lebens. Erinnerungen*. Berlin: Lothar Blanvalet Verlag, 1955.

Bertrams, Kurt U. *Der Kartell-Convent und seine Verbindungen*. Hilden: WJK-Verlag, 2009.

Bial, Henry. *Acting Jewish: Negotiating Ethnicity on the American Stage and Screen*. Ann Arbor: University of Michigan Press, 2005.

Biale, David. *Blood and Belief: The Circulation of a Symbol between Jews and Christians*. Berkeley: University of California Press, 2007.

Bilski, Emily D., ed. *Berlin Metropolis: Jews and the New Culture, 1890–1918*. Berkeley: University of California Press, 1999.

Body, N. O. *Memoirs of a Man's Maiden Years*. Translated by Deborah Simon. Philadelphia: University of Pennsylvania Press, 2006.

Boyarin, Daniel. *Unheroic Conduct: The Rise of Heterosexuality and the Invention of the Jewish Man*. Berkeley: University of California Press, 1997.

Boyarin, Daniel, Daniel Itzkovitz, and Ann Pellegrini, eds. *Queer Theory and the Jewish Question*. New York: Columbia University Press, 2003.

Boyarin, Jonathan, and Daniel Boyarin, eds. *Jews and Other Differences: The New Jewish Cultural Studies*. Minneapolis: University of Minnesota Press, 1997.

Boyarin, Jonathan, and Daniel Boyarin. "Self-Exposure as Theory: The Double Mark of the Male Jew." In *Rhetorics of Self-Making*, edited by Debbora Battaglia, 16–42. Berkeley: University of California Press, 1995.

Braun, Christina von, ed. *Was war deutsches Judentum? 1870–1933*. Berlin: De Gruyter Oldenbourg, 2015.

Brecht, Christoph, Armin Loacker, and Ines Steiner. *Professionalist und Propagandist: Der Kameramann und Regisseur Gustav Ucicky*. Vienna: Verlag Filmarchiv Austria, 2014.

Brenner, David A. *German-Jewish Popular Culture before the Holocaust: Kafka's Kitsch*. New York: Routledge, 2008.

Brenner, David A. *Marketing Identities: The Invention of Jewish Ethnicity in* Ost und West. Detroit: Wayne State University Press, 1998.

Brenner, Michael. *The Renaissance of Jewish Culture in Weimar Germany*. New Haven: Yale University Press, 1996.

Brenner, Michael, and Derek J. Penslar, eds. *In Search of Jewish Community: Jewish Identities in Germany and Austria, 1918–1933*. Bloomington: Indiana University Press, 1998.

Brenner, Michael, and Gideon Reuveni, eds. *Emancipation through Muscles: Jews and Sports in Europe*. Lincoln: University of Nebraska Press, 2006.

Bridenthal, Renate, Atina Grossmann, and Marion A. Kaplan, eds. *When Biology Became Destiny: Women in Weimar and Nazi Germany*. New York: Monthly Review Press, 1984.

Brod, Max. *Jüdinnen. Ein Roman*. 1911. Reprint, Leipzig: Kurt Wolff Verlag, 1915.

Bronner, Leila Leah. "From Veil to Wig: Jewish Women's Hair Covering." *Judaism* 42, no. 4 (1993): 464–77.

Browder, Laura. *Slippery Characters: Ethnic Impersonators and American Identities*. Chapel Hill: University of North Carolina Press, 2000.

Brown, Wendy. *Regulating Aversion: Tolerance in the Age of Identity and Empire*. Princeton: Princeton University Press, 2006.

Brunner, Constantin. *Der Judenhass und die Juden*. Berlin: Oesterheld & Co., 1918.

Brunner, Constantin. *Von den Pflichten der Juden und von den Pflichten des Staates*. Berlin: Gustav Kiepenhauer, 1930.

Brunotte, Ulrike, Anna-Dorothea Ludewig, and Axel Stähler, eds. *Orientalism, Gender, and the Jews: Literary and Artistic Transformations of European National Discourses*. Berlin: De Gruyter Oldenbourg, 2015.

Buber, Martin. "The Jewish Woman's Zion." In *The First Buber: Youthful Zionist Writings of Martin Buber*, edited and translated by Gilya G. Schmidt. Syracuse, NY: Syracuse University Press, 1999.

Budick, Emily Miller. *Blacks and Jews in Literary Conversation*. New York: Cambridge University Press, 1998.

Buerkle, Darcy. "Caught in the Act: Norbert Elias, Emotion, and *The Ancient Law*." *Journal of Modern Jewish Studies* 8, no. 1 (2009): 83–102.

Buerkle, Darcy. "Gendered Spectatorship, Jewish Women and Psychological Advertising in Weimar Germany." *Women's History Review* 15, no. 4 (2006): 625–36.

Buerkle, Darcy C. *Nothing Happened: Charlotte Salomon and an Archive of Suicide*. Ann Arbor: University of Michigan Press, 2013.

Bunzl, Matti. *Symptoms of Modernity: Jews and Queers in Late-Twentieth-Century Vienna*. Berkeley: University of California Press, 1999.

Butler, Judith. *Bodies That Matter: On the Discursive Limits of Sex*. New York: Routledge, 1993.

Cahnman, Werner J. "The Life of Clementine Kraemer." *Leo Baeck Institute Year Book* 8 (1964): 267–92.

Cahnmann, Werner. *Völkische Rassenlehre. Darstellung, Kritik und Folgerungen.* Berlin: Philo Verlag, 1932.

Campt, Tina M. *Other Germans: Black Germans and the Politics of Race, Gender, and Memory in the Third Reich.* Ann Arbor: University of Michigan Press, 2004.

Canning, Kathleen, Kerstin Barndt, and Kristin McGuire, eds. *Weimar Publics/Weimar Subjects: Rethinking the Political Culture of Germany in the 1920s.* New York: Berghahn Books, 2010.

Carlebach, Elisheva. *Divided Souls: Converts from Judaism in Germany, 1500–1750.* New Haven: Yale University Press, 2001.

Caughie, Pamela L. *Passing and Pedagogy: The Dynamics of Responsibility.* Urbana: University of Illinois Press, 1999.

Chin, Rita, Heide Fehrenbach, Geoff Eley, and Atina Grossmann. *After the Nazi Racial State: Difference and Democracy in Germany and Europe.* Ann Arbor: University of Michigan Press, 2009.

Clauß, Ludwig Ferdinand. *Von Seele und Antlitz der Rassen und Völker. Eine Einführung in die vergleichende Ausdrucksforschung.* Munich: J. F. Lehmanns Verlag, 1929.

Cohen, Arthur A., ed. *The Jew: Essays from Martin Buber's Journal* Der Jude, *1916– 1928.* Translated by Joachim Neugroschel. Tuscaloosa: University of Alabama Press, 1980.

Cohen, Deborah. "Who Was Who? Race and Jews in Turn-of-the-Century Britain." *Journal of British Studies* 41, no. 4 (2002): 460–83.

Colpet, Max. *Sag mir wo die Jahre sind. Erinnerungen eines unverbesserlichen Optimisten.* Gütersloh: Mohndruck Reinhard Mohn, 1976.

Conor, Liz. *The Spectacular Modern Woman: Feminine Visibility in the 1920s.* Bloomington: Indiana University Press, 2004.

Cowan, Michael. "Advertising, Rhythm, and the Filmic Avant-Garde in Weimar: Guido Seeber and Julius Pinschewer's *Kipho* Film." *October* 131 (Winter 2010): 23–50.

Cowan, Michael. "The Ambivalence of Ornament: Silhouette Advertisements in Print and Film in Early Twentieth-Century Germany." *Art History* 36, no. 4 (2013): 784– 809.

Cowan, Michael. "Fidelity, Capture and the Sound Advertisement. Julius Pinschewer and Rudi Klemm's *Die chinesische Nachtigall*." *Zeitgeschichte* 41, no. 2 (2014): 77–88.

Cowan, Michael and Kai Marcel Sicks, eds. *Leibhaftige Moderne. Körper in Kunst und Massenmedien 1918 bis 1933.* Bielefeld: Transcript Verlag, 2005.

Crim, Brian E. *Antisemitism in the German Military Community and the Jewish Response, 1914–1938.* Lanham, MD: Lexington Books, 2014.

Critchfield, Richard. *From Shakespeare to Frisch: The Provocative Fritz Kortner.* Heidelberg: Synchron, 2008.

Dalinger, Brigitte, Kurt Ifkovits, and Andrea B. Braidt, eds. *Gute Unterhaltung. Fritz Grünbaum und die Vergnügungskultur im Wien der 1920er und 1930er Jahre.* Frankfurt am Main: Peter Lang, 2008.

Dawkins, Marcia Alesan. *Clearly Invisible: Racial Passing and the Color of Cultural Identity*. Waco, TX: Baylor University Press, 2012.

Dick, Jutta, and Marina Sassenberg, eds. *Jüdische Frauen im 19. und 20. Jahrhundert. Lexikon zu Leben und Werk*. Reinbek bei Hamburg: Rowohlt, 1993.

Diedrich, Maria I., and Jürgen Heinrichs, eds. *From Black to Schwarz: Cultural Crossovers between African America and Germany*. Münster: LIT Verlag, 2011.

Diehl, Katrin. *Die jüdische Presse im Dritten Reich. Zwischen Selbstbehauptung und Fremdbestimmung*. Tübingen: Max Niemeyer Verlag, 1997.

Distelmeyer, Jan, ed. *Spaß beiseite, Film ab. Jüdischer Humor oder verdrängendes Lachen in der Filmkomödie bis 1945*. Hamburg: edition text + kritik, 2006.

Doane, Mary Ann. *Femmes Fatales: Feminism, Film Theory, Psychoanalysis*. New York: Routledge, 1991.

Döge, Ulrich, ed. *Hans Wollenberg. Filmpublizist. Mit Kritiken und Aufsätzen von Hans Wollenberg*. Munich: Edition text + kritik, 2013.

Dohrn, Verena, and Gertrud Pickhan, eds. *Transit und Transformation. Osteuropäisch-jüdische Migranten in Berlin 1918–1939*. Göttingen: Wallstein, 2010.

Doran, Sabine. *The Culture of Yellow: Or, the Visual Politics of Late Modernity*. New York: Bloomsbury, 2013.

Doty, Alexander. *Making Things Perfectly Queer: Interpreting Mass Culture*. Minneapolis: University of Minnesota Press, 1993.

Dunker, Ulrich. *Der Reichsbund jüdischer Frontsoldaten 1919–1938. Geschichte eines jüdischen Abwehrvereins*. Düsseldorf: Droste, 1977.

Dyer, Richard, with Julianne Pidduck. *Now You See It: Studies in Lesbian and Gay Film*. 2nd ed. London: Routledge, 2003.

Efron, John M. *Defenders of the Race: Jewish Doctors and Race Science in Fin-de-Siècle Europe*. New Haven: Yale University Press, 1994.

Efron, John M. *German Jewry and the Allure of the Sephardic*. Princeton: Princeton University Press, 2016.

Efron, John M. "Scientific Racism and the Mystique of Sephardic Racial Superiority." *Leo Baeck Institute Year Book* 38 (1993): 75–96.

Eigen, Sara, and Mark Larrimore, eds. *The German Invention of Race*. Albany: State University of New York Press, 2006.

Eikenberg, Gabriel. *Der Mythos deutscher Kultur im Spiegel jüdischer Presse in Deutschland und Österreich von 1918 bis 1938*. Hildesheim: Georg Olms Verlag, 2010.

Ellison, Ralph. *Shadow and Act*. New York: Random House, 1964.

Elon, Amos. *The Pity of It All: A History of Jews in Germany, 1743–1933*. New York: Metropolitan Books, 2002.

Elsaesser, Thomas, and Michael Wedel, eds. *A Second Life: German Cinema's First Decades*. Amsterdam: Amsterdam University Press, 1996.

Elswit, Kate. *Watching Weimar Dance*. New York: Oxford University Press, 2014.

Endelman, Todd M. *The Jews of Britain, 1656 to 2000*. Berkeley: University of California Press, 2002.

Endelman, Todd M. *Leaving the Jewish Fold: Conversion and Radical Assimilation in Modern Jewish History*. Princeton: Princeton University Press, 2015.

Erdman, Harley. *Staging the Jew: The Performance of an American Ethnicity, 1860–1920*. New Brunswick, NJ: Rutgers University Press, 1997.

Estraikh, Gennady, and Mikhail Krutikov, eds. *Yiddish in Weimar Berlin: At the Crossroads of Diaspora Politics and Culture*. London: Modern Humanities Research Association, 2010.

Evans, Jennifer V. "Introduction: Why Queer German History?" *German History* 34, no. 3 (2016): 371–84.

Fähnders, Walter. "Über zwei Romane, die 1933 nicht erscheinen durften: Mela Hartwigs *Bin ich ein überflüssiger Mensch?* und Ruth Landshoff-Yorcks *Roman einer Tänzerin*." Vol. 36 of *Chloe: Beihefte zum Daphnis, Regionaler Kulturraum und intellektuelle Kommunikation von Humanismus bis ins Zeitalter des Internet*, edited by Axel E. Walter, 161–90. Amsterdam: Rodopi, 2005.

Fanon, Franz. *Black Skin, White Masks*. Translated by Richard Philcox. New York: Grove Press, 2008.

Fauset, Jessie Redmon. *Comedy: American Style*. Edited and with an introduction by Cherene Sherrard-Johnson. New Brunswick, NJ: Rutgers University Press, 2009.

Fauset, Jessie Redmon. *Plum Bun: A Novel without a Moral*. Boston: Beacon Press, 1990.

Feld, Hans. "Jews in the Development of the German Film Industry: Notes from the Recollections of a Berlin Film Critic." *Leo Baeck Institute Year Book* 27 (1982): 337–65.

Fermaglich, Kirsten. "'Too Long, Too Foreign . . . Too Jewish': Jews, Name Changing, and Family Mobility in New York City, 1917–1942." *Journal of American Ethnic History* 34, no. 3 (2015): 34–57.

Fermaglich, Kirsten. "'What's Uncle Sam's Last Name?' Jews and Name Changing in New York City during the World War II Era." *Journal of American History* 102, no. 3 (2015): 719–45.

Finney, Gail, ed. *Visual Culture in Twentieth-Century Germany: Text as Spectacle*. Bloomington: Indiana University Press, 2006.

Foreman, P. Gabrielle, and Cherene Sherrard-Johnson. "Racial Recovery, Racial Death: An Introduction in Four Parts." *Legacy* 24, no. 2 (2007): 157–70.

Foucault, Michel. *Discipline and Punish: The Birth of the Prison*. 2nd ed. Translated by Alan Sheridan. New York: Vintage Books, 1995.

Franco, Dean. *Race, Rights, and Recognition: Jewish American Literature since 1969*. Ithaca: Cornell University Press, 2012.

Freeden, Herbert. *The Jewish Press in the Third Reich*. Translated by William Templer. Providence, RI: Berg Publishers, 1993.

Freidenreich, Harriet Pass. *Female, Jewish and Educated: The Lives of Central European University Women*. Bloomington: Indiana University Press, 2002.

Friedman, Jonathan C. *Rainbow Jews: Jewish and Gay Identity in the Performing Arts*. Lanham, MD: Lexington Books, 2007.

Fritzsche, Peter. *Reading Berlin 1900*. Cambridge: Harvard University Press, 1996.

Fuchs, Eduard. *Die Juden in der Karikatur. Ein Beitrag zur Kulturgeschichte*. Munich: Albert Langen, 1921.

Fuechtner, Veronika. *Berlin Psychoanalytic: Psychoanalysis and Culture in Weimar Republic Germany*. Berkeley: University of California Press, 2011.

Ganeva, Mila. "Fashion Photography and Women's Modernity in Weimar Germany: The Case of Yva." *NWSA Journal* 15, no. 3 (2003): 1–25.

Ganeva, Mila. *Women in Weimar Fashion: Discourses and Displays in German Culture, 1918–1933*. Rochester, NY: Camden House, 2008.

Garber, Marjorie. *Vested Interests: Cross-Dressing and Cultural Anxiety*. New York: Routledge, 1992.

Gay, Peter. *Freud, Jews and Other Germans: Masters and Victims in Modernist Culture*. New York: Oxford University Press, 1978.

Gay, Peter. *Weimar Culture: The Outsider as Insider*. 1968. Reprint, New York: W. W. Norton, 2001.

Gelbin, Cathy S. *The Golem Returns: From German Romantic Literature to Global Jewish Culture, 1808–2008*. Ann Arbor: University of Michigan Press, 2011.

Geller, Jay. *On Freud's Jewish Body: Mitigating Circumcisions*. New York: Fordham University Press, 2007.

Geller, Jay. *The Other Jewish Question: Identifying the Jew and Making Sense of Modernity*. New York: Fordham University Press, 2011.

Geller, Jay Howard, and Leslie Morris, eds. *Three-Way Street: Germans, Jews, and the Transnational*. Ann Arbor: University of Michigan Press, 2016.

Gemünden, Gerd, and Johannes von Moltke, eds. *Culture in the Anteroom: The Legacies of Siegfried Kracauer*. Ann Arbor: University of Michigan Press, 2012.

Gillerman, Sharon. *Germans into Jews: Remaking the Jewish Social Body in the Weimar Republic*. Stanford: Stanford University Press, 2009.

Gillman, Abigail. *Viennese Jewish Modernism: Freud, Hofmannsthal, Beer-Hofmann, and Schnitzler*. University Park: Pennsylvania State University Press, 2009.

Gilman, Sander L. *Difference and Pathology: Stereotypes of Sexuality, Race, and Madness*. Ithaca: Cornell University Press, 1985.

Gilman, Sander L. *Franz Kafka: The Jewish Patient*. New York: Routledge, 1995.

Gilman, Sander L. *Freud, Race, and Gender*. Princeton: Princeton University Press, 1993.

Gilman, Sander L. *Jewish Self-Hatred: Anti-Semitism and the Hidden Language of the Jews*. Baltimore: Johns Hopkins University Press, 1986.

Gilman, Sander L. *The Jew's Body*. New York: Routledge, 1991.

Gilman, Sander L. *Making the Body Beautiful: A Cultural History of Aesthetic Surgery*. Princeton: Princeton University Press, 1999.

Gilman, Sander L. *On Blackness without Blacks: Essays on the Image of the Black in Germany*. Boston: G. K. Hall, 1982.

Gilman, Sander L. "Salome, Syphilis, Sarah Bernhardt, and the Modern Jewess." In *The Jew in the Text: Modernity and the Construction of Identity*, edited by Linda Nochlin and Tamar Garb, 97–120. London: Thames and Hudson, 1995.

Gilman, Sander L., and Jack Zipes, eds. *Yale Companion to Jewish Writing and Thought in German Culture, 1096–1996*. New Haven: Yale University Press, 1997.

Ginsberg, Elaine K., ed. *Passing and the Fictions of Identity*. Durham, NC: Duke University Press, 1996.

Glaser, Jennifer. *Borrowed Voices: Writing and Racial Ventriloquism in the Jewish American Imagination*. New Brunswick, NJ: Rutgers University Press, 2016.

Gluck, Mary. *The Invisible Jewish Budapest: Metropolitan Culture at the Fin de Siècle*. Madison: University of Wisconsin Press, 2016.

Goffman, Erving. *Stigma: Notes on the Management of Spoiled Identity.* 1963. Reprint, New York: Simon and Schuster, 2009.

Grab, Walter, and Julius Schoeps, eds. *Juden in der Weimarer Republik.* Stuttgart: Burg Verlag, 1986.

Grady, Tim. *The German-Jewish Soldiers of the First World War in History and Memory.* Liverpool: Liverpool University Press, 2011.

Greene, Larry A., and Anke Ortlepp, eds. *Germans and African Americans: Two Centuries of Exchange.* Jackson: University Press of Mississippi, 2011.

Greenspahn, Frederick E., ed. *Women and Judaism: New Insights and Scholarship.* New York: New York University Press, 2009.

Greenspoon, Leonard J., ed. *Fashioning Jews: Clothing, Culture, and Commerce.* West Lafayette, IN: Purdue University Press, 2013.

Gronemann, Sammy. *Erinnerungen an meine Jahre in Berlin.* Edited by Joachim Schlör. Berlin: Philo Verlag, 2004.

Gronemann, Sammy. *Schalet. Beiträge zur Philosophie des "Wenn schon".* 2nd ed. Afterword by Joachim Schlör. Leipzig: Reclam Verlag, 1998.

Gronemann, Sammy. *Utter Chaos.* Translated by Penny Milbouer. Foreword by Joachim Schlör. Bloomington: Indiana University Press, 2016.

Grossman, Jeffrey A. *The Discourse on Yiddish in Germany from the Enlightenment to the Second Empire.* Rochester, NY: Camden House, 2000.

Grossmann, Atina. *Reforming Sex: The German Movement for Birth Control and Abortion Reform, 1920–1950.* Oxford: Oxford University Press, 1995.

Guenther, Irene. *Nazi Chic? Fashioning Women in the Third Reich.* Oxford: Berg, 2004.

Hahn, Barbara. *The Jewess Pallas Athena: This Too a Theory of Modernity.* Translated by James McFarland. Princeton: Princeton University Press, 2005.

Hake, Sabine. *Passions and Deceptions: The Early Films of Ernst Lubitsch.* Princeton: Princeton University Press, 1992.

Halberstam, Judith. *Female Masculinity.* Durham, NC: Duke University Press, 1998.

Hales, Barbara, Mihaela Petrescu, and Valerie Weinstein, eds. *Continuity and Crisis in German Cinema, 1928–1936.* Rochester, NY: Camden House, 2016.

Hall, Sara F. "Making the Case for German Police Films." *Historical Journal of Film, Radio and Television* 27, no. 4 (2007): 497–511.

Hammel, Andrea, and Godela Weiss-Sussex, eds. *'Not an Essence but a Positioning': German-Speaking Jewish Women Writers 1900–1938.* Munich: Martin Meidenbauer Verlag, 2009.

Hans, Anjeana K. *Gender and the Uncanny in Films of the Weimar Republic.* Detroit: Wayne State University Press, 2014.

Harrison, Kelby. *Sexual Deceit: The Ethics of Passing.* Lanham, MD: Lexington Books, 2013.

Harrison, Kelby, and Dennis Cooley, eds. *Passing/Out: Sexual Identity Veiled and Revealed.* Burlington, VT: Ashgate, 2012.

Harrison-Kahan, Lori. *The White Negress: Literature, Minstrelsy, and the Black-Jewish Imaginary.* New Brunswick, NJ: Rutgers University Press, 2011.

Hart, Mitchell B., ed. *Jews and Race: Writings on Identity and Difference, 1880–1940.* Waltham, MA: Brandeis University Press, 2011.

Hart, Mitchell B. *Social Science and the Politics of Modern Jewish Identity*. Stanford: Stanford University Press, 2000.

Hecht, Cornelia. *Deutsche Juden und Antisemitismus in der Weimarer Republik*. Bonn: Dietz, 2003.

Heikaus, Ulrike. *Deutschsprachige Filme als Kulturinsel. Zur kulturellen Integration der deutschsprachigen Juden in Palästina, 1933–1945*. Potsdam: Universitätsverlag Potsdam, 2009.

Heinsohn, Kirsten, and Stefanie Schüler-Springorum, eds. *Deutsch-jüdische Geschichte als Geschlechtergeschichte. Studien zum 19. und 20. Jahrhundert*. Göttingen: Wallstein Verlag, 2006.

Heinze, Andrew R. *Adapting to Abundance: Jewish Immigrants, Mass Consumption, and the Search for American Identity*. New York: Columbia University Press, 1990.

Helfer, Martha. *The Word Unheard: Legacies of Anti-Semitism in German Literature and Culture*. Evanston, IL: Northwestern University Press, 2011.

Hermand, Jost, and Frank Trommler. *Die Kultur der Weimarer Republik*. Munich: Nymphenburger Verlagshandlung, 1978.

Hertz, Deborah. *How Jews Became Germans: The History of Conversion and Assimilation in Berlin*. New Haven: Yale University Press, 2007.

Herzog, Todd. *Crime Stories: Criminalistic Fantasy and the Culture of Crisis in Weimar Germany*. New York: Berghahn Books, 2009.

Herzog, Todd. "Hybrids and Mischlinge: Translating Anglo-American Cultural Theory into German." *German Quarterly* 70, no. 1 (1997): 1–17.

Hess, Jonathan M. "Fictions of a German-Jewish Public: Ludwig Jacobowski's *Werther the Jew* and Its Readers." *Jewish Social Studies* 11, no. 2 (2005): 202–30.

Hess, Jonathan M. *Germans, Jews and the Claims of Modernity*. New Haven: Yale University Press, 2002.

Hess, Jonathan M. "Johann David Michaelis and the Colonial Imaginary: Orientalism and the Emergence of Racial Antisemitism in Eighteenth-Century Germany." *Jewish Social Studies* 6, no. 2 (2000): 56–101.

Hess, Jonathan M. *Middlebrow Literature and the Making of German-Jewish Identity*. Stanford: Stanford University Press, 2010.

Hobbs, Allyson. *A Chosen Exile: A History of Racial Passing in American Life*. Cambridge: Harvard University Press, 2014.

Hödl, Klaus. "The Blurring of Distinction: Performance and Jewish Identities in Late Nineteenth-Century Vienna." *European Journal of Jewish Studies* 3, no. 2 (2009): 229–49.

Hödl, Klaus, ed. *Nicht nur Bildung, nicht nur Bürger. Juden in der Populärkultur*. Innsbruck: StudienVerlag, 2013.

Hoffmann, Christhard, Werner Bergmann, and Helmut Walser Smith, eds. *Exclusionary Violence: Antisemitic Riots in Modern German History*. Ann Arbor: University of Michigan Press, 2002.

Hoffman, Warren. *The Passing Game: Queering Jewish American Culture*. Syracuse, NY: Syracuse University Press, 2009.

Holmes, Deborah, and Lisa Silverman, eds. *Interwar Vienna: Culture between Tradition and Modernity*. Rochester, NY: Camden House, 2009.

Honeck, Mischa, Martin Klimke, and Anne Kuhlmann, eds. *Germany and the Black Diaspora: Points of Contact, 1250–1914*. New York: Berghahn Books, 2013.

Houlbrook, Matt. *Queer London: Perils and Pleasures in the Sexual Metropolis, 1918–1957*. Chicago: University of Chicago Press, 2005.

Hurst, Fannie. *Imitation of Life*. Edited by Daniel Itzkovitz. Durham, NC: Duke University Press, 2004.

Hyman, Paula E. *Gender and Assimilation in Modern Jewish History: The Roles and Representation of Women*. Seattle: University of Washington Press, 1995.

Hyman, Paula E. *The Jews of Modern France*. Berkeley: University of California Press, 1998.

Idelson-Shein, Iris. *Difference of a Different Kind: Jewish Constructions of Race during the Long Eighteenth Century*. Philadelphia: University of Pennsylvania Press, 2014.

Isenberg, Noah. *Between Redemption and Doom: The Strains of German-Jewish Modernism*. Lincoln: University of Nebraska Press, 1999.

Isenberg, Noah, ed. *Weimar Cinema: An Essential Guide to the Classic Films of the Era*. New York: Columbia University Press, 2009.

Itzkovitz, Daniel. "Passing Like Me." *South Atlantic Quarterly* 98, nos. 1–2 (1999): 35–57.

Jacobs, Janet Liebman. *Hidden Heritage: The Legacy of the Crypto-Jews*. Berkeley: University of California Press, 2002.

Jacobs, Joela. "Assimilating Aliens: Imagining National Identity in Oskar Panizza's *Operated Jew* and Salomo Friedlaender's *Operated Goy*." In *Alien Imaginations: Science Fiction and Tales of Transnationalism*, edited by Ulrike Küchler, Silja Maehl, and Graeme Stout, 57–72. New York: Bloomsbury Academic, 2015.

Jacobson, Matthew Frye. *Whiteness of a Different Color: European Immigrants and the Alchemy of Race*. Cambridge: Harvard University Press, 1999.

Jelavich, Peter. *Berlin Cabaret*. Cambridge: Harvard University Press, 1993.

Johnson, James Weldon. *The Autobiography of an Ex-Colored Man*. Boston: Sherman, French & Company, 1912.

Joselit, Jenna Weissman. *A Perfect Fit: Clothes, Character, and the Promise of America*. New York: Metropolitan Books, 2001.

Judd, Robin. *Contested Rituals: Circumcision, Kosher Butchering, and Jewish Political Life in Germany, 1843–1933*. Ithaca: Cornell University Press, 2007.

Kaes, Anton. *Shell Shock Cinema: Weimar Culture and the Wounds of War*. Princeton: Princeton University Press, 2009.

Kaes, Anton, Nicholas Baer, and Michael Cowan, eds. *The Promise of Cinema: German Film Theory, 1907–1933*. Berkeley: University of California Press, 2016.

Kaes, Anton, Martin Jay, and Edward Dimendberg, eds. *The Weimar Republic Sourcebook*. Berkeley: University of California Press, 1994.

Kapczynski, Jennifer, and Michael D. Richardson, eds. *A New History of German Cinema*. Rochester, NY: Camden House, 2012.

Kaplan, Marion A. *Between Dignity and Despair: Jewish Life in Nazi Germany*. New York: Oxford University Press, 1998.

Kaplan, Marion A., ed. *Jewish Daily Life in Germany, 1618–1945*. New York: Oxford University Press, 2005.

Kaplan, Marion A. *The Jewish Feminist Movement in Germany: The Campaigns of the Jüdischer Frauenbund, 1904–1938*. Westport, CT: Greenwood Press, 1979.

Kaplan, Marion A. *The Making of the Jewish Middle Class: Women, Family, and Identity in Imperial Germany*. Oxford: Oxford University Press, 1991.

Kaplan, Marion A., and Deborah Dash Moore, eds. *Gender and Jewish History*. Bloomington: Indiana University Press, 2011.

Keun, Irmgard. *The Artificial Silk Girl*. Translated by Kathie von Ankum. New York: Other Press, 2002.

Kleeblatt, Norman L., ed. *Too Jewish? Challenging Traditional Identities*. New York: Jewish Museum, 1996.

Koller, Sabine. "*Mentshelekh un stsenes*: Rahel Szalit-Marcus illustriert Sholem Aleichem." In *Leket: Jiddistik heute/Yiddish Studies Today*, edited by Marion Aptroot, Efrat Gal-Ed, Roland Gruschka, and Simon Neuberg, 207–31. Düsseldorf: Düsseldorf University Press, 2012.

Kortner, Fritz. *Aller Tage Abend*. Munich: Kindler Verlag, 1959.

Kracauer, Siegfried. *The Mass Ornament: Weimar Essays*. Translated and edited by Thomas Y. Levin. Cambridge: Harvard University Press, 1995.

Krauss, Werner. *Das Schauspiel meines Lebens, einem Freund erzählt*. Stuttgart: Henry Goverts Verlag, 1958.

Kreimeier, Klaus. *The Ufa Story: A History of Germany's Greatest Film Company, 1918–1945*. Translated by Robert and Rita Kimber. Berkeley: University of California Press, 1996.

Kreutzmüller, Christoph. *Final Sale in Berlin: The Destruction of Jewish Commercial Activity, 1930–1945*. Translated by Jane Paulick and Jefferson Chase. New York: Berghahn Books, 2015.

Krobb, Florian. *Die schöne Jüdin. Jüdische Frauengestalten in der deutschsprachigen Erzählliteratur vom 17. Jahrhundert bis zum Ersten Weltkrieg*. Tübingen: Niemeyer, 1993.

Kroeger, Brooke. *Passing: When People Can't Be Who They Are*. New York: Public Affairs, 2003.

Kuzniar, Alice A. *The Queer German Cinema*. Stanford: Stanford University Press, 2000.

Landsberger, Artur. *Berlin ohne Juden*. Hannover: Paul Steegemann Verlag, 1925.

Landshoff-Yorck, Ruth. *Roman einer Tänzerin. Erstausgabe aus dem Nachlaß*. Edited and with an afterword by Walter Fähnders. Berlin: AvivA, 2002.

Larsen, Nella. *Passing: Authoritative Text, Backgrounds and Contexts, Criticism*. Edited by Carla Kaplan. New York: W. W. Norton, 2007.

Larsen, Nella. *Quicksand and Passing*. Edited and with an introduction by Deborah E. McDowell. New Brunswick, NJ: Rutgers University Press, 1991.

Lasker-Schüler, Else. *Star in My Forehead: Selected Poems*. Translated by Janine Canan. Duluth, MN: Holy Cow! Press, 2000.

Lässig, Simone. *Jüdische Wege ins Bürgertum. Kulturelles Kapital und sozialer Aufstieg im 19. Jahrhundert*. Göttingen: Vandenhoeck and Ruprecht, 2004.

Lerner, Paul. *The Consuming Temple: Jews, Department Stores, and the Consumer Revolution in Germany, 1880–1940*. Ithaca: Cornell University Press, 2015.

Levenson, Alan T. *Between Philosemitism and Antisemitism: Defenses of Jews and Judaism in Germany, 1871–1932.* Lincoln: University of Nebraska Press, 2004.

Levine, Emily J. *Dreamland of Humanists: Warburg, Cassirer, Panofsky, and the Hamburg School.* Chicago: University of Chicago Press, 2013.

Lieberg, Alice. *Remembrance of Things Past.* Dedham, MA: Sylvester Press, 1993.

Loberg, Molly. "The Streetscape of Economic Crisis: Commerce, Politics, and Urban Space in Interwar Berlin." *Journal of Modern History* 85, no. 2 (2013): 364–402.

Loentz, Elizabeth. "'The Most Famous Jewish Pacifist Was Jesus of Nazareth': German-Jewish Pacifist Clementine Krämer's Stories of War and Visions for Peace." *Women in German Yearbook* 23 (2007): 126–55.

Loevinson, Ermanno. *Roma Israelitica. Wanderungen eines Juden durch die Kunststätten Roms.* Frankfurt am Main: J. Kauffmann Verlag, 1927.

Loewenberg, Ernst L. "Jakob Loewenberg: Excerpts from His Diaries and Letters." *Leo Baeck Institute Year Book* 15 (1970): 183–209.

Loewenberg, Jakob. *Aus jüdischer Seele. Ausgewählte Werke.* Edited by Winfried Kempf. Hamburg: IGEL Verlag Literatur and Wissenschaft, 2011.

Loewenberg, Jakob. *Der gelbe Fleck.* Berlin: Philo Verlag, 1924.

Lowenstein, Steven M. *The Berlin Jewish Community: Enlightenment, Family, and Crisis, 1770–1830.* New York: Oxford University Press, 1994.

Ludewig, Anna-Dorothea, Hannah Lotte Lund, and Paola Ferruta, eds. *Versteckter Glaube oder doppelte Identität? Das Bild des Marranentums im 19. und 20. Jahrhundert / Concealed Faith or Double Identity? The Image of Marranism in the 19th and 20th Centuries.* Hildesheim: Georg Olms Verlag, 2011.

Lusane, Clarence. *Hitler's Black Victims: The Historical Experiences of Afro-Germans, European Blacks, Africans, and African Americans in the Nazi Era.* New York: Routledge, 2003.

Lybeck, Marti M. *Desiring Emancipation: New Women and Homosexuality in Germany, 1890–1933.* Albany: State University of New York Press, 2014.

Magilow, Daniel H. *The Photography of Crisis: The Photo Essays of Weimar Germany.* University Park: Pennsylvania State University Press, 2012.

Malinovich, Nadia. *French and Jewish: Culture and the Politics of Identity in Early Twentieth-Century France.* Oxford: Littman Library of Jewish Civilization, 2008.

Malkin, Jeanette R., and Freddie Rokem, eds. *Jews and the Making of Modern German Theatre.* Iowa City: University of Iowa Press, 2010.

Mancini, Elena. *Magnus Hirschfeld and the Quest for Sexual Freedom: A History of the First International Sexual Freedom Movement.* New York: Palgrave Macmillan, 2010.

Marhoefer, Laurie. *Sex and the Weimar Republic: German Homosexual Emancipation and the Rise of the Nazis.* Toronto: University of Toronto Press, 2015.

Matthias, Bettina. *The Hotel as Setting in Early 20th-Century German and Austrian Literature: Checking In to Tell a Story.* Rochester, NY: Camden House, 2006.

Maurer, Trude. "Die Juden in der Weimarer Republik." In *Zerbrochene Geschichte. Leben und Selbstverständnis der Juden in Deutschland,* edited by Dirk Blasius and Dan Diner, 102–20. Frankfurt am Main: Fischer Taschenbuch Verlag, 1991.

Maurer, Trude. *Ostjuden in Deutschland, 1918–1933.* Hamburg: H. Christians Verlag, 1986.

Maxwell, Alexander. *Patriots against Fashion: Clothing and Nationalism in Europe's Age of Revolutions*. New York: Palgrave Macmillan, 2014.

Mazón, Patricia, and Reinhild Steingröver, eds. *Not So Plain as Black and White: Afro-German Culture and History, 1890–2000*. Foreword by Russell Berman. Rochester, NY: University of Rochester Press, 2005.

McCormick, Richard W. *Gender and Sexuality in Weimar Modernity: Film, Literature, and "New Objectivity"*. New York: Palgrave, 2001.

McCormick, Richard W., and Alison Guenther-Pal, eds. *German Essays on Film*. New York: Continuum, 2004.

McLendon, Jacquelyn Y. *The Politics of Color in the Fiction of Jessie Fauset and Nella Larsen*. Charlottesville: University Press of Virginia, 1995.

Mellinkoff, Ruth. "Judas's Red Hair and the Jews." *Journal of Jewish Art* 9 (1982): 31–46.

Mellinkoff, Ruth. *The Mark of Cain*. Eugene, OR: Wipf and Stock, 1981.

Mendes-Flohr, Paul. *German Jews: A Dual Identity*. New Haven: Yale University Press, 1999.

Mendes-Flohr, Paul, and Jehuda Reinharz, eds. *The Jew in the Modern World: A Documentary History*. 3rd ed. New York: Oxford University Press, 2010.

Merback, Mitchell B., ed. *Beyond the Yellow Badge: Anti-Judaism and Antisemitism in Medieval and Early Modern Visual Culture*. Boston: Brill, 2008.

Meskimmon, Marsha. *We Weren't Modern Enough: Women Artists and the Limits of German Modernism*. Berkeley: University of California Press, 1999.

Meyer, Adam. *Black-Jewish Relations in African American and Jewish American Fiction: An Anthology*. Lanham, MD: Scarecrow Press, 2002.

Meyer, Adam. "Not Entirely Strange, but Not Entirely Friendly Either: Images of Jews in African American Passing Novels through the Harlem Renaissance." *African American Review* 38, no. 3 (2004): 441–50.

Meyer, Michael A., and Michael Brenner, eds. *German-Jewish History in Modern Times*. 4 vols. New York: Columbia University Press, 1998.

Mittelmann, Hanni. *Sammy Gronemann (1875–1952): Zionist, Schriftsteller und Satiriker in Deutschland und Palästina*. Frankfurt am Main: Campus Verlag, 2004.

Morris, Leslie, and Jack Zipes, eds. *Unlikely History: The Changing German-Jewish Symbiosis, 1945–2000*. New York: Palgrave, 2002.

Morris-Reich, Amos. *Race and Photography: Racial Photography as Scientific Evidence, 1876–1980*. Chicago: University of Chicago Press, 2016.

Mosse, Werner E., and Arnold Paucker, eds. *Entscheidungsjahr 1932. Zur Judenfrage in der Endphase der Weimarer Republik*. Tübingen: Mohr Siebeck, 1966.

Murray, Bruce. *Film and the German Left in the Weimar Republic: From Caligari to Kuhle Wampe*. Austin: University of Texas Press, 1990.

Nerad, Julie Cary, ed. *Passing Interest: Racial Passing in US Novels, Memoirs, Television, and Film, 1990–2010*. Albany: State University of New York Press, 2014.

Niewyk, Donald L. *The Jews in Weimar Germany*. New Brunswick, NJ: Transaction Publishers, 2001.

Oksman, Tahneer. *"How Come Boys Get to Keep Their Noses?" Women and Jewish American Identity in Contemporary Graphic Memoirs*. New York: Columbia University Press, 2016.

Otte, Marline. *Jewish Identities in German Popular Entertainment, 1890–1933*. New York: Cambridge University Press, 2006.

Otto, Elizabeth, and Vanessa Rocco, eds. *The New Woman International: Representations in Photography and Film from the 1870s through the 1960s*. Ann Arbor: University of Michigan Press, 2011.

Paucker, Arnold. *Der jüdische Abwehrkampf gegen Antisemitismus und Nationalsozialismus in den letzten Jahren der Weimarer Republik*. 2nd ed. Hamburg: Leibniz-Verlag, 1968.

Peiss, Kathy. *Hope in a Jar: The Making of America's Beauty Culture*. New York: Metropolitan Books, 1998.

Pellegrini, Ann. *Performance Anxieties: Staging Psychoanalysis, Staging Race*. New York: Routledge, 1997.

Petro, Patrice. *Joyless Streets: Women and Melodramatic Representation in Weimar Germany*. Princeton: Princeton University Press, 1989.

Pickus, Keith H. *Constructing Modern Identities: Jewish University Students in Germany, 1815–1914*. Detroit: Wayne State University Press, 1999.

Pierson, Ruth. "Embattled Veterans: The Reichsbund jüdischer Frontsoldaten." *Leo Baeck Institute Year Book* 19 (1974): 139–54.

Pierson, Ruth. "German Jewish Identity in the Weimar Republic." PhD diss., Yale University, 1970.

Prawer, S. S. *Between Two Worlds: The Jewish Presence in German and Austrian Film, 1910–1933*. New York: Berghahn Books, 2005.

Prell, Riv-Ellen. *Fighting to Become Americans: Assimilation and the Trouble between Jewish Women and Jewish Men*. Boston: Beacon Press, 1999.

Presner, Todd. *Mobile Modernity: Germans, Jews, Trains*. New York: Columbia University Press, 2007.

Prestel, Claudia T. "Die deutsch-jüdische Presse und die weibliche Sexualität: 'Freie Liebe' oder die Rückkehr zu traditionellem jüdischem Familienleben?" In *Frauen und Frauenbilder in der europäisch-jüdischen Presse von der Aufklärung bis 1945*, edited by Eleonore Lappin and Michael Nagel, 123–41. Bremen: edition lumière bremen, 2007.

Pulzer, Peter. *Jews and the German State: The Political History of a Minority, 1848–1933*. Detroit: Wayne State University Press, 2003.

Pulzer, Peter. *The Rise of Political Anti-Semitism in Germany and Austria*. London: Peter Halban, 1988.

Rabinbach, Anson. *In the Shadow of Catastrophe: German Intellectuals between Apocalypse and Enlightenment*. Berkeley: University of California Press, 1997.

Rahden, Till van. *Jews and Other Germans: Civil Society, Religious Diversity, and Urban Politics in Breslau, 1860–1925*. Translated by Marcus Brainard. Madison: University of Wisconsin Press, 2008.

Reinharz, Jehuda. *Dokumente zur Geschichte des deutschen Zionismus, 1882–1933*. Tübingen: Mohr, 1981.

Reinharz, Jehuda, and Walter Schatzberg, eds. *The Jewish Response to German Culture from the Enlightenment to the Second World War*. Hanover, NH: University Press of New England, 1985.

Reitter, Paul. *The Anti-Journalist: Karl-Kraus and Jewish Self-Fashioning in Fin-de-Siècle Europe*. Chicago: University of Chicago Press, 2008.

Reitter, Paul. *On the Origins of Jewish Self-Hatred*. Princeton: Princeton University Press, 2012.

Rentschler, Eric. *The Ministry of Illusion: Nazi Cinema and Its Afterlife*. Cambridge: Harvard University Press, 1996.

Reuveni, Gideon. *Reading Germany: Literature and Consumer Culture in Germany before 1933*. Translated by Ruth Morris. New York: Berghahn Books, 2006.

Reuveni, Gideon, and Nils H. Roemer, eds. *Longing, Belonging, and the Making of Jewish Consumer Culture*. Boston: Brill, 2010.

Reuveni, Gideon, and Sarah Wobick-Segev, eds. *The Economy in Jewish History: New Perspectives on the Interrelationship between Ethnicity and Economic Life*. New York: Berghahn Books, 2011.

Richarz, Monika, ed. *Jewish Life in Germany: Memoirs from Three Centuries*. Translated by Stella P. Rosenfeld and Sidney Rosenfeld. Bloomington: Indiana University Press, 1991.

Richarz, Monika, ed. *Jüdisches Leben in Deutschland. Selbstzeugnisse zur Sozialgeschichte 1918–1945*. Stuttgart: Deutsche Verlags-Anstalt, 1982.

Rippey, Theodore F. "Rationalisation, Race, and the Weimar Response to Jazz." *German Life and Letters* 60, no. 1 (2007): 75–97.

Robertson, Ritchie. *The 'Jewish Question' in German Literature, 1749–1939: Emancipation and Its Discontents*. New York: Oxford University Press, 1999.

Robinson, Amy. "It Takes One to Know One: Passing and Communities of Common Interest." *Critical Inquiry* 20, no. 4 (1994): 715–36.

Rogin, Michael. *Blackface, White Noise: Jewish Immigrants in the Hollywood Melting Pot*. Berkeley: University of California Press, 1996.

Rogowski, Christian, ed. *The Many Faces of Weimar Cinema: Rediscovering Germany's Filmic Legacy*. Rochester, NY: Camden House, 2010.

Rose, Alison. *Jewish Women in Fin de Siècle Vienna*. Austin: University of Texas Press, 2008.

Rosenblum, Warren. "Jews, Justice, and the Power of 'Sensation' in the Weimar Republic." *Leo Baeck Institute Year Book* 58 (2013): 35–52.

Ross, Corey. *Media and the Making of Modern Germany: Mass Communications, Society, and Politics from the Empire to the Third Reich*. New York: Oxford University Press, 2008.

Roth, Joseph. *The Wandering Jews*. Translated by Michael Hofmann. New York: W. W. Norton, 2001.

Roth, Laurence. *Inspecting Jews: American Jewish Detective Stories*. New Brunswick, NJ: Rutgers University Press, 2004.

Rottenberg, Catherine, ed. *Black Harlem and the Jewish Lower East Side: Narratives out of Time*. Albany: State University of New York Press, 2014.

Rottenberg, Catherine. *Performing Americanness: Race, Class, and Gender in Modern African-American and Jewish-American Literature*. Lebanon, NH: Dartmouth College Press, 2008.

Rürup, Miriam. *Ehrensache. Jüdische Studentenverbindungen an deutschen Universitäten, 1886–1937*. Göttingen: Wallstein Verlag, 2008.

Sánchez, María Carla, and Linda Schlossberg, eds. *Passing: Identity and Interpretation in Sexuality, Race, and Religion*. New York: New York University Press, 2001.

Sartre, Jean-Paul. *Anti-Semite and Jew: An Exploration of the Etiology of Hate.* Translated by George J. Becker. New York: Schocken Books, 1995.

Schlör, Joachim. *Das Ich der Stadt. Debatten über Judentum und Urbanität 1822–1938.* Göttingen: Vandenhoeck and Ruprecht, 2005.

Schnitzler, Arthur. *Fräulein Else.* Translated by F. H. Lyon. London: Pushkin Press, 2012. First published 1924 by Paul Zsolnay Verlag.

Scholem, Gershom. *The Messianic Idea in Judaism and Other Essays on Jewish Spirituality.* Foreword by Arthur Hertzberg. New York: Schocken Books, 1995.

Schönfeld, Christiane, ed. *Practicing Modernity: Female Creativity in the Weimar Republic.* Würzberg: Königshausen & Neumann, 2006.

Sedgwick, Eve Kosofsky. *Epistemology of the Closet.* Berkeley: University of California Press, 2008.

Seelig, Rachel. *Strangers in Berlin: Modern Jewish Literature between East and West, 1919–1933.* Ann Arbor: University of Michigan Press, 2016.

Seul, Stephanie. "Transnational Press Discourses on German Antisemitism during the Weimar Republic: The Riots in Berlin's Scheunenviertel, 1923." *Leo Baeck Institute Year Book* 59 (2014): 91–120.

Shahar, Galili. "The Jewish Actor and the Theatre of Modernism in Germany." *Theatre Research International* 29, no. 3 (2004): 216–31.

Shahar, Galili. *Theatrum judaicum. Denkspiele im deutsch-jüdischen Diskurs der Moderne.* Bielefeld: Aisthesis Verlag, 2007.

Sieg, Katrin. *Ethnic Drag: Performing Race, Nation, and Sexuality in West Germany.* Ann Arbor: University of Michigan Press, 2002.

Silverman, Eric. *A Cultural History of Jewish Dress.* New York: Bloomsbury Academic, 2013.

Silverman, Lisa. *Becoming Austrians: Jews and Culture between the World Wars.* New York: Oxford University Press, 2012.

Simonsen, Jon Gunnar Mølstre. "Perfect Targets—Antisemitism and Eastern Jews in Leipzig, 1919–1923." *Leo Baeck Institute Year Book* 51 (2006): 79–101.

Skolnik, Jonathan. *Jewish Pasts, German Fictions: History, Memory, and Minority Culture in Germany, 1824–1955.* Stanford: Stanford University Press, 2014.

Slezkine, Yuri. *The Jewish Century.* Princeton: Princeton University Press, 2004.

Smith, Jill Suzanne. *Berlin Coquette: Prostitution and the New German Woman, 1890–1933.* Ithaca: Cornell University Press, 2013.

Sneeringer, Julia. *Winning Women's Votes: Propaganda and Politics in Weimar Germany.* Chapel Hill: University of North Carolina Press, 2002.

Snorton, C. Riley. *Nobody Is Supposed to Know: Black Sexuality on the Down Low.* Minneapolis: University of Minnesota Press, 2014.

Sollors, Werner. *Neither Black nor White, Yet Both: Thematic Explorations of Interracial Literature.* Cambridge: Harvard University Press, 1997.

Sorkin, David. *The Transformation of German Jewry, 1780–1840.* Detroit: Wayne State University Press, 1999.

Spector, Scott. "Edith Stein's Passing Gestures: Intimate Histories, Empathetic Portraits." *New German Critique* 75 (1998): 28–56.

Spector, Scott. *Prague Territories: National Conflict and Cultural Innovation in Franz Kafka's Fin de Siècle.* Berkeley: University of California Press, 2000.

Spector, Scott. *Violent Sensations: Sex, Crime, and Utopia in Vienna and Berlin, 1860–1914*. Chicago: University of Chicago Press, 2016.

Spector, Scott, Helmut Puff, and Dagmar Herzog, eds. *After the History of Sexuality: German Genealogies with and beyond Foucault*. New York: Berghahn Books, 2012.

Spinner, Samuel. "Plausible Primitives: Kafka and Jewish Primitivism." *German Quarterly* 89, no. 1 (2016): 17–35.

Spreizer, Christa, ed. *Discovering Women's History: German-Speaking Journalists (1900–1950)*. Oxford: Peter Lang, 2014.

Stanislawski, Michael. *Zionism and the Fin de Siècle: Cosmopolitanism and Nationalism from Nordau to Jabotinsky*. Berkeley: University of California Press, 2001.

Steakley, James. "Cinema and Censorship in the Weimar Republic: The Case of *Anders als die Andern*." *Film History* 11, no. 2 (1999): 181–203.

Stiasny, Philipp. *Das Kino und der Krieg. Deutschland 1914–1929*. Munich: edition text + kritik, 2009.

Stratenwerth, Irene, and Hermann Simon, eds. *Pioniere in Celluloid. Juden in der frühen Filmwelt*. Berlin: Henschel, 2004.

Stratton, Jon. *Coming Out Jewish: Constructing Ambivalent Identities*. New York: Routledge, 2000.

Stratton, Jon. "Television Blackface: Jews, Race, and Comedy in the UK and Australia." In *The Routledge Handbook of Contemporary Jewish Cultures*, edited by Laurence Roth and Nadia Valman, 224–35. New York: Routledge, 2015.

Straus, Rahel. *Wir lebten in Deutschland. Erinnerungen einer deutschen Jüdin, 1880–1933*. Edited by Max Kreutzberger. Stuttgart: Deutsche Verlags-Anstalt, 1961.

Sundquist, Eric J. *Strangers in the Land: Blacks, Jews, Post-Holocaust America*. Cambridge: Belknap Press of Harvard University Press, 2005.

Sutton, Katie. *The Masculine Woman in Weimar Germany*. New York: Berghahn Books, 2011.

Sutton, Katie. "Sexological Cases and the Prehistory of Transgender Identity Politics in Interwar Germany." In *Case Studies and the Dissemination of Knowledge*, edited by Joy Damousi, Birgit Lang, and Katie Sutton, 85–103. New York: Routledge, 2015.

Sutton, Katie. "'We Too Deserve a Place in the Sun': The Politics of Transvestite Identity in Weimar Germany." *German Studies Review* 35, no. 2 (2012): 335–54.

Szilagyi, Charlotte, Sabrina K. Rahman, and Michael Saman, eds. *Imagining Blackness in Germany and Austria*. Newcastle upon Tyne, UK: Cambridge Scholars Publishing, 2012.

Thomas, Adrienne. *Katrin Becomes a Soldier*. Translated by Margaret Goldsmith. Boston: Little, Brown, 1931.

Thornham, Sue, ed. *Feminist Film Theory: A Reader*. New York: New York University Press, 1999.

Thurn, Nike. *"Falsche Juden". Performative Identitäten in der deutschsprachigen Literatur von Lessing bis Walser*. Göttingen: Wallstein Verlag, 2015.

Tucholsky, Kurt. *Berlin! Berlin! Dispatches from the Weimar Republic*. Translated by Cindy Opitz. New York: Berlinica Publishing, 2013.

Valman, Nadia. *The Jewess in Nineteenth-Century British Literary Culture*. New York: Cambridge University Press, 2007.

Vassogne, Gaëlle. *Max Brod in Prag. Identität und Vermittlung.* Tübingen: Max Nie-meyer Verlag, 2009.

Völker, Klaus. *Fritz Kortner. Schauspieler und Regisseur.* Berlin: Hentrich, 1987.

Volkov, Shulamit. *Germans, Jews, and Antisemites: Trials in Emancipation.* New York: Cambridge University Press, 2006.

Volkov, Shulamit. *Walther Rathenau: Weimar's Fallen Statesman.* New Haven: Yale University Press, 2012.

Wagner-Trenkwitz, Christoph, and Marie Th. Arnbom, eds. *Grüß mich Gott! Fritz Grünbaum (1880–1941). Eine Biographie.* Vienna: Brandstätter Verlag, 2005.

Wallach, Kerry. "Escape Artistry: Elisabeth Bergner and Jewish Disappearance in *Der träumende Mund* (Czinner, 1932)." *German Studies Review* 38, no. 1 (2015): 17–34.

Wallach, Kerry. "Observable Type: Jewish Women and the Jewish Press in Weimar Germany." PhD diss., University of Pennsylvania, 2011.

Walter, Dirk. *Antisemitische Kriminalität und Gewalt: Judenfeindschaft in der Wei-marer Republik.* Bonn: Dietz, 1999.

Ward, Janet. *Weimar Surfaces: Urban Visual Culture in 1920s Germany.* Berkeley: Uni-versity of California Press, 2001.

Warner, Michael. "Publics and Counterpublics (Abbreviated Version)." *Quarterly Jour-nal of Speech* 88, no. 4 (2002): 413–25.

Weinbaum, Alys Eve, Lynn M. Thomas, Priti Ramamurthy, Uta G. Poiger, Madeleine Yue Dong, and Tani E. Barlow, eds. *The Modern Girl around the World: Consump-tion, Modernity, and Globalization.* Durham, NC: Duke University Press, 2008.

Weinstein, Valerie. "Anti-Semitism or Jewish 'Camp'? Ernst Lubitsch's *Schuhpalast Pinkus* (1916) and *Meyer aus Berlin* (1918)." *German Life and Letters* 59, no. 1 (2006): 101–21.

Weinstein, Valerie. "Dissolving Boundaries: Assimilation and Allosemitism in E. A. Dupont's *Das alte Gesetz* (1923) and Veit Harlan's *Jud Süss* (1940)." *German Quar-terly* 78, no. 4 (2005): 496–516.

Weissberg, Liliane. *Hannah Arendt, Charlie Chaplin und die verborgene jüdische Tra-dition.* Graz: Leykam, 2009.

Weiss-Sussex, Godela, and Ulrike Zitzlsperger, eds. *Das Berliner Warenhaus: Ge-schichte und Diskurse/The Berlin Department Store: History and Discourse.* Frank-furt am Main: Peter Lang, 2013.

Weitz, Eric D. *Weimar Germany: Promise and Tragedy.* Princeton: Princeton Univer-sity Press, 2007.

Weniger, Kay. *"Es wird im Leben dir mehr genommen als gegeben . . .". Lexikon der aus Deutschland und Österreich emigrierten Filmschaffenden 1933 bis 1945.* Ham-burg: ACABUS Verlag, 2011.

Weniger, Kay. *Zwischen Bühne und Baracke. Lexikon der verfolgten Theater-, Film- und Musikkünstler 1933–1945.* Berlin: Metropol, 2008.

Wertheim, David J. *Salvation through Spinoza: A Study of Jewish Culture in Weimar Germany.* Leiden: Brill, 2011.

Wertheimer, Jack. *Unwelcome Strangers: East European Jews in Imperial Germany.* New York: Oxford University Press, 1987.

Whisnant, Clayton J. *Queer Identities and Politics in Germany: A History, 1880–1945.* New York: Harrington Park Press, 2016.

White, Walter Francis. *Flight*. Baton Rouge: Louisiana State University Press, 1998.

White, Walter Francis. *A Man Called White: The Autobiography of Walter White*. Athens: University of Georgia Press, 1995.

Yoshino, Kenji. *Covering: The Hidden Assault on Our Civil Rights*. New York: Random House, 2007.

Zackodnik, Teresa C. *The Mulatta and the Politics of Race*. Jackson: University Press of Mississippi, 2004.

Zadoff, Mirjam. *Next Year in Marienbad: The Lost Worlds of Jewish Spa Culture*. Philadelphia: University of Pennsylvania Press, 2012.

Zdatny, Steven. "The Boyish Look and the Liberated Woman: The Politics and Aesthetics of Women's Hairstyles." *Fashion Theory* 1, no. 4 (1997): 367–98.

Zemel, Carol. *Looking Jewish: Visual Culture and Modern Diaspora*. Bloomington: Indiana University Press, 2015.

Zimmerman, Andrew. "Anti-Semitism as Skill: Rudolf Virchow's 'Schulstatistik' and the Racial Composition of Germany." *Central European History* 32, no. 4 (1999): 409–29.

Zimmermann, Moshe. *Die deutschen Juden 1914–1945*. Munich: R. Oldenbourg Verlag, 1997.

Zipes, Jack. *The Operated Jew: Two Tales of Anti-Semitism*. New York: Routledge, 1991.

Zweig, Arnold. *The Face of East European Jewry*. Translated by Noah Isenberg. Berkeley: University of California Press, 2004.

Zweig, Arnold. *Juden auf der deutschen Bühne*. Berlin: Welt-Verlag, 1928.

Zwicker, Lisa Fetheringill. *Dueling Students: Conflict, Masculinity, and Politics in German Universities*. Ann Arbor: University of Michigan Press, 2011.

## FILMOGRAPHY

*Das alte Gesetz*. DVD. Directed by Ewald André Dupont. 1923. Berlin: Deutsche Kinemathek—Filmarchiv.

*Anders als die Andern*. DVD. Directed by Richard Oswald. 1919; New York: Kino Lorber, 2009.

*Arm wie eine Kirchenmaus*. DVD. Directed by Richard Oswald. 1931; Avondale, AZ: Rarefilmsandmore.com, no. 1638.

*Chad Gadjo*. DVD. Directed by Julius Pinschewer. 1930. *Julius Pinschewer. Klassiker des Werbefilms*. Berlin: ARTE edition, absolut MEDIEN, 2010.

*Doktor Bessels Verwandlung*. VHS. Directed by Richard Oswald. 1927. Berlin: Bundesarchiv-Filmarchiv.

*Dreyfus*. DVD. Directed by Richard Oswald. 1930; Eisingen: Morisel/KNM Home Entertainment, 2011.

*Die dritte Eskadron*. Directed by Carl Wilhelm. 1926. Film considered lost; still images and print material only. Berlin: Deutsche Kinemathek—Filmarchiv.

*Durchlaucht Radieschen*. Directed by Richard Eichberg. 1926/1927. Film considered lost; still images and print material only. Berlin: Deutsche Kinemathek—Filmarchiv.

*Fräulein Else*. DVD. Directed by Paul Czinner. 1928/1929; Rome: Raro Video, 2004. Restoration by Cineteca del Comune di Bologna, ZDF, and ARTE.

*Frühling in Palästina.* VHS. Directed by Willy Prager. 1928. Produced by Keren Hajessod and Keren Kajemeth organizations. Berlin: Bundesarchiv-Filmarchiv.

*Der Geiger von Florenz (Impetuous Youth).* Film. Directed by Paul Czinner. 1926. Berlin: Bundesarchiv-Filmarchiv.

*Ich möchte kein Mann sein.* DVD. Directed by Ernst Lubitsch. 1918. New York: Kino Lorber, 2006.

*The Jazz Singer.* DVD. Directed by Alan Crosland. 1927; Hollywood: Warner Home Video, 2007.

*Leichte Kavallerie.* Directed by Rold Randolf. 1927. Film considered lost; still images and print material only. Berlin: Deutsche Kinemathek—Filmarchiv.

*Makkabäer. Ein Film jüdischer Sportjugend.* VHS. Directed by Felix Simmenauer. 1929/1930. Berlin: Bundesarchiv-Filmarchiv.

*Mensch ohne Namen.* DVD. Directed by Gustav Ucicky. 1932. Berlin: Deutsche Kinemathek—Filmarchiv.

*Meyer aus Berlin.* VHS and YouTube. Directed by Ernst Lubitsch. 1918/1919.

*Moritz macht sein Glück.* DVD. Directed by Jaap Speyer. 1931. Berlin: Bundesarchiv-Filmarchiv.

*Überflüssige Menschen.* VHS. Directed by Alexander Rasumny. 1926. Berlin: Bundesarchiv-Filmarchiv.

# Index

*Note:* Page numbers in italics refer to illustrations.